Thomas Durand
Technology Strategies

Thomas Durand

Technology Strategies

—

Turning technological change into competitive advantage

DE GRUYTER

ISBN 978-3-11-139277-6
e-ISBN (PDF) 978-3-11-139797-9
e-ISBN (EPUB) 978-3-11-139905-8

Library of Congress Control Number: 2024944867

Bibliographic information published by the Deutsche Nationalbibliothek
The Deutsche Nationalbibliothek lists this publication in the Deutsche Nationalbibliografie;
detailed bibliographic data are available on the Internet at http://dnb.dnb.de.

© 2025 Walter de Gruyter GmbH, Berlin/Boston
Cover image: piranka/E+/Getty Images
Typesetting: Integra Software Services Pvt. Ltd.

www.degruyter.com
Questions about General Product Safety Regulation:
productsafety@degruyterbrill.com

To Martine, Marion and Alex, Quentin and Ioana, Thibaud and Alexandra, Anatole, Constantin, Cosma, Abel, Edith, and Ernest for being incredible sources of energy, joy and love.

Acknowledgements

This book results from the work and interaction over the years with many colleagues and friends from both academia and the world of practice in the business community. My thinking was nurtured by the combination of fascinating academic discussions, including with PhD candidates – especially those whose doctoral work I supervised – and the need to "touch base" with practitioners whom I had the opportunity to accompany over the years – and decades for some of them. I extend my thanks to my colleagues at CMI whose work triggered my thinking on so many occasions.

My thanks go to Saïd Ibrahimi, Eléonore Mounoud, Thierry Gonard, Jean-Pierre Rémy, Charles de Brabant, Lubomir Mortchev, Antoine Weil, Diane d'Arras, Michel Rapin, Marc Florette, Ronan Stephan, Antony Ricolfi, Armand Braun, Stépanie Dameron, Suzanne Berger, Yves Doz, David Teece, Klaus Jennewein, Alexander Gerybadze, Sebastien Ronteau, Silvia Guera Viera, Nicolas Pasquet, Nassef Hmimda, Staffan Hulten, Lassaâd Mezghani, Hai Chau Tran Cournede, Guillaume Tobler, Julien Deleuze, Brice Dattée, Benoit Tezenas du Montcel and Alexander Milodowski.

I am indebted to Nicolas Kandel, François Farhi, François Delay as well as Philippe Bassot and Julie Koeltz for their continuous support since the 1980s when I had my initial ideas that ended up populating the book as it stands today.

The EITIM team around Hugo Tschirky, David Probert, Cornelius Herstatt and Ove Granstrand worked as a stimulating lab to spur my thinking. I also benefitted from discussions with members of the IfM at the University of Cambridge around Sir Mike Gregory and Lord David Sainsbury, including through the international group of researchers gathered at the Babbage Forum.

I learnt a great deal with groups in executive education, e.g., with Orange, Danone and HEC Executive MBA – formerly CPA – (Jean-Claude Goaër), Chalmers University of Technology (Lars Trygg), the Stockholm School of Economics (Bengt Stymne) and CEDEP at INSEAD, Fontainebleau (Claude Michaud).

Part II of the book, especially Chapter 11, would simply have not existed without Brice Dattée.

A special word of appreciation for Hassan T'ber El Idrissi who remembered some of my teaching on technology strategy at Ecole Centrale Paris and contacted me years later, in the end leading me to write the book – though he does not know.

A friendly word to JC Spender whose role in triggering the writing of the book was essential – he knows.

My final thanks go to the team at De Gruyter around Stefan Giesen for a fluid and efficient work process.

https://doi.org/10.1515/9783111397979-202

Preface

While being a European from Continental Europe and the European Union, I have used in this book examples and references from around the world, though primarily from advanced economies and especially Europe. Yet, this is not a book about technology strategies in Europe.

As the book deals with technology strategies, I should stress that matters of selecting technologies for businesses are global, in the sense that companies around the world raise the same types of questions and answer in similar ways – although not necessarily in the same way. Unlike, e.g., HR policies that may be very "local" because they are dependent on the social, cultural, legal and political context, technology is global by nature.

This means that examples and case studies coming from specific parts of the world (in my case, Europe for a number of them) should not be seen as "locally biased" but as additional pieces of evidence on the topic, possibly bringing a bit of fresh air from the outside in a literature still largely dominated by north American influence. As we all know, the bulk of management research is indeed based in the US.

This book emerged as an output of my "in-between career", that is a career that took place in academia, as a strategic management scholar, while continuously working with practitioners in the business community. This is probably no longer compatible with the rules of the game that prevail today in business schools. I was fortunate enough to teach at Ecole Centrale Paris (for 30 years) and Le Cnam (for 14 years) where such professional positioning was not only made possible but even encouraged. That in-between positioning led me to make difficult choices along the way, including turning down offers from leading European business schools whose agenda could not fit my in-between stance.

The business situations that I faced while helping top managers struggle with complex strategic issues was of tremendous interest for me. It contributed to nurturing my teaching with concrete examples. It also helped me sieve through the academic literature with an acid test (among others): Does this research piece address an issue that one way or another relates to "real" situations encountered out there? Does the conceptual framework used in this piece of research do justice to the complexity of the situations top management face? I note that this cannot be the only test for academic relevance as theory building is an essential part of scholarly work. Along this line of thinking, this book is an attempt to address concrete problems that top managers face as technology evolves, while providing a theoretical framework to think about and strategize technological issues.

I also need to mention that I have been working "in between" in a different sense, namely in between technology and business studies. I was trained as an engineer before switching to the field of management, focusing on strategic management. As a result, I love to try to understand technology – how it works and what it can deliver. I also love to try to foresee what a new technology could do for a business and their

https://doi.org/10.1515/9783111397979-203

customers as well as why and how it could contribute to building a competitive advantage. This dual interest in digging into the content of both technologies and strategies may be seen as a personal bias that served as a useful capability in the context of this book.

I also need to signal another bias of mine in writing this book. Most of my work in the business realm took place in large organizations – in fact primarily large multinational firms. This does not mean that I have no familiarity with SMEs or start-ups. It means that my thinking was unavoidably influenced by large organizations equipped with sophisticated strategic processes, endowed with resources significant enough to help them create a path into their future. Nevertheless, I do believe the book can also help SME's top managers identify the key questions they need to address when facing technological choices.

On the research side, I have been strongly influenced by solid pieces of work including from Giovanni Dosi, David Teece, William Abernathy, James Utterback, Kim Clark and several others. In a way, I have consistently been trying to call upon the contributions stemming from economics of technical change into the field of strategic management. Let me insist on the debt that I owe to early writers in the field as well as to all those whom I was fortunate to work with, including PhD students.

All in all, this book comes as the final output stemming from a professional life spent primarily in Europe in between academia in the field of management and work with practitioners in the business world, with a combined interest in technology and business strategy. I have been thinking of writing this for several decades. Here it is.

Contents

Part IV: **Managerial Implications – Path Creation in Practice**

Chapter 1
General Introduction

This book is about technology strategy.

Carbon-free methanol vs electric cars?

Think of a European car manufacturer in the early 2020's having to address the emergence of electric cars spurred by the EU ban on sales of thermal engines beyond 2035 and the boldly move already made by Tesla, a new entrant shortly after the turn of the millennium. This meant a risky choice of abandoning their incumbent's position on thermal engines, where they held a competitive advantage built over decades, and switch to electric power (in whatever form: hybrid, hybrid rechargeable, full electric).

In the face of this new environment, several leading German car manufacturers became extremely worried by the risk of losing their competitive advantage on thermal engines. They felt they were being forced to give up what they had for something far less certain. In a defensive move, they lobbied their government to oppose the EU ban on thermal engines beyond 2035 and suggested another path forward.

Their proposed strategy was to stick to thermal engines by switching from petroleum to methanol. Methanol was presented as environmentally friendly and thus labeled as green fuel, with zero net carbon emissions (except for the manufacturing and disposal of the engine and transportation of the green fuel). They argued that while still being propelled by thermal engines, cars using green fuel would fulfill the target of carbon-free emissions imposed by the EU-planned 2035 ban. Indeed, the production process of methanol which consists of using CO_2 and combining it with hydrogen would *de facto* contribute to the capture of CO_2 upstream. In addition, the electricity required to produce Hydrogen (H_2) through the electrolysis of water would be carbon-free as it would be generated carbon free through renewable sources, typically wind turbines in areas such as southern Chile where there are strong and quasi-permanent winds. The carbon-free methanol would have to be stored locally before being shipped abroad.

Overall, the production cost of green methanol remains a major problem limiting its use to well-off car owners. This would mean that the whole green methanol scheme would be targeted to offer the high end of the market the possibility to circumnavigate the 2035 EU ban – a difficult objective to sell politically altogether. Clearly the German car makers promoting this scheme show their reluctance to abandon the strategic advantage they built around thermal engines.

How can we analyze and assess this strategy? its pros and cons (technically, strategically)? What to think of this strategic move by part of the German automotive industry? (I shall return to this mini case on pp 120–121 and then at the end of chapter 22, on p 257, in light of the concepts and frameworks presented in the book).

The purpose of this book is to provide firms facing technological change with concepts, frameworks, tools and methods to help them think about technology strategies. To this end, it is essential to rely on sound, well-documented and detailed representations of how technology unfolds. It is also important to use robust tools and methods to analyze the potential dynamics of situations like the one described above. This book is therefore about informing decisions regarding technological strategies.

Technology often evolves in unexpected ways. When technological change occurs or is about to occur, firms active in a business, the incumbents, face difficult strategic choices:

https://doi.org/10.1515/9783111397979-001

- Should they defend their activities, sticking to the still current dominant technology on which they built a competitive position?
- Or should they worry about their dominant technology becoming obsolete one day, if not soon? Hence, should they move on, accessing new technologies, hopefully fit for the future of their business (or paving the way for new businesses yet to be entered)?
  - Furthermore, funding the development or acquisition of many new options is likely to be too costly, thus preventing the firm from going for all potential candidate technologies.
- How to select the technological development projects to invest in?
- How to pick the hopefully future-winning technology among the many candidates that knock at the door? (Note that this wording assumes that the list of candidate technologies would be known as of today: the uncertainty would essentially be around which among them may win. Yet, it may well be that the future is so unclear that one cannot even tell what candidates to consider as of today. The first situation is uncertain. The second is indeterminate.[1] Obviously, indetermination makes it significantly more difficult to think of the future strategically). We shall see in Part III that a way to deal with uncertainty, and even to some extent to indeterminacy, is to work on the underlying competencies that may be needed for the firm to go for future technologies.

When in the 1980s Kodak made the mistake of ignoring the future of digital imaging, sticking instead to chemical (analog) photography, they chose to not prepare for the future of digital imaging (uncertain as it may have appeared to them at that time). Yet, they could have afforded to build internal competence, just in case, typically hiring a group of scientists, developers and engineers in electronics as a way to learn along the way. The future of technologies was unclear but they could have covered for the risk of a radical innovation coming in. There was no need to see in great details how the future digital technologies could shape up; it was just a matter of preparing for it, at low cost, just in case. Not going for that rather simple and affordable move turned out to be a deadly mistake for Kodak.

- How to go about accessing technologies for the future (through internal R&D, licensing-in, acquisitions, corporate venturing, partnering, etc.)?

All these questions are key issues for the strategic management of technology.

New entrants face similar issues as they consider surfing a wave of technological change when it comes to intruding into a market.

---

1 Frank Knight chose different wording to capture the same idea: risk and uncertainty. Risk would describe a situation where the value of outcomes and probabilities can be estimated and processed. Uncertainty would be about the "unknown unknowns", as Teece puts it. No assessment of options can be conducted because the options are unknown. Yet, in today's common language, risk and uncertainty are often used as equivalent terms. This is rather misleading. I thus prefer using indeterminacy for the second category and risk for the first.

I will clarify and amend this convention in Chapter 19 (Part III).

The car industry was known to protect itself behind high barriers to entry due to the large investments needed to access the technologies, build assembly plants, grow a brand, control distribution channels and a network of mechanics for maintenance and repair. Tesla surfed the wave of
technological change, namely electric cars, triggering the change when most incumbents were
still hesitant or considering they had plenty of time before going for it. Tesla triggered the
change, ahead of the pack. Since then, the entire industry has been running behind Tesla.

The entrepreneurial act is an act of creation. Creating a business that relates a socio-
economic need to a product or a service, say a solution, fulfilling all or part of the
need. Technology plays a role in creating a solution and, further down the road, in
regenerating the business and/or possibly creating new ones.

In this context, when thinking of technology strategically, top management needs
to create a path into the future for the firm. Some firms may try to limit themselves
on running operations effectively, remaining on the same technological track without
questioning what the firm does, essentially trying to do better what they have been
doing. This can do the job, at least up to a point. Such a strategy is no longer relevant
when competitors find better ways to run their own operations or to fulfill customers'
needs with innovative offerings or if a new technology comes in to substitute for the
firm's offerings, bringing in a range of aggressive new entrants. Instead of waiting for
the blow, the firm may anticipate proactively, trying to leverage technology to build a
unique path into the future, ahead of competition – or away from it. This is clearly
about strategy.[2]

In that sense, the strategic management of technology is not just about reacting
timely when technological change disrupts an industry or a business arena. It is about
the firm leveraging technology to create a path for itself into the future.

In other words, this book is about technology strategy for path creation.

The wording "path creation" aims at capturing the process for a firm to craft a
strategy that will find a way through the many (or few) technological options available (or at least thinkable) for the future of their businesses. In a jungle-like environment, there might be a mushrooming context of too many new technologies thinkable
for the future, where the issue will be to select among these to create the most appropriate path for the firm. In a desert-like environment, there might be not enough technological options for the future. The issue will thus be to find reasonable options "to
do the job" for the clients/users, ahead of competition, or away from competition. The
path does not necessarily exist ahead of time, hidden somewhere waiting to be uncov-
ered and followed. Most often the path needs to be designed, constructed and extended, to provide a specific answer to the key question of how to move forward
given the business and technological situation of the time.

---

2 Part of the above echoes Christensen's sustaining vs. disruptive innovations that I will discuss in
Part I, at the end of Chapter 8.

In so doing, the book focuses on corporate agency. That is, I primarily look at firms playing their part as agents. This means that I dig into the way firms can craft and implement creative strategies to shape their own future. However, this does not mean that other agents are not playing a part in the game. Typically, customers, government or society are also important players that use their agency to influence business and technology dynamics for their own sake, needs, concerns and priorities. Although these are not the focus of my attention here, when looking at firms crafting and implementing technology strategies, I obviously need to take into account the role of the other agents partaking in the game. In other words, I cannot ignore these other agents and their agency. Yet, this book will not dig into these in depth. Typically, public policy on technology (and thus research and innovation) is a much-investigated topic in industrial economics. Similarly, though from a different perspective, the field of marketing digs in particular depth into how customers exert their choice and preferences. While recognizing the importance of all forms of agencies that play a role on technological evolution, the focus of this book is on firms' agency as they design and implement their strategies by searching for and seizing opportunities in the middle of many pressures and constraints.

Major Shifts in the Way the Topic has been Addressed so far

For years, in both the world of practice and the academic literature, the theme of technology has been associated with R&D, innovation and the technical side of business.

From a practical viewpoint, technology was seen as a topic for scientists and engineers, thus best covered by R&D teams under the VP for research. For similar reasons, at least for companies in technical businesses, typically high-tech, innovation tended to be reduced to technological innovation and thus was considered as naturally falling under the responsibility of R&D as well. This kind of organizational arrangement ended up mixing the roles. More specifically, innovation and technology strategy were too often assimilated to R&D management, boiling down to budgetary choices among R&D programs.

A clarification appeared with the appointment of chief technology officers (CTOs). To some extent, this was initiated in the start-ups and venture capital community at the turn of the century. Typically, when venture funds would invest in a high-tech start-up founded by technology geeks, the venture capitalists would often recruit business developers as CEOs, pushing the founders to the side, while giving them the title of CTO to keep them on board. In the wake of this common practice, large companies started appointing CTOs, preferably apart from corporate R&D. The role of a CTO essentially deals with the issues described above (see Chapter 20). In other words, a CTO helps the top management read the complexity of potential future technologies to create a reasonable path into the future for the company.

From an academic point of view, the 1960s and 1970s were dominated by the theme of R&D (economics of technical change, national systems of innovation, public research-industry interfacing, management of R&D, etc.). Then the focus shifted to understanding the dynamics of technology in the 1980s and then the theme of learning and competence in the 1990s, hence managing a portfolio of technologies and competencies (or capabilities in Teece's sense). In turn, the theme of innovation emerged as dominant, including innovation beyond technology (e.g., organizational innovation, business model innovations, etc.). Overall, these various successive layers paved the way to integrate technology and innovation in strategic management. In this context, this book aims at digging further into the matter, offering a comprehensive picture to think about technology strategically for path creation.

More specifically, this book aims at taking stock of what we learnt along the way, leveraging the breadth of knowledge accumulated in the literature and through practice to help top management teams think about technology strategically. In short, the issue is both to adapt reactively to technical change and to use technologies proactively to find a way (in fact create a viable path ahead) for the firm towards its future.

The book provides three frameworks: a model of technological change and its strategic consequences; a framework for technological substitutions departing from the classic S-curve; and a framework of organizational competence underlying the technologies used in the firm. These three frameworks fit together into an overarching integrated framework to help think about technology strategically.

Illustrations

For the sake of illustration, I am introducing nine cases of radical technological shifts. Three of them are past cases, three are ongoing, three are future potential (yet expected) paradigmatic changes. These cover a variety of sectors and situations. The cases are essentially included here to provide illustrations of the concepts and frameworks developed in the book. I do not suggest in any way that they could capture or represent the variety of situations that may be encountered in practice.

I use the first three ("past cases": insulin, switchboards in the telecoms industry, recorded music) to illustrate the concepts and frameworks developed in the book. This helps keep the content as concrete as possible. These past cases are typical examples of past major technological change where the outcome of firms' strategies can already be observed.

The next three (the "ongoing cases": electric cars, 3D printing and Blockchain), offer situations where the reader can grasp concretely how the frameworks, concepts and tools presented in the book can help raise relevant issues to think about technology strategically. These three cases are ongoing situations ranging from "already shaping up" to "still uncertain". The case of electric cars is getting clearer every day, apart from the potential intrusion of hydrogen and the fuel cell. 3D printing is fuzzier because it covers a wide range of applications and several specific technologies to fulfill a variety of needs in a variety of sectors. The blockchain is emerging, already serving a few applications in specific sectors, but much remains uncertain, if not indeterminate. These three "in between" cases (ongoing cases) describe industries where the action is currently unfolding with outcomes yet to be seen, thus offering another kind of situation to grasp the analytical value of the insight stemming from the book's conceptual frameworks. While advancing through the book, I invite the reader to think how the framework, concepts and tools provided can help analyze those cases.

The last three (the "future cases": industry of the future, Molten-salt reactors and fusion in the future of nuclear energy, quantum computing) are at best uncertain (industry of the future, MSR and fusion) or indeterminate (quantum computing). They each essentially stand as a promise, with a long way to go before they could possibly come to application and become dominant. They illustrate typical situations where the future may still be so foggy that it is difficult to design a strategy in the face of too many "unknown unknowns". Yet, such situations need to be explored and assessed to monitor the dynamics as uncertainty vanishes. The point is to consider options – seen as of today – and then monitor them over time and look carefully for other options possibly emerging along the way. In doing so, the firm can start building competence early enough to prepare for some of these options that may be considered reasonable as things get clearer when the dynamics of technology progressively unfolds.

Past Cases

Insulin

Insulin is a substance produced by your pancreas to regulate the level of sugar in your blood. Diabetics have a failing pancreas. Treatment of diabetes used animal insulin that, once purified, was administered to diabetics. A technological revolution disrupted the industry when biotechnologies made the production of human insulin possible. That launched a technological race between two industry incumbents, Eli Lilly and Novo Nordisk. Novo won the race technologically but not commercially. In fact, Novo was essentially trying to survive to stay in a position to prepare for the day-after-tomorrow technology that, they believed, would be proinsulin. Things turned differently.

Switchboards in the Telecoms Industry

Telecom networks were made of three categories of systems: (1) terminals (phone sets, fax, mobiles, etc.); (2) transmission systems (copper line, underwater cables, satellites, terrestrial antenna and radio signals); and (3) switchboards, the heart of telecom networks. The switchboards dispatched the calls to create a specific temporary link between the caller and the respondent allowing the communication. In the early days, telecom operators would do the switching manually before electromechanical switchboards were introduced. At some point, the arrival of electronics generated another paradigmatic shift: the task of connecting/disconnecting to create/interrupt the continuity of a link was done electronically (the electric signal flows or is cut off). This paradigmatic shift prepared the floor for yet another shift, namely time-division multiplexing, that made it possible to carry several conversations in parallel on the same cable. This considerably saved cost on investments for network infrastructure. It turns out that CIT-Alcatel, a rather small player at that time, producing an electromechanical system under a license from Ericsson, chose to leapfrog directly to digital time-division multiplexing, the most advanced technology thinkable. They made a technological bet that turned out to be successful. As a result, they became for a while world leader of the telecom equipment manufacturers. The logical next technological generation was expected to be optical switching, except technology took the industry by surprise in the form of the internet protocol (IP) that carried with it packet switching and routers. This technology has been dominant since the end of the 1990s.

Recorded Music

Recorded music started as early as 1877 in the form of Thomas Edison's phonograph that used cylinders, followed ten years later by Emile Berliner's gramophone that introduced disks. The cylinders were abandoned in 1927, leaving the floor to the disk that became the dominant technology with full market development after World War II in its black vinyl form with 78, 45 and 33 rpm. Stereo music was introduced along the way, while new speakers kept refining the quality of the sound. The audiotape started cannibalizing the vinyl market in the 1970s before the CDs were launched based on laser technology. Then came a troubled period around the emergence of the internet, when downloads (not always paid for) in MP3 format hit the entire industry, before streaming took over. Along the way, show business shifted its model. While concerts had essentially been a way for artists to promote the sales of their records, live concerts (promoted through streaming) became the major source of revenue for artists. Labels turned into entities managing portfolios of rights, generating their revenues from the fees paid by the digital platforms streaming their stock of recorded music.

Ongoing Cases

Electric Cars

The first car to reach the speed of 100 km/h was electric.[3] It was in 1899 near Paris. Yet, the technology that subsequently dominated the auto industry for over a century was the internal combustion engine. High barriers to entry deterred candidate new entrants from coming into the sector. The only strategic moves that took place for decades were internationalization of activities by regional firms (US, Japanese, European, Korean and Indian primarily) and concentration through a sequence of acquisitions, mergers or formation of partnerships. Many technological

---

3 The case of electric cars was already touched upon in the box at the beginning of the introduction " Carbon-free methanol vs electric cars?". Here, I present the more general picture of the current dynamics of electric cars about to cannibalize thermal engines.

innovations contributed to improve the dominant technology of a sedan car powered by an internal combustion engine. Global warming and the need to decarbonize economies and human activities on the planet led to opening the door to electric power. Tesla went for it, with significant support from the US government, while the incumbents were still pondering. Some tried to develop cleaner diesel engines, others placed a bet on biofuel mixed to gasoline, others optimized fuel consumption, others developed dual or hybrid engines to achieve the same result, while others went for rechargeable hybrids, claiming that customers needed to experiment with electric cars before they would switch to 100% electric. Implicitly, this was also a way to recognize that autonomy of batteries was not sufficient for many buyers and the network of recharge stations was still too shallow. Yet, the switch to 100% electric power has been on its way in the auto industry since the 2010s, as suggested by the rapid increase of the market share captured by electric cars year after year. This dynamic is fueled by the public subsidies still allocated to buyers of new electrical cars in some countries, the increasing pressure put on car owners (including bans on gasoline cars in many urban centers), and the spectacular development of new models of electrical cars by most manufacturers. Still pending is the promise of the fuel cell (hydrogen technology) that could stand as the day-after-tomorrow technology.

3D Printing

3D printing is also known as additive manufacturing. This umbrella wording covers many process technologies that help design and produce parts and components by adding successive layers of material to form a desired object. One can identify about 37 families of such processes, including extrusion, photopolymerization, powder bed fusion, etc. These specific process technologies share two common traits: they add matter instead of taking matter off through drilling, milling, cutting or scraping; and they call upon digital technologies (computer-aided design and manufacturing). Firms on the supply side develop such specific process technologies to offer new solutions for a set of problems yet to be identified. On the demand side, companies interested by the promises of potential savings scan among those technologies to see which ones could help them for specific issues they face. In a way, 3D printing technologies are solutions in search of problems to be solved.

On the supply side, most firms are not capable of offering the whole spectrum of these technologies. Quite the opposite. Most technology providers offering 3D printing solutions are usually specialized in only one or two of them. On the demand side, users are primarily industrial firms wondering how they could benefit from 3D printing. The development of 3D printing requires the meeting and mating of problems to be solved (for firms unaware of the existence of 3D printing solutions to deal with specific problems they may have had for a long time) with solutions offered by technology providers and now rendered possible by the paradigm of additive manufacturing. This meeting and mating is an ongoing process that takes place at a decentralized level through some form of trial and error.

Blockchain

The blockchain technology stems from digital technologies that permit to create and follow distributed numerical registries. The idea is that the same information can be stored at many decentralized loci under the eyes of an entire community, thus offering an efficient way of keeping unchanged the records of an ecosystem with reliable tracing functionalities. This can be more efficient and reliable than a central system of certification, should the central power be tempted to erase and modify the past à la Orwell 1984. In a way, this is about some form of crowd certification or a libertarian philosophy suspicious of central power. This technology can prove useful in activities where transactions need to be recorded with trustworthy traceability: financial transactions, real estate and notaries, banking, cryptocurrencies, transactions in supply chains, etc. The applications are developing, encountering resistance from professions that have much at stake (as they could be substituted for – or at least significantly transformed).

Future Cases

Industry of the Future

Industry in several Western economies has been hollowed out through offshoring. The UK, the US and France, for example, have seen the share of industry in GDP fall from some 25–30% in the 1970s to around 10% in the 2020s (Italy and even Germany have also seen a decrease but not to the same extent). The fourth industrial revolution is seen as a wave of change, an opportunity to surf for those countries eager to reindustrialize by investing in, and leveraging, the new technologies that might constitute the backbone of a major industrial transformation.[4] The objective cannot be reshoring, as this would be more difficult and likely unsuccessful. This is about reindustrializing. The technologies likely to structure the industry of the future sound like an opportunity to regain part of the industrial ground lost by those advanced economies over the last decades. Although the overall idea of a fourth industrial revolution remains vague and somehow idealized as it will have to include a significant greening by those Western economies, should such a transformation take place, it will require serious preparation.

It is possible to list the key technologies that are candidates to structure the fourth industrial revolution: additive manufacturing (or 3D printing); machine learning and artificial intelligence; robots and cobots; internet of things and machine to machine; predictive maintenance; big data and big analytics; digital imaging and augmented virtual reality; smart manufacturing, etc. Yet, this is not just about technologies for manufacturing and operations. It is also about managerial orchestration of the change. This means strategizing rearrangements in the value chains, managing the organizational transformations attached, managing the greening – reindustrialization tension, etc.

---

4 The labeling "fourth industrial revolution" requires an agreement on what the first three industrial revolutions were – historians debate the number of industrial revolutions, their timing and content. Yet, it is commonly accepted that the first industrial revolution (end of the eighteenth century) stemmed from coal, steel and steam power, leading to railroads and mechanized looms. The second (end of the nineteenth century) stemmed from electricity, telephony, the beginning of the car industry and mass production. The third (after WWII up to the 1990s) surfed the waves of pharmaceuticals, aeronautics, nuclear energy, mass consumption, TV, electronics and computers. The fourth would stem from internet leading to the digitalization of the world, with biotechnologies supported by life sciences, plus the societal concern of greening the economy to save the planet. This would need to be nuanced, but this idea of a coming future technological revolution makes sense, although one can only tell for sure after the fact. This echoes the concept of the technical system developed by Bertrand Gille.

Molten-salt Reactors and Fusion in the Future of Nuclear Energy

Nuclear energy developed in the second half of the twentieth century. Fission of enriched uranium-235 is used in pressurized water reactors (PWRs) to heat water into vapor that propels turbines to generate electricity. The subsequent generation was meant to be the fast breeder reactor (FBR), except the technology has not made its way to full use despite its attractiveness (the principle was to collect the plutonium-239 generated by the PWR as a by-product or waste to reuse it as a fuel for the breeders). Note that the fuel used in some PWR plants is MOX, a mix resulting from adding some plutonium-239 to uranium-235. In any case, with or without MOX, the most commonly used technology today remains the PWRs that followed continuous improvement, especially on safety issues, typically leading to the European power reactor (EPR).

Seven technologies grouped under the 'Gen IV' family compete against each other for the nuclear power solutions of the next 40 to 50 years. The seven Gen IV candidates are: high-temperature gas-cooled reactor (HTGR); very-high-temperature reactor (VHTR); molten-salt reactor (MSR); supercritical water-cooled reactor (SCWR). These four belong to the thermal reactor family, while the fast reactor family is made up of three more candidate technologies: gas-cooled fast reactor (GFR); sodium-cooled fast reactor (SFR); and lead-cooled fast reactor (LFR). In the long run, beyond Gen IV, fusion may be the day-after-tomorrow technology, typically for the twenty-second century. Fusion is currently being investigated and to some extent developed at ITER, the international consortium based in the southeast of France.

The future of nuclear energy is a major question mark at the heart of a public debate internationally and sits at the crossroad of many fields: geopolitics, industrial strategies, science and application, nuclear physics, materials, biology, waste treatment, public acceptance, safety issues, political decision, leadership, etc. Some argue that humankind is taking too high a risk with such an industry that carries with it major safety issues for populations in the short term, and for humanity, biodiversity and the planet in the very long term (thousands of years). Some others argue that the world's energy equation does not look good without a significant energy storage solution readily available. Renewable energy is intermittent, leading to unreasonably high investment costs to cover the peak needs, thus justifying a base of nuclear energy to avoid overinvestment, costly energy and frequent shortages.

Quantum Computing

So far computers have been based on the binary distinction of [0] and [1]. Simple operations from logics (+, -, *, /, >, <, etc.) repeatedly combined and recombined have helped program a wealth of applications that made it possible to improve our lives (calculating quickly and accurately, implementing complex algorithms, storing and retrieving data, etc.). In this context, quantum computing stands as a potential paradigmatic shift in the computer industry. It draws on the specific behaviors of infinitely small particles in the realm of quantum physics. The state of a particle can be described by the superposition of [0] and [1], away from the binary dichotomy of current computers. While the current computers deal with bits, the quantum computer will deal with qubits. These properties of particles open the door to much faster computing. Several options can be dealt with in parallel, in the same operation, making it possible to discard many sub-options much faster.

Applications of quantum computing are envisioned in chemistry and the chemical industry to simulate molecules, financial modeling, weather forecasting, artificial intelligence and machine learning (to cope with massive data treatment), drug design and development in pharmaceutics, cryptography and cybersecurity, and supply chain optimization (logistics).

This is still a work in progress, but there are major R&D programs publicly (and, surprisingly, privately as well – a weak signal indeed) funded in the US, China and Europe.

Definitions of Key Terms

Technology is the daughter of science and techniques.[5] Yet, it cannot be reduced to the simple use of scientific discovery, nor is it just implementation of technical empiricism.

Science relates to basic knowledge produced through research activities. Science aims at identifying, characterizing and modeling natural phenomena taking place in our environment. These can be physical, chemical, biological, medical, social, etc.

Techniques relate to know-how built empirically through human action, as concrete experience builds up through learning by doing. Techniques are made up of human skills, recipes on how to operate, practical ways of producing an artefact or conducting a routine. To a large extent, techniques are tacit in Nonaka and Takeuchi's sense, i.e., they are not codified – or only in part – and thus difficult to replicate and imitate without previous experience. Transferring technical know-how requires some form of companionship, meaning working together with experienced masters who teach by demonstration. Techniques are embedded in practice and action. This represents both a strength and a weakness. Obviously, techniques are powerful precisely because they work, as they result from experimentation and accumulated experience. Conversely, techniques may be difficult to adapt and extend to new contexts and situations because no or too little explicit, articulated knowledge of why they work is available. Empirical know-how may be costly to transfer, with uncertain results.

Technology relates to the design, production and distribution of goods and services, in response to socio-economic needs. Technology is more than a technique: technology combines technical know-how with scientific knowledge (explaining how it works) to fulfil explicit socio-economic goals. In this sense, technology should be managed, even though it includes tacit knowhow that is by nature more difficult to manage.

Innovation may be defined as the making of the new. Invention is limited to expressing a new idea, a new concept, sketching a new way with no real confrontation with technical or marketing feasibility. A patent signals an invention. In contrast, innovation bridges the gap between the idea and its real implementation to serve a human

---

5 This section is adapted from Durand (2004), with kind permission from Palgrave Macmillan/ Springer.

need. Innovation is an idea put to work. It is change implemented, be it incremental or radical, for product design, manufacturing process or organizational matters etc. An innovation requires an invention to be further developed, industrialized and commercialized.

There is a natural link between technology and innovation. Technology improves continuously through a flow of incremental innovations that construct and shape a technological trajectory à la Dosi (see Part I): the trajectory exploits the potential of the technological seam or paradigm (dominant design, dominant process) until a radical innovation occurs, substituting a new dominant technology for the former dominant technology now becoming obsolete. This is what Schumpeter described as creative destruction. This will be presented in detail in Part I.

With these definitions in mind, I can now clarify what I mean by the strategic management of technology and innovation. The **strategic management of technology** includes the following:
– observation, identification, and assessment of competing technologies to fulfil a certain market need;
– selection of the most relevant technologies from the feasible options to help the firm build a sustainable, possibly long-lasting competitive advantage;
– access to the knowledge base required for the technologies selected, be it through internal development, R&D partnerships or acquisitions;
– management of research activities, development, feasibility studies and more generally project management;
– subsequent implementation and improvement of product and process technologies integrated in the firm's portfolio;
– and weeding out former technologies, progressively or suddenly rendered obsolete by new technologies.

Most if not all the issues listed above describe the extent to which the strategic management of technology gravitates around the theme of technical change. The main challenges have less to do with technology itself but more with the shift from old to new technologies. This is probably why the theme of innovation has been historically identified as equivalent to the management of technologies, even though not all innovations affecting firms are technological; far from it. Organizational or social innovations (which are sometimes called soft innovations) have in fact been as important, if not more important, in practice.

The strategic management of innovation thus goes beyond the limits of technologies to address the larger scope of change in general. Innovation can indeed deal with the technological side of human activities, thus with product design and manufacturing processes. Innovation may also deal with the organizational and social side, e.g., external interactions with suppliers, clients or partners,- as well as internal processes which became routine in the way the firm operates, as suggested by Nelson and Winter.

The **strategic management of innovation** includes:

- the promotion of innovation to facilitate and encourage the emergence of new ideas, both listening to proposals, regardless of where they originate from within the company or the outside, or how disturbing they may appear at first, and sponsoring subsequent development projects;
- selection of relevant innovations for the firm, managing a portfolio of innovative opportunities which are each financially accessible with reasonable expectations for their marketing relevance and technical feasibility;
- management of the resources and knowledge base of the firm required to conduct the innovation projects, including through external partnerships;
- and managing the social and organizational implications of innovations, including the sources of inertia and possibly the opposition which may arise when change is taking place.

As a result, the strategic management of technology and innovation addresses issues that are at the heart of strategic management: Which technologies should the firm select? Which technological change to promote against competition? How to access the necessary knowledge, especially the skills and capabilities that may be lacking? How to reinforce the innovative capability of the organization? How to select innovation projects, and according to which criteria?

The presentation of the frameworks developed in this book does not explicitly follow the steps used in theory building but implicitly draws from them. Observe phenomena, describe what is being observed, cluster the results of the observations into categories, identify patterns, conceptualize to offer some generality, represent and then, in academic work, model and test the relevance, accuracy and validity of the models. In fact, the frameworks that I present in this book stem from research that typically followed the above steps. I essentially put these research results together into an integrated, hopefully comprehensive, presentation. In this context, the examples discussed along the way come as illustrations to keep the content of the book as concrete as possible.

The flow of the book is as follows.

Part I presents a model of technological change, capturing how technology tends to evolve. Long periods of continuity (where a dominant technology improves through incremental innovation) are punctuated by radical change bringing about "disruption" (in the sense of turmoil) in the competitive dynamics.[6] Some of these changes are very radi-

---

[6] Note that, at this early stage, I use the word "disruption" in the sense of a significant change that affects the competitive dynamics in an industry. Hence, disruption may be seen as equivalent to the outcome of a revolution, a radical or almost radical innovation, a major or at least significant shift in

cal but rather rare, introducing a new technological paradigm and causing much turmoil in the competitive arena. The other technological changes, of intermediate intensity, stay within the current paradigm, contributing to shape the technological trajectory. Part I then discusses the strategic implications of each of these types of technological evolution on the competitive dynamics in industries or strategic arenas. Part I helps visualize technological trajectories, S-curves for technological substitutions, or dual technology trees that offer a representation of the intensity of technological change (from incremental to paradigmatic shifts).

Part II brings an additional layer of complexity to the model, focusing on paradigmatic shifts, i.e., radical innovations, showing how the dynamics of technological substitution can depart from the idealized S-curve to form a variety of patterns. Part II presents, maps, discusses and models ten observed patterns. Understanding these potential departures from the classic S-curve model is essential to grasp the corresponding dynamics and their strategic implications. The forces at work behind the ten patterns are identified and discussed. This is important to anticipate the risk of a technological substitution seemingly following the beginning of an S-curve but departing from that idealized basic pattern. In turn, Part II develops the idea of bifurcation windows and trigger relays. These two related concepts are key in the context of this book. Bifurcation windows are situations where technology evolution in an industry can suddenly bifurcate away from the dynamics that prevailed up to then, opening an unexpected new trajectory. In this sense, bifurcation windows are specific (and very sensitive) states of a socio-technological system where sudden shifts can occur. A trigger relay is a specific (potentially minor) evolution of a sub-part of the system, possibly a single element, often not standing at the heart of the system but on the side. Yet, given the sensitive state of the system within a bifurcation window, the trigger relay will sparkle and then amplify a bifurcation, somehow liberating the potential of change kept dormant in the system so far. Part II thus discusses how to identify the small signals that can help spot such bifurcation windows and potential trigger relays whose strategic consequences may be very significant.

Part III adds the competence perspective to the picture. The starting point is that technological forecasting is a risky activity. In fact, I argue that technology forecasting is too risky to stand at the foundation of strategic choices. Instead, my proposition is to think about technology via the underlying competence base (the knowledge and capabilities required by the technologies). The core proposition of Part III is to insure against technology uncertainty by building up competence ahead of time to cover the firm against technologies that may not seem to be the most probable winners in the race, yet spending some resources to get prepared for them, just in case, should one of these unexpectedly win in the end. This does not mean developing all candidate

---

key success factors in an industry. I will refine and amend this simplified view when discussing Christensen's innovator's dilemma (1997) and his sustaining/disruptive duality (see Part I, Chapter 8).

technologies (seen as of today) but making sure to secure enough of a competence base from which a catch-up race could take place if need be. I argue that organizational competence (knowledge, know-how, attitude) is what is being challenged by technical change. (Teece calls them capabilities.) This suggests analyzing the potential strategic effect of the arrival of new technologies by looking at their impact on the portfolio of competence of a company and that of its competitors (incumbents, new entrants, etc.). Part III thus suggests assessing the "competence gap" (the gap between the current portfolio of competence of the firm and that required by a potentially future dominant technology). The same analysis should be conducted for competitors as well. This leads to consider the options available to bridge the competence gap ahead of time and ahead of competitors (incumbents and potential new entrants).

Part IV discusses path creation, in the sense of thinking about technology strategically to build a path into the future for the firm, using roadmaps and adapting the competence base of the organization. Part IV discusses ways to identify and access the new set of competencies needed to compete under (potential) new technological regimes. This includes internal R&D; technology intelligence; identifying pervasive key technologies; intrapreneurship and the promotion of innovation in the organization to regenerate the portfolio of businesses (and competence) from within; leveraging the firm's technology ecosystems ("outside-in" perspective) through licensing technology from outside; corporate venturing; relational strategies, including partnerships and alliances; and acquisitions. Part IV calls upon the three frameworks presented in the book, adopting a practitioner's perspective.

In short, this book offers an overall framework made up of three components, each built in a specific part, followed by a part dedicated to the managerial implications of the framework, as represented below:

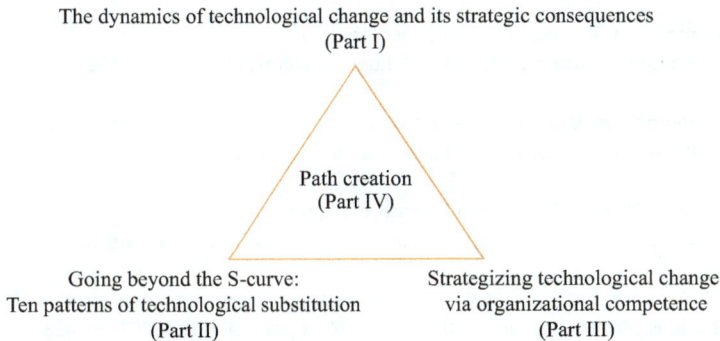

The dynamics of technological change and its strategic consequences
(Part I)

Path creation
(Part IV)

Going beyond the S-curve:　　　　　　　Strategizing technological change
Ten patterns of technological substitution　　via organizational competence
(Part II)　　　　　　　　　　　　　　(Part III)

Overall Structure of the book

References for Chapter 1 and Further Reading

Christensen, C. M. (1997). *The Innovator's Dilemma: When New Technologies Cause Great Firms to Fail*. Harvard Business School Press.

Dosi, G. (1982). Technology paradigms, technological trajectories. *Research Policy*, Volume 11, Issue 3, June 1982, Pages 147–162

Durand, T. (2004). The strategic management of technology and innovation. In *Bringing Technology and Innovation into the Boardroom: Strategy, Innovation and Competences for Business Value* (pp. 47–75). EITIM, Palgrave Macmillan.

Gille, B. (1978). *Histoire des techniques: technique et civilisation, technique et sciences*. Gallimard.

Knight, F. H. (1921). *Risk, Uncertainty and Profit*. Boston MA: Hart, Schaffner and Marx; Houghton Mifflin.

Nelson, R. R., & Winter, S. G. (1982). *An Evolutionary Theory of Economic Change*. Harvard University Press.

Orwell, G. (1949). *Nineteen Eighty-Four*. London, Secker & Warburg.

Further Reading

Abetti, P. A., (2000). Critical success factors for radical technological innovation: A five case study. *Creativity and Innovation Management*, *9*(4), 208–221. https://doi.org/10.1111/1467-8691.00194

Adner, R., & Kapoor, R. (2016). Innovation ecosystems and the pace of substitution: Re-examining technology S-curves. *Strategic Management Journal*, *37*(4), 625–648.

Christensen, J. F. (1995). Asset profiles for technological innovation. *Research Policy*, *24*(5), 727–745. https://doi.org/10.1016/0048-7333(94)00794-8

Cooper, R. G., Edgett, S. J., & Kleinschmidt, E. J. (2000). New problems, new solutions: Making portfolio management more effective. *Research-Technology Management*, *43*(2), 18–33.

Dosi, G. (2023). *The Foundations of Complex Evolving Economies*. Oxford University Press.

Eggers, J. P., & Kaplan, S. (2009). Cognition and renewal: comparing CEO and organizational effects on incumbent adaptation to technical change. *Organization Science*, *20*(2), 461–477.

Godet, M. (2006). *Creating Futures: Scenario Planning as a Strategic Management Tool* (2nd ed.). Economica-Brookings.

Grebel, T. (2009). Technological change: A microeconomic approach to the creation of knowledge. *Structural Change and Economic Dynamics*, *20*(4), 301–312. https://doi.org/10.1016/j.strueco.2009.05.003

Henderson, R. and Iain Cockburn (1994) Measuring Competence? Exploring Firm Effects in Pharmaceutical Research. Strategic Management Journal, volume 15, Issue S1, 63–84 https://doi.org/10.1002/smj.4250150906

Landini, F., Lee, K., & Malerba, F. (2017). A history-friendly model of the successive changes in industrial leadership and the catch-up by latecomers. *Research Policy*, *46*(2), 431–446. https://doi.org/10.1016/j.respol.2016.09.005

McEvily, S. K., Eisenhardt, K. M., & Prescott, J. E. (2004). The global acquisition, leverage, and protection of technological competencies. *Strateg. Manage. J. 25*(8–9), 713–722. https://doi.org/10.1002/smj.425

Nonaka, I., & Takeuchi, H. (1995). *The Knowledge-Creating Company: How Japanese Companies Create the Dynamics of Innovation*. Oxford University Press, New York.

O'Reilly, C. A., Tushman, M. L. (2011). Organizational ambidexterity in action: How managers explore and exploit. Calif. *Manage. Rev.*, *53*(4), 5–22. https://doi.org/10.1525/cmr.2011.53.4.5

Orlikowski, W. J. (2002). Knowing in practice: Enacting a collective capability in distributed organizing. *Organ Sci.*, *13*(3), 249–273. https://doi.org/10.1287/orsc.13.3.249.2776

Phaal, R., Farrukh, C., and Probert, D. (2004). Technology roadmapping—A planning framework for evolution and revolution. *71*(1–2), 5–26. https://doi.org/10.1016/S0040-1625(03)00072-6

Sainsbury David (2020) "Windows of opportunity - How Nations create wealth", Profile Books, London.

Tidd J. (2023) Radical Innovation, Edward Elgar, 124p

Tidd, Joe and John R. Bessant (2020). Managing innovation: integrating technological, market and organizational change, Wiley & sons, 7th ed, 624 p.

Teece D. J., Pisano, G., & Shuen, A. (1997). Dynamic capabilities and strategic management. *SMJ*, *18*(7), 509–533. https://doi.org/10.1002/(SICI)1097-0266(199708)18:7<509::AID-SMJ882>3.0.CO;2-Z

Yang, K.-P., Chou, C., Chiu, Y.-J. (2014). How unlearning affects radical innovation: The dynamics of social capital and slack resources. *Technological Forecasting and Social Change, (87)*, 152–163. https://doi.org/10.1016/j.techfore.2013.12.014

Part I: **Understanding the Dynamics of Technological Change and its Strategic Consequences**

If we are to think about technology strategically to create a path for a firm into the future, we first need to better understand how technology evolves and then how technological change affects competition. More specifically, we need to understand how technological change takes place and its impact on the firm's strategic position in the competitive dynamics of an industry (or a specific strategic arena). Part I develops a framework that brings insight into these two combined questions.

This is what the ten chapters of Part I are about. (The five chapters of Part II will present an add-on to the framework.) I am going to build the framework step by step. I will start with a simplified model and each subsequent chapter will add a layer of complexity and refinement to the model. This is drawn from empirical case studies that I conducted over the years as well as work conducted with colleagues, including PhD students whose theses I supervised. This, combined with theoretical contributions from the literature and my own observations when working with companies, leads to the framework presented hereafter. (See references and further reading at the end of each part.)

https://doi.org/10.1515/9783111397979-002

Chapter 2
A Simplified Smooth View of Technological Substitution

First, I start by presenting a stylized description of the dynamics of technologies with a simplified model.

Let us consider a generic need to be fulfilled in a market; this need is called function F hereafter. Take for example the need for a tool to make calculations easily and quickly with reliable results. Historically, this generic need has been covered by a sequence of solutions that were "dominant" in their own time, e.g., an abacus, a slide rule, an electronic calculator, a PC, a PDA or a smart phone (Fig. 1).

The x-axis on Fig. 1 is time, while the y-axis shows a cost/performance index for each of the technologies represented. This index gives an indication of the improvement of a technology along a curve over time – improvement in the sense of cost decrease and/or performance increase.

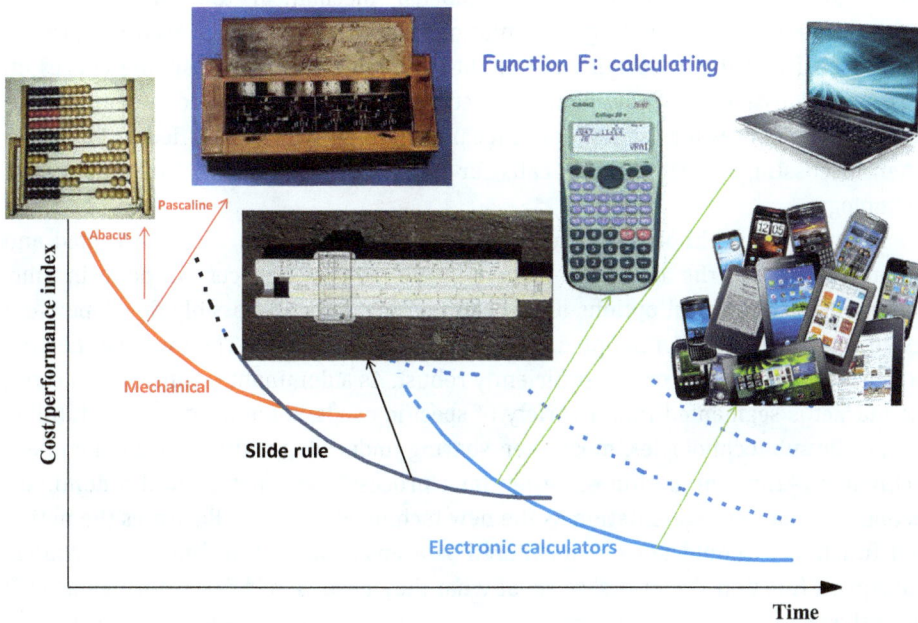

Fig. 1: Technological evolution in calculating tools.

https://doi.org/10.1515/9783111397979-003

Note that I added Blaise Pascal's calculator known as the Pascaline on Fig. 1.[7] Although this incredible invention never became dominant, it illustrates one among many technologies that could have played a role in the history of technologies for a specific function F, but never came even close to it. This illustrates that we are not discussing technological inventions, but innovations widely offered on the market and put to work – at least long enough to generate strategies among firms competing to fulfill function F.

In fact, the example of the Pascaline raises an important question: When is it that a solution is just a variation of a "main" technology? Typically, the Pascaline is a mechanical calculator that could be considered part of the same family as the abacus: Should it be presented as part of the curve labeled "mechanical" or with a specific curve (in fact a dotted line as it never went beyond prototypes)? In a way the question could apply to a slide rule as well because it is also mechanical – in its own way. Yet, the slide rule and the Pascaline have little to do with an abacus. A slide rule relies on the mathematical notion of logarithm that converts a multiplication into an addition (and vice versa with the exponential function). This would suggest that slide rules deserve their own curve. A similar argument could apply for the Pascaline as well. A way to go could be to rename the curve labeled "mechanical" to "abacus". Another way to solve the matter is to group solutions fulfilling function F according to the characteristics of the underlying dominant technology. In that sense, the curves on Figs. 1 and 2 essentially show dominant technologies, while variations would be attached to the curves for the dominant technology. This will be clarified in Chapter 5 when discussing Fig. 11. Yet, this calls for a preliminary definition of a dominant technology.

A **dominant technology** is the technology which has been widely accepted and adopted as state of the art by the players in the industry at a certain point in time. Competing technological options have been investigated and possibly developed and tested but have not been adopted, except possibly for niches. They were either too expensive, too futuristic or not sufficiently robust. As a dominant technology matures, the market is segmented into a variety of specific needs, some of which are fulfilled by specific sub-technologies, most often sharing underlying traits with the dominant technology – thus the notion of design (and process) variation around a dominant technology. Market segmentation as the new technology evolves illustrates the notion that function F should not be considered as a given. In fact, technological change transforms function F as users' sense of what they need is being transformed as well along the way.

---

7 This mechanical calculator invented by Blaise Pascal in 1642 made it possible to make additions swiftly, allowing for the carry. Several prototypes are displayed at the Musée des Arts et Métiers at Cnam in Paris.

For instance, an electronic calculator, a PC, a PDA or a mobile phone all stem from electronics while serving specific needs and specific market segments (everyday use, business application, engineering calculations, scientific use for programming algorithms, etc.).

In any case, the dominant technology remains the reference on the market. At least at that point in time, no other technology is in a better position to fulfil the generic need F. A process of maturation takes place, forming a continuous curve. All in all, this process of maturation is rather slow along the curve.

However, when a dominant technology is challenged and cannibalized by a radically new technology, radical change usually occurs much faster. A new curve appears and develops. More concretely, each of the solutions shown on Fig. 1 is attached to a technology (in the sense of a way to fulfill the need and a process to manufacture the product or to deliver the offering, including some services attached). One after the other, these technologies have substituted at some point for the previously dominant technology. Each technology shown cannibalized the market position of its predecessor, established itself as dominant and remained so for several years or decades – or sometimes even longer. This lasted until a radically new technology came out to disrupt the industry and replace the previously dominant technology.

In addition, as discussed above, *function F is in fact a moving target* co-evolving with technology and is likely to segment itself into sub-functions. The above example on electronic calculation suggests that function F should not be considered as a given. Function F tends to evolve over time. This results from customers' needs changing again and again. Typically, as the technology serving the initial function F improves, users learn and adapt their expectations. This means that function F (capturing market needs) and technology (fulfilling function F) co-evolve. Yet, a word of caution is needed here. Freeman used the analogy of a pair of scissors featuring the combined effect of the supply side and the demand side as two blades. I argue that this representation may be misleading because it suggests that the two sides operate symmetrically. Instead, I argue that the supply side is proactive while the demand side is reactive. Freeman's scissors do not do justice to the driving role of the supply side (including the dynamics of technology). Typically, when a very new technology disrupts an industry, like one of the curves on Fig. 1, users cannot specify their needs, given the potentialities of the new technology of which they know nothing. Hence, they wait for the supply side to offer new products and services stemming from the new technology. Then and only then can they react and contribute to express their needs by choosing the new offerings – or not. As a result, marketers (on the supply side) have no choice but to guess users' specifications on their own, iterating over time as the new technology unveils itself. Technological innovators search for users who search for their needs. This interactive process is a groping exercise altogether. It takes time.

Function F also evolves as it is segmented into a set of sub-functions, each corresponding to market sub-segments emerging along the way. This was the case in the example of electronic calculators where specific devices fit specific market needs: starting from a meta-function (calculating swiftly) and a meta-technology (electronics), we end up with an array of devices, all electronic, and a set of sub-functionalities, all having to do with calculation.

This suggests that function F is a moving target that should be looked at dynamically, not statically. In addition, function F may be decomposed and fragmented in a variety of sub-functions according to specific needs.

In short, technology on the supply side is not the only evolving player dancing the tango. The demand side plays its dynamic role as well – although in a more reactive mode.

Chapter 9 on market concept formation will discuss this matter around function F in further detail and I will introduce what I call the customer concept tree. In the meantime, the reasoning in Part I will keep referring to function F to develop a framework for the strategic significance of technological change.

A Simplified Model of Technological Change

Figure 2 presents the sequence of technological substitutions over time (the x-axis) according to a cost/performance index (the y-axis). Each technology is shown as a curve where the cost/performance index improves continuously (i.e., decreases) either because the performance increases or the cost decreases, or both. At the beginning of each of the curves, on the right steep part, the index improves quickly because of the potential of the new way of doing things, while the left part of the curves is flatter as most of the low-hanging fruit of the technology have already been picked for performance or cost improvements.

In practice, the cost/performance index is difficult to build. (The word "cost" is used here in the sense of what it costs to the user. In that sense, "price paid" could be used instead of cost. Yet I stick to the word cost as it stands for the user as the cost of fulfilling function F.) In most cases, the cost of various solutions may be compared across technologies and over time – with exceptions though.[8] In contrast, comparing the performance of technologies is trickier. Indeed, various technologies may not offer the same sub-functionalities. Going from point A to point B may be done by train, by plane, by car, by bus, riding a bicycle or by foot. The comfort, the speed, the carbon footprint, the flexibility (returning to departure if need be), the possibility to rest, work, eat during travel, all these aspects and many others combine into a mix that may be difficult to compare analytically among modes of transportation. The comparison may even be impossible when technologies offer totally different func-

---

8 Typically, the cost of fulfilling the function "accessing and listening to recorded music" is not easily comparable when buying a CD vs. subscribing to a streaming service.

tionalities: an electronic calculator offers programming or storing and retrieving of intermediate results. This is totally absent for a slide rule. These technologies are simply incommensurate (literally "not measurable one against the other").

In other words, the cost/performance index of each of the technologies shown on Fig. 2 is conceptual, giving a sense of the improvements of a technology in terms of both cost and performance but not fully measurable and most often not comparable. Note that many studies in industrial economics tried to come up with a method to grasp such an index, but those attempts essentially failed.

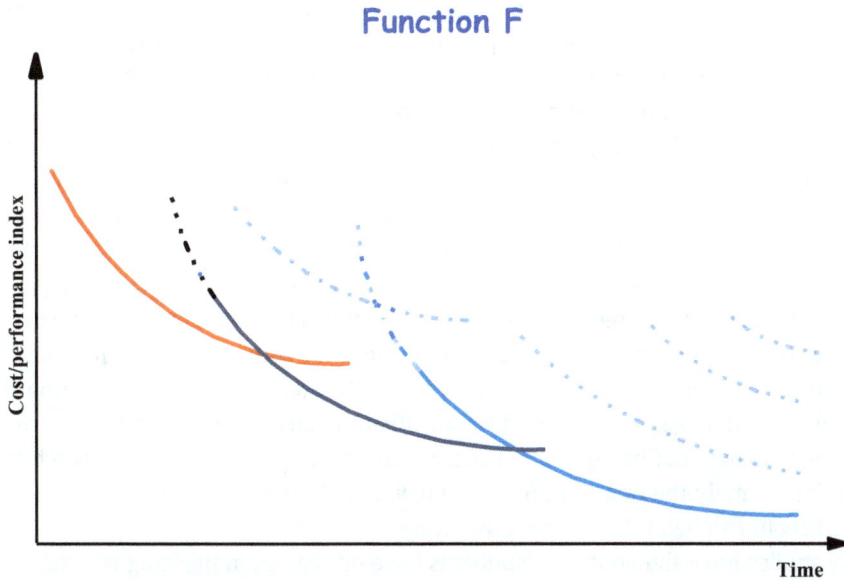

Fig. 2: A simplified model of technological evolution.

In Fig. 2, for the sake of clarity, many technical sub-options that may have been considered and possibly tested at some point by some competitors but without enough success are eliminated from the main paths shown, namely the trajectories. The Pascaline in Fig. 1 illustrated this point. One should thus keep in mind a diverse, mushrooming reality of technological innovation that unfolds in many different, contradictory directions at the same time, in unexpected ways.

Over time, new options may be considered to serve the same need. Among these, some promising options may emerge as the potential future dominant technology, with the promise of superior performance, reduced costs, new functionalities or a combination of these. Candidate new entrants are usually developing and promoting new technologies (one or a few) as they hope to put themselves in a position to surf the wave of change. The dotted lines on Fig. 2 show the emergence of a new technology, when it is not fully functional, nor fully reliable with not enough up times and still too many down times, still too costly – typically due to lack of volume. Some of these options actively developed by potential new entrants may never come to real life on the market (the dotted line remains dotted, instead of turning into a continuous line: outcomes simply fell short of expectations). When the dotted line turns into a continuous line, it signals that the battle starts raging between the modern and the old. Incumbents (those firms established in the business on the still dominant technology) watch out for new technologies that may threaten their position. Yet, studies show that they primarily tend to keep pushing hard to improve their dominant technology. New entrants tend to focus on specific market niches to bring the new technology into the business. The new technology is thus introduced focusing on specific needs that so far were improperly covered by the current dominant technology. Incumbents under such attacks are essentially eager to defend their technology on the bulk of their territory, possibly abandoning niches to new entrants. However, even though incumbents may not be fully aware of it, the still dominant technology runs in the flat part of the corresponding curve on Fig. 2. This means that the marginal return (index improvements on the y-axis) for the marginal euro invested in R&D on the dominant technology keeps decreasing. In contrast, new entrants launch the candidate new technology in the steep part of their curve, thus making significant improvements. The dynamic is likely to see the curves intersect, with the cost/performance index of the new technology diving below that of the soon-to-be-former dominant technology. At that stage, incumbents face a difficult choice of either sticking to the dominant technology that brought them success and performance so far, or switch to a new option, namely the one that, in their view, may become dominant. If they do, they are likely to run behind, becoming followers.

Many studies have shown that incumbents have difficulties in deciding whether to switch or not; inertia is at work. This may be due to uncertainty about the real potential of the technological options under consideration, fixed assets linked to the current dominant technology not fully amortized yet, emotional attachment to the current dominant technology that constitutes their comfort zone, candid hope to improve the current technology to resist the intruders, etc.

Figure 3 illustrates this point for the case of the computer industry. In the 1960s and 1970s, IBM's dominance over the industry was massive worldwide. Some even said that IBM "owned" the computer industry of the time. Yet, when Apple triggered the paradigmatic shift from mainframes to PCs, IBM staggered and came close to full collapse.

The subsequent major change took the form of the autonomous PC reconnecting back into a network, paving the way for a connected world with streaming and the platform businesses. (This could be seen as some form of a counterattack by the mainframe in the sense of a central network, with terminals at the periphery, except the nature of centralization had changed from distributed mainframes to a network.) By

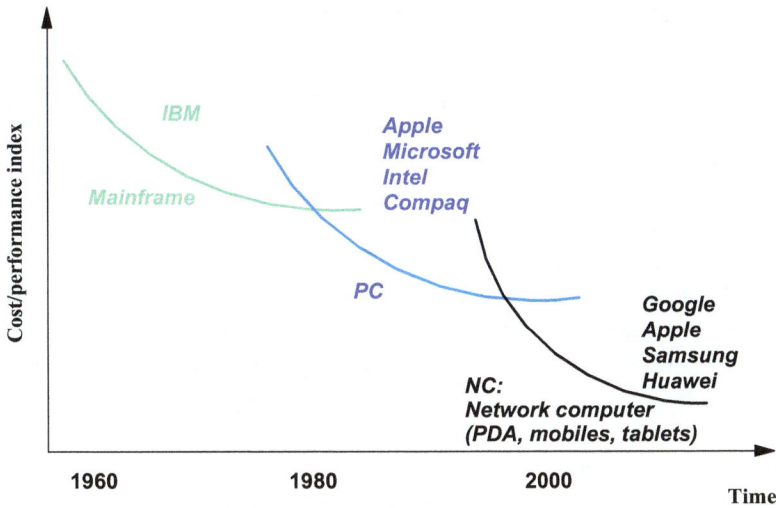

Fig. 3: Technological revolutions in the computer industry.

then IBM had reinvented itself in services and was too far out to come back into the game. In contrast, Apple and Microsoft managed to adapt to the new change.

Radical innovation shakes an industry, opening the door to newcomers and pushing out some incumbents, but not necessarily all of them. Chapters 6 and 7 in Part I and Chapter 19 in part III will discuss ways to anticipate the extent of a shakeout expected from a technological revolution.

Note that we look here at technology at a meta-level. A curve shown on Fig. 2 represents a technological trajectory in Dosi's terms, exploring a new technological paradigm. In a way, Fig. 2 offers a visual representation of the conceptual vision that Dosi brilliantly proposed as will be discussed next.

Dosi's Technological Paradigms and Technological Trajectories

Dosi borrowed the concept of paradigm used by Thomas Kuhn in science. Originally, a paradigm is a theory that explains phenomena observed in the world, at least to some extent.

For example, in Newtonian mechanics, the law of gravity helps understand how planets gravitate around stars according to predictable orbits or how galaxies are formed and evolve. The Newtonian paradigm is strong enough to explain most of what we see out in space. There are exceptions though. When it comes to very high speed or very small particles, Newtonian mechanics starts being inadequate. In such extreme situations, the classical law of gravity does not provide an explanation of what can be observed. It can no longer predict the trajectory, the position or the speed of objects. A new theory is needed to explain what the former theory cannot. This is the gap that the theories of general relativity and quantum mechanics offered to bridge. As progress is made in science, a new paradigm emerges to deal with the phenomena improperly explained by the former dominant paradigm. The new paradigm usually encompasses the previous paradigm. (Note that a grand theory of everything is still missing in physics. There is a grand unified theory accounting for three of the four basic interactions known, but researchers in physics are still working hard to unify the four interactions. A new umbrella paradigm is still missing.)

With the concept of technological paradigm, Dosi proposes a metaphor, importing concepts developed for science into the realm of technology. The dominant technology reflects the state of the paradigm prevailing at a point in time. To fulfill some specific socio-economic need, captured by function F on Fig. 2, new development may then offer a completely renewed and improved way of doing things, a radically new technology stemming from a new paradigm. As the new paradigm is being explored, through iterations between supply and demand, as needs and solutions meet and mate, the technology evolves, creating a path that Dosi calls a technological trajectory. This is what is shown visually on Fig. 2. I use the term "technological seam" – as in mining – to describe Dosi's technological trajectory exploring the paradigm, following the vein where the richest ore can be mined.

In this sense, radical innovation occurs when moving from a previous paradigm to the next, i.e., when a paradigmatic shift takes place. The simplified model of technological evolution presented here identifies two polar extremes of the intensity of technological change. On the one hand incremental innovation (continuous improvements), on the other hand radical innovation (a revolution or paradigmatic shift). This simplified model suggests that technology evolves through incremental innovation in long periods of continuity disrupted from time to time by radical innovation in the form of paradigmatic shifts.[9]

This simplified vision should be immediately nuanced in the case of meta-paradigms that stem from the convergence and aggregation of sub-paradigms. Paradoxically, and though it might seem oxymoronic, in such cases, a paradigm can evolve incrementally. This is interesting and worth digging into, even briefly at least for completeness' sake. Two cases from the nine presented in the introduction of the book can illustrate the matter.

Pedota, Grilli and Piscitello argue that a new paradigm can emerge from the aggregation of sub-paradigms. They studied the case of additive manufacturing (AM), also known as 3D printing. AM is composed of an array of mechanical, material and chemical process sub-technologies to add layers of material to form a part or a component – e.g., binder jetting, directed energy deposition, material extrusion, material jetting, sheet lamination, powder bed fusion, or photopolymerization. Tezenas du Montcel also discusses the matter in detail. The digital side of AM comes from computer-aided design (CAD) and computer-aided manufacturing (CAM). From their own obser-

---

9 This resonates with punctuated equilibrium and gradualism in the theories of evolution of life on Earth. Gradualism mirrors incremental innovation, while the notion of punctuation echoes radical innovation and vice versa.

vations, Pedota, Grilli and Piscitello suggest that the meta-paradigm may form and evolve incrementally, while the sub-paradigms bring in their radicalness into the new meta-paradigm through aggregation and convergence.

They argue that the convergence process of 3D printing with CAD/CAM forms AM as a new meta-paradigm that carries Dosi's properties of a paradigm. "AM can be framed as a technological paradigm, being consistent with the epistemological notion of 'an outlook, a set of procedures, a definition of the relevant problems and of the specific knowledge related to their solution'. The outlook is clear-cut and revolutionary, creating a direct bridge between digital and physical objects."

Pedota, Grilli and Piscitello further argue that AM has already started to revolutionize businesses (e.g., aeronautics or automobile to design and manufacture lighter parts) and is expected to continue to do so in a variety of sectors (from fashion and clothing to electronics and biotech/pharma). Yet, as they rightly point out, AM evolves incrementally from the convergence and aggregation of sub-paradigms while its origins carry the radicalness of the sub-technologies fulfilling business needs in a variety of applications. In that sense, the idea that a paradigm means radical change needs to be reformulated. More precisely, a new paradigm emerging from the convergence and aggregation of sub-paradigms may evolve essentially incrementally.

I add to the above the case of the fourth industrial revolution. Again, we have here a new paradigm stemming from the convergence and aggregation of a set of disruptive technologies (artificial intelligence, machine learning, cobots, big data, big analytics, internet of things, preventive maintenance, etc.). All these technologies have been around for some time, but each carries their radicality boosted by the increasing speed and volume of data that information systems can handle. In a way, the new industry of the future paradigm tends to evolve incrementally as the radical new technologies attached to sub-paradigms converge and aggregate, themselves continuously fueled by the expanding capacity of digital technologies to capture, store, retrieve, process, compute and visualize data and information. I would even argue that the aggregation of the sub-technologies sounds more powerful in the industry of the future paradigm than in the AM case. In the case of the industry of the future, technologies are very likely to recombine to create new opportunities. This is less so in the case of AM as technologies find a variety of applications distributed across sectors, suggesting an additive mode of aggregation more than a potential for recombinations. However, Pedota, Grilli and Piscitello are right in using the word aggregation when pointing to AM sub-technologies combining to CAD/CAM digital technologies.

I will come back to the intensity of innovation in detail as I add layers of complexity to the overall model of technological change. This is important from a strategic viewpoint because the intensity of technological change directly relates to the strategic consequences to be expected from the change, namely the impact on competition. Indeed, technological change can be both a threat for incumbents and an opportunity for intruders. This was already illustrated by the new entrants' battle against incumbents when it comes to introducing a new technology to substitute for the current dominant technology. A paradigmatic shift creates a wave of change that can be surfed by new entrants to displace incumbents. In contrast, incremental innovations tend to entrench the incumbents in their dominance.

In this context of continuity vs. discontinuities, Teece challenges Dosi on the grounds of the latter focusing too much on trajectories and not enough on paradigmatic shifts. Teece argues that entrepreneurial decisions made within the firm should not be limited to the current paradigm. He urges managers to consider a wide spectrum of solutions, even outside the current paradigm. I agree with Teece on his recommendation, but I disagree on his critique. I argue that Dosi's description of paradigms and trajectories strikes a proper balance between continuity (being stuck on a trajectory) and discontinuities (as his vision also captures the idea of switching to radically new technological options via the concept of a paradigm shift). In that sense, I challenge Teece's critical point of view on Dosi's visionary contribution. In contrast, I fully support Teece's concept of dynamic capabilities (those very specific capabilities that firms need to extract themselves from the habits and routines attached to the soon-to-be-former dominant technology), a key theme that I will discuss at length in Part III. Given that this controversy on Dosi's contribution is important for the topic of the book, I briefly dig into the matter below.

> While otherwise supporting Dosi's insight, Teece points out the constraining nature of technological paradigms. He thus urges managers to think about technological progress not only along the trajectories within the current dominant paradigm, but also along other technological paths attached to other paradigms. "Dosi's perspective of how R&D or other decisions get made is of course at odds with a rational unitary actor making optimal decisions about innovation. The paradigm recognizes that path-dependent learning and decision heuristics can confine technological advance to accepted avenues. Often this is desirable, but there are occasions when it is not." Teece goes one step further suggesting that firms should not focus their innovation thrust within the current dominant paradigm as if this was part of Dosi's proposition: "Another useful extension would involve juxtaposing entrepreneurial actions with decisions that come out of accepted and embedded paradigms operating inside the firm. Clearly, a good deal of what we think about as entrepreneurial decision-making takes place in a manner orthogonal to Dosi's paradigmatic representation of technological development. As already discussed, breakthrough solutions to a problem are often defined as ones that lie outside the paradigm." It seems to me that Teece pushes Dosi's insight a bit too much into a normative exploration of the current dominant paradigm only. Instead, I argue that Dosi's framework clearly opens the door to reimagining the future of a business through scanning for renewed technological paradigms instead of sticking to the "normal" current dominant paradigm. This does not mean that Teece's idea of dynamic capabilities is not needed. Quite the opposite. Anytime a firm is going to explore new territories, away from the current dominant paradigm, there will be a need for the ability to move out of the tracks of the trajectories followed up to that point. There will be a need for dynamic capability. I argue that Dosi's framework includes both continuity and incremental innovation along trajectories exploring the current dominant paradigm and the opportunities of disruption attached to paradigmatic shifts.

Teece regrets that Dosi's technological paradigms have had a much more significant impact in economics than in management. I could not agree more. In a way, my writing of this book was triggered by the same concern.

From a different, although related, perspective, a series of early studies on technological evolution led to a set of very useful representations that stand as a landmark in the field. This will help add a layer of complexity to my initial, simplified model of technological evolution. (One could in fact compare this simplified model to Bore's model of atoms. It helps shape a first acceptable description of an atom, while not doing justice to the complexity of what constitutes matter.)

Chapter 3
The Abernathy-Utterback (A-U) Model

Abernathy and Utterback looked at industries disrupted by radical innovation. Their observations can be summarized as follows:

Following a paradigmatic shift, they identify three stages. Their studies show that there tend to be first many innovations that gravitate around the product design: innovation focuses on what it is that is offered, with a variety of new functionalities and sub-functionalities brought about by the many new options rendered possible by the new paradigm. Then, the rate of major innovations as they call it (y-axis on Fig. 4) tends to decrease for product design while it grows for the production process. They suggest that a dominant design has emerged from the first stage. The dominant design is a design of the product that most competitors adopted because it seems to be the best fit to users' needs. On top, its current (or anticipated) cost and thus its price make it the best offering given the variety of options offered to and tested by the users throughout stage one. (Other competitors making a different choice, away from the dominant design, may survive on niches or be thrown out from the market.) In stage two, a high rate of major innovations is observed on the production process. This suggests some form of trial and error in search for the best process (cost, quality, reliability) to produce the dominant design. In other words, stages one and two help converge towards a dominant design and a dominant process, respectively. Once this is done, in stage three, a much lower rate of major innovation is observed, with essentially incremental innovations that improve the dominant design and optimize the dominant process.

Note that the wording "rate of major innovation" (y-axis on Fig. 4) is ambiguous. It indicates both the quantity and intensity of innovations, i.e., some notion of significance. The interpretation above suggests that the y-axis indeed relates to a combination of both: fairly high numbers of innovations in stages one and two, with significant improvements of the design or process, respectively; lower significance of (incremental) innovations, possibly still in large numbers, but not changing much on the design or process in stage three.

Also note that Abernathy and Utterback do not suggest that innovation first takes place on design and then on process. They observe a higher rate of introduction of major innovations on design first and then on process. This should not be seen as a sequence that would always go "design then process then incremental innovation". This may explain the use of the word "stage" instead of "phase" in the model. Nevertheless, I argue that the A-U model does convey a bit of sequential flavor in the way the new paradigm is being explored and the way the technological trajectory forms.

The A-U model further describes the cycle composed of the three stages, naming them "fluid", "transitional" and "specific", respectively.

The fluid stage takes place just after a radical innovation struck in an industry, opening the exploration of a new paradigm. The potential of the new technology is

https://doi.org/10.1515/9783111397979-004

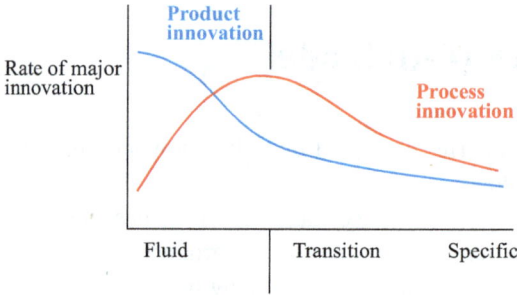

Fig. 4: The A-U model.

still to be understood. Yet, on the demand side, users cannot fully express their needs because they are not aware of the many new functionalities that could be offered within the new paradigm. The firms designing offerings on the supply side search for a demand side – the users – who are not able to express their needs in new ways given the new paradigm. Marketing has a hard time to get a sense of what the users would expect. Indeed, users have no or too little experience in new offerings brought about by the paradigmatic shift. Users cannot say whether this may or may not fit their needs better than the former dominant technology and whether they are interested or not in new functionalities rendered possible by the change, and at what price. The name of the game in that fluid stage is about learning about users' needs and users' technical inputs. As a result, the firms on the supply side keep changing the product design to test users' reactions. Thus, the word fluid. The product line is diverse, with custom designs, meaning the production process needs to be flexible to cope with frequent changes on the product design. The equipment is general purpose, with a highly skilled workforce able to adapt to constant change. The production setting is flexible but inefficient and costly.

The main point in that fluid stage is for the organization to be able to cope with change resulting from constant trial and error as providers search for users who are revisiting their own needs in a new context. Fluidity is what matters, not productivity and formal organizational control.

I already mentioned (in chapter 2) that the respective roles of supply and demand described above departs from Freeman's scissors of innovation. (Freeman argues that supply and demand operate as two blades forming a pair of scissors. This metaphor gives a feeling of symmetry, with some sort of shared responsibility in the innovation process and its outcome.) In contrast, I argue that the supply side is proactive, while the demand side is reactive. Both are indeed important but not in the same way, and firms on the supply side are in most cases the engine providing energy to the process of innovation. (Von Hippel showcased situations where users are the innovators. The point is well taken as this indeed happens, but I view these as a minority of special cases.)

The transitional stage deals with the search for the best process to produce the dominant design that emerged from the fluid stage. This stage is about scaling up to reach higher volumes and efficiency, at least around one or a few dominant product designs. Islands of automation emerge along the way. As a result, the production process becomes more rigid, and the sourcing of materials and equipment is more focused and specialized. The transitional stage leads to a dominant process which, combined to the dominant design, constitutes the dominant technology.

The specific stage ends the exploration of the new paradigm by entrenching the dominant technology in an organization dedicated to operational efficiency, mass-producing the dominant design through a dominant process that is constantly improved – incrementally. The label "specific" attached to this last stage reflects how everything is specifically attached to the dominant concept and process: the equipment, the materials sourced, the work organization are all specific to permit high productivity, low cost and high quality and reliability. In this context, incremental innovation is welcome, but more significant changes are rejected because they would disturb the setting that has been carefully optimized over the years. The cost of change is high. The organization has become rigid and conservative.

This lasts until a new paradigm breaks in. This is what Fig. 5 illustrates. An A-U cycle (see below) unfolds until a new technological revolution comes about, starting a new cycle.

The A-U model adds a layer of refinement to the simplified model of technological evolution presented in Chapter 2. The technological trajectory unfolds as the new paradigm is being explored. The A-U model suggests that each continuous curve of Fig. 2 or Fig. 5 are in fact composed of three stages (fluid; transitional; specific). In turn, each stage is characterized by a more frequent type of innovation (product design; process; incremental), respectively; each generating an outcome of its own (dominant design; dominant process; optimized but rigid organization).

This model has direct managerial implications, as illustrated by the short case below:

In the early 1990s, Valeo, the tier one supplier in automotive, had a very profitable business in clutches. A clutch is essentially a mechanical sub-system that transmits the power of the car engine to the driving wheels. Two discs face each other, one powered by the engine, the other connected to the driving wheels. When the clutch is engaged, the two discs are pressed one against the other so that the power of the engine goes to the wheels. When the clutch pedal is pushed, the clutch is disengaged; the two clutch discs separate, the driving wheels are no longer powered. One of the traditional problems of clutches relates to the sliding of the clutch discs against one another when engaged. This results in frictional wear and loss of energy. When the first application of electronics entered the world of automotives, the idea emerged of controlling the sliding of the clutch discs electronically. This meant triggering a paradigmatic shift. There was typically no engineering competence in electronics in Valeo's clutch division at that time. Top management at Valeo sensed that such a technological revolution could not be managed within the mechanical world (the mechanical paradigm) of the clutch division. In a group organized in a profit center, the decision was made to create a new unit that was in fact going to operate as a cost

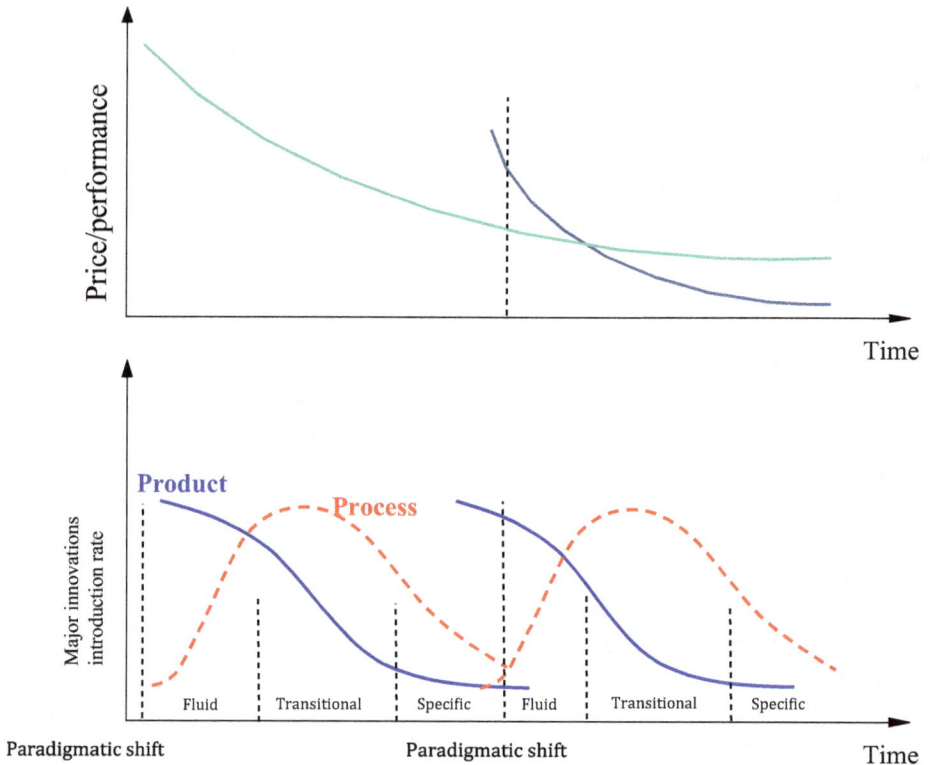

Fig. 5: Relating the A-U cycle to technological trajectories in the simplified model of technological change.

center for three years or so – the time needed to develop the technology, design new clutch offerings and launch the new business. The top management at Valeo had no idea of the A-U model. In a way, however, they had the intuition of what the model suggests: when a paradigmatic shift occurs, the incumbent's business is still in the specific stage (the end of the A-U cycle on the soon-to-be-former dominant technology). It is about to enter a fluid stage to start an iterative process of trial and error to search for the best applications (and thus product design) rendered possible by the new technology. The culture, the organization and the managerial style of a specific stage – constantly looking for optimization of the dominant design and process – are likely to be counterproductive for a fluid phase where flexibility and agility are vital. When the firm enters a new paradigm, the profiles of the managers in place would typically match the requirements of a specific stage. They would anticipate too early what they would see as the future dominant design and dominant process. They would be tempted to invest too early in equipment and a work organization specific to a "wrong" product design and its manufacturing process. They would not allow for enough time for the fluid and transitional stages to search and select the dominant technology among the many options made possible in the new paradigm. In Valeo's case, after naming the new clutch technology "mechatronics", they thought it would apply perfectly to Formula 1 racing cars. As a matter of fact, in the middle of the fluid stage, they paradoxically found out that a great segment for launching the new clutch offering would be on the low-end segment of the car market – and so they did, successfully. Allowing more time to conduct the search through the fluid stage proved very useful.

In short, a clear managerial implication of the A-U model is to protect the teams in charge of exploring the new paradigm from applying managerial recipes of a specific stage to a fluid stage.

More generally, the A-U model helps understand the formation of a technological trajectory while a new paradigm is being explored. This is also what the S-curve model has to offer, although from a different perspective.

Chapter 4
The Process of Technological Substitution and the S-curve

When a technological revolution occurs, most often the new paradigm is *terra incognita*. As there is no path in the pristine forest, there are no such things as pre-existing technological trajectories in the new paradigm. Trajectories are still to be formed. They are not hidden somewhere, waiting to be unearthed. They will result from the choices made by firms on the supply side and by users on the demand side. More generally, they will result from the interaction among stakeholders. As the Spanish poet Antonio Machado put it, *"Caminante, no hay camino, se hace el camino al andar"* [Walker, there is no path, the path is made by walking"].

In any case, this implies that the technological trajectories shown on Figs. 1–3 and 5 can only be represented *ex post*. This means that the model of technological evolution presented here should not be interpreted as deterministic. The cases studied are historical and the model discussed is a reconstruction offering representations of how technology unfolded in such cases. The model does not aim at forecasting. It brings light on the dynamics at work in the wake of a paradigmatic shift. Nevertheless, uncertainty and bifurcations remain part of the process. This will become even clearer as I keep adding layers of complexity (and hopefully refinements) to the model, especially with the concept of windows of bifurcation in Chapter 14 (Part II).

Yet, the above presentation where stakeholders and, even more so, market dynamics would play a key role in shaping the evolution of technology needs to be downplayed a bit. Dosi suggests that once a paradigmatic shift has taken place, the subsequent direction of change is somewhat constrained by the shift. The paradigmatic shift indeed opens a new set of possibilities, but subsequent development is limited to the boundaries of the space opened within the new paradigm. The trajectory is yet to be shaped, but the overall direction of the trajectory is somehow predefined.

> When the car industry went for internal combustion engines instead of electric cars at the beginning of the twentieth century, the overall direction of technological advancement was constrained for decades to come – gas stations along the roads, cooling systems to keep the engine temperature low enough, etc. Surely there were subsequent variations around the dominant technology (e.g., four cylinders, six or eight cylinders were variations of the same generic technology – the thermal engine). However, the direction of technological change was defined when entering the thermal engine paradigm and remained so for most of the twentieth century.

The A-U model brought some light on the technological trajectories. Nevertheless, more can be said about how trajectories form while the new paradigm is being explored.

We saw that the new technology is often first introduced in a market niche that operates as a beachhead. From that initial basis, the technology rapidly improves and

https://doi.org/10.1515/9783111397979-005

can expand to other segments. More iterative trial and error generates cumulative improvements. This contributes to accelerate the learning process of technology adaptation and diffusion. This can be reinforced by followers who enter the market with similar offerings, eager to get a slice of the growth potential.

The new technology progressively cannibalizes the soon-to-be-former dominant technology. The substitution process is both explosive and irreversible, taking an S-shaped form as shown on Fig. 7. (In fact, there are many exceptions that depart from the S-curve. This will be discussed in great detail in Part II). As the S-curve unfolds, incumbents have a final chance to revisit their strategic choice: keep spending even more resources to improve the soon-to-be-obsolete technology or being late in adopting the new dominant technology, accepting the new rules of the game, and, with them, the newly required set of competencies.

Given the potential of the new technological paradigm and the sub-technologies attached, a new segmentation process takes place on the market. Some sub-technologies (variations in product design and manufacturing process) fit the specific needs of groups of users, forming new segments. In so doing, new applications and new segments emerge, blurring traditional market and industry borders. As the new technology establishes its dominance, the technological trajectory shapes up. A maturation process takes place, until the next episode of de-maturation brought about by the next radical innovation.[10] Indeed, another technological revolution will eventually strike, as this is the life of technologies.

The S-curve

The S-curve is widely used in many social sciences.[11] In management, it is used to capture several important dynamics. A logistic or S-shaped curve results from the tension and shift over time in the dominance between two forces: (1) a potential for growth; and (2) a saturation effect. In the management literature, three phenomena resulting from such a tension are typically modeled through a logistic framework (S-curve):
- the diffusion of innovations (to what extent have targets adopted the innovation over time);
- technological performance trajectories (how much performance has been gained over time);
- and technological substitutions (to what extent has the new technology cannibalized the former technology on a market, and how fast).

---

10 The concept of de-maturation is discussed in Chapter 10.
11 The first part of this section stems from Dattée (2006) and Dattée and Durand (2009) with kind permission from Brice Dattée.

As shown on Fig. 6, three stylized S-curves are graphical representations over time of, respectively:
- diffusion (the cumulative number of adopters of an innovation until market saturation);
- technology performance (the improvements in the performance of a technology before reaching an upper limit);
- and substitution (the share of a new technology substituting over time for a former dominant technology in a market.

Given the theme of this book, the focus is put here on the third case, i.e., the substitution S-curve.

Phenomenon	Underlying		Graphical S-curve of the:
Diffusion	An innovation is adopted through a social system	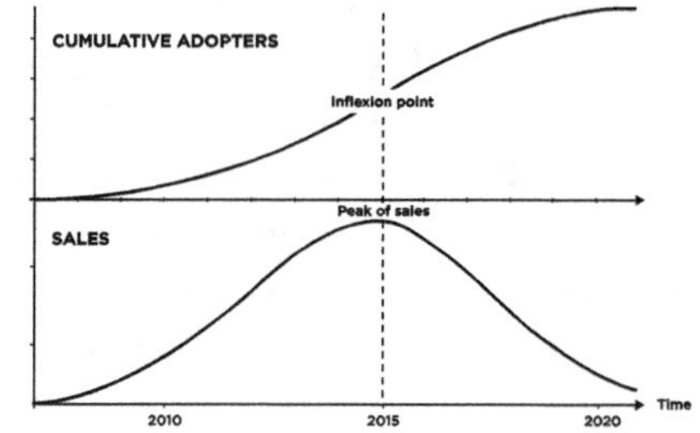	Cumulative adopters *(reaching saturation)*
Technology performance	Improvement in the performance of a technology	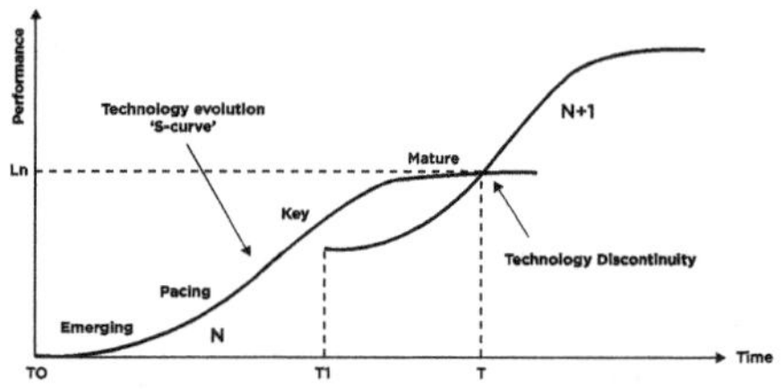	Performance trajectory *(reaching upper limit)*
Substitution	Subsitution of one technology for the other	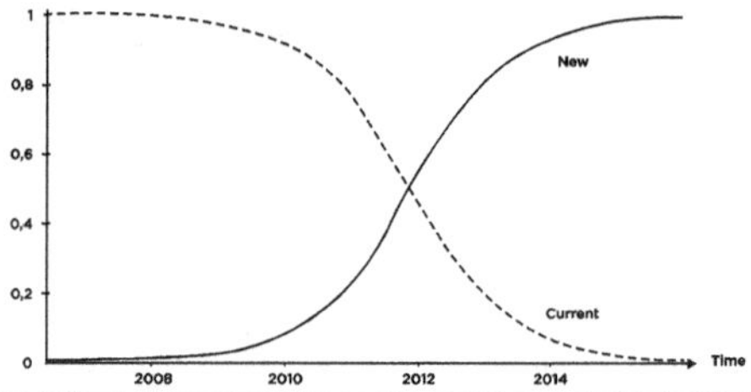	Relative market share *(reaching dominance)*

Fig. 6: The three classic S-curves: Diffusion, technology performance and substitution/adoption. (Source: Dattée, 2006)

In fact, these three elements are interrelated. The evolution of a technology performance (performance S-curve) is in part driven by cumulative volume of sales (substi-
tution/adoption S-curve) which in turn is often driven by the expected utility of the
technology's features. Aggregating across competing technologies will yield their respective market share over time (substitution S-curve).

As I focus here on technology substitution, it is worth summarizing what the literature tells us about the substitution/adoption S-curves (the third curve on Fig. 6).

Unlike a diffusion curve that plots the absolute number of adopters over time, a
substitution curve represents the fraction of a social system (a population, a market, an
industry, etc.) which has shifted to a new technology. Fisher and Pry developed an analytical model to gain a temporal representation of the substitution between two technologies. The Fisher-Pry model states that the substitution rate of the new technology N+1
for technology N is proportional to the remaining amount of N left to be substituted for.
More specifically, the log of the market share of technology N+1 to that of the technol-
ogy N ratio is a linear function of time; so that $\ln\left[\frac{m}{1-m}\right] = \alpha + \beta^* (t - t^*)$ with m the market share of technology N+1 and t^* the start date of the substitution.

The full S-curve model for technology N+1 substituting for technology N is presented on Fig. 7.

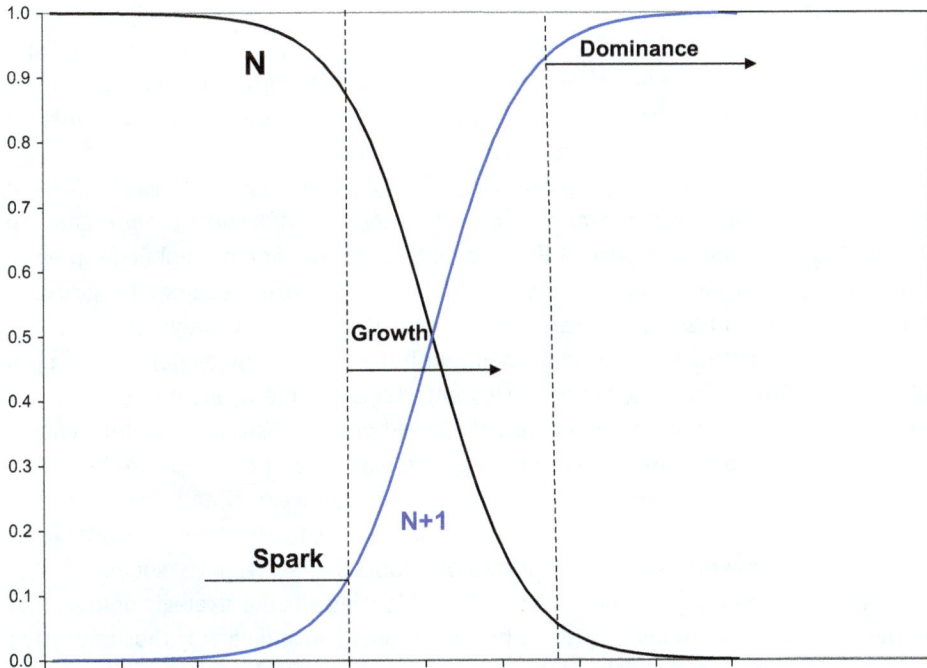

Fig. 7: Three time-phase S-curve of a technological substitution.

The substitution curve is a normalized view of a technology life cycle (i.e., in %: market share).

When technology N+1 comes in to challenge technology N, there is first a period needed for N+1 to emerge. This is a time of spark and emergence. Then, at some point, technology N+1 takes off, capturing more and more market share, cannibalizing technology N in an explosive and irreversible process of substitution. The intruders surfing the wave of change enjoy high growth while incumbents who did not go for the switch to N+1 will need time to react and prepare for it. In the meantime, they are bound to remain on what is left of the market for technology N. By the time they are finally ready for N+1, competition having surfed N+1 is likely to have occupied the distribution channels and taken the market share. Incumbents live through the same process as those who placed their bets on N+1 but from an opposite perspective. For the incumbents, the process is implosive and irreversible. The second phase is thus a growth phase for the proponents of N+1 and a decline phase for the incumbents sticking to N. The third and final phase displayed by the S-curve model of technological substitution is that of N+1 reaching dominance while the defenders of N have been excluded from the market or marginalized to limited residual market niches.

It appears that the Fisher-Pry model suggests a smooth curve of substitution and essentially focuses on the speed of the substitution, i.e., on β as the key parameter indicating the slope of the curve.

In other words, when it comes to grasping the time path of technological substitutions, the tradition of the S-curve conveys the idea of a smooth continuous phenomenon, essentially characterized by its slope β. This is interesting and explains the success of the S-curve. However, this creates two problems.

First, this is only partially consistent with what can be observed empirically. Several cases of substitution that significantly depart from the smooth S-curve are presented in Part II. This might not be important if we could be assured that the simplified representation stemming from the Fisher-Pry model properly informs strategy by grasping enough of the substitution dynamics. In many cases, it does not – as shown in Part II.

However, and this is a second problem with the S-curve, the model may be seen as an oversimplification that can be misleading. Arguably, it only identifies one factor characterizing the phenomenon, namely the speed of the substitution. It thus ignores other potentially important dimensions (e.g., the existence of a plateau in the curve, or the disruption of the smooth substitution process between N and N+1 by yet another technology N+2 that will result in the initial S-curve to abort: see an example on Fig. 8 below). These problems are important limitations of the S-curve model.

The time dynamics of technological substitutions affects the strategic options that are left open to firms competing in the middle of such transitions. It is thus important to recognize that technological adoption is not a phenomenon leading to uniform substitution patterns. The key point is that differences in the patterns do not only come from the speed of the substitution but also from other variables driving the shape of the substitution trajectory. While the literature says little about the time path of substitutions, except for the S-curve, it is important to better describe how substitution trajectories may unfold.

A good example stems from the music recording industry. Figure 8 shows the sequence of dominant technologies that made up the industry of music recording over time in France. The vinyl records took off in the 1950s to become mass market, peaking in 1978 with 78 million units sold. At that point in time, the vinyl was already seriously challenged by the audiotape that had captured a market slice of 20 million units. (In fact, car manufacturers had started preinstalling audiotape players in new cars: the audiotape opened the car market which was unfit for vinyl record players). Interestingly enough, at first the audiotape captured about a fifth of the total market volume as of 1978. Yet, strangely, when the vinyl record started its downturn in 1978, the audiotape suddenly plateaued for some nine years and even decreased a bit before starting a second phase of quick development that led to a peak of 41 million units sold in 1990. One possible explanation of the plateau may be linked to the early announcement by Japanese firms of the arrival of the next technology, the laser CD. This new offering was announced as early as 1980, launched in 1983, while not taking off before 1986. Users still considering a switch from vinyl to audiotape may have been worried about going for the wrong technology. This may have put them in a standstill position. The paradoxical result is that the audiotape started its second growth in 1986, exactly when the CD started cannibalizing the entire market. The audiotape kept growing until 1990 when the CD took a clear lead on the audiotape that subsequently followed a downturn. All in all, although it opened a sizable new market segment (listening to recorded music in cars), the audiotape technology never reached full dominance on the French market. The arrival of the CD cut short its cannibalizing of vinyl.

This is a typical example of a substitution trajectory that is rather poorly modelized by the smooth S-curve, at least when it comes to the audiotape vs. vinyl record substitution. An awkward technological trajectory for audiotapes resulted from: (a) a new market segment (the car market) created by preinstalled audiotape players in cars; and (b) the early announcement of the laser CD. The audiotape growth was stopped for nine years before it took off again, paradoxically when the CD became the clear next dominant technology, thus shortening the life duration of the audiotape technology.

Finally, the shift from laser CDs to streaming (briefly with both legal and illegal MP3 downloads in the middle – not shown on Fig. 8) followed a more classic substitution trajectory.[12] Note that the streaming platform paradigm cannot be easily compared to the recorded music sold in the form of an album (vinyl, audiotape or CD). With streaming, available measures are in numbers of subscriptions, turnover generated or numbers of online listening and numbers of downloads per song or piece of music, away from the number of albums sold. Again, the new paradigm is incommensurable with former technologies (the plot shown for streaming results from data for sales in euros [see the scale on the right] instead of units sold – a tricky way to simplify a complex issue).

---

12 It is difficult to find data for MP3 because they do not compare with data for previous technologies. We face the same issue for streaming. Yet, for streaming, I opted for a convention that permits an approximate plot.

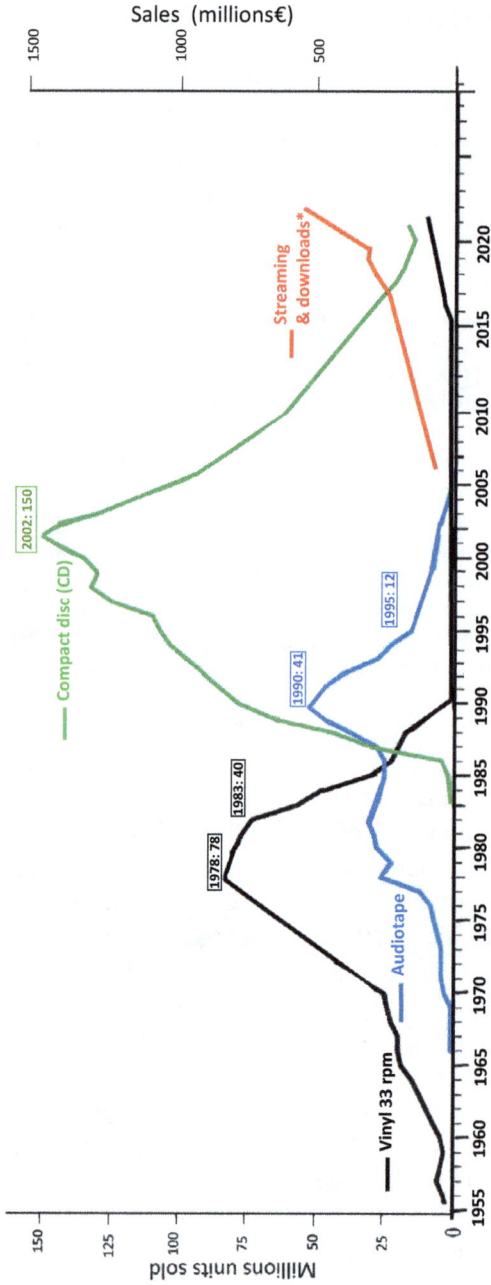

Fig. 8: Dominant technologies over time in the music recording business in France.
Source: SNEP
*Measured in sales (Millions €)

The shape of the technology substitution trajectory matters. Depending on the antici-pated shape of the trajectory, firms may decide to accelerate or postpone part or all of their investment to develop and deploy the new technology. New entrants hoping to surf the wave of change may no longer bet on technology N+1; incumbents may not strongly defend technology N. Instead, firms may envisage a variety of potential out-comes, thus choosing to place a combination of bets while monitoring the dynamics of the substitution. *The trajectory matters.* Therefore, a better description of the po-tential dynamics of substitutions is essential for strategy and path creation.

There can be a variety of trajectories departing from the pure, stylized case of the S-curve.

Moore proposed an interesting view of the time path of a technological substitu-tion, around the concept of chasm (See fig 9). He suggested that the substitution follows a sequence of phases, including a critical step when the firms promoting a new technol-ogy need to cross what he calls the chasm, meaning that they need to go beyond con-vincing the usual limited groups of innovators and early adopters. While early adopters are keen to test any new technology, thus providing a spearhead into the market, the new technology needs to find more adopters for the substitution to unfold. The critical phase is to bridge the gap between this initial market niche of early adopters and a cannibalization process on the bulk of the market. This is crossing the chasm. This model is interesting because it remains one of the very few attempts to address the time dynamics of technological substitutions from a different viewpoint than that of the S-curve. However, Moore's model falls short of providing a framework to describe and understand the overall phenomenon, nor does it identify the key dimensions that help characterize the time path of technological substitutions. However, Moore's chasm helps explain the plateau shape that was described earlier when discussing the difficult development of audiotapes (Fig. 8). Chapter 15 in Part II will discuss the matter further.

Another limitation of the substitution S-curve is that it fails to capture any market growth induced by a new technology. If technology N remains best adapted to a spe-cific set of applications (a situation described in the "partial base case" of Part II) and if technology N+1 increases the market size by creating new applications (such as the car market for audiotapes), by considering the moving boundaries of the overall mar-ket, the share of N will still appear to be decreasing – even though it resists on the market. Thus, it is important to be aware of technological segmentation and to be spe-cific about the scope of the market considered when studying a substitution. (Never-theless, the normalized view of the S-curve allows to grasp technological substitutions even in the case of market expansion due to the creation of new segments.)

All in all, the S-curve is a simple and powerful representation. It offers a synoptic view of the different time phases of technological transitions. Yet, this may not actu-ally capture the diversity of substitution pathways which result from broad and inter-dependent socio-technical dynamics. In other words, the S-curve is a very simplified model that does not properly account for the variety of time dynamics observed in technological substitutions. While the S-curve is more than a straw man, its descrip-

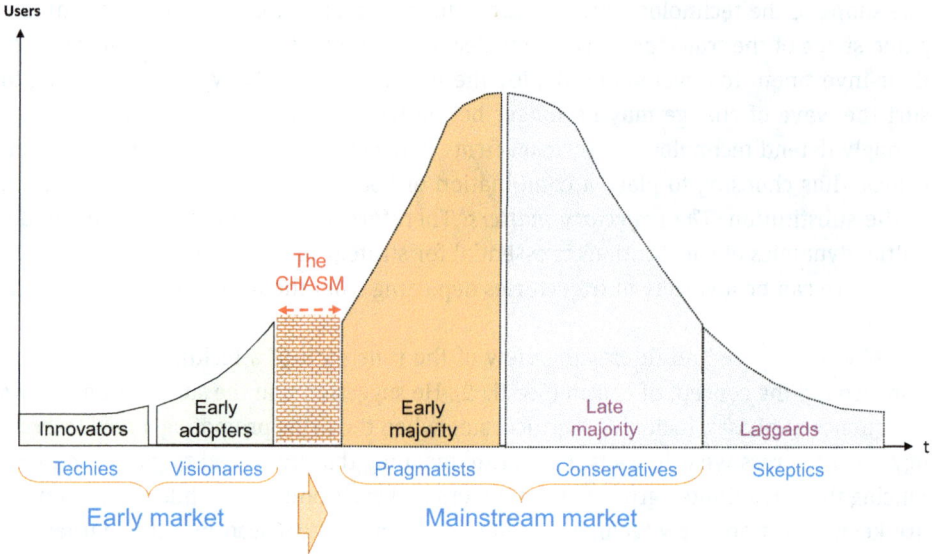

Fig. 9: The technology adoption life cycle and Moore's chasm.
Source: adapted from Moore (1991)

tive and prescriptive limitations are usually acknowledged. Yet, the alternative substitution time paths are seldom discussed, Moore being an interesting exception. Part II brings more light on the matter. This is important because technology and strategy interact dynamically: the transition periods between the different phases need to be managed with particular care. Tripsas highlighted that "understanding the origins and timing of discontinuous technological change is extremely important for managers trying to better weather transitions". This is exactly what we are after.

Chapter 5
A Continuum of the Intensity of Technological Change

A major problem that arises from the Abernathy-Utterback model discussed in Chapter 3 lies in their binary categorization of the intensity of innovation: Are there not indeed innovations that are neither radical nor incremental?

Abernathy and Clark acknowledged this point. They clearly suggest a continuum for technological change defined by "polar extremes": their scale ranges from incremental to radical innovation. They do not say, however, what falls in between.

The studies that I conducted over the years suggest that there is indeed a continuum of the intensity of change. All radical innovations are not equally radical; all incremental innovations are not just an additional small improvement of what already exists. There are some intermediary changes that both disrupt and continue. The "order-breaking/order creating" distinction suggested by Tushman and Anderson should allow for an order breaking/creating category.

Moving from 64k DRAM's electronic memories to 128k then to 256k, etc., were by no means radical changes, nor were they simply incremental evolutions. Similarly, four-cylinder, six-cylinder and eight-cylinder engines are all internal combustion engines in the car industry. They offer significantly different performance (power, acceleration, torque) or even, for the connoisseur, the pleasure of listening to the sound of the engine.[13] Yet these are essentially variations within the same technological paradigm, in the same seam: not radical innovation nor incremental innovation either – but in between.

I have a name for these in-between innovations. I call them "micro-radical" innovations.

The Schumpeterian "creative destruction" may thus be only partial in some instances.

As an illustration of micro-radical innovations, Fig. 10 shows the case of public switching technologies in the telecoms industry. The main curves shown (manual, electromechanical, space division, time-division multiplexing, internet protocol [IP]) are technological trajectories in Dosi's sense. To be more precise, I would say that these are the seams that were followed to explore each successive paradigm. (I justify this point below.)

Figure 10 displays micro-radical innovations (e.g., Strowger, rotary, panel, crossbar) and their relation to the trajectories (electromechanical switching in this case). Each technological seam was exploited through successive micro-radical innovations that brought about sub-technologies.

---

13 A passion that is no longer politically correct at a time when saving the planet is a collective priority for humankind.

https://doi.org/10.1515/9783111397979-006

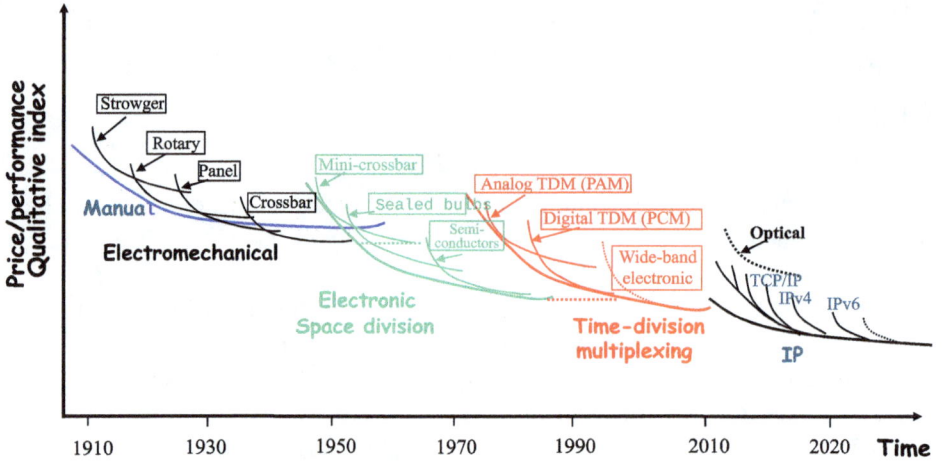

Fig. 10: Technological trajectories and micro-radical innovations in the telecoms industry.

> Each of them was then progressively improved, one after the other, through incremental innovation until a new sub-technology took over, or a new paradigmatic shift occurred introducing a new trajectory.

In this sense, a technological trajectory appears to be the "envelope curve" of the sub-technologies introduced through micro-radical innovations. This describes the way the promise of a particular technological seam is explored.

> (I note in passing that it is the IP technology that became dominant at the turn of the millennium. Yet, most telecom equipment manufacturers had been preparing for optical switchboards because it was the logical next step after space- and then time-division electronic switching. Indeed, the network had already made the transition to optical fiber for cost reasons. The voice was thus transmitted via photons until it was converted into an electronic signal to go through electronic switchboards and converted back again to a photonic signal onto the next switchboard, etc. The logical next step should have been optical switching to avoid those many converters before and after electronic switchboards in the network. However, the IP technology took the industry by surprise, sweeping those issues away.)

The synthetic representation of Fig. 11 enriches the simplified model visualized on Fig. 2 in Chapter 2 with the A-U model and its cycle of three stages (fluid: product innovation; transition: process innovation; specific: incremental innovation), the notion of a continuum of innovation (radical; micro-radical; incremental) as well as Dosi's technological paradigms and trajectories following seams. In addition, the technological trajectory is the envelope of sub-technologies that shape the trajectory as they unfold in exploring a paradigm.

This provides a much richer conceptual representation than the simple vision behind Fig. 2.

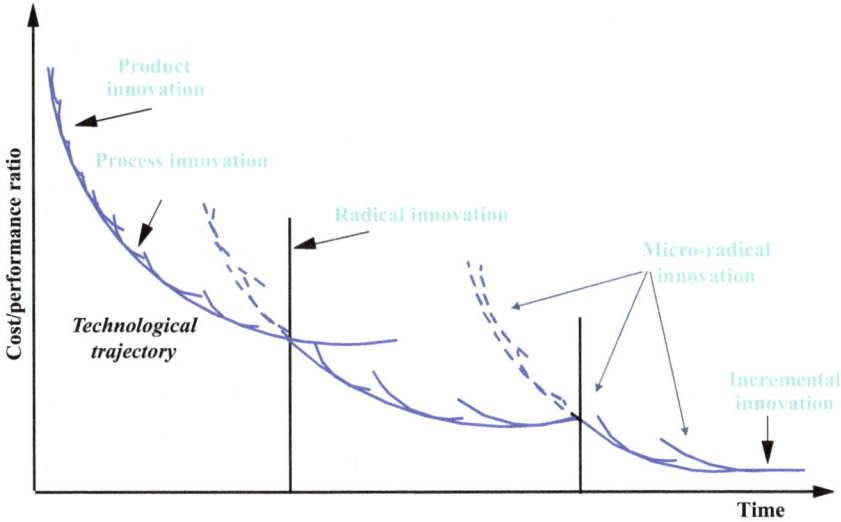

Fig. 11: Innovation and technological seams – Radical, micro-radical and incremental innovation.

This helps clarify the discussion following Fig. 1 in Chapter 2 where the definition of candidate and dominant technologies for the curves shown was rather impressionistic and loose. I can now try to do a better job conceptually.

I need first to clarify an important point. There is a conceptual difference between a seam and a trajectory. A mountain road follows valleys, circumnavigating high peaks as much as possible, sometimes going through a pass to go from one valley to the next. The sequence of valleys and passes make the seam, the road is the trajectory. In other words, the seam is the notional direction of advancement, the promise of a way through, while the trajectory is the concretization of the path followed.

From there, I can clarify the concepts used in the framework that I am building in this Part I: a paradigm, a seam, a trajectory, a technology, radical revolutionary innovation and micro-radical innovation, a dominant technology. These concepts can be described via the mountain road analogy used above. The paradigm is the region or landscape. The seams are the sequence of valleys, with some passes in between, indicating a notional direction of advancement in exploring the paradigm. The trajectory is the road that makes it possible to travel across the paradigm, following valleys and passes. The sub-technologies (those enveloped by the trajectory) are the stretches of road that follow the valleys. Micro-radical innovations are the passes that permit to go from one valley to another. Radical innovation (in the sense of a paradigmatic shift) is the entry into a whole new region. (Dosi is quite right in asserting that choosing a paradigm constrains future technological choices. Choosing the region predefines the landscape, thus predetermining the seams, at least in part, and in turn the trajectories.)

As a result, the dominant technology is at the same time the sub-technology (the road stretch that we are currently driving on), and by extension the trajectory (the road driven on), the seam (the sequence of valleys and passes) and even the paradigm (the region that we are driving through). Of all those concepts, the dominant technology is the trickiest as it is a source of ambiguity because it can designate any of the other concepts above. Let me clarify why.

Presenting a trajectory, and even more so a seam, as if it were a technology is inappropriate. The trajectory of electromechanical technologies in telecom switchboards is like the last name of a family made up of quite different technologies, each with their own "first name": Strowger, rotary, crossbar. Their physical difference is shown on Fig. 12. These are indeed all electromechanical. That does not mean that the electromechanical trajectory is a technology. It encompasses several technologies that have something in common. For practical reasons, however, when speaking of a technological paradigm, the corresponding technological trajectory may be considered as some form of a meta-technology. Yet, as an envelope curve, the trajectory (electromechanical switch) that follows a seam is just a family name – not the full detailed name of a sub-technology such as an electromechanical rotary switch. This helps better understand the difference between a trajectory (and thus a seam) and the sub-technologies that formed it. From that perspective, note that the grouping of sub-technologies into technological families becomes a sensitive issue. This will be addressed with the discussion of relatedness between technologies in the dual technology trees introduced in Chapter 8.

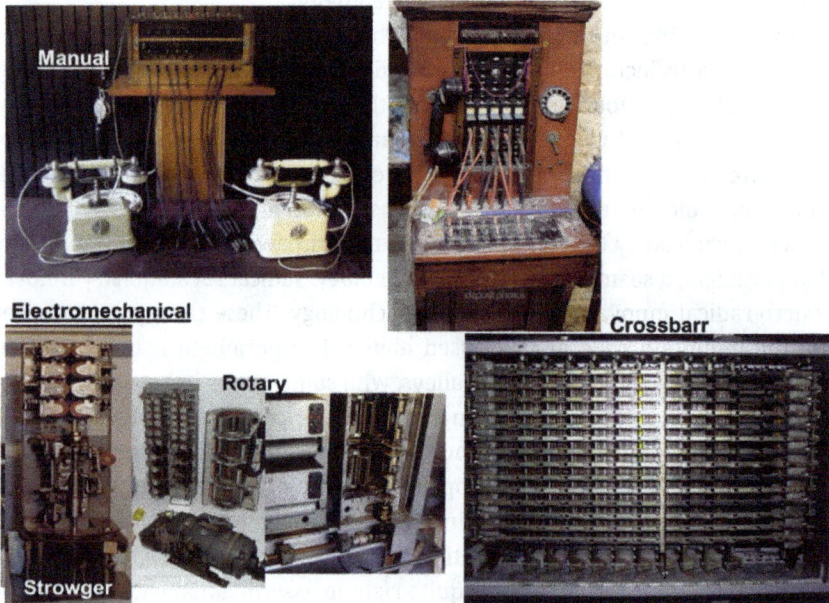

Fig. 12: Illustration of telecom switches in the twentieth century.

In short, the concept of a dominant technology should apply to a combination "paradigm/seam/trajectory/sub-technology". Yet, we can understand that, in practice, it may designate a trajectory or a seam or a sub-technology, or even a paradigm.

We now better understand the statutes of technology curves initially shown on Figs. 1 and 2. In addition, we have a continuum of the intensity of technological change:

Incremental innovations ⋘ Micro-radical innovations ⋘ Radical innovations (paradigmatic shifts)

From there, we can start grasping the link between the intensity of technological evolution and its strategic consequences – the focus of the next three chapters.

Chapter 6
The Strategic Consequences of Technological Change

In time, the path followed in exploring a seam in the paradigm generates the technological trajectory. Moving from one paradigm to the next (or one seam to the next) corresponds to radical innovation. These are big steps, significantly disturbing competition. Moving from one sub-technology to the next (within a technological trajectory as the envelope curve) corresponds to micro-radical innovations. These are intermediate steps with less impact on competition. They can range from low to significant, but nothing revolutionary. Along the trajectory, once a dominant technology reached the "specific" stage, with no more micro-radical innovations and no more variation around product design and process, there is essentially room left for incremental innovations. These do not disturb competition. They even tend to entrench the leaders dominating the business.

All of this means that technology evolves in stages, with a variety of strategic consequences.

As Dosi puts it, technological trajectories combine both "continuous changes and discontinuities in technological innovations: continuous changes are often related to progress along a technological trajectory – the direction of advancement within a technological paradigm – while discontinuities are associated with the emergence of a new technological paradigm". Note that I adapt this wording by introducing the concept of seam as the direction of advancement.

The A-U model brings its share with its three stages essentially describing the evolution along a trajectory. And the cycle starts again when moving from one technological paradigm to the next.

Electromechanical vs. electronic switchboard systems in the telecoms industry, chemically extracted and purified animal insulin vs. biotechnologically produced human insulin and vacuum tubes vs. semiconductors in electronics are all technological seams. Each was explored through successive micro-radical innovations that brought about sub-technologies which were themselves progressively improved, one after the other, by incremental innovation.

In time, the path followed in exploiting the seam generates the technological trajectory. Moving from one paradigm to the next (and from the corresponding seam to the next) corresponds to radical innovation.

Technological evolution in diabetes treatment illustrates the above. It is presented on Fig. 13 with firms' strategies subsequently discussed in more detail.

Diabetes is a disease related to the level of sugar in the blood. Your pancreas produces insulin on demand to convey the sugar from the blood to the body cells as energy fuel. Insulin thus regulates the level of sugar in your blood. If your pancreas does not do its job properly, for genetics

https://doi.org/10.1515/9783111397979-007

reasons (type I diabetes) or if your body becomes resistant to insulin because of fatigue due to overconsumption of carbohydrate food (type II diabetes), you have diabetes. Historically doctors treated diabetics by administering animal insulin.

Animal insulin was extracted from the pancreas of animals. Shots of animal insulin administered to patients (first in Canada) was found effective and reasonably safe in treating hyperglycemia. Industrial production of animal insulin started in the 1920s. The insulin was extracted from the pancreas of cows and pigs and then purified through rounds of crystallization (gel filtration) and then by chromatography (ion exchange). The first significant innovation that came next in the business stemmed from a problem: the effect of that insulin was too short in time, thus requiring up to several shots in a day, according to the degree of the patient's illness. New developments led to long-acting insulin (protamine first and then zinc suspension). As a result, patients could be treated with about a shot a day because the effect of the new insulin was delayed, covering a longer time lapse. Note that this progress improved considerably the comfort of diabetics but had little impact on competition in the industry. All competitors were almost instantly able to adjust and produce the new long-acting insulin. In other words, a very significant innovation from the perspective of the customers (the patients) had no real impact on the competitive dynamics. This means that, contrary to common belief, customers do not necessarily have the final say, at least as far as competitiveness is concerned. (This point will be discussed in more detail later, around Fig. 15.)

Another significant innovation followed, spurred by a serious problem attached to animal insulin. Despite the purification process applied to the insulin extracted from bovine and porcine pancreases, the resulting insulin was not pure enough for some of the patients. There were about 10% of the patients who were found intolerant to the product injected. There again, a significant progress was made by modifying the process, leading to a highly purified insulin and then monocomponent insulin or monopeak insulin, reducing resistance and allergic reactions. Then came the big bang of human insulin brought about by the first application of biotechnologies. The animal insulin paradigm was to leave the floor to the paradigm of human insulin.

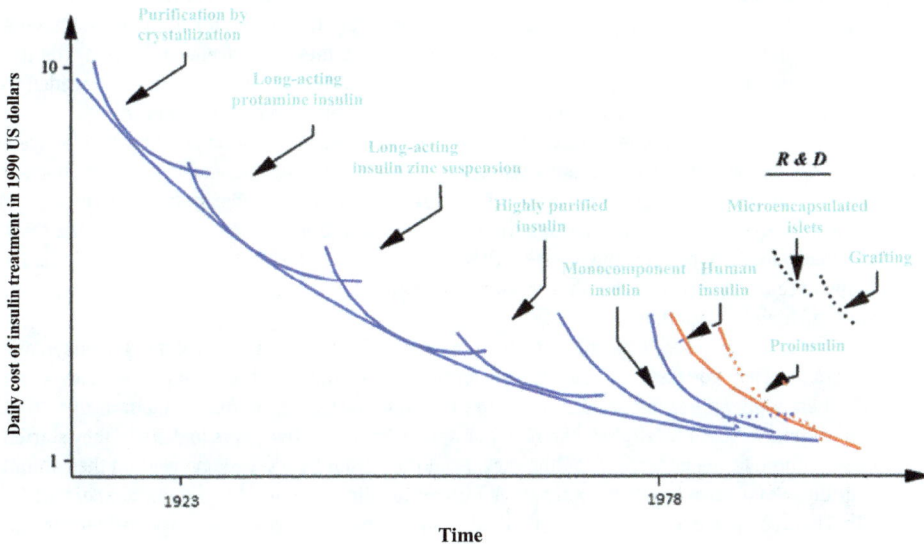

Fig. 13: History of the production of insulin/treatment of diabetes (1923–present).

What we have for the technological trajectories of diabetes treatment is in clear accordance with the A-U model: the innovations characterizing the early stage of a technological trajectory are essentially product-oriented, then become more process-oriented and eventually are essentially incremental as product and process innovations are both said to decline in frequency and significance. A radical innovation may then occur, introducing a new trajectory and thus a new cycle.

In other words, this confirms the proposition of the A-U model suggesting that a paradigm is being explored through major innovations on the product design first (here, long-acting insulin) and then on the process (here, to better purify the animal insulin), thus selecting the dominant technology (dominant design and dominant process) subsequently improved incrementally. This shapes the trajectory until a paradigmatic shift occurs (human insulin).

It should be stressed at this point that technology is by nature complex and unpredictable as it results from the changing combinations of many different elementary possibilities evolving in time, some of them being still unknown. Technological trajectories thus only appear afterwards as a pattern in a flow of past technological innovations.

More can be learnt from the insulin short case study, especially regarding technology strategies.

Human insulin turned out to be the prehistory of what was called at that time biotechnologies. In 1978, Eli Lilly announced that they had bought an exclusive license from Genentech to produce human insulin through cloning techniques and fermentation. They further announced that the development, clinical test studies, approval by the various drug regulators of the world, industrialization and ramp-up of production would require five years for the product to reach market.

The Danish company Novo had been and still was the historical leader of the insulin business. Novo had made most of the technology development of insulin over the decades. When they learnt about Eli Lilly having secured a technology from Genentech for human insulin, with a product planned for commercialization within five years, they got extremely worried. The tradition in big pharma was that everything was slow due to the regulatory constraints needed to protect public health. This meant that firms could see the blow coming to them in slow motion but did not have enough time to dodge the blow because slow motion applied to them as well. Drug development was like running a marathon, not a sprint. (Since then, things have changed with the Covid-19 pandemic and the successful rush to develop vaccines in a year.) Yet, at that time, Novo knew they were in serious trouble. Novo could not ask Genentech to provide them with the technology because the license sold to Eli Lilly was exclusive. Novo had no real in-house competence in cloning and could not even consider following Eli Lilly on that technology, never mind catching up with them.

However, Novo had a specific set of competencies (knowledge and know-how) in enzymatic conversion. They got the idea of starting from purified animal insulin, a technology they knew well, then apply an enzymatic conversion to the animal insulin to produce human insulin. That path was risky, but they felt they had no other option. They had five years to deliver; they started the marathon. In the end, they won the race. Even though Eli Lilly saved one year on their initial planning, Novo turned out to obtain their human insulin accredited two months ahead of Eli Lilly. That took place in the UK. In fact, Eli Lilly was trying to leverage their expected technological advantage to enter the European market on diabetes treatment. As it turned out, Novo won the technological race – quite unexpectedly.

Yet the story is not over. When the human insulin was launched on the UK market, the new offering did not take off, contrary to what both Eli Lilly and Novo had hoped for. Marketers were asked to conduct field studies. They soon found out that diabetics who had been treated for years with animal insulin and did well with it were not ready to switch to a new treatment. Their doctors were not too keen on it either. This led to targeting the sub-segment of those newly diagnosed with diabetes. The "new" diabetics and their GPs were kindly informed hat it would be risky to use animal insulin – an interesting solution for sure, but outdated and with a track record plagued with allergies, intolerance and accidents. Something new and secure was finally available: a human insulin, logically fitter for human beings than animal insulin. After six months campaigning with such a pitch, over 50% of the newly diagnosed diabetics had gone for the human insulin. The new technology would thus slowly substitute for the former over time. The new technology was bound to become the future new dominant technology.

Soon after, however, it appeared that the sales of Eli Lilly took off much faster than Novo's on the new market of human insulin. In other words, Novo had won the technology race but was losing the commercial battle for sales and market share. It turned out that there was a cost reason behind it – the price of a drug used daily or so cannot be ignored by the patient, health insurers or the GP.

When both firms launched their new product on the British market in 1982, Eli Lilly's price was about 10% below that of Novo, and the price difference was bound to widen over time. When starting the technological race four years earlier, Novo found no other option but to choose a technological path consisting of transforming animal insulin through an enzymatic conversion. This meant that the cost of the product resulted from the cost of animal insulin (collecting bovine and porcine pancreases, extracting the animal insulin, purifying it) plus the additional added-value step, namely the enzymatic conversion. Novo had over 60 years of experience in producing animal insulin, which means that most of the cost decrease on those steps had already been obtained. Adding an additional step (enzymatic conversion) was not helping costs either, especially for an activity on which they had built a solid experience already. All in all, the prospects of cost reduction on Novo's human insulin were rather bleak. In sharp contrast, Eli Lilly's technology acquired from Genentech started from scratch. That was the promise of a fast decrease in cost for the human insulin produced by Eli Lilly. The price difference at product launch between Novo and Eli Lilly was bound to widen.

In other words, Novo had selected a technology that was not cost-competitive vs. Eli Lilly's. The most fascinating part of the story is yet to come. When going for the enzymatic conversion, Novo was in fact aware of betting on the wrong horse. Nevertheless, they did it. Why?

I need another tool to explain the rationale behind Novo's technological strategy for human insulin.

Chapter 7 deals with understanding the impact of innovation on competitive dynamics in industries. This leads to the introduction of the dual technology tree (Chapter 8). This is the tool that I will use to conclude the discussion of technology strategies in the case of diabetes treatment. For more on Novo's surprising technology strategy in that instance, stay tuned.

Chapter 7
Qualifying the Intensity and Strategic Significance of Technological Change

This book aims at helping think about technology strategically. I suggest doing so through the lens of competence.

A first step in that direction is to better grasp the consequences of technological innovation on competitive dynamics in industries. For that, we need to recognize that it is the competence, capabilities and resources of the firm that are being changed, disrupted or entrenched by technological innovation. This leads to giving a closer look at the underlying competence of the firm (both individual and organizational).

Broadly speaking, it is possible to analyze technological innovation from two different angles:
– On the *technology side*, innovation may be looked upon through its technical content or through the requirements it puts on the firm's capabilities.
– On the *market side*, innovation may be assessed through the customer's perception or through the impact it may have on the competitive dynamics.

Hence, four different perspectives may be adopted to look at the intensity and strategic significance of technological change.
– *technological input*: technical novelty or scientific merit;
– *competence throughput*: new or reinforced requirements on the competencies (resources, skills and knowledge) relating to the concept of transilience (resilience through the transition);
– *market perception*: market novelty, new functions proposed to the customers;
– *strategic outcome*: impact on the competitive positions of the firms.

We are interested in understanding the impact of technological change on competitive dynamics in industries. We look at innovation from the strategic business perspective, i.e., how does technological innovation affect the competitive game? How can it help create (or conversely destroy) sustainable competitive advantages stemming from technology, namely technological rents?

Thus, gauging innovation from the technological input is of little interest. The scientific merit of a new technology does not guarantee that it will help increase your market share or profitability. McGee and Thomas define technology essentially as "information – the specifications for a product or a process which when built will 'work'"; Tushman and Anderson define "order-breaking discontinuities as those that fundamentally alter either the core product or process of a product class". I argue that the significance and the intensity of technological changes should be gauged

https://doi.org/10.1515/9783111397979-008

using criteria other than the weight of the 'set of blueprints' that are to be replaced when the innovative technology is implemented.

Technical novelty does not mean much in terms of competitive advantage. When a splendidly engineered technology can be imitated and adopted easily by any competitor in the industry, it brings no durable leadership.

The situation may be different if patents and similar legal protections enter the picture. However, it is not so much the characteristics of the technological input that might then make a difference, but rather the ability of competitors to gain access to the technological resource, namely the patent. I thus suggest analyzing such situations under the competence throughput category. Teece specifically addressed this issue in his discussion of the "appropriability regime", as he called it. Mansfield argues that patents tend to be circumnavigated, making them rather weak in protecting owners' rights.

At the other end of the spectrum, one could analyze the significance of innovation from its strategic outcome, measuring *a posteriori* how innovation affected competition. One could indeed scrutinize competitors before, during and after technological change has occurred, study their respective strategies, analyze their strategic positions at the outcome and thus gauge the innovation intensity and significance from its competitive implications. From a competitive perspective, this would be remarkably adequate. It would, however, be of little interest for the strategist: there is no way to be predictive about the significance of innovation if we intend to wait for the strategic outcome to measure its impact.

Alternatively, one might thus want to rely on the market perception to assess the intensity of the change as well as its strategic significance. Customers are often regarded as the judges in the marketplace. Should they strongly welcome an innovation, it would thus mean that it is a great technological change with much strategic content attached to it. This, however, can be very misleading.

The long-acting insulin (protamine and then zinc suspension) in the early days of animal insulin offered much more comfort to the diabetics since it helped reduce the treatment to only one shot per day or so. The innovation was extremely well received by the market. However, it had very little strategic significance. Market perception only indicates that the customers enjoy new features offered by the new technology. It does not necessarily give any kind of long-term competitive advantage if the innovation can be imitated in a few months' time. This again relates to Teece's appropriability regime.

Keeping in mind that we look at innovation from a competitive perspective, I suggest that the only strategically meaningful perspective on the significance of innovation turns out to be the intermediary step of competence. Will the firm's competence base be reinforced and entrenched by the change, or will it be disrupted and rendered obsolete?

This is captured by the notion of transilience proposed by Abernathy and Clark (the word transilience results from the contraction of transition and resilience, thus conveying the idea of what remains or resists through the change). In adopting this perspective, I follow Abernathy and Clark as they define transilience: "The significance of innovation for competition depends on its capacity to influence the firm's existing resources, skills and knowledge – What we shall call its 'transilience'". Similarly, in Dosi's words: "Progress upon a technological trajectory is likely to retain some cumulative features." Therefore, continuity, i.e., progress along a trajectory, would accumulate competence while discontinuity, i.e., a change of trajectory, would disrupt competence. Teece adopts a somewhat similar perspective when he develops his complementary assets framework for the innovative firm: he points out that the firm's ability to develop, implement and translate innovation into a competitive advantage requires resources and skills that may or may not be available to the organization. His subsequent concept of dynamic capabilities points to the same direction.

While the rationale of this book will obviously tend to connect the strategic outcome to the competence throughput, it is fair to recognize that the first three perspectives discussed above (technical merit, market perception, competence throughput) are often correlated to one another. For an innovation of great technical novelty, chances are that the market novelty will be significant and that the change in competence required by the new technology will be important. This is, however, not always the case. Henderson and Clark have shown that apparently incremental innovations relying on architectural change may have a strong competitive impact. They define architectural change as a new way of integrating the very same components into a new product design. They suggest that competence inherited from routine improvements of a previously stable architecture may end up as a handicap for the organization unable to unlearn and then relearn new architectural ways.

In fact, unlearning is often more complicated than learning. More specifically, past learning results in stocks of knowledge and beliefs that prevent new learning, making it very difficult to adapt to change. This is at the heart of the dynamic capabilities framework. A dominant technology and its paradigm operate like rail tracks. They both habilitate and constrain. They habilitate because they make operations possible, continuously improved through incremental innovation as long as the firm follows the track. However, when it comes to changing direction, the track locks the firm in. Specific capabilities are needed to divert the firm from the existing track, very much as an exogenous force would be needed to extract the moon from its trajectory around the Earth.

My point is that a firm's ability to compete on a given current or future technology depends heavily on the fit of its portfolio of competence to the requirements of the technology. In other words, when facing technological change, a firm should raise two sets of questions:
- What part of my existing competence base will be entrenched or rendered obsolete by the change?
- What existing competitors/new entrants may enjoy a strong competitive advantage when implementing the new technologies, given their specific competence base?

Note that I use here the word "competence" as a generic concept which includes individual and organizational expertise, skills and knowledge, namely the ability to deploy resources. I will clarify the matter with definitions, categories and a model for competence in Part III. Also note that these many forms of in-house capabilities are usually built internally over the years through experience. This means that they are likely to be difficult to acquire or contracted from the outside. Abernathy and Clark underline the differences among the three types of competence that they consider (resources, skills, knowledge) and insist on the cost, time and means required to gain access to them. More specifically, since this book is about reaping the benefits of technology, I argue that competence that can be acquired or contracted in is not likely to make a difference strategically, at least not to the same extent as competence rooted in the depth of the organization. In addition, when facing technological change, the more costly and the longer it takes to access the newly required set of competencies, the more strategic impact it may have on the competition within the business.

Going one step further, I suggest gauging innovation by assessing not only what competencies will be reinforced and entrenched by the change, and what others will be disrupted and rendered obsolete, but more importantly how wide the gap is for a firm between its current portfolio of competence and the newly required competence portfolio. The same portfolio of competence would mean business as usual, while a significantly renewed portfolio of competence would sound like strategic turmoil (typically an opportunity for some new entrants – and trouble for most incumbents). The next chapter aims at bringing light on the matter.

Chapter 8
The Dual Technology Tree

When considering the long list of past, present and potential technologies that did, still do or could fulfil a generic need (function F), I suggest the construction of a "dual technological tree" (DTT) that organizes technological choices in the product/process duality as shown in Fig. 14.[14] One technology is shown as a path in the tree from the top (the function to be satisfied on the marketplace) down to one branch at the bottom. Horizontal branches represent product designs, while vertical branches show process technologies.

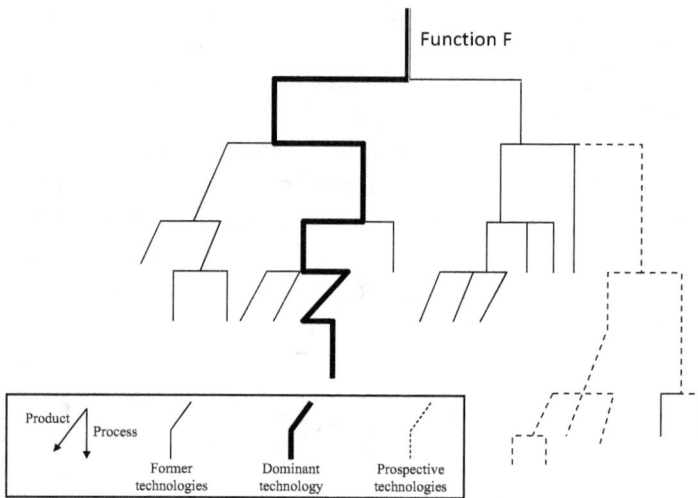

Fig. 14: The dual technology tree.

Starting from the function to be satisfied (what I called function F in Chapter 2), the tree organizes the major technological choices that one would face when redesigning from scratch products to fulfil the need and the corresponding production processes. Former, existing (dominant or not) as well as prospective technologies should be considered. A former technology appears as a continuous line; the current dominant technology appears in dark and a prospective technology is shown as a dotted line.

The set of technological options may not be fully known as of today. In that sense, the future is not just uncertain, it is also indeterminate, with unknown boundaries. Yet, I argue that it is possible, as of today, to grasp at least part of it by structuring the wide spectrum of the technically possible into potential seams and plausible trajectories,

---

14 This chapter draws from Durand (1992) with kind permission by Elsevier.

https://doi.org/10.1515/9783111397979-009

what Dosi calls "some notional technical future". The idea is to sort out and visualize the current understanding of how technological seams and trajectories might look in the future, even though we should expect technology to follow other unanticipated paths. It should be stressed again at this point that future technologies are not known ahead of time as they will essentially result from the combination of a great number of technical variables, some of them being still unforeseen and unforeseeable.

It was thus by no means suggested above that the DTT adopts a deterministic view of technology. Instead, I recognize the complex and unpredictable nature of technology and essentially suggest mapping the various major technological options and sub-options that one would think plausible at the present time, keeping in mind that technology will end up finding its own peculiar ways.

The tree is built according to the principle of "technical competence relatedness": the closer the branches, the more common the competencies required and thus the smaller the change for the firm from one technology to the other. In that sense, the DTT is built according to the proximity of the competence portfolio required by two different technological branches in the tree. In other words, the DTT gives a visual sense to the concept of transilience – and thus the extent of the competitive turmoil generated by a jump from one branch to the other, close to one another or far apart. Two closely linked branches low in the tree represent two slightly different versions of the same technology and share most of the same competence requirements. A small jump from one branch to the other would mean a small technological change in the sense of no or little strategic consequences to be expected. Two branches far from one another with no close links in most cases have little competence in common. A big jump from one branch to the other would mean a significant strategic impact of the technological change.

Starting from the top, the most basic design options to fulfill function F are considered first, generating the earlier major branches in the upper part of the tree. The smaller variations around a technological design are presented at the bottom of the branches.

Technological change thus appears as a jump from one branch to another. The jump may be small or large, meaning that the extent of the competence change needed will be small or large. The further and the more unrelated the branches are from one another, the more intense the change from one technology to the other since more competencies will have to be renewed. Such branches are rather unrelated in the sense that one has to go back rather high in the tree to connect them together. One could even imagine defining a technological metric to evaluate the competence relatedness of two technologies in the tree. (It is a bit like in a family tree: the proximity between branches in a family tree qualifies the degree of relatedness between family members.)

A challenging new technology may thus be evaluated in terms of its potential impact on the firm's competence: its distance or unrelatedness to the current dominant technology in the tree illustrates graphically the degree of vulnerability of the established firms facing the potential innovation. This will be developed in Part III.

Similarly, incumbents can assess potential new entrants by evaluating the relative fit of intruders' portfolios of competence to the requirements of the current dominant technology (or the foreseeable next dominant technology).

A dual technology tree for the case of the treatment of diabetes is presented on Fig. 15.

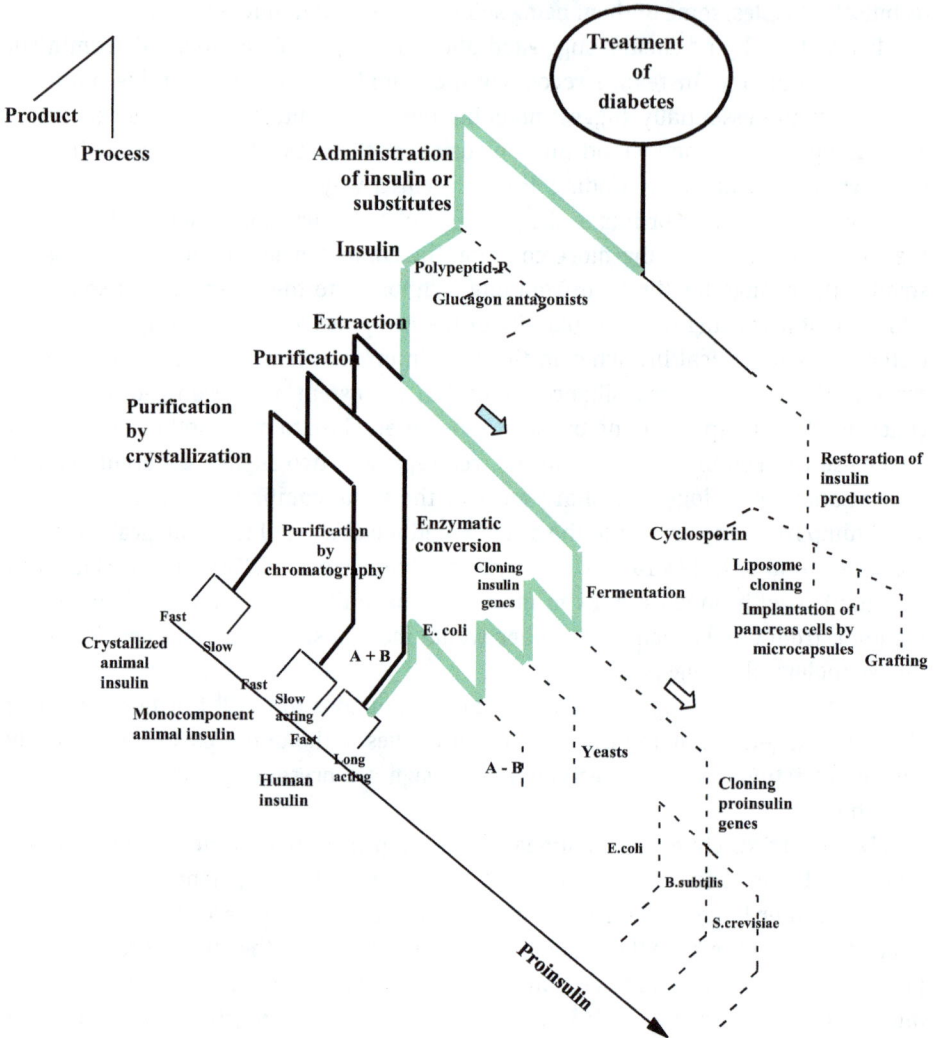

Fig. 15: Dual technology tree for the treatment of diabetes (and insulin technologies).

Reading the tree from top to bottom (according to the impact of a jump from one branch to another) and from left to right (over time):

At the top, the function F to be fulfilled covers diabetes treatment.

Broadly speaking there are two basic options to treat diabetes. The first (traditional) way has been to administer insulin to diabetics. A second option, an interesting alternative, would be to restore the production or the acceptance of insulin in the patient's own body. This, shown as the top right branch, has been and is still under investigation. It could be done through grafting a pancreas, with the usual limitations on the donors and the numbers of organs available compared to the needs. It could also be done through some form of artificial pancreas, such as implanting pancreas cells in microcapsules in the body of diabetics. The cells produce insulin, the insulin can flow out from the microcapsules while the substance that forbids diabetics' pancreas cells to produce insulin cannot enter the microcapsules. (The latter are like diodes in electricity or one-way streets: the flow can go one way but not the other way.) At the end of the spectrum of sub-options, cyclosporine was at some point seen as a promising option of a drug that could rehabilitate diabetics' bodies to produce or tolerate insulin. (This sub-option is shown horizontally as if it would be a product.) All these sub-options on the "restoration" main branch are not functional yet and most may never be. They thus appear as dotted lines on Fig. 15.

Coming back to the first basic option at the top of the tree, the top left branch in the tree corresponds to offering insulin or a substitute to the diabetics. The candidate substitutes (e.g., polypeptide-P or glucagon antagonists) are shown as horizontal dotted lines because they are still candidate technologies for products. The main historical solutions were animal insulin, produced from porcine and bovine pancreases through extraction and purification (first by crystallization and then chromatography) leading to monocomponent highly purified insulin. The fast vs. slow acting insulin sub-branches are shown as horizontal lines at the very bottom of the tree. Indeed, these turned out to have minimal strategic impact despite their bringing significant comfort to the patients. Then came the revolution of human insulin via the cloning of the genes of insulin and fermentation (Eli Lilly) or enzymatic conversion (Novo). The latter appears as some sort of a shortcut between animal insulin and human insulin. Human insulin via cloning turns out to be the current dominant technology. Additional prospective options are also shown (dotted lines), including for pro-insulin. Pro-insulin is what your pancreas produces, a precursor of insulin that your body then transforms into insulin. Diabetics' bodies can transform pro-insulin into insulin. This made pro-insulin an interesting candidate seam for the future.

Note that branches for long-acting insulin have been placed as product designs at the very bottom of the tree. As discussed earlier, they represented tremendous progress for the patients, but their strategic significance was very low because the new technology required very little new competence and was thus imitated rather easily.

Also note that the starting point at the top of the tree is not "insulin production" but rather "treatment of diabetes", which turned out to be the real generic functional need in the marketplace. Attention should be paid to properly identify the function for which a tree is built. More specifically, by simply changing the definition of the function at the top of the tree, one may transform a product into a process technology and vice versa. For example, an electric generator may be either regarded as a product on the electrical equipment market or as a process to produce electricity. Similarly, a switchboard may be seen either as a transparent process for the telephone user or as a product sold by telecom equipment manufacturers to telcos. (This situation is actually very similar to the concept of duality in linear programming, thus giving some legitimacy to the term "dual technology tree").

We have now a tool to end the case discussion on Novo's technological strategy for human insulin.

We saw that Novo deliberately chose to develop a technology that they knew would be inferior to the cloning technology that Eli Lilly was implementing. Novo felt cornered, with no option available, except the enzymatic conversion – not a cost-competitive path as we saw. However, they anticipated that the human insulin revolution brought about by Genentech's early work in biotechnologies would only be a first step. They foresaw the potential subsequent step, that of producing pro-insulin. They knew that diabetics' bodies can transform pro-insulin into insulin. In addition, they anticipated that it would be cheaper to produce pro-insulin than insulin. Hence that meant that the next logical step in diabetes treatment was likely to be producing pro-insulin.

On that basis, Novo's strategy becomes crystal clear. They were on animal insulin, technology N, already announced to be soon challenged by technology N+1 (cloning and fermentation) to offer human insulin. And technology N+2, pro-insulin, was believed to come next. Novo saw the opportunity to surf the wave of N+2, a way to strike back to Eli Lilly's announced attack with N+1 on human insulin. Novo thought that the only way to possibly play N+2 was to remain in the business of diabetes treatment in the meantime, surviving on the market for the time human insulin would be dominant, while actively preparing pro-insulin for the next radical innovation. Hence, choosing to compete on human insulin with an inferior technology, at least cost-wise, was nothing but a gap filler.

However, Novo did not properly anticipate that developing and producing pro-insulin would require the very same competence (cloning and fermentation) that Eli Lilly was going to build for human insulin. I argue that this is something Novo should have been able to spot by looking at the competence requirements. However, I recognize that it was much more difficult to properly see the next bifurcation that subsequently came on top of everything else.

Indeed, it later appeared that the future of diabetes treatment was a changing priority. The next focus ended up not being pro-insulin but the mode of administration and the monitoring of diabetics' glycemia in real time. "A continuous glucose monitor (CGM) is a compact medical system that continuously monitors your glucose levels every 5 minutes or so. A small sensor is inserted into your arm with a tiny plastic tube (a cannula) penetrating the top layer of skin. An adhesive patch holds the sensor in place, allowing it to take glucose readings in interstitial fluid. The data can be displayed via a smartphone app . Alert can be sent about your blood sugar levels. CGM revolutionized diabetes care.[15]"

This is another interesting feature of the technology story of insulin. While the early days of insulin meant injecting the product into the diabetic's body (arms or belly), Novo introduced an innovation with the Novo Pen, a miniature kit in the form of a pen with a cartridge for the needle and the insulin dose. That innovation helped simplify the life of diabetics, regardless of the insulin used. This was a service bundled to the product offered to the diabetics. In a way, with continuous glucose monitoring (CGM), the industry went a step further in the direction of better and more service. Monitoring the level of sugar in the blood in real time introduced significant progress for the users. "This changed my everyday life" is the most heard comment about CGM. In a way, while the technological battle had been on the product injected and manufacturing process technologies for decades, the new focus moved to improving the comfort of diabetics. Another form of paradigmatic shift indeed. While industry experts expected the next revolution to strike via pro-insulin, the change came from a very different angle.

---

15 https://www.healthline.com/diabetesmine/what-is-continuous-glucose-monitor-and-choosing-one (march 2023).

Note that it is difficult to show CGM as a new technology on both Figs. 13 and 15. This matter will be addressed in Chapter 9 when introducing the customer concept tree (CCT) and the interactions between the DTT and the CCT.

A Discrete Continuum of the Intensity of Technological Innovation

It is now possible to put together the two graphs of Fig. 11 (Chapter 5) and Fig. 14 (Chapter 8), thus leading to the combined image of Fig. 16-A. Each technological trajectory and even sub-technology shown on the upper part of the graph can actually be traced in the DTT.

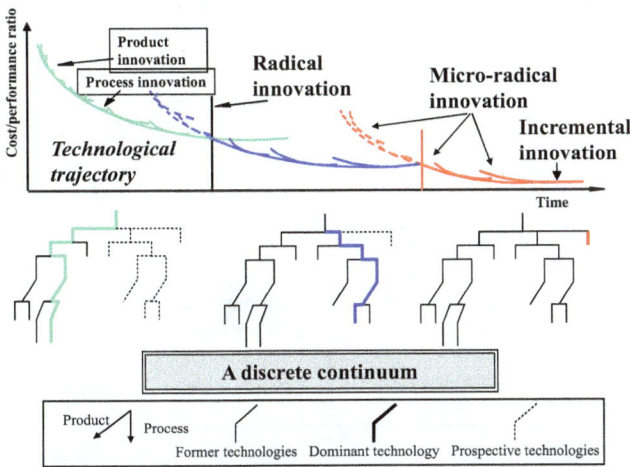

Fig. 16-A: Innovation and technological seams – Radical, micro-radical and incremental innovations and dual technology trees: A discrete continuum.

The tree representation visualizes a wide spectrum (a continuum) of technological change: the intensity of an innovation depends on the height of the corresponding jump in the tree from one branch to another. It may be small (incremental innovation), large (radical innovation) or intermediate (micro-radical innovation) with several different intensities and strategic consequences.

Conversely, the tree shows that technological change occurs through rather discrete steps. In a somewhat paradoxical sense, there is a "discrete continuum" of technological change.

The format of the DTT opens the door to a discussion of real options when it comes to thinking about technology strategically.

Real options analysis is a useful approach to decision making about options that can be clearly identified, described at least to some extent – that is, enough to assess expectations of outcomes and probability of occurrence. (In other words, this is a useful perspective in contexts of risk – not of indetermination, or uncertainty in Knight's sense.) Typically, investment decisions can be reassessed beyond the classic net present value (NPV) calculations based on comparing the cost of investment to a stream of discounted future cash flows. Real options can end up showing that it may be better to wait before investing or stagger a plan of investment over time, despite a preliminary conclusion favorable to an immediate full investment according to NPV. Indeed, discounted cash flows are by construction transformed into today's money by using a risk-neutral rate. However, they ignore the important information that may be gathered if the investment decision is postponed (in full or in part). In this context, the DTT is indeed a visualization of all the technological options thinkable as of today. In that sense, the DTT seems to pave the way for real options calculations. However, to do so, one needs to assess the probability of occurrence of each option and their expected outcome. When it comes to technology, such assessments are in most cases far from being graspable in practice. In short, real options are likely to be useless for technology strategy in contexts of indetermination, and even in contexts where one can list and draw options on a DTT, the probability and outcome measures are likely to be out of reach.

Table 1-A summarizes the continuum of the intensity of technological change (from radical innovation to incremental innovation with micro-radical in between) and the corresponding strategic significance of innovation.

Tab. 1-A: Intensity of technological change and strategic significance.

	Radical innovation	Micro-radical innovation	Incremental innovation
Intensity of change	A whole new game	Intermediate	Business as usual
Step size	Giant step	Several discrete steps	Continuous flattish slope
Transilience	Competence base renewed	Some new competence	Same competence reinforced
Strategic significance	Turmoil - incumbents likely to lose vs. new entrants	Some potential strategic change	Incumbents reinforce their positions
Examples	Human vs. animal insulin IP (packet switching) vs. TDM switch boards Electric cars/fuel cells-H2 vs. Thermal engines	3G-4G-5G-6G-…in GSM mobile telephony Strowger-rotary-crossbar in electro-mechanical public switching	Kaizen-like improvements

Note at this point that it is no longer obvious to define what a trajectory is, where it starts or where it ends.

Is Novo's human insulin (obtained through an enzymatic conversion from animal insulin) part of the human or animal technological seam? Does mini-crossbar, one of the first electronically monitored switchboards, belong to the electromechanical or electronic seam? Will pro-insulin (assuming it is developed and commercialized one day) form a new seam, or does it belong to the human insulin seam?

Once Fig. 16-A made it clear that the intensity of technological change is a continuum, it is no longer acceptable to force innovations into a binary categorization (i.e., revolutionary vs. incremental change). This issue somewhat relates to the mathematical concept of noticeable differences. Dosi acknowledges this difficulty and suggests considering technological clusters instead of his trajectory metaphor. I argue that the hierarchical format of the DTT clarifies this point.

Figure 16-B shows the case of public switching in the telecoms industry. Note that to make it simpler, the technological tree presented here is not dual; it simply shows the product technologies (and not the corresponding manufacturing process technologies). This keeps the graph readable.

Interestingly, Martinelli came out with the same sequence of paradigms in the switchboard business since the beginning of telephony in the nineteenth century. She used data from patents and looked at the set of patents cited by subsequent patents, thus hinting that these belonged to the same trajectory (in the sense of technologies displaying cumulative features). She also looked for key patents that would depart from the clusters mapped around a trajectory. She would thus dig into these key patents, once identified, to search for qualitative information that would substantiate (or not) the emergence of a new paradigm. Conceptually, Martinelli was investigating a way to clarify whether a new technology was simply an extension of a "normal" trajectory (typically a sub-technology introduced by a micro-radical innovation in the sense of Tab. 1-A) or whether it signaled a new paradigm, à la Dosi, (meaning a change of trajectory as a result of a paradigmatic shift). Her point was that looking at the artifacts (typically the switchboards) is not enough. One also needs to dig below the surface of the physical appearance of objects and systems, to look at what she called the "knowledge space" (including the engineering knowledge, of which engineering heuristics is a sensitive part).[16] Calling upon patent data bases turned out to be a very relevant approach, combining quantitative data with qualitative information. Her conclusion is interesting: "We can conclude that a paradigmatic shift is always (almost by definition) competencies destroying (Anderson and Tushman), whereas a genera-

---

[16] This echoes the life science situation where two animals (such as muntjac deer) can look alike while sharing very little in common as, through evolution, they have lost most of the genetic patrimony of their ascendants. The observation that the artifacts, products or apparatus (the animals in our analogy) look alike does not mean that the underlying competencies and knowledge (the DNA material and chromosomes in our biological analogy) are shared.

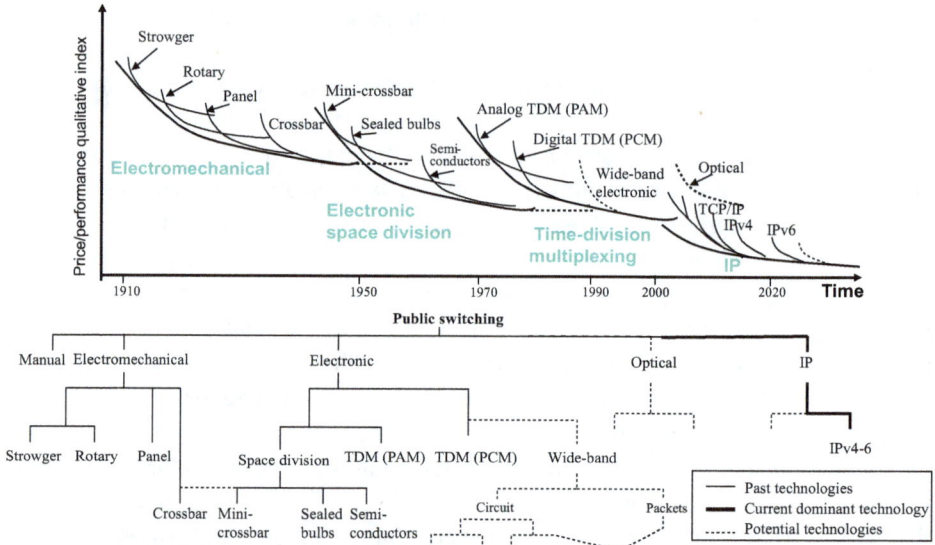

Fig. 16-B: Nature and intensity of technological innovation – Radical, micro-radical and incremental innovations in public switching.

tion shift [micro-radical innovation introducing a new sub-technology along the same envelope trajectory][17] only sometimes. Therefore, engineering heuristics are characteristics of a paradigm defined at competence level and not at artifact level." This is exactly the point of view that I develop in detail in Part III.

Sustaining vs Disruptive Innovations

At this stage, it is useful to call upon the ideas that Christensen developed around what he identified as the innovator's dilemma. Christensen starts by observing that many firms are so focused on improving the dominant technology in a business, that they can get carried away – possibly going too far in their quest for performance improvement. As a result, they end up overshooting, that is reaching levels of performance that may go significantly beyond market needs. In that sense, this is a waste of resources: offering value not perceived by customers. Christensen uses the word "sustaining" to qualify such strategy (more of the same, improving permanently, incrementally or even radically at times, focusing on the same dimension of product performance). In this context, Christensen suggests another strategic option. He observes that while some firms may be sticking to their endless effort to improve prod-

---

17 My addition.

uct performance on what they see as the key feature expected by customers, some astute competitors play it differently, via the business model. New entrants, or even incumbents, may innovate by bringing in a new way of fulfilling customers' needs, apart from (though complementary to) the product/service functionality that stood so far at the heart of the competitive arena. This was typically the case when Novo introduced the Novo Pen to facilitate the injection of insulin for diabetics, making it somehow user-friendly to administer the medication. This was even more so with the introduction of CGM that turned out extremely convenient for the users. Being informed in real time of the sugar level in their blood is indeed a major new functionality offered to diabetics – although not changing anything to the product injected and its intrinsic performance to regulate blood sugar levels (animal insulin, human insulin, pro-insulin, long acting or short acting, very purified or less so, etc.). For these "lateral" innovations (in the sense of not aiming at the core function that most competitors still focus on), Christensen uses the word "disruptive". Clearly, the disruption qualifies the extent of the turmoil resulting from the innovation in the competitive arena.

In addition, and this point is key, such disruptive innovations may stem from straightforward applications of existing technologies or solutions to the specific context of the business. CGM technologies are a typical combination of existing digital technologies and existing biological sensors to measure the sugar level in interstitial fluids of the skin – a good proxy for the sugar level in blood. Along the way, some improvements of these existing technologies can be made, be it incrementally or more radically. This means that disruptive innovations in the sense of Christensen can be of any intensity along the incremental/micro-radical/radical continuum. Their disruptive effect comes from the change in value perception brought to users for another sub-functionality of the generic need F. The novelty thus stems from the target and focus of the innovation, possibly ignoring (though complementing) the traditional criteria of performance adopted by those many competitors that do not sufficiently question the relevance of their sustaining strategy (improving the performance on a main criterion only). Christensen insists that what counts is to find a new ("better") way of "doing the job" for the customers/users. This new way may happen to be much less costly than the still dominant technology, the cost of which being possibly penalized by a useless overshooting on performance.

This means that Christensen's disruptive innovations may in fact undermine the incumbents from below, that is, with lower costs, bringing something significantly new (e.g., convenience and comfort to the users in the case of insulin for diabetics), not just performance on a single functionality.

In addition, Christensen suggests that competitors blinded on their sustaining track may not recognize the deadly challenge stemming from such business model innovations from below. As the disruptive innovations target some other component(s) of market needs, competitors may not see the threat because they consider such sub-functionalities as unimportant. As they see it, the disruptive innovation (on something else, seen as minor) does not directly affect their core effort of improving the performance of what they keep viewing as the primary users' needs. As a result, they may not see the blow coming, even though it is already there. All in all, Christensen identifies a dilemma:

- going for (1) the sustaining path (more of the same – improved) with the risk of overshooting;
- going for (2) the disruptive path (identifying better ways to do the job for the customers, fulfilling function F and its sub-functionalities in innovating ways to displace/disrupt competition not via the intensity of innovation but from its target and focus).

Note that the sustaining path is tempting as the market is already known and occupied ("we are already in business"), thus minimizing risks, while the disruptive path includes the risk of offering some different features or functionalities that may not find market buoyancy despite high expectations.

In short, Christensen suggests a way to compete through innovation from below on something different "to do the job" for the users. He calls it disruptive.

This leads me to compare my categories of technological innovations summarized in Tab. 1-A to Christensen's duality (which he rightly sees as a dilemma): sustaining and disruptive innovations.

First, innovations can be technological (the focus of this book), or not necessarily (typically, Christensen's disruptive innovations do not need to be technological, although they can be, while sustaining innovations are more likely to be technological but may not be as well). In addition, technological innovations range from incremental to radical along the discrete continuum identified on Fig. 16-A and summarized on Tab. 1-A.

Second, an innovation can be characterized by where it strikes, that is its target, in the sense of the locus of application: the target can be the main criteria of performance identified by most, if not all, competitors as users' key expectation. (This is typically the case for sustaining innovations in Christensen's sense.) Yet, innovations can also be directed at one or several complementary components of the value perceived by customers. In doing so, firms competing in the arena offer something new, not necessarily impressive per se, but transforming the business model nonetheless. Such targets that recombine to reshuffle the business model may be one or several specific sub-functionalities that complement the main criteria of performance that has prevailed so far in the competitive game.

When the fax, then emails via internet, SMS and the social networks emerged as a new way to interact in written form, postal services (snail mail) were progressively displaced. In the case of France, the CEO of La Poste (the French Post office) reported that the peak of postal services was reached around 2002 with about 24 billion letters being delivered compared to 6 billion in 2022. This is a typical business model innovation where physical presence and coverage of geographies or the reliability in delivery the next day (at D+1) were no longer relevant criteria of performance when the fax and even more so email, not to speak of WhatsApp and the social networks, were quasi-immediate. In addition, the new services were already paid for in most cases, making them look as if they were for free. The postal mail was displaced by solutions that transformed a mix of sub-functionalities into a whole new service (theses sub-functionalities that combined into function F that could be captured as "delivering a written message to a correspondent"). Note that the new solutions to fulfill function F were not developed to compete against postal mail. They simply emerged and happened to undermine the historical postal services.

Third, innovations can be characterized by their outcome in terms of competitive dynamics. What may be the extent of the turmoil generated on the competitive positions in the arena? This can range from a very high rate of turmoil (typically radical innovations on Tab. 1-A or disruptive innovation in Christensen's sense) to business as usual (typically incremental innovation in Tab. 1-A).

In fact, Christensen's choice of using the word "disruptive" to qualify the innovations targeted at another/other dimension(s) of the business model stems from his intent to qualify the outcome of the innovations, more than its input.

This book is about technological strategy when thinking about technological options for the future. Hence, I also aim at anticipating the outcome of a strategic choice selecting a technology. I thus also look at the potential consequences to expect from the irruption of a new technology N+1 (and subsequently N+2, etc.) on the competitive dynamics. This is what this chapter discussed.

In Christensen's sense, disruptive means significantly changing the rules of the game and thus significantly affecting competition. However, it does not mean that the disruptive innovation needs to be radical. It is not a matter of the intensity of the innovation (as an input). Instead, by focusing on a different feature of the offering, disruptive innovations bring about change that transforms the competitive dynamics – even if the trigger is incremental innovation on that complementary feature. In a way, disruptive innovations in Christensen's sense deal with other components of the business model, regardless of the intensity of those innovations.

Tab 1.B recaps the comparison between the three categories of technological innovations shown on tab 1.A (radical, micro-radical and incremental technological innovations) to Christensen's two (sustaining vs disruptive) categories of innovation. All in all, it appears that these two perspectives, while partly related, belong to two different conceptualization of innovation (including technological change) and their impact on the competitive dynamics in an industry.

This discussion leads me to suggest using the words disruptive and disruption with much care, given the specific sense Christensen introduced. In the rest of this book, I keep using these words in the following sense that extends Christensen's view: a disruption is a significant change (or turmoil) in the competitive dynamics in a business arena; disruptive qualifies a change, including but not only a new technology, an innovation that will generate disruption at the outcome. Further, I suggest avoiding equating disruptive with radical. While disruption conveys the notion of turmoil in the competitive position of firms, Christensen pointed to the disruptive power (on competitive dynamics) of incremental change

Tab. 1-B: Clarifying the difference and linkages between the intensity of innovation framework and Christensen's sustaining/disruptive categories.

	Input		Outcome	
	Technological innovation & intensity	**Target/locus of innovation**	**Intensity of turmoil induced in competitive arena**	**Category**
Table 1-A	Radical techno innovation	Any	Very high: a new game brought about by technology	Technological paradigmatic shift
	Micro-radical techno innovation	Any	Significant turmoil "intermediate impact"	Same techno paradigm, new or same envelope trajectory, new sub-trajectory
	Incremental techno innovation	Focus on same core performance as before	No or small impact "business as usual"	Continuous improvement along a trajectory within same paradigm
Innovator's dilemma (Christensen)	"Sustaining" Techno or not, of any intensity	Focus on same core performance as before	Risk of overshooting performance beyond market needs	Christensen's sustaining
	"Disruptive" Techno or not, of any intensity	Targeted to "lateral" sub-functionalities: "doing the job differently"	Potentially very high "Game Changer"	Christensen's disruptive

as well, when it applies to a new, very sensitive sub-functionality of F (that is, a very sensitive market expectation, not recognized as such by most competitors so far).

In short, radical technological innovations are likely to lead to a major disruption (corresponding to paradigmatic shift in my framework shown as Tab. 1-A). Hence, radical technological innovations are likely to be very disruptive (although not necessarily in Christensen's sense – where the focus/target is not the intensity of the trigger but the business model).

Micro-radical innovations are likely to lead to significant disruption (same paradigm, new trajectory in my framework shown as Tab. 1-A). Hence, micro-radical technological innovations are likely to be significantly disruptive (although not necessarily in Christensen's sense – where the focus/target is not the intensity of the trigger but the business model).

Incremental technological innovations are likely to lead to no disruption (business as usual because the competence base required remains the same) except if the innovations are targeted to new dimensions of the business model, away from what was the focus of competition so far.

Decomposing function F into an upstream tree

I mentioned the importance of properly choosing the wording for function F at the top of the DTT. In some situations, an "upstream tree" may be needed to define and organize the customer functions to be satisfied around certain needs, thus focusing on the construction of several DTTs, each of them for a clearly specified function or sub-function. This matter needs to be explored and discussed in more detail because it deals with the most fascinating – and still poorly understood – aspect of innovation. This is about the key market mechanism that governs the search for a match between technological possibilities and solutions on the supply side, and market concepts and customer needs on the demand side. This is what Chapter 9 is about.

Chapter 9
The Customer Concept Tree (CCT) – Market Concept Formation

Given the theme of this book, I clearly adopted a supply-side viewpoint. I am building a way for firms to understand how technology evolves, how such evolution affects competition in a business arena and thus what a firm can do to create a path for itself into the future. It is thus natural that my writing leans towards technologies and firms in the competitive game, i.e., the supply side. Yet, this does not mean that the role of the demand side should be downplayed. The whole field of marketing has clearly shown the importance and the relevance of better understanding what the users and customers want and need – a key component of innovation.

I already discussed the oversimplification of reducing the demand side to a target named function F (Chapter 2). I insisted that function F should not be considered as a given. I recognized that function F is in fact a moving target co-evolving with technology and likely to segment itself into sub-functions. In fact, technological change leads to revisiting function F as users' sense of what they need is being transformed as well along the way. In other words, a deep dive into the technology dynamics and its strategic impact on competition (the focus of this book) requires a closer look at the user/customer side as well. I start by recognizing that market concepts are being formed throughout the whole process of technological evolution that I primarily described so far from the offering side. This leads me to the idea of a customer concept tree that subdivides function F. In a way, thinking about technology strategically requires understanding how the dual technology tree (DTT) and the customer concept tree (CCT) meet and mate.

I suggest a CCT to visualize the second half of the evolution process – the part representing the demand side. It should start from what Dosi calls some generic technological tasks or generic 'needs', i.e., a very upstream function to be satisfied in the marketplace (what I have called function F since Fig. 2 in Chapter 2), e.g., the treatment of diabetes, switching, transportation, etc. The CCT should then organize the different combinations of specific needs (characteristics, performance, price, etc.) that may be expressed (explicitly or not) on what would thus form customer concepts to serve market segments that appeared along the way. This would mean transforming function F into an array of $F_1 \ldots F_i$ specific sub-functions. In this sense, each market segment would then represent a specific customer concept. This would lead to a CCT.

Before going further in that direction, I need to add a layer of complexity as offerings serving specific market segments may result from the combination of a variety of sub-systems stemming from sub-sub-functionalities. Let me clarify this point.

https://doi.org/10.1515/9783111397979-010

Decomposing Function F

As I address the demand side, I need to refine the gross approximation made so far by using a single meta-function F. The first refinement appeared early on as I immediately stressed that function F is not a given. Users' needs tend to co-evolve with technology. A second and then a third refinements comes from the need to decompose the single meta-function F. This is done in two ways that recombine to one another.

The first decomposition of F stems from the dynamics of market segmentation. Segments appear in the form of clusters of users sharing the same type of needs around customer concepts. In this sense, a variety of customer concepts (each covering clusters of users' specific needs) are reassessed and reformulated over time. Typically, if the need for an offering can indeed be summarized in a single generic function F (like going from point A to point B), sub-functions will soon appear to decompose such an overall meta-function into customer concepts (here expressed in terms of offerings) such as a car, bike, plane, train, bus, walking, etc. In this sense, those customer concepts are nothing but sub-functions of F. I will name these F_1 ... F_i. Obviously, the corresponding technologies for each of these customer concepts are likely to differ significantly. This means that we need to draw a specific DTT for each customer concept with a specific F_i at the top (see Chapter 8).

Yet, there is more to it.

A second decomposition of F needs to be accounted for. Among the customer concepts for F ("going from A to B"), one corresponds to a specific customer concept called automotive, say sub-function F_u. There comes the inevitable complexity of sub-function F_u. As an offering fit to the task (going from A to B), a car is made up of several sub-systems that serve specific sub-sub-needs such as autonomy, speed, power, adaptation to road conditions (e.g., rain, snow), safety, media and connectivity, heating, comfort, etc. This means that F_u can itself be decomposed into an array of sub-sub-functions F_{u1} ... F_{ui}.

The Customer Concept Tree (CTT)

This leads to a structure of a CCT that includes an array of specific sub-functions, themselves decomposed into sub-sub-functions. See Fig. 17-A.

Conceptually, this leads to view the function F to be fulfilled on the market as a set of sub-functionalities such as F_u. In turn, these are themselves a set of sub-sub-functionalities F_{u1} ... F_{ui}. This means that a specific DTT will be needed for each such sub-sub-functionality.

In turn, this also means that the conceptual description of dynamic interactions between a CCT and a DTT can be viewed from two different levels of granularity. At the finer-grain level, the CCT boils down to the sub-sub-functionality F_{ui} that happens to be standing at the top of its corresponding DTT in the way described in Chapter 8.

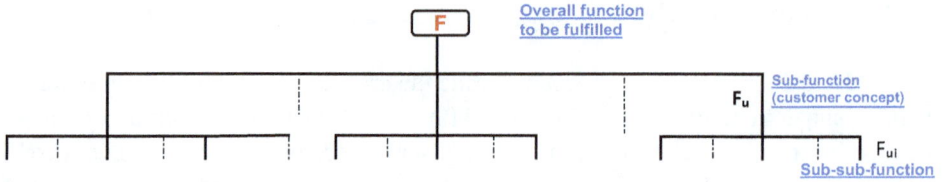

Fig. 17-A: A customer concept tree (CCT).

At the coarser level of granularity, it is possible to view the overall CCT (where F stands at the top) with all the sub-functionalities and their sub-sub-functionalities attached, as shown on Fig. 17-B. In such cases, each F_{ui} (the latter category) sits at the top of its corresponding DTT. This leads to some form of a forest of DTTs nurturing the global CCT via the sub-sub-functions. Figure 17-B offers a visual representation of such CCT-DTT interactions. This representation is essentially an illustration of a conceptual metaphor.

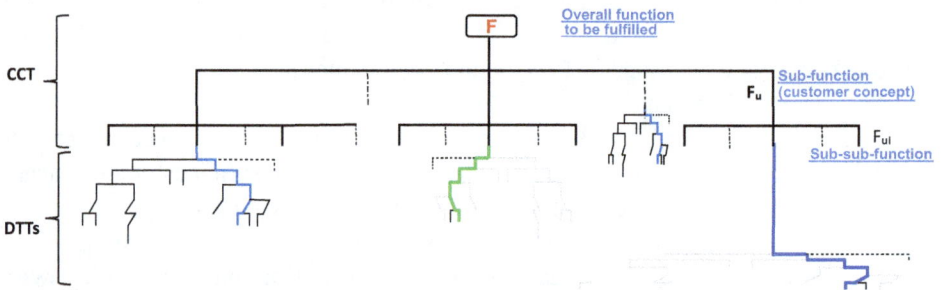

Fig. 17-B: The meeting and mating of the customer concept tree (CCT) and its dual technology trees (DTTs).

Note that the same technological options can appear in several of the DTTs. This opens the door for optimization via mutualization and sharing in the technology resource development programs.

All in all, this means that our goal is to think about technology strategically to fulfil a moving target of needs, in fact a function that may be just one among an array of sub-functions or sub-sub-functions to be looked at when dealing with a firm's businesses. Each of these sub-(sub-)functions should be dealt with, one after the other, building their corresponding DTT. Conceptually, it is a matter of replicating the same logic as the one discussed around DTT and CCT interactions.

There is a caveat though. The analysis needs to consider the integration of several technologies into the same offering. There may be issues of compatibility, interference, overall size, weight, cost (never a detail), etc. Such matters need to be taken care of, not just as a final step but by anticipation for the sub-sub-specific solutions that could make the integrated system vulnerable, uncertain, unreliable or even faulty.

Kim Clark looked at the interactions between design hierarchies and market concepts. He built upon Alexander's notion that "every design problem begins with an effort to achieve fitness between two entities: the form in question and its context". Clark analyzed the evolutionary pattern of technological innovation arguing that it is "the result of two related processes. The first is the logic of problem solving in design; the second is the formation of concepts that underly customer choice". He further argued that "both processes impose a hierarchical structure on the evolution of technology". He looked at the logic of product design, then customer concept formation and finally technological design for the logic of process development.

The above sequence of presentation of the three hierarchies (product design, market concepts, process) is rather surprising since it seems to separate product and process design hierarchies. However, Clark ends up reunifying product design and processes, recognizing "the important influence of process innovation on product design" and, I will add, vice versa. Also, Clark exclusively mentions problem solving as the innovative engine on the design side. To problem solving, I add chance and non-programmed creativity.

I essentially agree with Clark on everything else. On that basis, I already offered to visualize the hierarchies on the technological side in the form of the DTT for both product design and processes. I suggested here going one step further, offering to visualize the demand side via a CCT. In a way, the DTT/CCT representation helps visualize Clark's conceptual argument.

Regarding the hierarchies on the technology side, we saw that:

- The DTT recognizes the hierarchical nature of the design logic: it even maps it out.
- The DTT merges the product/process designs in a highly interrelated, intricate tree.
- The concept of duality used in the DTT further strengthens the argument against the idea of a chronological sequence (product design then process) in the A-U model.

The dual format of the DTT takes the last point into account in an explicit, visual way: a change from one branch to another may come from a process change but still affects the product design (and vice versa). However, I also acknowledge what the A-U model simply reports: on average the fluid phase is (statistically) experiencing more product innovations while the transition phase is more characterized with process innovations (again statistically). This leads to qualify the A-U model by adding that process changes may in turn interact with product designs.

It is then possible to describe an iterative dynamic fitting process between the DTTs and the CCT.

The whole picture of the evolutionary process would go more or less as follows:

- A certain technological seam is adopted for a given market segment associated with a specific customer concept representing a certain expression of the generic functional need (function F).
- The market concept can be viewed as a sub-functionality of F and may have to be itself subdivided into sub-sub-functionalities related to the various sub-systems that compose the complex offerings materializing the market concept.
- For each sub-functionality or sub-sub-functionality, the technology is then being adapted through trial and error, as the cumulative search mechanism converges in the branches of that seam to shape the trajectory.
- In the meantime, the market segmentation also evolves as customer concepts are being formed, refined and modified, thus looping back on the technological design choices.

As Teubal and Twiss, cited by Clark, put it, "consumers learn about what they want or need, and producers learn to innovate." In this sense there may be at the same time several different dominant technologies serving specific customer concepts on specific market segments. Each of those technologies is thus dominant with respect to a specific sub-function of a specific market concept – if not a sub-sub-function.

> Tezenas du Montcel studied the development of 3D printing, also known as additive manufacturing. He showed that there are many 3D printing technologies, identifying about 37 families. In a way, these are solutions in search of problems to be solved. No single firm is capable of offering the whole spectrum of these technologies. In fact, most technology providers offering 3D printing solutions are usually specialized in only one or two of them. On the demand side, users are industrial firms wondering how they could benefit from the potential of 3D printing, scanning their own unfulfilled needs in search of candidate applications. Their needs are many, each being specific. For instance, Michelin looked at 3D printing to manufacture tires. They soon realized that no solution would be relevant. However, they saw the opportunity to manufacture their own molds via a specific additive sub-technology. This would help them gain agility and speed to develop and experiment new models of tires. Unable to find a technology provider capable of developing a technical solution fit to their need, they ended up developing it on their own. As a result, they now offer their specific 3D printing expertise on the market. Tezenas du Montcel describes several other use cases where two firms (a technology provider and a user) chose to form an alliance to apply a specific additive sub-technology to a specific need.
>
> Tezenas du Montcel proposes a meta-process to describe the meeting and mating of problems to be solved (for firms unaware of the existence of 3D printing new solutions fit to specific problems they may have had for a long time) with solutions offered by technology providers and now rendered possible by the paradigm of additive manufacturing. He looks in detail at the relational strategies at work in the meta-process of many such strange encounters between techno providers and users. This illustrates what I mean by the dynamic interaction between a DTT and a CCT.

Clark was obviously looking for a model of this kind. In a similar way, Larue de Tournemine suggested that technological innovation takes place as a changing set of market needs faces a varying set of elementary technologies: these may be combined in many different and changing ways to yield new products/processes. On a more theoretical wavelength, Dosi is also thinking along the same lines. He suggests that "economic forces operate as a selective device (the focusing device of Rosenberg)" to choose technological paths "in a much bigger set of possible ones". He views technology as "a perception of a limited set of possible technological alternatives and of notional future development". He argues that the selective device draws upon multidimensional trade-offs among both technological and socio-economic variables. One may recognize in this description a segmentation process with buying criteria – and similar variables synthesizing the customer behavior – operating as the selective device among technological alternatives.

This discussion of the interaction between market concept formation and technological choices illustrated by the mating of a DTT with a CCT leads to the issue of the chronological order of technological development. As an early reader of this section put it: "There is a very significant difference between the logical structure of the technology and the temporal sequence of developments that characterize designs actually introduced in the marketplace."

Typically, the DTT for diabetes treatment shown on Fig. 15 (Chapter 8) presents the various technological options from left to right in temporal order which is an *ex post* historical presentation, while future potential technologies are presented in what may seem to be (as of today) a reasonable sequence of development. Yet again, I do not mean to convey any form of a deterministic view of the time sequence.

This suggests stressing again that conventions were used in designing the DTT and can be extended to the CCT. A typical convention chose to visualize technological options in the DTT hierarchically. Another convention was also used to present the historical sequence of emergence of past options from left to right. In fact, the sequence of the introduction of technologies and sub-technologies results from a combination of many factors, including the complex interaction between forces on the users' side and technology providers' proactivity on the supply side. However, displaying potential future technological options using the same convention, from left to right, does not anticipate the order of appearance of these options in the future.

Preventive Functionalities

I have discussed the evolution of needs over time, insisting on function F as a target not being a given.

An interesting idea concerning the thinking process regarding technological strategy suggests anticipating future needs beyond the current target F (and the corresponding sub-functionalities).

Kuperstein et al. call this "preventive quality of innovations". Examples of such deliberate overshooting can be found in engaging in the greening of the economy, by selecting energy-saving solutions beyond current regulations to both anticipate on future norms compliance and voluntarily contribute to a major societal challenge, assuming that customers (and regulators) may encourage such moves. Their study suggests positive market responses in terms of perception and adoption of the new offerings.

Such preventive functionality options are interesting as they can in fact accelerate technology substitutions, serving the planet, market expectations and the strategic position of those firms going for preventive quality technologies.

Modalities: Paradigms-trajectories-modalities

This discussion of the idea of a CCT and the interactions of the CCT with the DTTs leads to the concept of *modality* that Benoit Tezenas du Montcel and I put forward.

By modality, we mean a "nesting space", a "window of encounter", where and when a specific business opportunity for a technology is framed and materializes as an application. This is where and when a technology and a user need meet and mate in some form of a fertilization and developmental process.

A modality can be further defined by adopting a variety of points of view, typically below: space, time, materiality, organization, theory.

Space-wise, the modality can be seen as a cocoon where firms and users interact, nurturing and transforming an opportunity into a specific new offering (product/service) or a new production/distribution process.

Time-wise, a modality starts with some form of pollination (when the wind or insects carry the pollen of a plant to the stigma of a plant), encompasses fertilization, seeding, incubation, fruiting, germination, water capturing to nurture the early growth, and ends before the plant further develops. In other words, a modality includes the identification of a new technology to serve a need, the design of a solution that is technically feasible, relevant marketing-wise and financially viable, and the developmental process attached before the new offering can be sold or the new process implemented.

From the point of view of materiality, the end result of a modality is a new product/service offering, partly tangible, partly intangible, or a new production process that contributes to produce an offering. While traditionally a technological innovation project was often viewed through the lens of its outcome, the concept of modality makes it possible to capture the various antecedents of the outcome. A variety of forms of boundary objects[18] (marketing briefs, sketches, plans, mock-ups, prototypes, business plans, etc.) create a sequence of milestones before reaching the outcome, thus building the materiality of the technological innovation along the way. Pregnancy is a long process that cannot be reduced to giving birth – a critical moment indeed but with many other steps that took place and shape before; and many as well afterwards.

---

18 I discuss the concept of boundary objects in Part III at the end of Chapter 19.

From the point of view of the organization, the modality is (1) a process that leads to the development of the new, in a way similar to pregnancy. It is also (2) the interactions among organizations. (These include the identifier of a business opportunity behind a specific need; the provider of technological solutions and capacities to adapt the technology to the specifications of the need; the providers of equipment fit to manufacture the new artifacts; the distributors to put the new offering on the market; the agency capable of setting up the ads and the campaign needed prior to market launch). Organizationally, a modality covers both the process and the inter-organizational iterative and interactive arrangements.

From a theoretical point of view, the concept of modality makes it possible to grasp a technology at three levels: the paradigm; the trajectory (the envelope of subtechnologies exploring the paradigm); and the modalities (where the technology finds its applications for specific needs). This extends Dosi's twofold vision of "technological paradigm, technological trajectory" into a trilogy "paradigm-trajectory-modalities".

The traditional representation of market mechanisms views technology as a broad concept bringing solutions on the supply side to fulfill needs on the demand side. This perspective has two limits. First, it is general and rather vague, providing little insight on how technology and user needs meet and interact in search of a fit. Second, this traditional view ignores the process side of a modality, focusing essentially on the outcome (an artefact in the form of a product and/or a service) and/or a production process. In fact, by lack of a concept, the modality tended to be too often designated by its outcome as if the naming of a new product/service or production process was enough to inform about its fertilization, birth and emergence.

The concept of modality extends and complements the paradigm-trajectory representation of technological change, providing a finer grain of analysis. In doing so, the user needs are included in the representation via the modalities in the trilogy paradigm-trajectory-modalities. In this extended perspective, the need is not a given. In fact, in many cases, if the need seems to drive the way technology evolves, the need also co-evolves with technology.

The concept of modality relates to, though differs from, the notion of affordance that has been introduced in marketing after the initial idea was proposed by Gibson from a psychology perspective. Affordance stems from users' actions with an object, say a new offering, in a way it had not been designed for, possibly opening new applications of a product and/or service. The concept of affordance extends the concept of user needs and design beyond the target of functionalities. I would argue that the functionalities are designers' representations of market needs seen from the supply side. In that sense, it is interesting to observe and follow what users actually do with offerings – possibly beyond what the designers aimed for, namely the intended functionalities. In turn, Felin et al. discuss "perception and affordances" in the sense of the ability of actors in an environment to perceive business opportunities. They argue that this entrepreneurial creative task cannot be done purely analytically, as intuition and serendipity are part of the process. They thus argue that factors that combine into such intuitive and serendipitous potential new offerings (the future materialization of the business opportunities) cannot be priced on the market if the list of all applications of the factors is not known ahead of time. From there, they challenge the resource-based view (see Part III) as a theory that pre-assumes market efficiency. This discussion also relates to Teece's trilogy (notion of sensing, seeing, seizing). In a way, I argue that modalities correspond to the process of materializing Teece's trilogy.

In short, the concept of modality is a lens that permits a closer look at each of the many occurrences of encounter of the DTT and the CCT as they interact dynamically.

In the case of 3D printing discussed earlier in this chapter, Tezenas observed a very large number of modalities. Many firms in a variety of sectors find unique ways to call upon 3D printing sub-technologies as they search for innovative solutions to fulfil their needs. (This indeed applies to the firms' internal manufacturing processes). Tezenas argues that such a large diversity of modalities (due to many opportunities of specific application of additive manufacturing in many sectors) explains why he observed a large number of dyadic alliances while studying the development of 3D printing. By dyadic alliances, he simply means an alliance between two partners. The two partners are both from a supply side, but not in the same way. One partner supplies specific 3D printing sub-technologies. The second partner brings in the identification and understanding of some unmet or poorly met customer need on a specific market (and/or their own manufacturing process needs). Tezenas sees those dyadic alliances as the strategy selected by both partners: the technology supplier looking for problems to be solved, and the firm active on a market looking for new technologies to serve its customers (or its own internal manufacturing processes).

In fact, Tezenas identified three complementary interfirm relational strategies that firms use to explore the 3D printing paradigm: networking clubs; dyadic alliances; and transactional relationships. Networking clubs are professional association types of collective gathering to raise awareness about the new technological paradigm and grasp its potential. Networking clubs gather suppliers of technology as well as firms looking for new technological solutions. Dyadic alliances form to explore technological modalities as discussed above. Transactional relationships are classic B2B transactions taking place in value chains once the modalities have led to specific offerings (product/services) and/or new manufacturing processes. Based on these three types of interfirm relational strategies and using the concept of modality, Tezenas provides an insight into the way interfirm relations contribute to shape trajectories in exploring a new technological paradigm.

In short, his observations lead him to suggest that the emergence and exploration of the new paradigm (3D printing) took place as follows. First, a technological breakthrough on a very specific modality triggered attention to some new opportunities. Some visionaries suddenly anticipated the promises of this early signal. They started searching for additional applications and extended technological solutions in the same vein (in the same paradigm), meaning they searched for additional modalities. In so doing, they made noise and attracted more attention. While the process had been essentially the result of individual initiatives, on an entrepreneurial mode, the interest raised led some professions to launch networking clubs to raise awareness and help their members get a feel for what the new paradigm could be about (what may be in it for them). From there, some sort of spin-offs of the networking clubs were be generated in the form of dyadic alliances where a technology supplier and a need bearer entered into a partnership to explore specific modalities. In a way, the networking club proved unable to deal with concrete modalities because such a setting cannot cope with the very large diversity at hand (too many sub-technologies and too many specific potential applications). However, the networking club will have permitted participants to identify a fit with a potential partner. In a way, the networking clubs operated as dance floors or dating platforms where couples can form.

The above description provides an understanding of how a selective device operates for a specific case (3D printing) at the interface of DTTs and CCTs.

The question of the *relevance* of the choice that comes out of the selective device operating between technological possibilities and customer concepts is an interesting one. There is a whole body of literature on the economics of technical change that addresses this issue.

More specifically, it appears that market forces (the selective device mentioned above) do not always seem capable of selecting the "best" technology and may embark an entire industry and their customers onto "wrong" (or at least "not the best") track. This has been pointed out decades ago. Yet, this is a sensitive proposition as it challenges market efficiency in our Western economies. This is discussed in Chapter 10.

Chapter 10
Technology Selection, Technological Bifurcation, Small Events, Lock-in, De-maturation

Market economies assume that market mechanisms are the best way to select among competing offerings or allocate resources among investment projects. Yet, there is plenty of empirical evidence of market failure when it comes to selecting technologies. In several sectors, it is not the "best" technology that became dominant. More specifically, when it came to choosing a technology among the options available, the "selective device" failed to properly operate as a filtering mechanism among technological branches of the DTT.

This can be explained with the concepts of increasing rate of adoption, bifurcation or small event, and lock-in.

Increasing Rate of Adoption

The concept of increasing rate of adoption may seem ambiguous. Increasing rate of adoption of what and adoption by whom? In the context of this book, the "what" question is rather simple; we deal here with adoption of a new technology. The "adoption by whom" question is slightly trickier. This is because the concept of increasing rate of adoption is twofold.

On the one hand, when selecting a technology for their product design and/or process, firms on the supply side may end up attracting competitors who can benefit from spillover and network effects (e.g., learning that leaks through the equipment offered by suppliers to the industry). More firms end up choosing a specific technology because it is becoming the industry dominant technology.

On the other hand, when selecting a product or service, customers on the demand side end up attracting still hesitant customers who can benefit from network effects (typically, in platforms' business models, the more subscribers the more attractive the offer becomes to customers and users).

In both cases, supply and demand sides, there can be increasing rates of adoption. New adoption at some stage of technological change generates increasing adoption at a later stage. This can be either on the supply side or the demand side, or even both, via a combined effect.

> The first car to ever reach 100 km/hour speed was an electric car. The record was set in 1899 in Achères in the Yvelines district in France, just northwest of Paris. Designed and driven by Camille Jenatzy, a Belgian engineer and pilot, the car prototype was called La Jamais Contente (literally, "the never satisfied"). Yet, the car industry subsequently grew with the internal combustion engine. Typically, once some of the first car manufacturers had picked that technology, away

https://doi.org/10.1515/9783111397979-011

from the electric car, the experience gained made it ever more attractive, especially cost-wise, thus fueling demand. In addition, the more adopters on the demand side, the more incentives for investing in gas stations along roads, thus encouraging slow followers on the demand side to adopt the technology. It took over a century and the environmental concerns over CO_2 emissions in transportation to reconsider this early choice made at that time for the internal combustion engine.

For the demand side, the concept of increasing rate of adoption captures the essence of network effect or snowballing. The more customers in the network, the more adopters (new customers) will follow. (The more profiles on Facebook, the more attractive Facebook became to newcomers.) In addition, for the supply side, when a new technology is selected and implemented by some of the competitors, its industrialization and commercialization will help attract early adopters/customers and thus build a preliminary experience base for the firms on the supply side. This means reaching superior functional performance and/or much lower costs than competing technologies. The early accumulation of experience on that technology thus induces improvements that will subsequently make it likely to be more competitive and attractive than any other options at any point in time. This lasts for a period of time that can be prolonged. Indeed, this effect will reinforce itself over time, thus leading to a lock-in situation.

A lock-in situation emerges when an ecosystem is in place: thermal engine cars assembled by car manufacturers; gas station along the roads, properly supplied by petroleum companies; a dense network of mechanics for maintenance and repair; logistics for parts; an extensive user base driving cars powered by internal combustion engines; etc. Once this is in place, cost and quality can improve continuously through incremental innovation and optimization of operations. There is no simple way for a new technology to compete with the current dominant technology because it requires to set up another ecosystem to reach the same level of costs and performance. This describes a lock-in, a situation where change is difficult to promote unless there is a very significant gap in price or performance brought in by the new technology, or major regulatory or societal forces to push for it.

Note that the argument around an increasing rate of adoption goes in the opposite direction of Moore's concept of chasm (see discussion in Chapter 4 around Fig. 9). Under a regime of increasing rate of adoption, once the early adopters have opted in, the early followers (to be) should be attracted as well. However, there may be a tension between attractiveness stemming from the effect of increasing rate of adoption and worries of potential early followers not fully convinced to opt in, at least not immediately. These are opposing forces. Thus, the opportunity for a chasm to emerge. However, once the chasm is crossed, the dynamics around early followers is likely to be amplified by the increasing rate of adoption, reinforcing what Moore calls the "bowling alley".

Bifurcations and Small Events

In case of subsequent increasing rate of adoption, the initial choice of a technology by some players can be of utmost importance on the rest of the technology dynamics. Whatever the reasons behind the early choice (by some firms on the supply side and early adopters on the demand side), the technology first introduced is very likely to be the natural candidate to become dominant.

The word "bifurcation" is used to describe the moment of emergence of the new technology that takes off; and the adoption of this technology will accelerate if it takes off under a regime of increasing rate of adoption. This can be modeled as follows.

> Two colored balls are in a bowl. One is red, the other is white. A blind draw takes place. If the ball drawn from the bowl is red, two red balls are put back into the bowl. If it is white, two white balls are put in. Then another round of blind draw takes place. Again, two balls of the same color as the ball drawn are put back into the bowl, and so on for many rounds of blind draw. As one can anticipate, at the end of a sequence of many draws, the bowl will be essentially unicolor. The first draw gives a 50/50 probability on the color of the draw. The second round faces a 33.33/66.66 probability split. Chances are that the next draw will confirm the first draw, thus still increasing the probability of the same color to be drawn once more at the next round, and so on. If the second draw picks the other color, the two colors come back to parity and the system returns to a 50/50 initial stage. With the next draw, the process starts again. In the end, an almost unicolor outcome is still expected.
>
> In other words, a system with two fully equivalent options (50/50) will bifurcate for one or the other, just because of the early draws.

This simple model captures the dynamics for both the supply and demand sides. It illustrates how a final choice of a technology may result from an initial bifurcation that is subsequently amplified by an increasing rate of adoption. The bifurcation can stem from a strong push from a proponent on the supply side, or a sudden momentary belief spreading among early adopters on the demand side, or a prescriptive effect of an opinion leader expressing a preference at some stage (well informed, poorly informed or deliberately biased).

In this context, Paul David and Brian Arthur have both argued that a "small event" may cause the bifurcation.

The origin of QWERTY (the sequence of letters from the left on the top row of English-language keyboards), QUERTZ (for German) or AZERTY (for French), illustrates how a small event created a lock-in.

> When the first typewriters were introduced, fast-typing users frequently jammed the arms of the letters used to press ink onto the paper. To solve the jam problem, technicians had a strange idea. They chose to organize the letters on the keyboard in such a way that it rendered typing very difficult, thus slowing down the speed of use of the typewriters. That simple trick solved the technicians' problem by shifting the issue onto the users. This obviously solved the jamming matter at the cost of complication for the typists. Over a century later, the complication remains because generations of typists have been trained on the same keyboards. Thus, reorganizing the

letters on the keyboards is today simply a non-starter. Social inertia entrenched the lock-in. Although computer keyboards can be easily reprogrammed, experience shows that this functionality is seldom used. A radical change such as voice interface to dictate text to a PC seems to be the only way to escape the lock-in.

Another illustration of a small event generating a lock-in stems from electronuclear technologies.

The first nuclear reactor to produce electricity in the US started operations in 1957 in Shippingport, Pennsylvania. The reactor's design and technology (pressurized light water) came directly from the first US nuclear submarine, Nautilus. A key player in the choice of the technology was Admiral Hyman Rickover. This brilliant marine officer, born in 1900 in what was to become Poland, joined the US navy in 1918 and climbed up the ladder thanks to his engineering talent. During WWII, he oversaw the US submarines' electrical systems. After the war, he participated in the development of the Nautilus reactor and subsequently supervised the development of reactors for nuclear-powered surface ships (aircraft carriers). He was soon appointed to the US Atomic Energy Commission. In that commission, Hyman Rickover supported the pressurized water reactor technology for electronuclear power plants. This was quite logical for him as this technology had been successful for submarines and aircraft carriers. He managed to convince the commission. As a result, the US went for pressurized water nuclear technology in the civil application of atomic energy. In turn, the entire Western world, under US leadership, followed suit. A small event made the bifurcation: the appointment of Admiral Rickover to the US Atomic Energy Commission turned out to strongly influence the selection of pressurized water nuclear reactor technology for nuclear electricity – one could even say that the small event "selected" the technology.

Most of the nuclear engineering literature suggests that pressurized water nuclear reactors were probably not the best technological option. However, once implemented successfully in the first electronuclear power plants, it had gained obvious superiority against any other technology not yet implemented.

Selecting a second-best technology or missing the "best" technology would not be a problem if a correcting mechanism could operate at a later stage. In fact, it appears that increasing rates of adoption of the first technology selected led that technology to spread because it became increasingly attractive at any point in time compared to any other technology. The other technologies cannot compete because they have not been implemented, or not to the same scale. This leads to a situation of lock-in. The new dominant technology remains dominant because its dominance reinforces itself over time. It may subsequently appear to have been an intrinsically inferior technology that should not have reached dominance, but it is too late.

This raises the sensitive question of escaping from a lock-in.

Technological Lock-in, Escaping the Lock-in, Going Over the Threshold

The dynamics of technology in a regime of increasing rate of adoption tends to embark an industry into tracks. As I discussed earlier, tracks both habilitate and constrain. The dominant technology became dominant as it fulfilled the needs attached to function F. In that sense, the technology selected habilitates the firms on the supply side: The technology works and makes it possible to meet users' expectations, at least to a certain extent. Yet, because the dominant technology kept constantly improving and built volumes as it developed, no other candidate technology may be in a position to reach the same level of cost, reliability and quality. In that sense, the tracks constrain: it is increasingly difficult to consider other options. The technological dynamics leads to a situation of lock-in.

It should be stressed here that not only does history matter, but also strategic decisions made by competitors and other players involved, including users/customers. As discussed earlier, lock-in situations may result from norms setting, increasing returns to adoption following a move by a major competitor, government intervention through procurement or publicly funded R&D, or even one of the somewhat overemphasized "small events".

In any case, a lock-in situation benefits the incumbents as it keeps new entrants out.

Yet, keeping in mind the way the current dominant technology was selected in the first place, chance and small events having possibly had a significant role, it may appear along the way that the technology selected is not fully adequate. Players may be keen on switching to another technology. However, the situation of lock-in impedes such switching.

Escaping the lock-in requires one or more of the five items discussed below.

(1) New entrants boldly try to push for a new technology, even though the business case is not easy to sell because, the new technology being new, it may not yet be in a position to compete against the established dominant technology. This is because of uncertainty: the candidate new technology has not been implemented and there may be unexpected technical roadblocks ahead, costs may be high, investments may take longer than planned, users may not adopt the new solution, etc.

Comparing the potential of a new candidate technology to the reality of the current dominant technology is likely to turn to the advantage of the latter, precisely because it is well established. A significant step improvement of the cost/performance index of Fig. 2 in Chapter 2 is needed. By "significant" I do not mean a marginal improvement but going beyond a *threshold* that will permit the buy-in by decision makers on both the supply side and demand side.

(2) Dynamic capabilities needed to exit the tracks. Most incumbents may not have these dynamic capabilities. No slide rule manufacturer was able to reinvent itself

into the business of electronic calculators. The Eastman Kodak Company could not move to digital photography. IBM missed the boat on PCs. I would argue that the roadblock for Kodak and IBM was primarily cultural. Their internal beliefs, built on decades of industrial success, prevented them from accepting the idea of the change. They disregarded the change.

In contrast, when radiologists had to surf the wave of echography first in obstetrics and then in many other medical applications they felt they had been hit by a revolution. The parallel development of the Computed tomography scan (CT scan) and its subsequent deployment was another form of revolution, although still based on X-rays. All in all, the arrival of the CT scan was managed, obviously with much improvement for the patients. Later, when nuclear magnetic resonance (NMR) appeared, radiologists had become used to coping with major technological change. This does not mean that radiology was the only sub-field of medicine that made significant progress over the last 50 years! Nevertheless, for the years to come, one should expect radiologists to be particularly receptive to innovation. Information technologies – storing images, digital networks, etc. – already diffuse very easily in radiology. Radiologists are clearly on the move, learning and ready to learn again. In a way they have built dynamic capabilities. The next revolution for them may already be on its way, with Artificial Intelligence. I would add that the dynamic capabilities that they built for themselves over the last 4 or 5 decades should prepare them to navigate change provided it stays within the realm of digital imaging. More radical change bringing radiologists into yet another technological world (IA is about information technologies – not so much about digital imaging) may not be so easy for them to cope with.

(3) New regulation that reopens the search agenda for new technological options and public support. Bans on diesel and then on all internal combustion engine cars opened the door for electric cars (hybrid and 100% electric). While big car makers pondered what to do and when exactly, Tesla rushed into the breach. That move was typical of the entrepreneurial side of the Tesla coin.

One could argue that the Tesla success story is in fact the result of the US government's industrial policy strongly pushing for electric cars in the name of environmental concerns. An entrepreneur with bold visionary ideas for the car industry was identified in Elon Musk, with all the traits of the North American entrepreneurs, regardless of him being born abroad. His venture was heavily supported by public funding, including when Tesla was on the verge of bankruptcy.

(4) A sudden economic shock that disturbs the established rules of the game. The oil shocks of 1973 and 1979 forced car manufacturers to revisit their offerings towards more compact cars with lower gas consumption.

(5) A paradigmatic shift that shakes the industry, opening the door for change. In the hospitality business, worldwide hotel chains faced the arrival of Airbnb as a major threat. The intrusion of a business model based on two-sided digital platforms was a breach that obliged the incumbents to revisit their old business models. A bold move from a start-up towards a new hospitality paradigm unlocked the industry lock-in.

This discussion of the ways to escape a situation of technological lock-in suggests digging two specific points in more depth: threshold for triggering substitution and de-maturation.

Threshold for Triggering Substitution

As briefly mentioned above, I suggest that there is a threshold effect that prevents firms from switching from one technology to another unless there is a significant cost/performance gain in the switch. A candidate new technology (A) just at par with the current dominant technology is likely to be a lost cause (and even more so if it is below par). A candidate new technology (B) offering new functionalities, lower cost, increased flexibility and better quality than the current dominant technology is more likely to pass the test and trigger a substitution process. In between option A at par or below par, a situation that is a non-starter, and the obvious promises of option B, I argue that there is a threshold. Below, the technology will not fly; above, it may.

However, implementing this concept of threshold would require a workable way of assessing and comparing cost/performance indexes, as discussed in Chapter 2. This echoes the discussion on the comparability between technology performance. Yet, conceptually, the notion of a threshold makes sense, even though it may not be easily implemented in practice.

De-maturation

Escaping a lock-in means searching for or promoting a de-maturation process.

The above discussion on escaping a lock-in, together with the DTT, makes it possible to further understand the concept of technological de-maturation.

The A-U model suggests a slow convergence towards the dominant technology. This is named maturation. The seam-trajectory metaphor links successive A-U cycles together: the DTT integrates these models in a hierarchical format. Maturation is a slow process searching for a dominant technology through iterations leading to a downward convergence in the hierarchy (the DTT).

In contrast, de-maturation is a *jump up* in the DTT. As Clark puts it, "Movements up the hierarchy are associated with departure from existing approaches". De-maturation can be visualized in the DTT as a new search for new technological paths in the tree. De-maturation means reopening the search agenda for a dominant technology.

De-maturation rarely comes from a single firm's strategic initiative. Instead, it tends to stem from a shock (regulatory, environmental, economic, geopolitical, pandemic) that is shaking an industry (and sometimes several industries if not the entire economy). It reopens the search agenda in the DTTs, away from the dominant technology of the time. Obviously, some firms can opportunistically use the shock to enter the market, accompanying, if not promoting, the change. However, in the absence of a driver for de-maturation, it is risky for a single firm, even if powerful, to attack a dominant design head-on as incumbents are entrenched in their strategic position. Start-ups may be exceptions. They are bold, having little to lose. They may successfully displace the dominant technology and the incumbents. They may trigger a paradigmatic shift. SpaceX in launch vehicles or Airbnb in the hospitality business provide good examples, recalling what Apple achieved in the computer industry. Yet these are exceptions. I argue that de-maturation relates more to the industry dynamics than it is the result of a firm's competitive strategy. However, when de-maturation is in the air, firms have a window of opportunity to try to benefit from the change. To achieve this, they need to understand de-maturation.

The process of de-maturation can be sketched as follows.

The previous dominant technology – corresponding to a "specific" A-U stage – was clearly recognized and adopted over the years by most, if not all competitors in the industry. The competitors refusing to adopt that dominant technology were either thrown out of the market or marginalized into small niches. All the neighboring branches in the DTT, within the same seam, were explored or at least tested and abandoned. The dominant technology has thus clearly become the winning technology – at least for a given customer concept/market segment, expressed by the generic function F selected at the top of the DTT.

In Chapter 9, I discussed the process of technological selection at the interface between technological possibilities on the supply side (the DTT) and specifications of customers' needs on the demand side (the CCT). I have also pointed out earlier in this chapter that the governance mechanism that operates the selecting process may not always pick the best technology to yield the winning, dominant technology. However, the fact is that the search process converges and stabilizes, at least for some time, around a dominant technology visualized in the DTT as a clear dark line going deep down in the tree.

Then, and this is the key point, when de-maturation occurs, an entirely new search process is about to take place, beginning the exploration of a new seam, up somewhere else in the tree. As Clark puts it: "New technical options or changes in customer concepts may reopen certain items on the agenda and may in fact unleash search and learning with renewed vigor". As a new search is on, no immediate convergence mechanism can operate. It takes time to explore the many possible branches that are already available in the new seams as well as the sub-options that may appear along the way. The industry thus sees a wide variety of sub-technologies – product designs and processes – being offered in what appears to be a fluid stage of a new cycle on the A-U model. The frequency of innovation is high. De-maturation appears in the tree in the form of many competing branches being tried by many different players in the industry at the same time. In turn, this diversity eventually slowly decreases, and a new dominant technology is likely to emerge as the trial-and-error search process takes place and converges downwards in the tree.

The oil shocks of 1973 and 1979 operated as an exogenous mechanism to modify customer behavior with respect to energy. As a result, de-maturation occurred in several industries, including automotive. Amouyal counted the number of different technical combinations (engine/transmission/gear shaft) sold in cars on the US market over the years. His data show a clear increase in the diversity of technical options offered in the late 1970s and early 1980s as compact-size automobiles and other energy-saving designs were increasingly put to market in that period. Apart from the effect of import designs, I see in this increasing diversity the result of US car manufacturers searching for new designs up in the automobile DTT and not converging at once. One might argue that the 1986 oil counter-shock had an opposite effect on the industry, although this effect had to be combined with both environmentalist concerns on car technology and Japanese pressure on competition. The subsequent development of SUVs shows that market preference played a role in counter-influencing product designs.

More recently, the growing awareness of the limited resources of our planet and global warming operated as a major driver of de-maturation in a variety of sectors, from cement to steel to automotive to aeronautics, tourism or logistics, to name a few.

De-maturation somewhat relates to the idea of being reborn, at least partially, which is tantamount to losing a part of the organization's experience, accepting to learn all over again.

One should thus expect recently de-matured industries to be more receptive to radical innovation than mature ones. Packing your personal belongings and losing your friends are known to be the two most difficult things to do when moving; however, once you have been on the move, you are usually much quicker to accept moving away again before you settle down making new friends and growing roots. Similarly, the tennis player keeps bouncing on their feet when the opponent hits the ball because this is the only way to react fast. Some firms have proven to be very successful in keeping innovating regularly in the long run; developing some organizational skills to keep changing technology, bouncing from one branch in the DTT to another without taking the time to reach the "specific" stage of the A-U model on any branch, i.e., to mature. They seem to remain permanently on a de-matured mode. This echoes the concept of dynamic capabilities.

Summary of Key Points of Part I

(1) Seen at the meta-level of technological paradigms and technological trajectories, technology evolves in long periods of relative continuity punctuated by paradigmatic shifts. (See Fig. 2.)

(2) However, there is a continuum of the intensity of technological change with indeed two polar extremes (incremental innovation and radical innovation) that need to be complemented by some intermediary intensity of change (micro-radical innovation) in between.

(3) On that basis, having a closer look at it, technological evolution appears to take place as a series of technologies substituting for one another. Each becomes dominant for a period, fulfilling users' needs around a function F. Radical technological innovation strikes when a new paradigm emerges to displace the former paradigm (as technological progress offers radically new ways of addressing function F). This opens a period of exploration of the new paradigm by following a seam. This is when the apparently continuous evolution is in fact made up of a succession of micro-radical innovations that form and shape technological trajectories as their envelope. This is then followed by incremental innovation to improve the dominant sub-technology of the time, thus leading to a period of real continuity. This lasts until another micro-radical innovation takes place, if not another paradigmatic shift bringing radical change – and strategic turmoil. (See Fig. 11.)

(4) The framework built in Part I to represent technological evolution combines several concepts: technological paradigm, seam, trajectory, sub-technology, dominant technology, incremental innovation, micro-radical innovation and radical or revolutionary innovation. Typically, in time, the seam followed to explore a paradigm generates the technological trajectory made up of sub-technologies brought about by micro-radical innovations.

(5) The A-U model describes stages of innovation that search for a dominant design (fluid) and a dominant process (transitional) before optimizing the dominant technology (specific). (See Fig. 5.)

(6) The S-curve is a widespread tool used to grasp the dynamics of technological substitution whereby a dominant technology N is cannibalized by a new technology N+1 that will in turn become dominant. (See Fig. 7.) Yet, S-curves do not properly capture the variety of dynamics observed empirically, a matter discussed in Part II.

(7) The intensity of technological innovation drives the strategic consequences of the change on competitive dynamics in the corresponding business arenas. Moving from one paradigm to the next corresponds to radical innovation. These are big steps, significantly disturbing competition. Moving from one sub-technology to the next (within a technological trajectory as an envelope curve) corresponds to micro-radical innovations. These are intermediate steps with less impact on com-

https://doi.org/10.1515/9783111397979-012

petition. They can range from low to significant but nothing revolutionary. Along the trajectory, once a dominant technology reached the "specific" stage, with no more micro-radical innovations and no more variation around product design and process, there is essentially room left for incremental innovations. These do not disturb competition. They even tend to entrench the leaders dominating the business. (See Tab. 1-A.)

Christensen points to what he calls the innovator's dilemma (sustaining vs. disruptive innovations). He also points to an innovation strategy "from below", especially when incumbents tend to overshoot product/service performance beyond market needs, by focusing on the same specific feature again and again. Yet, in the rest of this book, I keep using the words disruptive and disruption in their full original sense: a disruption is a significant change (or turmoil) in the competitive dynamics of a business arena; disruptive qualifies a change, a new technology or an innovation that will generate disruption at the outcome. This does not mean that we should ignore the specific meaning that Christensen gave to disruptive innovation as an innovation of any intensity that is targeted to some new element(s) of the business model, thus generating disruption, including from below.

(8) The conceptual way to explain how the intensity of technological change drives its strategic significance calls upon the concept of competence of a firm. (The competence can be individual or organizational. A significant part of the competence base was built over time through learning via experimentation and action.) Competence is what change disrupts. Thus, the need to assess the competence gap when considering technological innovation: How far is our firm's competence base from the newly required set of competencies? And how far is it for competitors (incumbents or new entrants)? Competence is what to look at to assess the strategic significance of technological change. The DTT aims at offering a visual map of the many technologies (past, present – including dominant and prospective) that may fulfill function F. The bigger the jump in the tree imposed by technological change, the more violent the strategic turmoil is likely to be. (See Fig. 14.)

(9) The concept of modality extends and complements the paradigm-trajectory representation of technological change, providing a finer grain of analysis. As a result, technological change can be grasped at three levels: the paradigm, the trajectory (the envelope of sub-technologies exploring the paradigm) and the modalities (where the technology finds its applications for specific needs). In addition, the user needs appear explicitly in the representation of technological change via the modalities in the trilogy paradigms-trajectories-modalities. In this extended perspective, the need is not a given. In fact, in many cases, the need drives the way technology evolves or at least co-evolves with it. The concept of modality is a lens that permits a closer look at each of the many occurrences of encounter of the DTT and the CCT as they interact dynamically.

Part II is going to discuss further the variety of patterns of technological substitution departing from the oversimplified model of the S-curve. Part III will dig into the concept of competence: What is it exactly that is disrupted by technological change? How to think about technology strategically via the concept of transilience (the competence that will be rendered obsolete vs. the competence that will still be needed despite the change)? Part IV will discuss how to operationalize the framework resulting from Parts I, II and III.

References for Part I and Further Reading

Abernathy, W. J. & J. M. Utterback (1978). Patterns of industrial innovation. *Technology Review, 80*(7), 40–47.

Abernathy, W. J., & Clark, K. B. (1985). Innovation: Mapping the winds of creative destruction. *Research Policy, 14*(1), 3–22.

Adner, R. (2002). When are technologies disruptive? A demand-based view of the emergence of competition. *Strateg. Manage. J. 23*, 667–688. https://doi.org/10.1002/smj.246

Alexander, C. (1964). *Notes on the Synthesis of Form*. Harvard University Press, Cambridge MA. 15–16

Anderson, P. & Tushman, M. L. (1990). Technological discontinuities and dominant designs: a cyclical model of technological change. *Administrative Science Quarterly, 35*, 604–634.

Amouyal, P. (1982). La dématuration technologique dans l'automobile. S&T, Working Paper, Ecole Centrale Paris.

Arthur, B. W. (1989). Competing technologies, increasing returns, and lock-in by historical events. *Economic Journal, 99*(394), 116–31.

Christensen, C. M. (2003). *The Innovator's Dilemma*. New York, HarperCollins.

Dattée, B. (2006). The dynamics of technological substitutions. PhD thesis, Ecole Centrale Paris/University College Dublin.

Dattée, B., & Durand, T. (2009). Patterns of technological substitutions. Working paper, S&T, Ecole Centrale Paris.

David, P. A. (1985). Clio and the economics of QWERTY. *The American Economic Review, 75*(2), 332–337.

Durand, T. (1992). Dual technological trees: Assessing the intensity and strategic significance of technological change. *Research Policy, 21*, 361–380.

Gibson, J. J. (1977). The theory of affordances. In R. Shaw and J. Bransford (Eds.) *Perceiving, Acting, and Knowing, 67–82*. Hillsdale: Lawrence Erlbaum (hal-00692033)

Klepper, S. (1997). Industry life cycle. *Industrial and Corporate Change, 6*(1), 145–181.

Kuhn, T. S. (1962). Historical structure of scientific discovery. *Science, 136*(3518), 760–64.

Kuperstein Blasco, D., Saukkonen, N., Korhonen, T., Laine, T., & MuiluMäkelä, R. (2021). Wood material selection in school building procurement – A multi-case analysis in Finnish municipalities. *Journal of Cleaner Production, 327*, 129474.

Larue de Tournemine, R. (1988). Comment évaluer les stratégies technologiques. *Revue Française de Gestion*, (June–July) 26–36.

Mansfield, E. (1985). How rapidly does new industrial technology leak out? *Journal of Industrial Economics*, Wiley Blackwell, vol. 34(2), pages 217–223, December.

Martinelli, A. (2012). An emerging paradigm or just another technological trajectories? Understanding the nature of technological change using engineering heuristics in the telecommunications switching industry. *Research Policy, 41*(2), 414–429.

Moore, G. A. (2002). *Crossing the Chasm: Marketing and Selling High-Tech Products to Mainstream Customers*. New York, HarperCollins.

Pedota, M., Grilli, L., & Piscitello, L. (2021). Technological paradigms and the power of convergence. *Industrial and Corporate Change, 30*(6), 1633–1654.

Rosenberg, N. (1976). *Perspectives on Technology*. Cambridge, Cambridge University Press.

Schumpeter, J. A. (1941). *Capitalism, Socialism and Democracy*. New York, Harper and Row Publishers.

Teece, D. J. (2008). Dosi's technological paradigms and trajectories: insights for economics and management. *Industrial and Corporate Change, 17*(3), 507–512.

Tézenas du Montcel, B. (2019). Relations inter-firmes pour l'exploration d'un nouveau paradigme techno-industriel. Comment les entreprises s'y prennent-elles pour tirer parti de la fabrication additive? Thèse de doctorat en Sciences de Gestion, Conservatoire National des Arts et Métiers. https://theses.hal.science/tel-04368440v1

https://doi.org/10.1515/9783111397979-013

Tripsas, M. (1996). Surviving radical technological change: an empirical study of the typesetter industry. PhD thesis, Sloan School of Management, Massachusetts Institute of Technology.

Tushman, M., & Anderson, P. (1986). Technological discontinuities and organizational environments. *Administrative Science Quarterly, 31*(3), 439–465.

Further Reading

Bass, F. M. (1969). A new product growth model for consumer durables. *Management Science, Vol 15*, No. 5, 215–227.

Bessant, J., Öberg, C., & Trifilova, A. (2014). Framing problems in radical innovation. *Industrial Marketing Management, 43*(8), 1284–1292. https://doi.org/10.1016/j.indmarman.2014.09.003

Bhargava, S. C. (1995). A general form of the Fisher-Pry model of technology substitution. *Technology Forecasting and Social Change, 49*(1), 27–33.

Blackman, A. W. (1971). The rate of innovation in the commercial aircraft jet engine market. *Technological Forecasting and Social Change*, Vol *2*, 269–276.

Blackman, A. W. (1974). The market dynamics of substitutions. *Technological Forecasting and Social Change*, Vol 6, 41–63.

Blanc, A., & Huault, I. (2019). The maintenance of macro-vocabularies in an industry: The case of the France's recorded music industry. *Industrial Marketing Management, 80*, 280–295. https://doi.org/10.1016/j.indmarman.2018.06.004

Chandrasekaran, D., Tellis, G. J., & James, G. M. (2022). Leapfrogging, cannibalization, and survival during disruptive technological change: The critical role of rate of disengagement. *Journal of Marketing, 86*(1), 149–166. https://doi.org/10.1177/0022242920967912

Christensen, C. M., Suarez, F. F., & Utterback, J. M. (1998). Strategies for survival in fast-changing industries. *Manage. Sci., 44*(12-part-2), S207–S220. https://doi.org/10.1287/mnsc.44.12.S207

Christensen, C. M. (1992). Exploring the limits of the technology S-curve. Part I: Component technologies. *Production and Operations Management, 1*(4), 334–357.

Christensen, C. M. (1992). Exploring the limits of the technology S-curve. Part II: Architectural technologies. *Production and Operations Management, 1*(4), 358–366.

Christensen, C. M., & Rosenbloom, R. S. (1995). Explaining the attacker's advantage: Technological paradigms, organizational dynamics, and the value network. *Research Policy, 24*(2), 233–257. https://doi.org/10.1016/0048-7333(93)00764-K

Christensen, C. M., & Overdorf, M. (2000). Meeting the challenge of disruptive change. *Harvard Business Review* 78, no. 2 (March–April 2000): 66–76.

Clark, K. B. (1985). The interaction of design hierarchies and market concepts in technological evolution. *Research Policy, Vol 14*, issue 5, 235–251.

Coccia, M. (2005). Measuring intensity of technological change: The seismic approach. *Technological Forecasting and Social Change, 72*(2), 117–144. https://doi.org/10.1016/j.techfore.2004.01.004

Cooper, A. C., & Schendel, D. (1976). Strategic responses to technological threats. *Business Horizons, 16*(1), 61–69.

Cowan, R. (1991). Turtoises and Hares: Choice among technologies of unknown merit. *The Economic Journal, vol 101, (407)* 801–814.

Cozzolino, A., Gianmario, V., & Rothaermel, F. T. (2018). Unpacking the process: New technology, business models, and incumbent adaptation. *Journal of Management Studies, 55*(7), 1166–1202.

Dattée, B., & Weil, H. B. (2007). Dynamics of social factors in technological substitutions. *Technological Forecasting and Social Change, 74*(5), 579–607. https://doi.org/10.1016/j.techfore.2007.03.003

Dijk, M., & Yarime, M. (2010). The emergence of hybrid-electric cars: Innovation path creation through co-evolution of supply and demand. *Technological Forecasting and Social Change, 77*(8), 1371–1390. https://doi.org/10.1016/j.techfore.2010.05.001

Donald, N. (2013). *The Design of Everyday Things*. Basic Books.

Dosi, G. (1982). Technological paradigms and technological trajectories: A suggested interpretation of the determinants and directions of technical change. *Research Policy, Vol 11*, Issue 3, 147–162.

Durand, T., & Gonard, T. (1986). Stratégies technologiques: le cas de l'insuline. *Revue Française de Gestion*, n° 60 (novembre-décembre), 89–99.

Durand, T., & Stymne, B. (1988). Lessons from the public switching past technologies in the telecoms, Proceedings Prince Bertil Symposium, Stockholm, 9–11 November.

Durand, T. (1988). Programs competencies matrix: Analyzing R&D expertise within the firm. *R&D Management, 18*(2), 169–180.

Durand, T., & Stymne, B. (1991). Technology and strategy in a hitech industry. In L. G. Mattson and B. Stymne (Eds.), *Corporate and Industry Strategies for Europe. Adaptations to the European Single Market in a Global Industrial Environment* (pp. 193–215). Elsevier Science Publishing.

Durand, T. (2000/2006/2016), L'Alchimie de la Compétence. *Revue Française de Gestion, 32*(160), 261–292. (Originally published in 2000; republished for special issue *RFG* 30th anniversary in 2006 and 40th anniversary in 2016.)

Felin, T., Kauffman, S., Mastrogiorgio, A. & Mastrogiorgio, M. (2016). Factor markets, actors, and affordances. *Industrial and Corporate Change, 25*(1), 133–147.

Fisher, J. C., & Pry, R. H. (1971). A simple substitution model of technological change. *Technological Forecasting and Social Change, 3*, 75–88.

Foray, D. (1989). Les modèles de compétition technologique. *Revue d'Economie industrielle*, Vol *48*, Q2 1989, 16–34. doi.org/10.3406/rei.1989.2244

Foster, R. (1986). *Innovation: The Attacker's Advantage*. New York, Summit Books.

Freeman, C. (1979). The determinants of innovation: Market demand, technology, and the response to social problems, *Futures*. Vol.11, No. 3 (*1979*), 206–215.

Gibson, J. J. (1979). *The Ecological Approach to Visual Perception*, Boston: Houghton Mifflin.

Gort, M., & Klepper, S. (1982). Time paths in the diffusion of product innovations. *The Economic Journal*, Vol *92*, Issue 367, 630–653.

Grebel, T. (2009). Technological change: A microeconomic approach to the creation of knowledge. *Structural Change and Economic Dynamics, 20*(4), 301–312. https://doi.org/10.1016/j.strueco.2009.05.003

Griliches, Z. (1957). Hybrid corn: An exploration in the economics of technological change. *The Econometric Society*, Econometrica, Vol. 25, No. 4 (Oct., 1957), pp. 501–522

Henderson, R., & Clark, K. B. (1990). Architectural innovation: The reconfiguration of existing product technologies and the failure of established firms. *Administrative Science Quarterly, 35*(1), 9–30.

Hill, C. W. L., & Rothaermel, F. T. (2003). The performance of incumbent firms in the face of radical technological innovation. *Academy of Management Review, 28*(2), 257–274. https://doi.org/10.5465/AMR.2003.9416161

Itami, H., & Numagami, T. (1992). Dynamic interaction between strategy and technology. *Strategic Management Journal, 13*(S2), 119–135.

James, S. D., Leiblein, M. J., & Lu, S. (2013). How firms capture value from their innovations. *J. Manag., 39*(5), 1123–1155. https://doi.org/10.1177/0149206313488211

Kandel N., Remy, J. P., Stein, C., & Durand, T. (1991). Who's who in technology: Identifying technological competence within the firm, *R&D Management*, 21, 3, July 91, 215–228.

Klepper, S. (1996). Entry, exit, growth and innovation over the product life cycle. *The American Economic Review, 86*(3), 56–583.

Klepper, S., & Graddy, E. (1990). The evolution of new industries and the determinants of market structure. *Rand Journal of Economics, 12*(1), 27–43.

Klitkou, A., Bolwig, S., Hansen, T., & Wessberg, N. (2015). The role of lock-in mechanisms in transition processes: The case of energy for road transport. *Environmental Innovation and Societal Transitions, 16*, 22–37. https://doi.org/10.1016/j.eist.2015.07.005

Kuhn, T. S. (1962). *The Structure of Scientific Revolution*. University of Chicago Press.

Linstone, H. A., & Sahal, D., (Eds.) (1976). *Technological Substitution: Forecasting Techniques and Applications*. New York, Elsevier.

Loveridge, R., & Pitt, M. (Eds.) (1990). *The Strategic Management of Technological Innovation*. New York, Wiley.

Martino, J. P. (1993). *Technological Forecasting for Decision Making*. New York, McGraw-Hill.

McGee, J., & Thomas, H. (1989). Technology and strategic management: Progress and future directions. *R&D Management, 19*(3), 205–213.

Nelson, R. R., & Winter, S. G. (1982). *An Evolutionary Theory of Economic Change*. Harvard University Press.

Nightingale, P., von Tunzelmann, N., Malerba, F., & Metcalfe, S. (2008). Technological paradigms: Past, present and future. *Industrial and Corporate Change, 17*(3), 467–484.

Nonaka, I., & Takeuchi, H. (1995). *The Knowledge-Creating Company: How Japanese Companies Create the Dynamics of Innovation*. Oxford University Press, New York.

Rogers, E. M. (2003). *Diffusion of Innovations*. New York, The Free Press.

Ryan, B., & Gross, N. C. (1943). The diffusion of hybrid seed corn in two Iowa communities. *Rural Sociology, 8*(1), 15–24.

Sahal, D. (1981). *Patterns of Technological Innovation*. Reading, MA, Addison-Wesley Publishing Company.

Saviotti, P. P., & Metcalfe, J. S. (1984). A theoretical approach to the construction of technological output indicators. *Research Policy*, vol. 13, issue 3, 141–151 http://www.sciencedirect.com/science/article/pii/0048-7333(84)90022-2

Sierzchula, W., Bakker, S., Maat, K., & van Wee, B. (2012). Technological diversity of emerging eco-innovations: A case study of the automobile industry. *Journal of Cleaner Production, 37*, 211–220. https://doi.org/10.1016/j.jclepro.2012.07.011

Song, C. H., & Aaldering, L. J. (2019). Strategic intentions to the diffusion of electric mobility paradigm: The case of internal combustion engine vehicle. *Journal of Cleaner Production, 230*, 898–909. https://doi.org/10.1016/j.jclepro.2019.05.126

Souitaris, V. (2002). Technological trajectories as moderators of firm-level determinants of innovation. *Res. Policy, 31*(6), 877–898. https://doi.org/10.1016/S0048-7333(01)00154-8

Stoneman, P. (2001). *The Economics of Technological Diffusion*. Wiley-Blackwell.

Sull, D. N. (1999). The dynamics of standing still: Firestone Tire & Rubber and the radial revolution. *Business History Review, 73*(3), 430–464.

Teece, D. J. (1986). Profiting from technological innovation: Implications for integration, collaboration, licensing and public policy. *Research Policy, 15*(6) 285–305.

Teece, D. J., & Pisano, G. (1994). The dynamic capabilities of firms: An introduction. *Industrial and Corporate Change, 3*(3), 537–556.

Teece D. J., Pisano, G., & Shuen, A. (1997). Dynamic capabilities and strategic management. *SMJ, 18*(7), 509–533. https://doi.org/10.1002/(SICI)1097-0266(199708)18:7<509::AID-SMJ882>3.0.CO;2-Z

Teubal, M. (1979). On user needs and need determination: Aspects of the theory of technological innovation. In M. J. Baker (Ed.), *Industrial Innovation*. 266–293. Palgrave Macmillan, London. https://doi.org/10.1007/978-1-349-03822-0_14

Tidd, J. (2023). *Radical Innovation*. Edward Elgar.

Tripsas, M. (2008). Customer preference discontinuities: A trigger for radical technological change. Managerial and Decision Economics, John Wiley & Sons, Ltd., vol. 29(2–3), 79–97.

Tushman, M., & Anderson, P. (1986). Technological discontinuities and organizational environments. *Administrative Science Quarterly, 31*(3), 439–465.

Vīgants, E., Blumberga, A., Timma, L., Ījabs, I., & Blumberga, D. (2016). The dynamics of technological substitution: The case of eco-innovation diffusion of surface cleaning products. *Journal of Cleaner Production*, 132, 279–288. https://doi.org/10.1016/j.jclepro.2015.10.007

Von Hippel, E. (1988). *Sources of Innovation*. New York, Oxford University Press.

Williamson, O. E. (1975). *Markets and Hierarchies*. New York, The Free Press.

Winter S. G. (2018) History-friendly modeling. In R. R. Nelson, G. Dosi, C. E. Helfat, A. Pyka, P. P. Saviotti, K. Lee, K. Dopfer, F. Malerba, & S. G. Winter, *Modern Evolutionary Economics: An Overview* (pp. 129–142). Cambridge University Press.

Part II: **Going Beyond the S-curve: Ten Patterns of Technological Substitutions**

In this book, I discuss technology as one of the ingredients of competitive advantage.

Part II is primarily about technological paradigmatic shifts (radical innovation) and micro-radical innovations that bring about technological substitutions. In fact, Part II is essentially a discussion of the simplified S-curve model of substitution. More specifically, Part II describes variations around the S-curve, including variants that can significantly depart from the S-curve. Understanding the variety of shapes for substitution trajectories is very important for strategy because the careful selection of technologies to place bets on and the timing and volume of investments need to be thought through accordingly. Part II brings an important addendum to the framework developed in Part I because radical change is where most of the action is, meaning that this is where there is plenty of room for strategy.

From a strategic standpoint, technological change affects competitive dynamics in two ways. It can reinforce existing competitive advantage by entrenching the dominant technology and the firms well established in the competitive arena; incremental innovation typically feeds this form of dynamics, namely continuity. Conversely, it can challenge and even destroy existing competitive advantages while bringing in a new dominant technology as a source of a new competitive advantage. This is typically what happens in case of radical innovation (and to a lesser extent for micro-radical innovations that in a way renew the dominant technology).

In Part I, I presented a framework to better understand technological evolution at large. This aimed at providing a conceptual representation to think about technology strategically. The framework presented showed how technological evolution combines change and continuity. In fact, technological evolution appears to be made of long periods of continuity with the same dominant technology, punctuated by radical innovations striking as paradigm shifts. Yet, the framework built in Part I also accounts for micro-radical innovations introducing sub-technologies that partake in the shaping of a technological trajectory à la Dosi (Tab. 1-A in Part I).

Given my focus in this book on leveraging technology strategically, although there is room for other forms of strategy in periods of technological continuity, I argue that technological discontinuities are particularly important cases when it comes to strategizing technology. Hence, Part II focuses on radical innovations and to a lesser extent micro-radical innovations.

Since technological discontinuities (brought about by radical and micro-radical innovations) end up in technologies being replaced by other technologies in all or in part, I will use here the word "substitutions". Hence, Part II focuses on the technological substitutions side of the framework for technological evolution presented in Part I.

In this sense of technological substitutions, Part II focuses on change – that is, radical innovations and micro-radical innovations that disrupt the competitive game, at least to some extent. The aim is to better understand how successive waves of technical change break into an industry, forcing stakeholders, incumbents and new en-

https://doi.org/10.1515/9783111397979-014

trants to choose among a set of radical (or micro-radical) new technological options that are introduced over time.

By radical and micro-radical new technologies (the latter being what I have called sub-technologies so far) and the radical and micro-radical innovations that bring them, I mean first paradigmatic shifts opening a new trajectory in the sense of the envelope curves of Fig. 11 and Tab. 1-A. Second, I mean the micro-radical innovations that are part of the envelope trajectory in the same model. In fact, if most of the cases used to illustrate the patterns presented in Chapter 11 below are radical innovations, some others relate to micro-radical innovations as well, thus including sub-technologies in the scope of analysis.

More specifically, one can think of the typical sequence where technology N is taken over by technology N+1 in an industry, before being itself taken over by technology N+2, and so on, until N+i stands as the current dominant technology in that industry. This is what I call here technological substitutions. This has been extensively researched, but the many cases and models discussed in the literature lack a common framework to capture the variety of dynamics at hand. Typically, the time path of the substitution of N+1 for N is too often viewed as an S-curve. Geroski commented that such a mental model has an amazingly powerful effect on how people think about this particular phenomenon and that "the literature on new technology diffusion is really a literature about S-curves, and in many ways this is rather limiting". I could not agree more.

In this context, Part II stands as an addendum to the framework presented in Part I. More specifically, while the overall framework developed in Part I describes the dynamics of technological evolution at large, Part II is dedicated to radical innovations when paradigm shifts take place, while also covering, though to a lesser extent, micro-radical innovations (those introducing sub-technologies along a trajectory in the sense of Fig. 11). Part II thus discusses in more detail the phenomenon of repeated technological substitutions and their strategic implications – when technology N, N+1, N+2, N+i successively substitute for each other on a market over time. Although a variety of trajectories beyond the classic representation of the S-curve have been described, a consistent framework to capture and integrate the diversity of substitution patterns encountered is still needed. This is what Part II is about.

The path followed over time by technology N+1 matters because it influences the nature and timing of strategic decisions in firms, e.g., regarding technology development and product launch and the duration of the competitive advantage attached to each technology.

Using past cases, Chapter 11 presents and discusses ten patterns of technological substitution. In Chapters 12 and 13, two key variables and four shape factors are identified that help describe the trajectories of the patterns, offering variations around the S-curve model of substitution. In fact, some variations are so significant that the corresponding patterns clearly depart from this simplified model of the S-curve. This is very important for us here because this variety of patterns calls for a variety of strategic responses for the firms that compete in the corresponding business arena. In addition, a mapping of the patterns is presented. In a way, the ten patterns, the variables and shape factors and the mapping offer some sort of a grammar of technological substitutions. Chapter 14 introduces the idea of "bifurcation windows", during which an otherwise smooth trajectory may suddenly be substituted by another trajectory attached to another paradigm, thus yielding a radically different strategic situation. Finally, Chapter 15 discusses the underlying mechanisms that drive the variables and shape factor, and thus shape the patterns. Overall, this addendum to the main framework presented in Part I provides a conceptual structure to think about radical technological substitutions strategically.

Chapter 11
Ten Patterns of Technological Substitution

It is important to recognize that all technological substitutions are not alike, with, in fact, a variety of time dynamics involved. While I supervised his doctoral work, I encouraged Brice Dattée to study historical cases.[19] He collected a set of ten patterns of technological substitutions that describe the life cycle of technologies N, N+1, N+2 and N+i. Each of the ten patterns is given a name, represented, described and documented. Some of the patterns turn out to bring less disruption or at least at a slower pace than usually expected from a radical innovation. Some other patterns turn out to be so bumpy, speedy and disruptive that they represent a significant challenge for firms to surf the dynamics of change. The shape of the trajectory shows how competitive advantages may survive longer or be swept away by the next waves of technical change. In that sense, the shape of the trajectories really matters.

The name given to each of the ten patterns aims at capturing the specificity of the corresponding trajectory. The time span of each historical case varies from a few years to half a century or more (this says something about long periods of continuity in technological evolution). While technology strategy and path creation require a forward look, the chapter aims at learning the lessons from the past in the way historians do.

Please note that, in describing these patterns, when I write that "technology N+1 launches an attack on N" or "N has to withdraw", the wording used aims at simplifying the text. It is obviously the players (firms, users, scientists, developers, investors, regulators, etc.) who act, not the technologies per se. There are promoters and opponents (and many neutral players) to a given technology. It is their respective actions and interactions that make the fate of a technology. Yet, for the sake of readability, I keep writing about technologies as if they were thinking and acting entities, while fully recognizing that this is not the case. Hence, no personification of technology nor anthropomorphism here.

The Pattern of Reference

Pattern 1: Base Case

The *base case* is a binary straightforward substitution that occurs when an emerging technology N+1 is substituted for the current technology N which had reached market dominance. This is where the S-curve is at its best.

---

19 This chapter borrows heavily from Brice Dattée's doctoral work (Dattée, 2006) and a working paper that we jointly wrote (Dattée & Durand, 2009), with kind permission from Dattée.

https://doi.org/10.1515/9783111397979-015

Empirical case: The transition from the Bessemer to the open-hearth process in the steelmaking industry offers an example of a base case. This substitution has already been modeled by Fisher and Pry and Blackman. Historical data were collected from Hendriksen and the American Iron and Steel Institute (AISI) annual reports to present this classic example. The first phase of technological change covers 1880 to 1950. At the end of the nineteenth century, the dominant method of steelmaking was the Bessemer process, invented by Sir Henry Bessemer in the late 1850s. The rapidly expanding railroad industry provided a stimulus for heavy demand and the Bessemer converter was the foundation of the industry. Yet, the process had technical difficulties in part because the reactions involved in a Bessemer blow were sudden and very violent. The open-hearth process, first proposed by Carl Wilhelm Siemens in 1861, overcame many of these difficulties and began substituting for the Bessemer equipment.

By 1930 in the United States, the Bessemer process accounted for only 12% of total output, and by the mid-1950s was completely overshadowed by the open-hearth process. The historical substitution pattern of this binary substitution in the US industry is shown in Fig. 18.

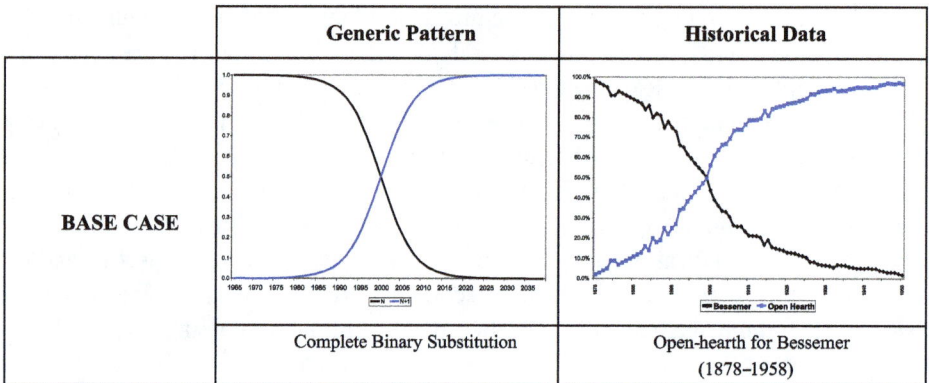

Fig. 18: Pattern of a base case of technological substitution (US, 1878–1958).

The subsequent nine patterns depart from the base case according to specific traits.

The next three patterns (N°2 to 4) are variations of the base case around the extent of the substitution, i.e., the final share of the market captured from N by N+1.

The next group of three patterns (N°5 to7) gravitates around the timing of arrival of N+2 with respect to the focal substitution, namely N+1 vs. N.

The final group of three patterns (N°8 to 10) results from explicit strategic moves from incumbents to defend N (and oppose N+1) or reaction from the demand side or external pressures from the environment.

Extent of the Substitution: Three Patterns

There are many situations where technology N+1 successfully substitutes technology N, except for a share of the market (specific segments or low vs. high end of the market, etc.). Technology N+1 becomes dominant, or partly dominant as N does not fully disappear, keeping part of the business even in the long run, at least before a new technology comes in to take over N+1 (and what remains of N).

The next group of three patterns stems from variations of the base case according to the extent of the N+1 vs. N substitution at the outcome:

Thus, beyond full substitution (pattern 1-the "base case", seen above),

– (2) partial substitution: a "partial base case",
– (3) marginal substitution: a "burst",
– (4) initially marginal, eventually significant substitution: a "pathfinder".

Pattern 2: Partial Base Case

The base case assumes that N+1 fully takes over N. In fact, in many instances, the substitution is only partial as N+1 may not fit part of the spectrum of use. (For example, N+1 may be too expensive or may lack some specific features of technology N, while offering new features.)

Empirical case: This pattern is illustrated by looking at over-current protection devices for electrical circuits. There are two main types of technologies to address that core function in a large array of applications: fuses and circuit breakers. The primary advantages of fuses are their low cost and their small package size. Circuit breakers are electromechanical devices which are actuated either magnetically or thermally to unlatch a contact. With a wide range of available types, circuit breakers are extremely versatile products. Thanks to improvements in dielectric material, high-voltage circuit breakers were first introduced by Westinghouse in the late 1950s. This allowed them to be successfully used in nearly any kind of electrical power system. However, fuses have relative merits which helped them to maintain a significant stronghold in low-voltage applications.

Based on annual shipment data from the United States Census Bureau, Fig. 19 shows that circuit breakers captured around 75% of all circuit protection applications, while fuses have defended their strongholds, accounting for 25% of the industry. Figure 19 shows the results of the partial substitution corresponding to technological segmentation from 1992 to 2006.

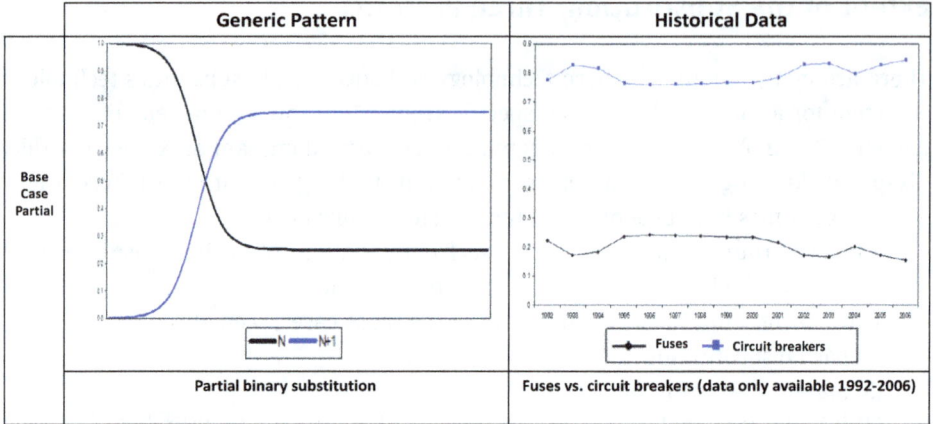

Fig. 19: Pattern of a partial base case technological substitution.

Pattern 3: Burst

As we move from a base-case view of complete substitution to one of partial substitution, we are in fact considering the penetration potential of each technology across industry segments. Here, we discuss the case not of complete failure, but of extremely low penetration. In some cases, promoters of technology N+1 claim to push the performance limits so far that the new technology is expected to completely revolutionize the industry and become widely adopted. Yet, this revolution just does not take place, or only very marginally. The outcome falls short of expectations. This may be because the new technology, whose higher performance overshoots the requirements of many market segments, only interests a sub-part of the market that is reduced to a small niche. (Note that Christensen confirmed and significantly dug into this tendency of firms to overshoot the performance of their offerings compared to customer needs and expectations. Yet, Christensen does not point to promoters of N+1 as the over-shooters, but to the incumbents that, in overshooting the performance requirements, open the door for some radical N+1 to come in.)

A burst is an extreme case of a partial base case.

Empirical case: The Iridium satellite system provides a prominent example of a technological burst. In the late 1980s, Motorola engaged in developing a satellite mobile phone system. In 1991, there were only 11 million mobile phone subscribers worldwide. Cellular service was very limited and there was limited international roaming. The complete Iridium satellite system promised to allow communication "with anyone, anytime, virtually anywhere in the world". Motorola's faith in the satellite paradigm was unshakable. By the late 1990s, relatively good-quality cellular phone service from the GSM technology that brought international roaming and equipment compatibility was much more prevalent than the planning of Iridium had anticipated. It took 12 years, five billion US dollars and more than 20 million lines of computer code to build the system. Iridium communication service was launched on November 1, 1998. Cumulative sales were expected to reach 1.6 million subscribers by 2000 and 27 million by 2007. By 2000, there were a mere 55,000 subscribers. Compared to the explosive growth of the mobile industry, Iridium's 150,000 subscriber base in 2005[20] accounted for only 0.006% of worldwide mobile subscribers (Fig. 20). A costly burst indeed.

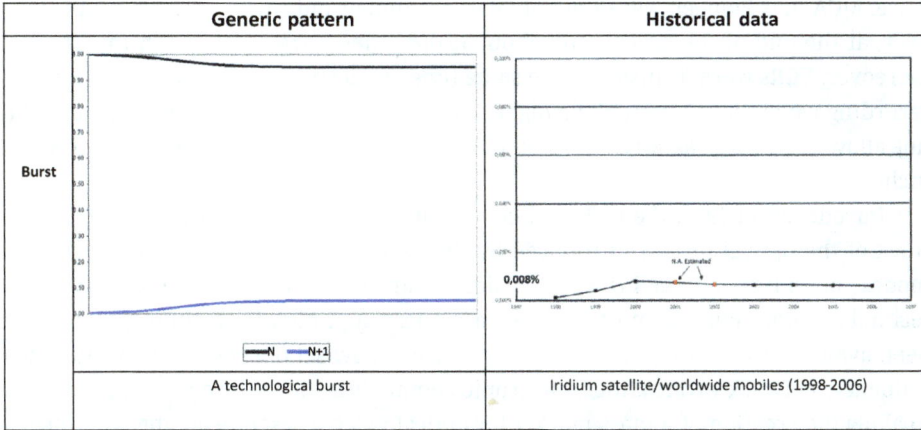

	Generic pattern	Historical data
Burst		0,008%
	A technological burst	Iridium satellite/worldwide mobiles (1998-2006)

Fig. 20: Pattern of a technological burst.

Pattern 4: Pathfinder

In some cases what initially appeared to be a technological burst (a shy takeoff followed by an endless plateau at very low market share) eventually reaches the growth phase. As I already mentioned, Abernathy and Utterback describe the phase after the introduction of a disruptive technology as a fluid phase during which many product innovations occur. When the dominant design (and its dominant process) is established, then the diffusion rate increases because of reduced uncertainty.

In the case of a pathfinder, it seems that this fluid phase is abnormally long. Only a very few players, and for an unusually long time, are making attempts at the technology. But then, somehow, the set of contextual conditions necessary for creating a massive adoption by users appears in the setting. A pathfinder is thus an initial *burst* stuck in a niche, which eventually reaches the growth phase; like a sleeping beauty who finally wakes up.

---

20 Based on Iridium Satellite LLC's first quarter 2006 results.

Empirical case: The optical video disc offers an example of a technology which followed a pathfinder trajectory. The home video market was started in the 1980s by the video cassette recorder (VCR) using analogue magnetic tapes (the VHS standard that we shall here refer to as technology N). The Laserdisc (LD) technology (an early form of the DVD, hereafter technology N+1) was introduced in the retail market in 1978. It offered a very high image quality by using frequency modulation of an analogue signal while audio was already recorded digitally in separate tracks. Because of their superior image and sound quality, players and disc titles were kept at a fairly high price. MCA and Pioneer were the only two prominent industrial players in LD. However, at the end of the 1990s, only about 15,000 titles were available in this format. Moreover, VCRs were diffusing at the same time and a strong emphasis was placed on recording capability. Despite their higher quality, LDs were still cumbersome and did not allow recording; as a result, they did not reach outside of the video enthusiast niche.

Introduced in 1997, the DVD format was, in effect, the digitalization of the video track of the optical format introduced by the Laserdisc and was considered to be "a modest net advance over LD and a major advance over VHS".[21] In a way, the DVD technology was some form of LD+, i.e., a modest upgrade of a technology that had been available for many years. Moreover, a whole new set of conditions (institutional influence, network externalities, electronic commoditization) were suddenly in place to allow the creation of a mass market for optical video discs. Indeed, the DVD format was really pushed by an unprecedented cooperation from the computer industry, music companies, Hollywood studios and consumer electronics companies which had formed a consortium – the DVD Forum – and launched an institutional communication campaign to promote the format. The amazingly rapid commoditization of the DVD player, the availability of titles, the rental infrastructure already in place (via the VHS technology) and the familiarity that consumers had developed with home video (again through the VHS) made adoption easier.

By 1998, the US installed base of VCRs had reached 80 million units. In contrast, laserdiscs, which were introduced in 1978, had by 1990 only reached an installed base of two million units. Monthly sales data from 1997 to 2006 for DVD players in the US from the Consumer Electronics Association show that less than ten years after their introduction, the installed base of DVD players in the US had reached 106 million. Figure 21 shows that despite its superior quality, the optical video disc in its LD form stayed for an initial burst in the video enthusiast niche until a rather limited additional innovation and a new set of conditions made it possible for the optical video disc in its DVD form to explode into a mass market.

In short, the three patterns described above (2–4) are variations of the pattern of reference, the base case (pattern 1 above), according to the extent of the substitution:

---

21 Laser Magic 1998 edition of Widescreen Review magazine, cited by Dattée.

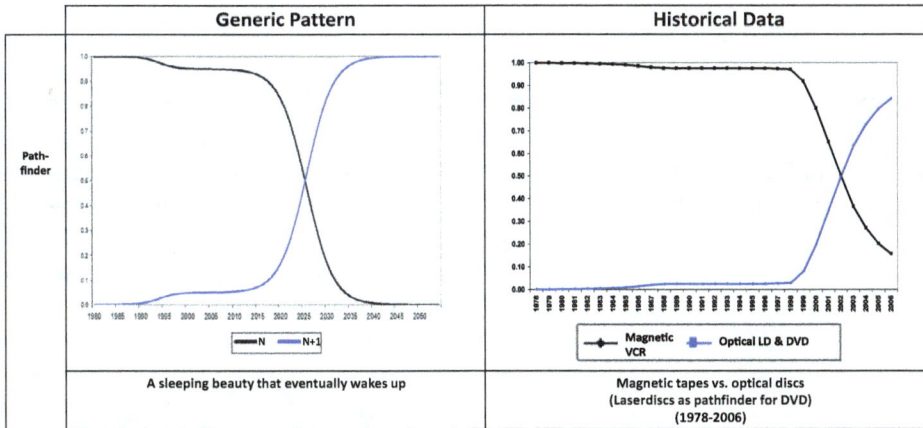

Fig. 21: Pattern of a pathfinder technological substitution.
Source: Dattée (2006)

the base case is a full substitution of N by N+1. The partial base case is most common, when technology N+1 wins while leaving some remaining space on the market for N, even for long periods of time until a new technology eventually strikes to disrupt the industry once more. The burst is a sparkle of N+1 that captures a very limited share of the market, leaving most of it to N. The pathfinder is a burst remaining marginal for a long period of time but eventually taking off to cannibalize a significant share of the market, leaving only a slice to N, if anything.

The Arrival of N+2 Disturbs the N+1 vs. N Struggle: Three Patterns

The next group of patterns gravitate around the effect of the arrival of N+2 on our focal substitution, namely N+1 vs. N:
- (5) if N+2 comes in late enough: this is a "concatenation of base cases" (N+1 has time to live its life);
- (6) if N+2 comes in a bit early: this causes an "overlap" (N+1 lifetime is shortened);
- (7) if N+2 arrives very early on: this is a "double shift" (squeezed between N and N+2, N+1 aborts).

Pattern 5: Concatenation of Base Cases

The base case relates to a binary technological substitution. Yet, in an industry, successive generations of technologies replace each other over time; and the sequence of substitutions between these generations is often expected to look like a concatenation of base cases. Indeed, in most of the literature, authors offer a stylized representation of a technological discontinuity which occurs during the mature phase of the previous technology.

Empirical case: The steelmaking case can be used once again to illustrate this pattern. While the dominant steelmaking technology throughout the post-war period was the open-hearth furnace, the mid-1950s saw the beginning of an entirely new approach, the basic oxygen process (BOP). It was found that the introduction of oxygen into the furnace would greatly speed up the refining process. The first BOP plant in the United States was built in 1954. By 1987, BOP accounted for 95% of the steel output from the chemical combustion processes. Figure 22 illustrates this concatenation effect.

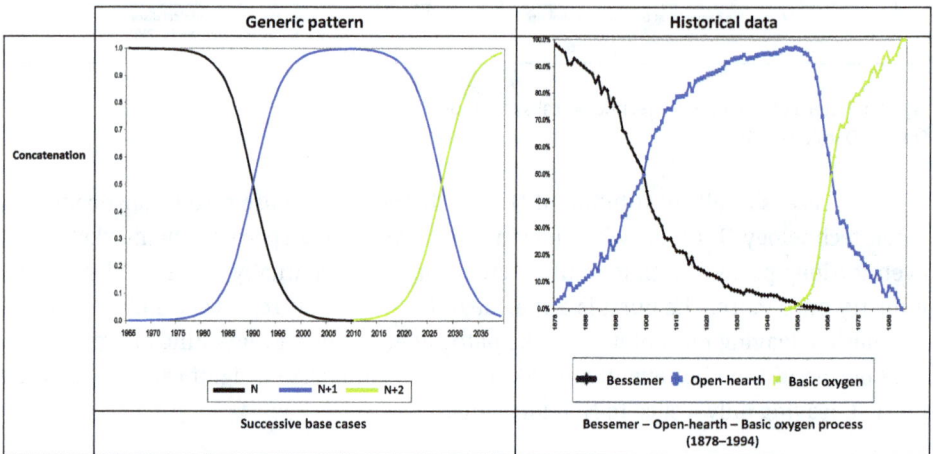

Fig. 22: Pattern of a concatenation of technological substitutions.

Pattern 6: Overlap

A *concatenation* of base cases occurs when each technological generation has time to reach full dominance before being substituted by the next generation. However, the timing of emergence of the new technologies often means that several technologies overlap. The overlap pattern can be created deliberately by industry leaders to impose a fast pace to competitors left in the difficult position of running behind, trying to keep up with the tempo. Some analytical models address these "multilevel" substitutions, i.e., between more than two technologies at once (Norton & Bass; Mahajan & Muller; Sohn & Ahn).

Empirical case: IBM mainframe computers offer such examples of overlapping cases. Here, the data were collected by Phister to describe the overlapping of the successive generations of IBM mainframes. The performance per price ratio of these generations can be estimated with a generic index of the number of operations per second per dollar. The first generation of IBM mainframes started with the 650, first introduced in November 1954. It yielded an average of 77 kops/$. In November 1959, the second generation of IBM mainframe was introduced with the IBM 7090 which already yielded 1,472 kops/$. This second generation included six systems from the 7090 to the 707x series. In 1962, the 7094 system offered 6,898 kops/$. But already the 360 generation was introduced. Its performance characteristics set a new standard that its 11 models kept improving. By 1965, the 360/20 offered some 11,232 kops/$. A fourth generation of 370 systems started in February 1971 with the 370/150. It was already performing 28,106 kops/$.

Historical data provided by Phister for the substitutions of IBM mainframe systems illustrate, as shown in Fig. 23, that each of these overlapping generations had not reached complete dominance when the next generation started substituting. This was obviously managed strategically by IBM to impose the tempo on the entire computer industry of the time.

For the sake of clarity, it is important to stress here that the example of IBM mainframes during the period 1954–1974 corresponds to sub-technologies, the envelope curve of which forms the mainframe trajectory. Hence, the innovations in between the generations of mainframes are more micro-radical innovations than radical innovations. As shown on Fig. 3 in Chapter 2, Part I, the subsequent radical innovation was the shift to the PC paradigm, a disruptive transition triggered by Apple that IBM was unable to cope with.

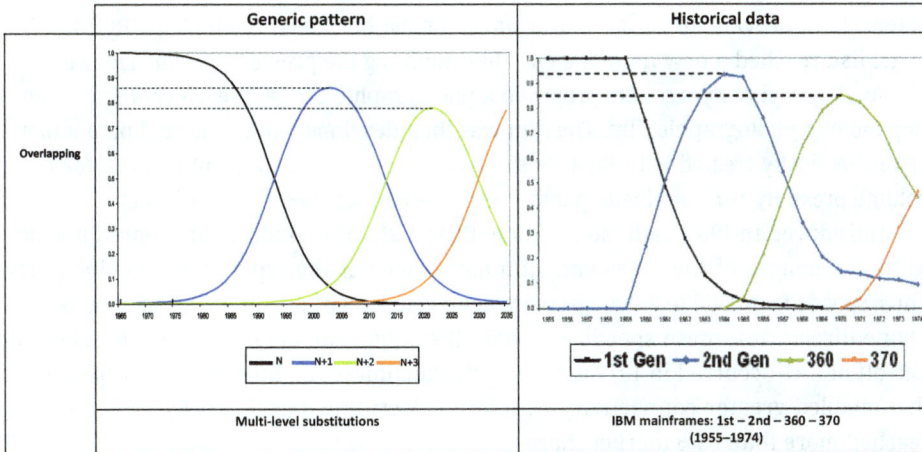

Fig. 23: Pattern of overlapping technological substitutions.

Pattern 7: Double Shift

Moving from a concatenated view of life cycles to one of *overlap* means considering shorter intergenerational time periods. This can lead to the case of extreme overlaps where the substitution dynamics of generation N+1 is cut short during the growth phase by a third generation N+2 which ends up dominating the market before N+1 had a chance to reach maturity.

This pattern of technological change, labeled as a double shift, can be observed in a few industries. For example, Tushman and Anderson report that the transistor architecture, which in 1962 had started substituting for minicomputers based on vacuum tubes, was itself replaced within two years by a second shift to integrated circuits. Similarly, when public switches in the telecommunication industry moved away from electromechanical technologies, analogue space division would most probably have become the next dominant technology if digital Time Division Multiplexing (TDM) had not become the new challenge".

Empirical case: An impressive double shift also occurred in the typesetter industry. Dattée collected primary and secondary data on the successive generations of typesetting technology. The substitution data collected by Tripsas help illustrate the double shift pattern. From 1886, the industry moved from the manual process invented by Gutenberg around 1440 onto keyboard typesetting systems like the Mergenthaler Linotype. A matrix of types was composed, and a slug was cast by tapping a reservoir of molten lead, hence the name "hot metal". Until 1930, the speed of hot metal typesetters, measured in characters per second (cps), followed a very clear S-shape (technological performance) trajectory from around 1.5 cps to a limit of 3.5 cps which was reached by 1910. In 1946, analogue phototypesetters appeared, and this induced a very noticeable defensive improvement in the performance of the hot metal technology. By 1965, hot metal had reached a new limit of 8 cps, thus doubling the previous performance limit.

Analogue phototypesetters projected a photographic image of each character onto a step-moving photographic film. The film was then developed and projected onto a metal plate chemically treated with light-sensitive emulsion to create a printing plate for high-volume press. By 1975, analogue phototypesetters had reached speeds of 80 cps.

Introduced in 1965, cathode-ray tube (CRT) systems digitalized and stored magnetically the images of the types and eliminated most of the typesetters' moving parts. Thus, speeds from 500 to 3,000 cps were achieved. Except for the printing of large telephone directories, these speeds exceeded the requirements of most users. The real takeoff of CRT occurred in 1977 with the introduction of the Intel 8080 microprocessor that enabled greater connectivity with large electronic databases. By 1985, CRT had reached more than 65% market share.

Introduced in 1976, laser technology offered a significant development for setting pages complete with text and graphics. Nevertheless, by 1985 the technology had slowly captured less than 10% of the market and did not represent a significant threat for the rapidly growing CRT generation. Because a laser writes text across the breadth of a page in a raster fashion by spinning a polygonal mirror, it requires a page description language. In 1982 John Warnock and Charles Geschke formed Adobe Systems after leaving Xerox PARC. They developed PostScript, a simple and "on-the-fly" raster image processing software that specifies the outline of a typeface in terms of straight lines and Bézier curves. The release of the PostScript language in 1985 created tremendous externalities by linking the growing base of personal computers and the printing industry, effectively sparking the desktop publishing revolution. PostScript acted like a trigger relay and generated an explosive substitution; by 1988 laser imagesetters had pre-empted the growth of CRT and reached 60% of the market share.

Figure 24 offers a longitudinal view of this sequence of substitutions based on data from Tripsas. It illustrates how the shift from analogue (N) to CRT (N+1) was cut short by laser technology (N+2). Finally, the typesetter industry was subsequently disrupted by yet another technology (N+3): computer-to-plate (CTP). Instead of striking a film which must be developed and then projected onto a plate, the laser is used directly on a light-sensitive printing plate. Another development eliminated the process of developing printing plates altogether. With the advent of the digital press, as Woods observed, "rather than exposing data to an off-press plate via laser, these new machines allow for sending pages to photopolymer plates mounted directly on the press, thus saving time, printing waste and labor". Expectedly, CTP incumbents responded to this threat by improving their technology by developing processless and even rewritable plates.

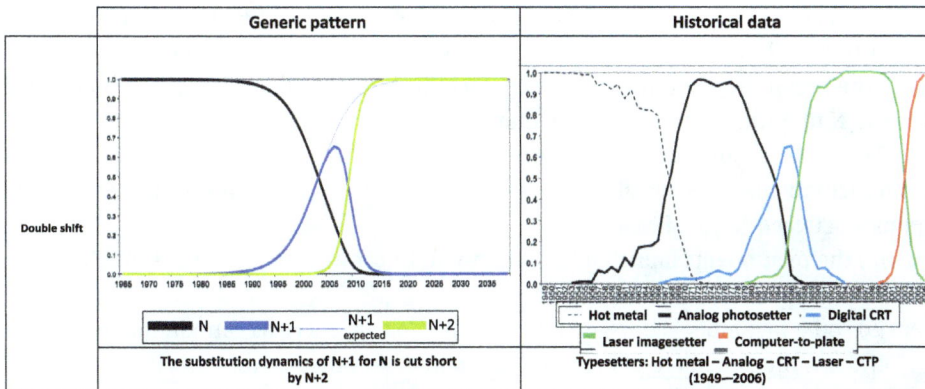

Fig. 24: Pattern of a double shift technological substitution.

The shape of the CRT time path (technology N+1) illustrates an aborted trajectory of a technology squeezed in between N (analogue) and N+2 (laser).

In short, this second group of patterns (N°5 to 7) gravitates around the timing of arrival of N+2 with respect to the N+1 vs. N battle.

The specific time of emergence of N+2 affects the transition of N+1 from the growth phase to the dominance phase at the right-hand side of a base case substitution curve (Fig. 18). We thus have here three patterns numbered 5 to 7:

- (5) If N+2 comes in late enough, i.e., at a time when N+1 has already succeeded in substituting for N, reaching dominance to the maximum extent possible, this leads to a "concatenation" pattern whereby the N+1 vs. N battle is not affected by the subsequent arrival of the next technology N+2 (although the life of N+1 is obviously shortened).

- (6) If N+2 comes in a bit earlier, this causes some "overlap". N+1 has the time to approach dominance but possibly not enough time to yield significant return on the investment, if any.

- (7) If N+2 arrives very early, N+1 is squeezed between N and N+2 and cannot fully develop. The N to N+1 shift is overtaken by the N+1 & N to N+2 shift. This is a "double shift". N+1 is an early victim of N+2.

When Incumbents Defend their Beloved Technology N: Two Patterns Plus One

I already discussed the most encountered stance of incumbents when technology N+1 concretizes as a threat: before anything else most incumbents desperately try to resist N+1. This can be done by improving the performance of N or by developing an intermediate technology, often hybridizing technology N with some features of N+1. And, there is a special case when it is not so much the resistance to N+1 by the incumbents that will save N, but an awkward situation where pressures in the environment will push the previously winning technology N+1 out, with no other alternative than going back to N to fulfill the need because there is no N+2 available yet.

This final group of three patterns covers the effect of explicit strategic moves from incumbents or external pressures from the environment on the substitution dynamics between N+1 and N:

- (8) the incumbents launch a last attempt to improve their beloved technology N: a "last gasp" delays the arrival of N+1;

- (9) some incumbents develop a N+½ technology to serve as cannon fodder against N+1: an "intermediate hybrid" hinders and delays the arrival of N+1;

- (10) external forces in the environment impose N+1 to withdraw: in the absence of any N+2 to take over, this leads to "reverting" to N as the only feasible technology available.

Pattern 8: Last Gasp

I pointed out earlier that incumbents established on technology N tend to defend themselves by improving N to prevent or at least delay the arrival of N+1. Rosenberg noted that a dominant technology which is threatened by a new technology will often undergo a final set of innovations in an attempt to compete. This refinement of the current technology N allows it to maintain its performance advantage over the new technology N+1, at least temporarily. Sull studied different mechanisms that can lead to what he calls the "last gasp" phenomenon. He notes, however, that the usual effect of such a last gasp is only to postpone the traditional technology's displacement. Famous last gasp examples include the improvements of ice harvesting techniques when mechanical refrigeration emerged (Utterback); the longer than expected survival of optical photolithography after the entrance of x-ray photolithography (Henderson); or the last gasp by the carburetor technology when electronic fuel injection was first introduced (Snow). Whilst this phenomenon is often represented by plotting the surge on the performance trajectory (the second type of S-curve discussed in Part I, Chapter 4, around Fig. 6), data are seldom provided to substantiate the delay on the substitution trajectory.

Empirical case: A stereotypical and often eponymous example (the "sailing ship effect") for this pattern of the last surge of performance is the evolution of the sailing ship into fast clippers as the steam engine emerged. The clippers were novel and faster sailing vessels introduced in 1845 as a defensive move by the incumbents. They delayed the substitution by still relatively inefficient steam ships by three decades.

At the beginning of the nineteenth century, sailing ships were cumbersome and slow. The use of steam engines for ocean navigation began in 1819 but the first boilers were pretty dangerous as they could not withstand pressures higher than three bars. They could explode violently. On long routes such as from Europe or the US to China for the tea trade, speed was a vital consideration. In the face of the paddle wheel and low-pressure boilers, sailing ships had to hold their supremacy as cargo carriers. They managed to do so at least until 1870. During the late 1840s, in response to the arrival of steam power, the sailing ships evolved with completely new and original naval design characteristics, carried large amounts of sail relative to their displacement and were capable of remarkable speed. This was the beginning of the clippers era which ran roughly from 1845 to about 1870.

However, better steel produced with the open-hearth process mentioned earlier and the improvements brought by the compound engine marked a notable advance in marine engineering. In the 1870s, the lead of clipper ships became precarious, and the substitution of powered ships resumed at its previous rate. Figure 25 shows the historical data of the substitution of powered boats for sailing ships for US ocean cargo from 1797 to 1964. Figure 25 also shows that a classic Fisher-Pry logistic curve can be fitted ($R^2 = 0.89$) to the time period 1797–1845: $\ln\left[\frac{m}{1-m}\right] = -4.9 + 0.085*(t - t^*)$ with m the market share of powered boats and $t^* = 1797$. One can easily imagine that by 1845, the binary substitution trajectory would have been expected to follow a classic logistic shape.

However, with a 31-year delay into the t^* time reference constant ($R^2 = 0.91$), it appears that the substitution was delayed by clipper ships but resumed around 1875 as steam engines became economically efficient for marine trade. Typically, the classic models in the literature fit an S-curve to the entire dataset and ignore this step-like delay (or plateau), despite its significant duration of three decades, because it cannot be captured with a single logistic curve (S-curve).

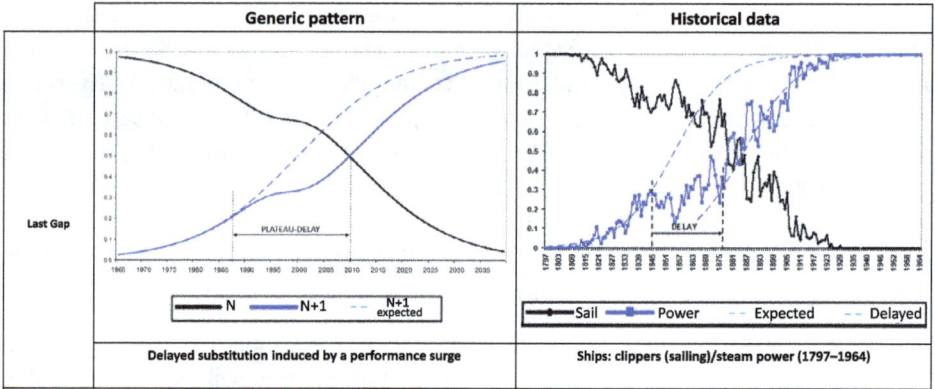

Fig. 25: Pattern of a delayed technological substitution induced by a last gasp.
Source: Dattée (2006) 25, adapted from Graham (1956) and US Bureau of the Census

Pattern 9: Intermediate Hybrid

In some cases, incumbents respond to the substitutive threat of N+1 not by a defensive surge of technology N, but by developing an *intermediate hybrid,* that I suggest naming N+½, trying to combine the best of both technologies.[22] Hybrid technologies may be difficult to pinpoint and identify as independent generations. This is because a hybrid often exhibits what Michel Foucault describes as "convenientia": it blends with both the end of the previous technology and the start of the new one. In any case, it is important to note that the hybrid technology is introduced *after* the emergence of N+1, that is once it becomes clear that N+1 attacked N. Note that naming the hybrid technology N+½ distorts the labeling convention implicitly used so far (i.e., naming technological generations by order of appearance on the market). The reason to do this is that N+½, although appearing after N+1 on the market, is designed as an intermediary technology between N and N+1.

In the middle of the shift from thermal engines to electric batteries, German car manufacturers kept looking for a way to hold onto their competitive advantage on thermal engines. (This minicase was introduced at the very beginning of the book). They imagined an almost carbon-free source of energy in the form of e-fuel (adapted from methanol produced via hydrogen, obtained by electrolysis of water, using wind-generated electricity – in southern Chile where winds blow all year long). The aim is to use the e-fuel in thermal engines, thus circumnavigating the EU ban on the sales of new cars with thermal engines

---

22 In rare cases, the hybrid technology may have a beneficial combination of traits which, as in evolutionary biology, allows it to succeed in a niche market (marginal habitat) where the two parent technologies (species) are disadvantaged.

beyond 2035. However, this defensive move means a very high price of the e-fuel, a poor mileage per watt compared to batteries, a waste of scarce green electricity at a time when there will be crucial needs for decarbonized electricity. Suarez et al. observe that incumbents' imaginations are limitless but prove inadequate in most cases. (See more on this intermediate hybrid attempt on electric cars: end of Part IV, p.257.)

Empirical case: The US tire industry provides an interesting example. Before 1960, the bias-ply tire was the dominant technology. In bias-ply tires, the body cords are layered in the body of the tire at an angle to the direction of rotation. In radial tires, the body cords are perpendicular to the direction of rotation.

Because of these characteristics, the two tire technologies differ substantially in performance (comfort, safety, mileage); radials represented a better deal for the consumers. But US incumbents considered that radials' longer life would decrease unit demand in the profitable replacement market. In addition, they feared that radial tires would provide an opportunity for foreign companies to enter their market. Moreover, when radial tires were introduced, they represented a significant challenge for the contemporary industrial capacity because the new technology required an enormous investment to upgrade the existing production capacity. In 1967, Goodyear introduced the belted-bias tire, an extension of the existing bias technology. Belted-bias tires could be manufactured with minor modifications of the existing production equipment. Firestone also increased its capital spending for retooling its factories. Goodyear aggressively promoted the belted-bias tire, claiming that it conferred significant performance improvements over bias tires and launched an advertising campaign questioning the benefits of the new radial tires. But with credible foreign suppliers such as Michelin, Detroit's automobile manufacturers – which together purchased 30% of all tires – demanded in 1972 that the American suppliers provide radial tires or lose market share to foreign competitors. Thus, by 1973, the rapid adoption of radials was inevitable.

Figure 26 draws from Sull, showing data on the shipment of tires by construction type – from bias to radial via hybrid belted-bias – between 1961 and 1988 as an example of a hybrid intermediate substitution pattern. The hybrid intermediate (belted-bias as N+½) may be seen as a sacrifice technology or cannon fodder aimed at blocking, or at least delaying, the technological substitution of N by N+1. A key point is to observe that N+½ arrives after the attack launched by N+1 on N; it comes as a consequence of that attack in the form of a counterattack (in fact a defensive move).

Pattern 10: Reverting

In previous patterns, it is the emergence of a new technology (supported by new entrants or incumbents, or other market and/or non-market forces such as regulators or public policy makers) that triggers the substitution process. However, there are partic-

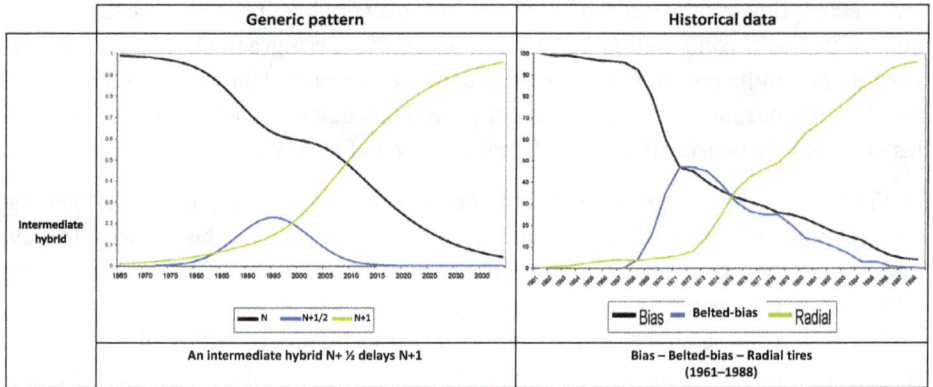

Fig. 26: Pattern of an intermediate hybrid technological substitution.
Source: Dattée (2006), adapted from Sull.

ular cases where these dynamics are triggered even in the absence of a newer and improved alternative. Maguire suggests a socio-political view: "changes to any of the organizational or scientific or regulatory or natural components of a technological system could also trigger a substitution [. . .] Therefore, existing artifacts can be socially reconstructed as a response to changes in other elements of the system of which they are part". Sometimes these institutional changes can even make an industry abandon the new technology N+1 and, in the absence of a readily available N+2 candidate, revert to the previous technology N. This pattern is thus named *reverting*. This may, for example, be due to "long-term feedbacks". The observed pattern thus has the shape of a concatenated case, but where N+2 is N.

Empirical case: The case of organochlorine insecticides illustrates the case of a reverting substitution triggered by long-term feedbacks. The rise and fall of the organochlorine insecticides and especially DDT[23] is a famous and extensively described example of a reverting substitution due to long-term environmental feedbacks. Prior to the 1940s, inorganic natural substances such as sulfur, lead, arsenic or mercury were used to control pests in agriculture. From the 1940s, synthetic organic compounds were used. These included organophosphates, carbamates, pyrethroids and organochlorines. Within the class of synthetic organic compounds, DDT is an organochlorine that was first synthesized in 1874. Its effectiveness as an insecticide was only discovered in 1939. Shortly after 1945, DDT started to be used in agriculture. Recommended by the US Department of Agriculture, its usage became widespread in the US because it was "effective, resilient, versatile and available at a reasonable price" according to the US Environmental Protection Agency (EPA). For 30 years, it remained the top-selling insecticide in the US.

---

23 Dichlorodiphenyltrichloroethane.

However, certain characteristics of DDT which initially contributed to its early popularity started to become the basis for public concern over environmental effects. The persistence of DDT, which was a solution by 1945, became a problem in the 1960s. Toxicologists raised questions about DDT's chronic toxicity to humans; and increasing resistance to DDT was documented by economic entomologists. From 1964, many federal actions were taken, and in 1972 the EPA announced the final cancellation of all remaining crop uses of DDT in the US. But the EPA ban was not the sole or even most important cause for DDT's dis-adoption. Indeed, Maguire explains that insecticide efficacy and safety had different social meanings over the years, resulting from changes in the social construction of DDT and other insecticides. As a result, the use of DDT in cotton production (not an agro-food product) went from 23.6 million pounds in 1964, to 19.2 in 1966, to 13.2 in 1971 and was not used anymore afterwards, see Fig. 27.

Data from the US Department of Agriculture indicates that organochlorines fell steadily from 70% of synthetic organic pesticides used in 1966 to only 6% in 1982. This self-induced loss of performance for DDT reverted the substitution dynamics: the other main synthetic organic pesticides bounced back from 20% in 1966 to almost dominance in 1982.

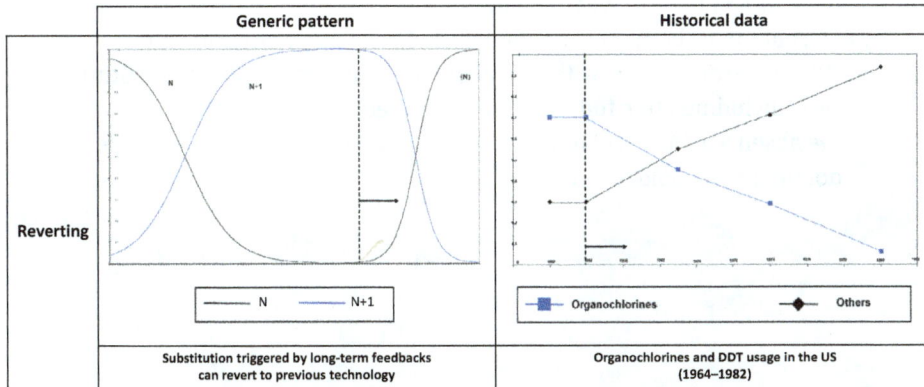

Fig. 27: Pattern of technological substitutions reverted by long-term feedbacks.
Source: Dattée (2006) adapted from US department of agriculture

Note that a variant of the reverting pattern takes place when technology N comes back to recreate a market niche for itself, leading to some form of a partial base case.

The comeback of the vinyl disc since the mid-2010s is no longer marginal and un-significant. With over 5% of the revenue generated by the industry (streaming, CD, vinyl) in 2021 in France, it appears as some form of partial reverting. A combination of factors drives this rebound: nostalgia for those who enjoy the memory of their youth (long-term feedback); the sound that was recorded analogic (before digitalization casted a veil on the world of music) is best reproduced in a vinyl analogic form.

Obviously, there was and still is the unwanted sound of the sapphire on the vinyl, but the connoisseur accepts this small nuisance because the analogic sound reproduced is of better quality; there is also a human need to own and hold a disc as to own and read from a physical book. On top, a physical object is more fit to marketing and promotion on TV, when the star waves the new album in front of the camera.

In any case, the revival of the vinyl disc can be interpreted as a reverting ending up in a partial height as if technology N had had a second thought and came back to limit N+1 as in a partial base case. This illustrates the explanatory/combinatory power of the patterns presented here.

In short, the three last patterns described above (8–10) represent situations of proactive defense of technology N
– by the incumbents:
  – (8) A "last gap" is a desperate attempt to sufficiently improve the performance of N to keep N+1 out, at least causing enough delay before N+1 succeeds, thus leaving more time to get a longer return on N and/or to develop an alternative.
  – (9) An "intermediate hybrid" is a proactive attempt to block or at least hinder the access of N+1 to dominance by hybridizing technology N with some features of N+1 to form what I name N+½.
– by external forces in the socio-economic and regulatory environment
  – (10) "Reverting" is the withdrawal of N+1 (at any stage of the substitution process, including after full successful completion of the substitution), which, in the absence of any N+2 to fulfill the generic market need F, reinstalls N as the dominant technology.

Chapter 12
Recap of the Ten Patterns, Interrelations and Recomposing Trajectories

Altogether, ten patterns of technological substitutions have been identified, named, described and illustrated. Figure 28 recapitulates the patterns.

Case	Pattern	Historical case	Specific feature
Base case		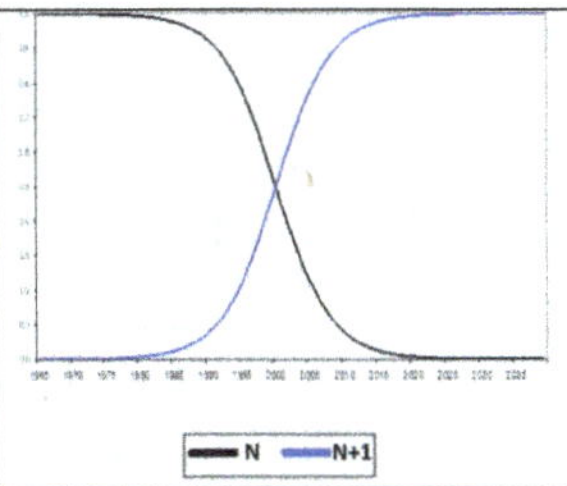 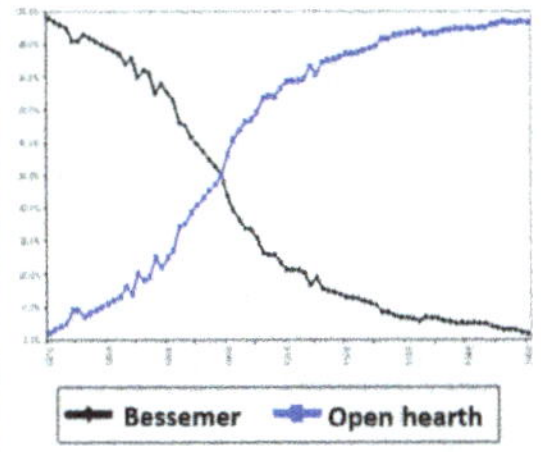 Steelmaking	New technology following an S-curve
Partial base case		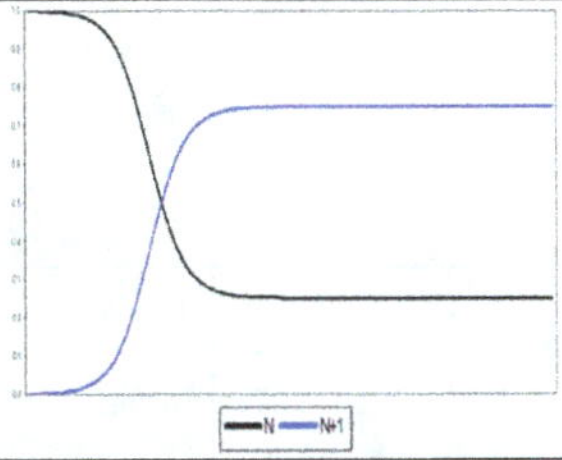 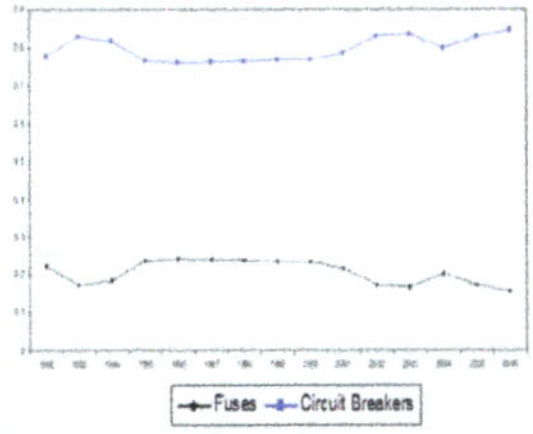 Fuses vs. circuit breakers (data only available 1992–2006)	Partial binary substitution
Burst		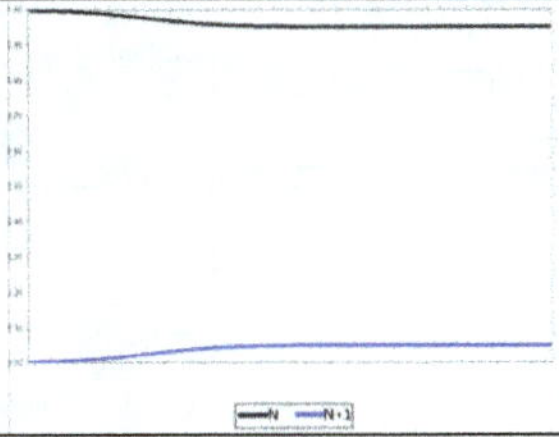 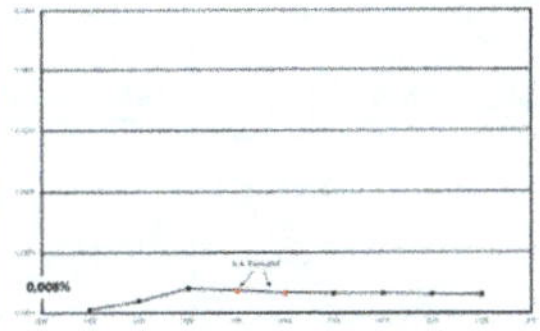 Iridium satellite phones	Overshooting performance which stays only in a niche and fails to reach growth
Pathfinder		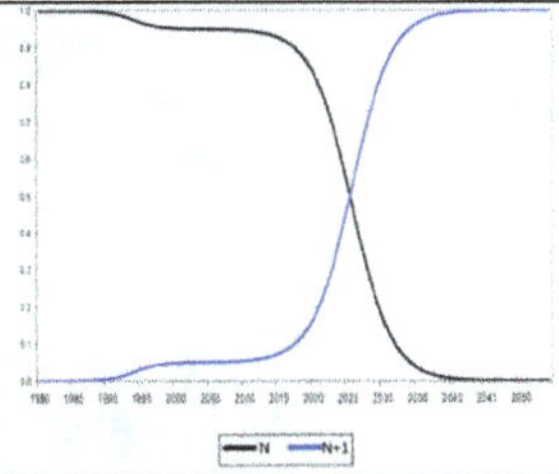 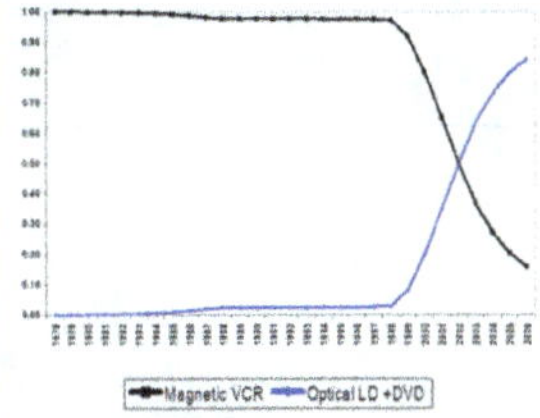 Laserdisc pathfinder for optical video DVD	New tech stays in niche for an unusually long time, but finally reaches growth

Fig. 28: Ten patterns of technology substitution.

https://doi.org/10.1515/9783111397979-016

Pattern	Chart (legend)	Chart (legend)	Example	Description
Concatenation	N — N+1 — N+2	Bessemer — Open Hearth — Basic Oxygen	Steelmaking	Successive generations each reaching dominance
Overlapping	N — N+1 — N+2 — N+3	1st Gen — 2nd Gen — 360 — 370	IBM mainframes	Successive generations overlapping. Multilevel substitutions
Double shift	N — N+1 — N+1 expected — N+2	Hot Metal — Analog Photosetter — Digital CRT — Laser Imagesetter — Computer To Plate. Typesetters: Hot Metal – analog – CRT – Laser – CTP (1949–2006)	Typesetters	N+1 squeezed between N and N+2
Last gasp	N — N+1 — N+1 expected	Sail — Power — Expected — Delayed	Sailing ship into clipper against steam engine	"Last gasp" of performance on N delays the substitution
Intermediate hybrid	N — N+1/2 — N+1	Bias — Belted Bias — Radial	Bias, belted-bias, radial tires (1961–1988)	An intermediate hybrid N+½ is launched as a counterattack against N+1, delaying N+1
Reverting	N — N+1	Organochlorines — Others	Organochlorine and DDT usage in the US (1964–1982)	Substitution triggered by long-term feedbacks against N+1. In the absence of candidates, N+2 can revert to previous technology N.

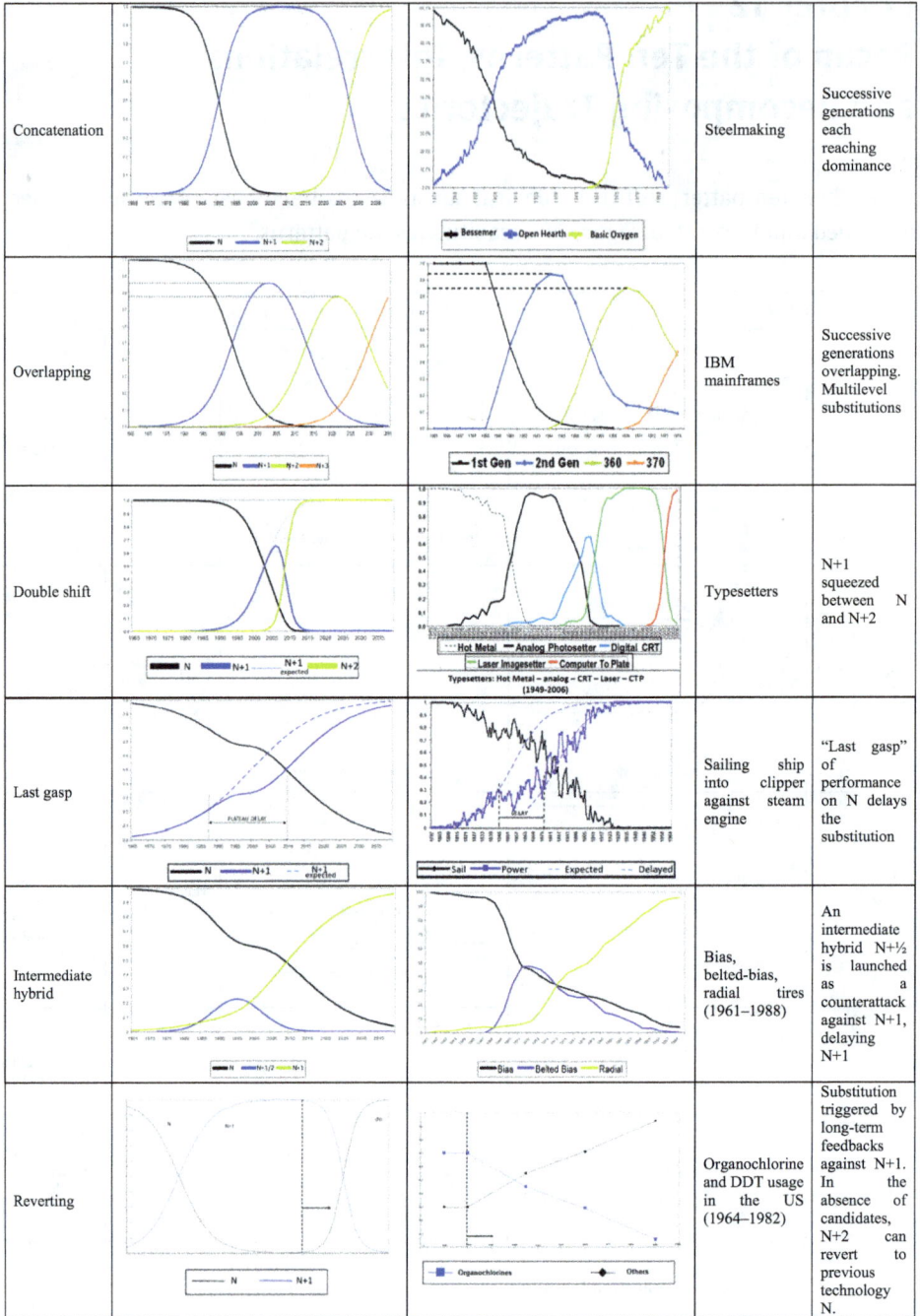

Fig. 28 (continued)

Interrelations among the Patterns

The ten patterns relate to one another in many ways. Here are a few illustrations of those interrelations.

A concatenation is a sequence of base cases. This is the traditional view of evolutionary economics of technological change. This is where the classic stylized S-curve offers a useful representation of the substitution dynamics over time. In this view, the competitive advantage attached to technology lasts long enough to be considered as stable along each of the technological trajectories. These are periods of "linear strategic dynamics" as Burgelman and Grove called them.

An overlap is a concatenation where N+2 emerges a bit early. N+1 had the time to unfold but the life cycle of N+1 is slightly shortened by the arrival of N+2. The competitive advantage of N+1 is thus more temporary than in a standard concatenation pattern. In an overlap, firms promoting N+1 do not have the time to extract the counterfactual[24] full rent stemming from the competitive advantage attached to their technology.

A double shift is an overlap where N+2 comes very early. In fact, N+2 comes in so early and diffuses so suddenly that there is barely a time window to deploy N+1 and basically no time to take advantage of it. New entrants, and possibly some incumbents, are still in the process of investing in N+1 when the prospects of return on N+1 are suddenly shadowed by the unexpected uprise of N+2. In such dynamics, N+1 is squeezed between N and N+2, with no time available to reap the benefits of the investments in N+1.

A hybrid intermediate is a last gasp where N needs to hybridize to counter N+1. Because the hybrid form creates a new technology, it needs to have its own curve to show that it has a separate life cycle. Conversely, a *last gasp* is a *hybrid intermediary* where N+½ remains N itself. In a last gasp, N does not need to hybridize to counter the arrival of N+1 and delay its growth. N is sharply improved as the incumbents' innovativeness and efficiency are spurred by the arrival of N+1. The competitive advantage for incumbents is prolonged but remains temporary as N+1 eventually wins. If the last gasp is successful, N+1 fails and the pattern may become a technological *burst* or a *partial base case* for N+1.

A reverting pattern is a concatenation where N+2 is N. Technology N+1 overthrew N and became dominant. Yet, at some point N+1 is finally rejected, not because some N+2 technology takes over, but because N+1 no longer fits the socio-economic environment. In this particular concatenation case, the need to abandon N+1 in the absence of N+2 candidates forces the industry to revert back and resurrect technology N. Note that a reverting pattern can in fact take place faster in the form of an *overlap* or even a *double shift*, but with this unique feature that N+2 is in fact N.

---

24 In the sense used by Dupuy – that is if N+2 had not emerged.

A burst is a (very) partial base case that failed to capture market dominance. Many of the potential technological bursts are not even launched and thus "N+1 to be" never reached the market. When they are launched, however, the substitution process is triggered by a spark but falls short of expectations. The competitive advantage is not even temporary, it never establishes itself. This may be due to a *last gasp* from technology N which succeeds beyond the intent, or a successful *hybrid intermediate* that takes over the market, or a performance of N+1 that disappoints the early adopters and/or fails to convince the mainstream market.

A pathfinder is a burst that finally succeeds, or a base case that takes a very long time to reach the growth phase, or an almost successful last gasp by technology N. If the burst is quite common, the pathfinder is less frequent. In a pathfinder, the initial spark is there as some players choose to invest in N+1 but the trigger of the growth phase does not ignite for some time; until it does. In a pathfinder, crossing the chasm (see Chapter 15) is long and difficult. It may be that N+1 has some difficulties to convince additional users beyond early adopters or N significantly resists via a fairly long last gasp.

Another situation is an *intermediate hybrid* where N+½ takes it all. Initially, when N+1 was launched against N, incumbents launched N+½ as cannon fodder to slow down the growth of N+1. Yet, it may be that N+½ succeeds beyond expectations and stops N+1. In doing so, N+½ is likely to take the market share of both N+1 and N, thus becoming the new dominant technology. If one decides to regard N+½ as a simple variant of N, it means that the incumbents won over the intruders and N+1, meaning that this is a case of *no substitution at all,* which in fact is the most common pattern. However, should one decide to interpret N+½ as a variant of N+1 (because it hybridized N thanks to N+1 features), then, it is a *double shift* where N+½ played the role of N+2. In this case, short-lived N+1 was defeated in a squeeze between N and N+½ (in the role of N+2).

The above comments simply illustrate the interrelations among the patterns presented.

Recomposing Complex Trajectories

The ten patterns can be combined into a variety of sequence of technological substitutions. Figure 29 provides an illustration of the combinatory power of the patterns.

Figure 29 presents a speculative sequence where technology N resists technology N+1 via a defensive *last gasp*, but the substitution of N by N+1 resumes; soon after, the emergence and diffusion of technology N+2 creates an *overlap*; technology N+2 then rapidly diffuses and substitutes for both technology N and N+1; however N+2 is suddenly cut short by a *double shift* to technology N+3; In turn, N+3 subsequently follows a *base case* trajectory and eventually reaches dominance; finally another technology

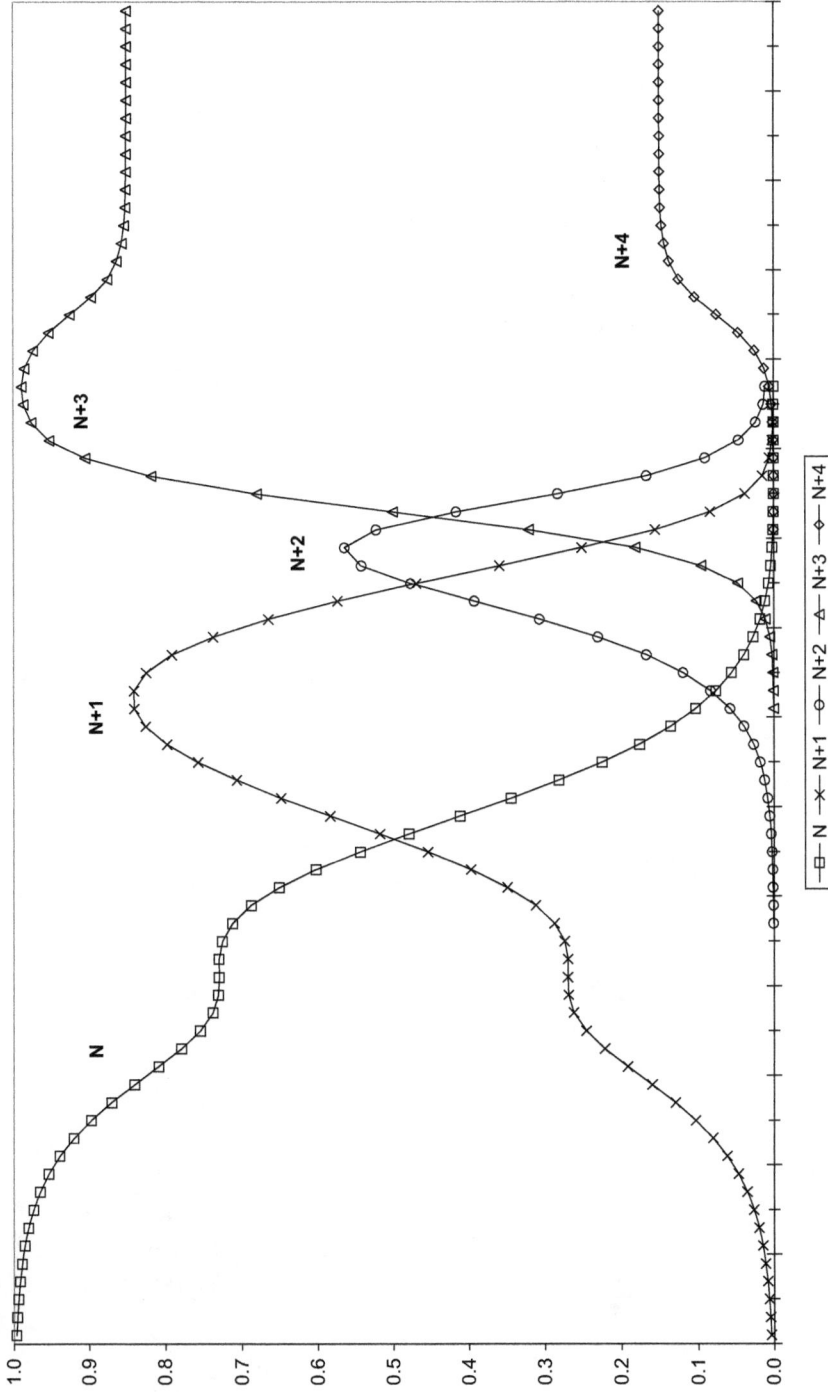

Fig. 29: Combination of patterns into a sequence.

N+4 emerges but only penetrates certain segments of the industry as for a *partial base case* that almost looks like a *burst*.

In fact, I argue that the ten patterns may help reinterpret a complex trajectory as a combination/sequence of some of the patterns. As an example, the longitudinal description of technological change in the typesetter industry (Fig. 24) illustrates such a combination of patterns (last gasp, pathfinder, double shift, base case.). Time will say whether the ten patterns carry with them some form of genericity or not – in the sense that they could help decompose/recompose many, if not most, substitution trajectories. To start with, it will be interesting to see whether additional patterns are identified beyond the 10 described here.

Chapter 13
A Model for Technological Substitutions

This chapter presents a model of technological substitutions stemming from the observation and description of the ten patterns. First the boundary conditions of the set of patterns are discussed, then two key variables driving four shape factors are identified to capture the shape of the patterns before an integrated mapping is presented. Altogether, with the content of this chapter, I argue that the ten patterns, the two variables and the four shape factors, plus the mapping, constitute some form of a grammar of technological substitutions.

Boundary Conditions and Focus on the Patterns as Representations

Each of the ten patterns identified describes a situation where:
- A single technology N is fully dominant on a given market in a given industry.
- While N is established as the dominant technology, previous technologies N-1 or N-2, now obsolete, may still have some marginal market share, e.g., via niches.
- Some promising new technologies N+1, N+2, . . . N+i are envisaged for the future with a variety of players actively developing one or several of them: incumbents optimizing the current dominant technology N and possibly preparing "their own next generation", or new entrants hoping to surf the wave of a change via a new technology they are preparing to intrude into the industry with.
- By technology N and N+1, N+2, I mean technologies brought in by radical innovation (a paradigmatic shift) or at least micro-radical innovation, thus shaping the envelope curve known as the trajectory exploring a paradigm (see Part I). In other words, the technologies considered here are either trajectories à la Dosi, or sub-technologies shaping the Dosian trajectory as discussed around Fig. 11 and Tab. 1-A in Part I.
- Some other potentially promising technologies may also be in the picture, but they are still at the preliminary stage of the idea, with no prospect of any marketing or commercial activities in the period under consideration.
- Technology N which won over former technologies (N-1, N-2, . . .) is now being challenged by an array of promising technologies (N+1, N+2, . . . N+i). Eventually N is substituted for by a technology that will be named N+1. In turn, technology N+1 is challenged by an array of technologies (N+2 to N+i) until one of them (named N+2) substitutes for N+1, and so on.

https://doi.org/10.1515/9783111397979-017

Note that some of these simplifying assumptions may be slightly relaxed in several ways:

- N+1 may not always win in the end, or only to a limited extent (partial base case, including burst);
- some intermediate technology N+½, designed and triggered by incumbents defending N against N+1, may interfere in the N+1 vs. N battle; or N+2 may arrive while the N+1 vs. N battle is still raging.

Again, in studying technological substitution in this context, the choice is to focus on *the fate of technology N+1*, and the duration of market activity for N+1. The description thus focuses on the initial battle of N+1 substituting for N, and to some extent on the subsequent battle, when some N+2 technology arrives to substitute for N+1. (The situation of N+2 vs. N+1 is similar to that of N+1 vs. N, so that the framework can "slide" to the subsequent dynamics. This does not preclude looking at the "overlapped" substitution dynamics between N and N+1 vs. N+2 if N+2 arrives early, typically in the middle of the N vs. N+1 battle). Note that the focus is on the life cycle of N+1. In that sense, the arrival of N+2 is important, not so much because there would be a specific interest in N+2 *per se* but to find out about the termination of N+1. In other words, the observation looks at the substitution dynamics essentially by adopting the focal perspective of N+1 struggling for dominance between N and N+2.

The numbering of the various technologies stems from the sequence of arrival on the market: there may be several technologies facing N, yet the name N+1 goes to the technology that leads the charge against N, i.e., the one that is the first to start a new Dosian trajectory. Then comes N+2 etc. Obviously, this labeling can only be done *ex post* but this is intended to help read into the framework. (The only exception to this labeling convention is the case of technology N+½ in a *hybrid intermediate*: as previously discussed, N+½ appears in reaction to the launch of N+1, after N+1 started its attack against N. Yet, N+½ stands in between N and N+1 as an attempt by the incumbents to delay the substitution of N by N+1.)

Another important aspect of the analysis is that it looks at the dynamics in terms of market shares, meaning that the market can grow with the arrival of N+1 and/or N+2: additional market needs can be served thanks to new functionalities brought in by the new technologies. The normalized view of the market share (using percent shares of total market instead of absolute volumes) helps deal with changing market size without having to go into the details of each specific application being served on the market.

Finally, the observation and discussion of the phenomenon of technological substitution are limited here to the *description of the shape of the trajectory* for market penetration over time, at least as far as this chapter is concerned. The analysis here does not go into the complex and interdependent socio-technical determinants of the resulting dynamics (behavior of early adopters, word of mouth in social networks, perceived utility, social acceptance, defensive strategic response, etc.). This will be discussed in Chapter 15. The intent in this chapter is primarily descriptive, not explanatory. The overarching objective is to provide a framework representing technological substitutions as part of technological evolution to help managers think about technology strategically. Thus, the model conceptualizes and integrates what is observed. In addition, it identifies key descriptive characteristics of the phenomenon of technological substitution: as these patterns cover a variety of shapes (penetration levels, plateau effect, timing, downturn) and can be combined into complex trajectories, it is worth discussing their relations and underlying features. This is done by describing a small set of variables, in fact two, that capture the shape of the patterns via four shape factors, and by mapping the patterns to get an overall integrated representation.

Variables and Shape Factors to Describe the Patterns

The last two sections of Chapter 12 discussed how some of the patterns relate to one another and how they can be combined. I now turn to look for descriptive variables that help characterize the patterns, typically whether N+1 wins over N or not (aborted substitution?), to what extent (partial substitution?), how fast (slope and plateau?), for how long (when is N+2 coming in to take over, thus provoking a downturn for N+1?).

Given the boundary conditions discussed earlier, when a new technology N+1 breaks into a market to challenge the dominant technology N, what are the foreseeable scenarios?

Scenario 1: First is the case of non-disruption. Technology N remains dominant, which is the most common situation. This is primarily a world of incremental innovation whereby the current dominant technology N is mostly improved continuously and remains dominant.

Scenario 2: Second is the case of full takeover by technology N+1 that offers higher benefits to the users. Technology N+1 substitutes for technology N over a period through a diffusion process. Users progressively convert to the new technology and new users possibly join in. The substitution curve is the typical S-curve extensively discussed in the literature. This is the *base case*.

Note that one could adopt these two basic scenarios (1 and 2) as a simplified dichotomous view of technological change: on the one hand, continuity and incremental innovation, i.e., no disruption; on the other hand, straightforward and complete substitutions where radical innovation strikes, moving the competitive arena from technology N to N+1 via an adoption process following a logistic time path. To a certain extent, this is the macro view that the evolutionist literature conveys.

Scenarios 3: Third, as discussed above, things can depart from the apparently smooth dynamics of the base case, generating four additional scenarios (3-A to 3-C, and 4). I start with 3A to 3C.

Incumbent firms, who enjoy a competitive advantage by leveraging technology N, may react to the strategic threat represented by the arrival of technology N+1 as it is likely to destroy their strategic position. Other forces may also come into play to support N and oppose N+1, such as users heavily committed to N, e.g., due to fixed assets. This leads to the three next scenarios 3-A to 3-C:

Scenario 3-A: The incumbents' renewed efforts to improve and promote technology N combined to some users' preference for N may end up slowing down the speed of the substitution. This is typically captured by the β coefficient of the Fisher-Pry model for the S-curve – namely the "slope" of the ascending left part of the S-curve for N+1.

Scenario 3-B: Alternatively, the slowdown might be so significant that the substitution comes to a halt for a certain period of time before the process resumes, thus yielding a "plateau" in the substitution trajectory.

Scenario 3-C: In other instances, technology N+1 might have the potential of displacing technology N on some applications but not for the entire spectrum of use on the market. The substitution takes place, but not to the full extent of the market that N previously dominated. The extent of the final substitution is only "partial". The final height of the S-curve for N+1 at maximum market penetration does not reach 100%.

These three variations may thus change the "slope" of the S-curve (the focus of an immense literature) or introduce a "plateau" or limit the extent of the substitution to a "partial" height. These three variations (scenarios in fact) are the first three cases of the left part of Fig. 30. Each of these cases in fact covers a continuum of situations around a specific factor (slope, plateau, partial). These are "shape factors" as they can contribute to describe the shape of a pattern. And these factors can combine.

These first three shape factors on Fig. 30 capture, in a general sense, the resistance to the penetration of N+1 by technology N, or more precisely by a mix of forces opposing N+1, including not only the incumbents but also those players active in exploiting/using technology N, as well as regulators and society at large. This resistance

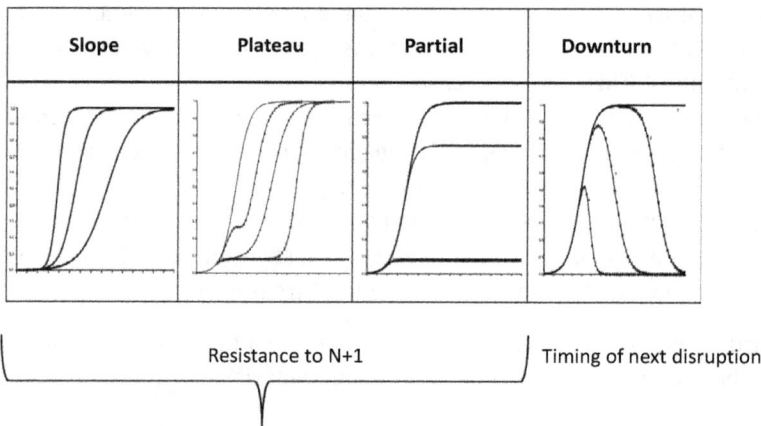

Fig. 30: Four shape factors and their effect on the trajectory of N+1.

may be due to a combined effect of a variety of forces and may be weak to strong; unsuccessful to very efficient; affecting the speed and the extent of the substitution as well as generating a plateau effect; thus, yielding a variety of outcomes.

The resistance to N+1 is thus a first variable that stands behind the first three shape factors shown on Fig. 30 to help describe the patterns. More specifically this variable affects the left-hand side of the trajectory of N+1, i.e., the trigger and growth phase of N+1.

Finally, something else can happen, this time affecting the right-hand side of the trajectory.

Scenario 4: A technology N+2 may arise in the middle of the N+1 vs. N struggle and affect the subsequent part of the process. Typically, some new entrants may have triggered the deployment of technology N+1 when some others may have subsequently chosen to bet on N+2, a more futuristic option which they perceived as even more promising. This intrusion of N+2 may be early or late, quick or slow, allowing N+1 to live its full life or not before reaching the downturn, again yielding a variety of outcomes. This is shown as the fourth case on the right part of Fig. 30. It corresponds to another shape factor, "downturn": How long will N+1 last? When will N+1 start being substituted for? How fast will N+1 hit the downturn? This fourth shape factor depends upon a second variable which has to do with the time of intrusion of N+2 into the competitive game.[25]

The timing of next disruption is thus the second variable that can be used to describe the patterns. Is the arrival of N+2 taking place after N+1 has successfully substituted for N? Or is it at the end/in the middle/at the beginning of the N+1 vs. N substitution process?[26]

The timing of next disruption is meant with respect to the N+1 vs. N substitution. In other words, what matters is the time of appearance of N+2 relative to another timing, that of the N+1 vs. N battle.

Concretely, if the next disruption (typically the time of arrival of N+2) is late, N+1 has the time to enjoy full dominance. If the time of arrival is a bit earlier, the pattern is an overlap. If the time of arrival is even earlier, the pattern becomes a double shift.

Note that the second variable is not named "timing of N+2 arrival" because, in case of *reverting*, the downturn does not result from N+2 but from other forces in the environment. The "timing of next disruption" is a wording that includes the case of reverting.

This provides two variables (resistance to N+1, timing of next disruption) and four shape factors shown on Fig. 30 (slope, plateau, partial, downturn), respectively meaning: How fast? With a delay along the way? To what extent? For how long once dominance is reached? I argue that the two variables and four shape factors provide descriptive analytical tools to capture the variety observed through the ten patterns.

---

25 Or the time of forced self-withdrawal by N+1 in the case of reverting.
26 In the case of reverting, the same applies for the need to abandon N+1, despite the absence of N+2.

Mapping the Patterns

This section presents a mapping of the patterns of technological substitution based on the two variables driving the four shape factors discussed above.

First comes the resistance to N+1. To do this, I look at a situation where N+2 does not come in to interfere (and where N+1 does not have to self-withdraw). I suggest viewing the variable "resistance to N+1" with a value ranging from low to medium, strong and very strong. The aim is to explore how the shape of the substitution pattern evolves, according to the intensity of the resistance to N+1, via the first three shape factors (slope, plateau, partial).

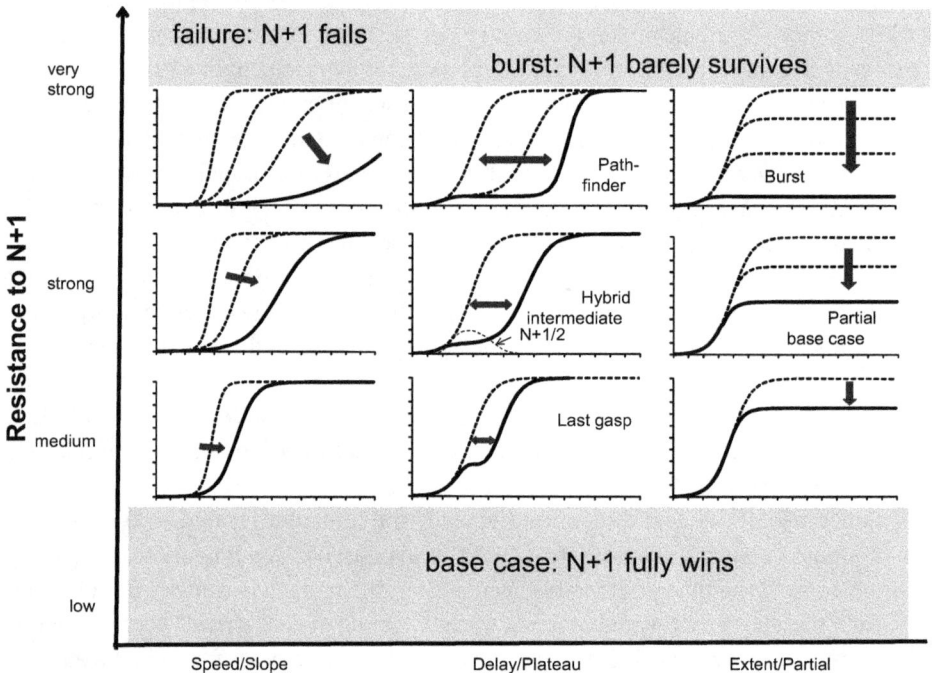

Fig. 31: Resistance to N+1 – The effects of three shape factors on trajectory for N+1.

In this setting, when the resistance to N+1 is low, technology N+1 simply substitutes for N at a rather fast pace via a base-case pattern. This is shown on the lower left corner of Fig. 31. From there we can explore Fig. 31 column by column.

Slope or *Speed* (the left column on Fig. 31): As the resistance to N+1 increases, the trajectory still follows a base-case pattern, but the speed of the substitution is slower. The slope of the curve is less steep. This is shown on the lower left "medium" box of Fig. 31. This is where the S-curve model works best, with the speed of the substitution captured as β, the parameter representing this shape factor. When the resistance to N+1 is even stronger, the same can hold: the shape is even flatter, but again N+1 eventually wins. However, when the resistance to N+1 is very strong, then the S-curve is just flat. N+1 ends up as a very partial base case, (or a burst or even does not make it: N remains dominant. The N+1 vs. N substitution process aborts).

Plateau or *Delay* (middle column on Fig. 31): The resistance to N+1 can lead to yet another form of variation from the base case. This is when, after an initial takeoff, the penetration by N+1 is so much slowed down that it comes to a halt. This leads to a delay in the growth of N+1 resulting in a plateau. The resistance to N+1 is observed this time via the second shape factor on Fig. 30, plateau. This is shown in the center "medium" box on Fig. 31 and the box below as well. The plateau can, for example, capture the difficulty of crossing the chasm to the main market or be generated directly by the supporters of N via a last gasp or a hybrid intermediate. (It is important to stress that, in a hybrid intermediate, technology N+½ is viewed as a deliberate attempt by incumbents to resist the arrival of N+1). If the resistance to N+1 gets stronger, the plateau may be very long until the substitution process can nevertheless resume, leading to a *pathfinder* shape (upper part of middle column on Fig. 31). If the resistance to N+1 is even stronger, the process remains stuck on a plateau at a certain level of penetration. Depending on that level of penetration, it may be a *partial base case*, a *burst* or even a *failure*, that is no substitution at all. This connects to the third shape factor, namely partial (or the extent of the substitution) discussed below.

Partial or *Extent* (right column on Fig. 31): Finally, N+1 may not be able to go beyond the plateau that it reached at a certain level of penetration. The substitution process came to a halt that eventually becomes a final stop. This is a *partial base case*. The third shape factor, partial, on Fig. 30 captures the extent of the substitution. This is shown on the right-hand side of Fig. 31. The maximum level of penetration (the partial height) attained decreases as the intensity of the resistance to N+1 increases. When the resistance to N+1 is very strong, the plateau takes place at a very early stage, thus at a low level of penetration, and stays there. This is a *burst*. Again, the extreme case of a burst is a *failure*, i.e., no substitution at all.

As a result, Fig. 31 presents a mapping of six of the patterns (again this assumes no intrusion by N+2 and no forced self-withdrawal of N+1). The six patterns covered are: base case; partial base case; burst; pathfinder; last gasp; intermediate hybrid.

Figure 31 illustrates how the intensity of the resistance to N+1 can affect the shape of a substitution pattern, via the slope, a plateau and/or the partial height. Note that the map was described vertically, i.e., via the three columns corresponding to the first three shape factors. Despite some form of discontinuities introduced by the nature of the columns, it is also possible to move across the map of Fig. 31 horizontally or diagonally. Typically, starting from the bottom left and moving towards the right and up, as the base case becomes slower and thus flatter, it can give shape to a plateau. And if that plateau lasts long enough, it gradually takes the shape of a partial base case. And if the plateau appeared very early on because of a fierce resistance to N+1, the pattern may take the shape of a *pathfinder* or may even stay in the form of a *burst*. At the extreme, a *burst* with so low a level of penetration simply means that the N+1/N substitution did not take place, thus resulting in a failure for N+1.

In this sense, the map shown on Fig. 31 suggests that a pattern can evolve into another as the intensity of the resistance to N+1 varies, triggering the first three shape factors (slope, plateau, partial).

Overall Mapping: Second Variable and Fourth Shape Factor

As discussed earlier, there is another variable that needs consideration (timing of next disruption) and the related fourth shape factor (downturn). These will affect the right-hand side of the substitution curves. The downturn is the final touch to describe the fate of N+1. Whatever happened since the trigger and growth of N+1, how does it terminate?

The setting is known: N+1 is substituting for N (or has already successfully substituted for N) when something more happens. N+2 arrives as a new challenger on the market. (Note that to extend the discussion to a *reverting* pattern, one essentially needs to follow the same line of reasoning and replace N+2 by N.) In addition, for the sake of clarity, the discussion below assumes that N+2 will follow a base-case pattern because it encounters low resistance by previous technologies N and N+1. Note that this does not preclude more complex scenarios where N+1 and other forces would resist N+2. Such cases would require one to "slide" the framework.

In order to provide an integrated view of all the patterns, Fig. 32 combines the intensity of the first variable, "resistance to N+1", on the y-axis, like in Fig. 31, and the squeezing intensity of the second variable, "timing of next disruption", on the x-axis. There is a squeeze in the sense that N+1 is squeezed between N and N+2. The variable "timing of next disruption" goes from "very late" (low interference) on the left-hand side to "very early" (much interference from N+2) on the right-hand side. Note that the left part of Fig. 32 (when N+2 comes in very late, in the sense that the N+1 vs. N battle is over) is in fact Fig. 31. This allows viewing the combined effect of the two variables (with their respective shape factors) on the substitution patterns of N+1.

Fig. 31 was built using the three first shape factors (slope, plateau, height) as columns on the x axis. The second mapping shown in Fig 32 added the fourth shape factor (downturn). Note, however, that this requires choosing which one of the three shapes emerged from the development of N+1 in the first place. In the example of Fig. 32, the right part shows the effect of a downturn (early or not so early) on a "partial" substitution (height) of N by N+1. A similar mapping could be drawn if the emergence of N+1 had led to a standard shape (slope) or a temporary halt in the growth of N+1 (a plateau).

As a result, the mapping on Fig. 32 captures the effect of the intensity of the resistance to N+1 combined with the effect of the intensity of the "squeeze" by N+2 onto N+1.

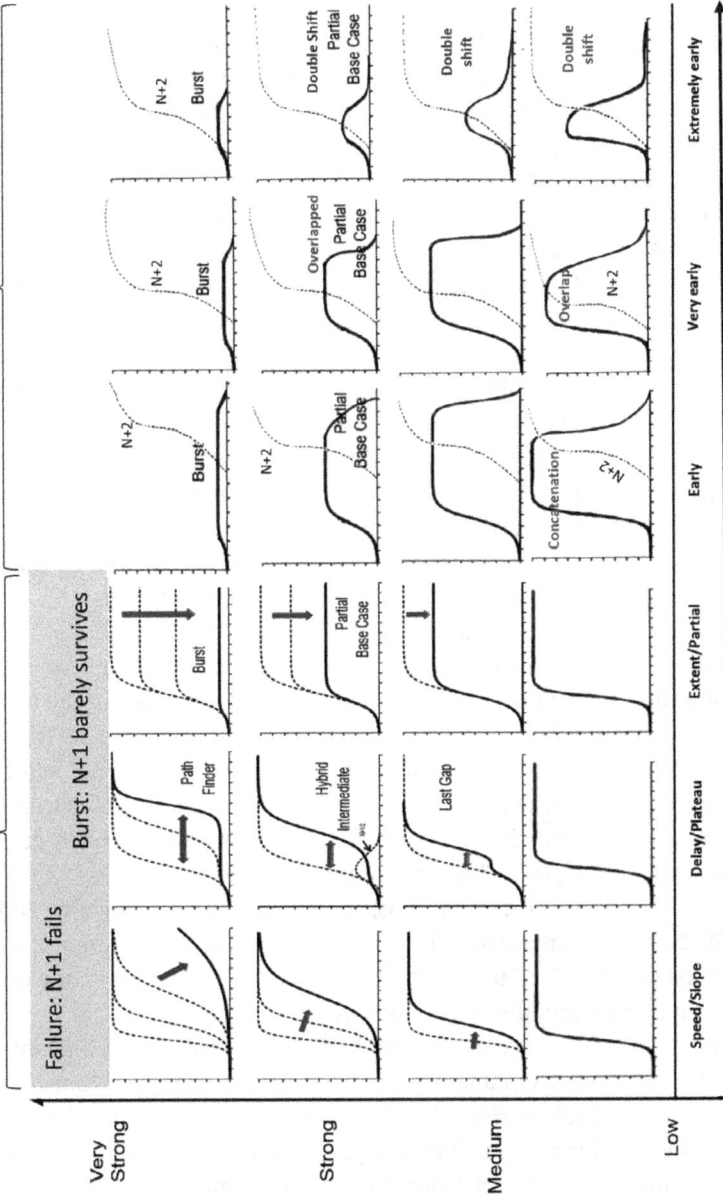

Fig. 32: Mapping patterns of techno substitution – Resistance to N+1 and timing of N+2.

Note that the right part of Fig. 32, i.e., downstream of the substitutions, is when N+2 became dominant. Symmetrically, the very left part of Fig. 32, upstream of the substitutions, is when N was still dominant. (These two extremes are the initial and final boundary conditions set up above for the model.) N+1 is active in between. This structure for the mapping is consistent with the choice made to focus the discussion on the fate of N+1 and thus on the shape of the curve for N+1.

Again, keep in mind that the right-hand side of Fig. 32 represents the downturn effect striking N+1 after a *partial* factor effect (right column of Fig. 31, also shown as the third column from left on Fig. 32). Again, variants of Fig. 32 can also be drawn when N+1 developed under a regime initially attached to one of the other two shape factors (slope and plateau). More generally, this applies for a downturn affecting a trajectory resulting from any combination of the three shape factors (slope, plateau, partial) that may have resulted from the specific conditions prevailing in the resistance to N+1.

Also note that N does not appear on Fig. 32 because the diagram essentially aims at describing the trajectory of N+1. In this context, N+2 is only shown to capture the timing of the downturn. However, it is worth keeping in mind that, in case of early downturn, N is still part of the story (although not shown on the diagram) because the N+1 vs. N substitution was not over yet when N+2 came into the picture.

We can now go through Fig. 32, starting with the bottom left area.

The situation is a low resistance to N+1 and a very late next disruption (no squeeze) by N+2. More specifically, N+2 arrives late enough for N+1 to have been fully deployed through a *base-case* pattern, having taken full market dominance over N. This is the "no squeeze" value of the variable "timing of next disruption". N+2 does not interfere in the N+1 vs. N substitution and the promoters of N+1 enjoy enough time of market dominance to reap the benefits of their technology. Another substitution process may then start – this time N+2 attacking N+1. This is a standard *concatenation*.

Moving right along the horizontal axis, with still low resistance to N+1, the squeeze from N+2 onto N+1 increases. The bottom row of Fig. 32 represent the effect of the fourth shape factor of Fig. 30 (downturn). As the squeeze increases, the *concatenation* becomes an *overlap* and then a *double shift*.

A convention may be useful to distinguish between an *overlap* and a *double shift*. In an *overlap*, the duration of dominance for N+1 is shorter than in a *concatenation*, but the promoters of technology N+1 still have the time to extract enough rent from the market to go beyond breakeven. Conversely, I suggest defining a *double shift* as a case where the timing of arrival of N+2 does not permit the promoters of N+1 to reach breakeven on the investments made to develop, market and deploy N+1. Obviously, this convention is primarily conceptual as it is difficult to assess ahead of time when breakeven might be reached in practice.

Moving up from the bottom of Fig. 32, as N+1 is encountering increasing resistance, N+1 will need more time to win over N, leaving more time for the next disruption to strike. Relatively speaking, this means that a squeeze via the next disruption (on the right-hand side of N+1) is more likely to interfere, transforming a potential *concatenation* into an *overlap* or even a *double shift*. In fact, both variables (resistance to N+1 and timing of next disruption) can combine to squeeze (i.e., narrow) the window of opportunity for N+1. (Should we map zones of Fig. 32, dropping the "boxes" format, this combined effect of the two variables on both axes x and y would lead to rounded shapes. Outside a large quarter of a circle centered on the base-case pattern [lower left corner], N+1 fails. Immediately inside it, N+1 exists at least for a while, more as a burst than anything else, possibly cut short by a very early downturn. Then would appear the *break-even* line that separates a double shift from an overlap as defined earlier. In the core of the quarter circle stands the base case and the concatenation case that play the role of reference, meaning the oversimplified view of the S-curve or a sequence of S-curves.)

Looking at an extreme case offers a consistency check: when the resistance to N+1 is very strong, there are situations where the only substitution dynamics that are observable are N+2 vs. N, meaning that N+1 fully failed. As simple as it is, N+1 did not really exist on the market. The situation boils down to N having defeated N+1 then struggling against N+2. This can thus be analyzed using Fig. 31, with N+2 in lieu of N+1.

The map on Fig. 32 suggests that the ten patterns can be seen as forming a continuum (more precisely a variety of continua): a *concatenation*, an *overlap* or a *double shift* are conceptually of the same nature and fit a continuum depending on the timing of next disruption. The same holds for a *reverting*. Similarly, for the left part of Fig. 32 corresponding to Fig. 31 (and as discussed earlier): a *base case*, a partial *base case*, a *last gasp*, an *intermediate hybrid*, a *pathfinder* and even a *burst* cover a continuum according to the intensity of the resistance to N+1 via the effect of the first three

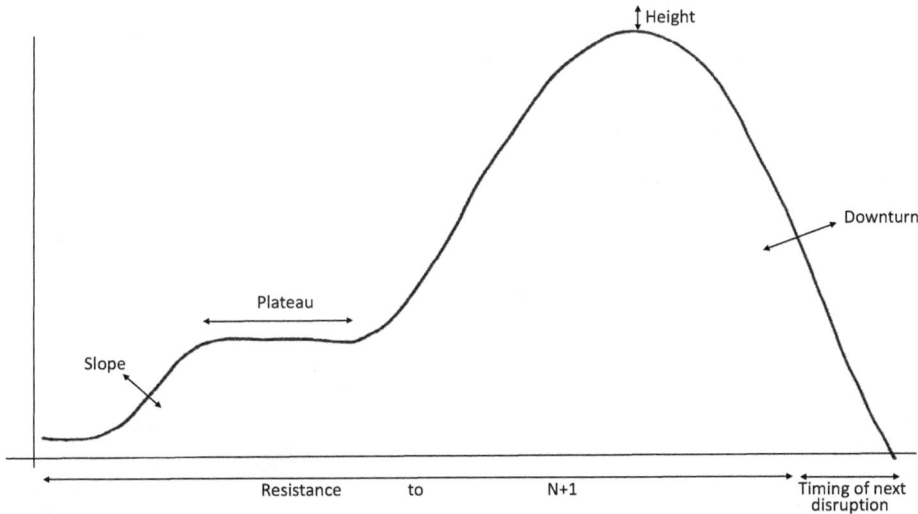

Fig. 33: The two variables and four shape factors describing the substitution pattern for N+1.

shape factors. In the in-between zones, the partial substitution of N+1 for N can be due to any combination of the resistance to N+1 and the early intrusion of N+2 which comes in to interfere.

In other words, *the map of* Fig. 32 suggests that *the ten patterns* can be seen as forming a continuum (more precisely a variety of continua). This confirms and generalizes the descriptive elements presented in Chapter 12 about interrelations between the patterns.

In this context, the *base case* and the *concatenation of base cases* – and thus the S-curve – can be viewed as the patterns of reference from which other patterns depart according to the variation of two variables (resistance to N+1 and timing of next disruption) driving the four shape factors (slope, plateau, partial and downturn).

All in all, the ten patterns, the two variables and the four shape factors (Fig. 33), and the mapping (Figs. 31 and 32) provide a richer descriptive framework of technological substitutions than the traditional S-curve representation.

Chapter 14
Windows of Bifurcation and Trigger Relays

In this context, an interesting topic emerges from the discussion of technological change. At some points in a sequence as the one shown on Fig. 29, the dynamics lead to sudden bifurcations in the trajectory, with shifts from one pattern to another. I argue that this does not just happen randomly. Pasquet suggested that there are typical moments or situations or zones in a techno-socio-economic-political system where the dynamics of change may bifurcate.

> Consider a flow of cars and trucks on a motorway heading north. The traffic is dense. An accident happened on the other side of the motorway, heading south. The police came in to secure the zone. A rescue team is taking care of the injured. A tow truck is on its way to remove the cars damaged in the accident. As this takes place on the other side of the motorway, it should not affect the flow heading north. Yet, it does. Out of curiosity, drivers unconsciously slow down to look at what happened on the other side. In dense traffic, their slowing down propagates up to the point of creating a traffic jam. Still, the northbound had nothing to do with the accident. Now, imagine the same situation with a very fluid traffic heading north. The accident on the other side is much less likely to lead to a traffic jam on the northbound.
>
> The accident affected first the people who were directly part of the accident (sorry for them), second those heading south who are very likely to be held for a long period of time, third those on the northbound having nothing to do with it. Yet, this third group may be negatively affected as well by the consequences of the traffic jam (missing a plane, a date, a sale, a wedding ceremony, an exam, a recruitment interview, etc.). Depending on the state of the system (fluid or dense), a trigger (an accident) quasi-external to the system (the flow heading north), may or may not generate a bifurcation, and amplify or not the effect (a jam that builds up and lasts).

These specific situations (dense traffic in the situation just described) can be viewed as windows during which, initiated by some form of a trigger, the dynamics of the system is more likely than in other periods to bifurcate into another state with significantly different strategic consequences. These windows can be called bifurcation windows. The triggers can be called trigger relays. The proposition is as follows.

As the techno-socio-economic-political system in which the technological substitution takes place enters a bifurcation window, it reaches an unstable state that makes it more likely for the trajectory to suddenly respond to some form of trigger relay that may appear, thus shifting away from the foreseeable dynamics that prevailed so far, leaving a pattern for another. The trigger relay is an element of the system, apparently of minor importance and often seating at the margin, that will first ignite and then amplify and extend a specific change, generating a bifurcation.

For players in the competitive arena, the strategic context may shift dramatically according to the bifurcations and thus the trajectories. This means that bifurcation windows can open the floor for potentially radically new strategic conditions.

Two of the cases presented earlier illustrate this idea. In the typesetting industry, the expected concatenation from analogue to CRT and then eventually from CRT to

https://doi.org/10.1515/9783111397979-018

laser was suddenly changed into a double shift. It may be argued that it was the conditions prevailing at that time in the system that led the release of Adobe PostScript to trigger such a bifurcation from a concatenation to a double shift. The second case is that of the optical video disc. The Laserdisc (LD) was on its way to a burst when a rather marginal additional innovation – the digital storing of the video part on the disc – permitted a sudden wakening up of a sleeping beauty into a pathfinder, leading to the success of the DVD. Again, the proposition is as follows. The specific conditions prevailing in the context combined with a trigger relay (the release of Adobe PostScript, in the first illustration above, or the digital storing of the video part in the second illustration) made the bifurcation possible.

This does not suggest that no bifurcation could occur outside a bifurcation window. A violent exogenous blow can destabilize an otherwise stable system, suddenly generating a bifurcation that was difficult to anticipate. Symmetrically, crossing a bifurcation window does not mean that a bifurcation will necessarily occur. The bifurcation also needs a trigger relay. In other words, a trigger relay is an otherwise marginal element that becomes significant due to the special context. It simply means that there are special states of the system where trigger relays can find an echo chamber making such bifurcations more likely to happen.

This raises the question of how to spot a bifurcation window. If it is only possible to tell *ex post* that the industry crossed a bifurcation window, then the concept is of little practical interest. In addition, if the probability for a technological bifurcation to take place is the same for any moment in the life of an industry, the concept of window of bifurcation is also irrelevant.

Instead, I argue that a set of factors in the socio-technical system combine to create the conditions prevailing in a bifurcation window. A typical list of questions should be raised and carefully answered to assess if and when a bifurcation window could be in the process of being crossed:

- *Technology N not progressing anymore*: Is technology N still making progress (cost-wise and/or in terms of performance) or did it reach an asymptote, thus leaving the door wide open for a new technology to come in?
- *Pending technologies*: Are there serious options pending among the long (or short) list of candidate technologies that could substitute for our current dominant technology? Have we been able to set up the list or is it too foggy? Did we notice the filing of new patents that relate to some of the technologies on the list? Did we see R&D contracts signed by incumbents or potential new entrants with universities or technology providers?
- *New entrants massing troops at the border*: Are there potential new entrants sharpening their own candidate technology and very likely to consider our industry to start a new business? What about start-ups? If we were a prospective new entrant in the industry, would we do it now (or soon)? If not, what would we wait for and why?

- *Moves by incumbents*: Do we observe incumbents frantically improving their dominant technology to deter any attempt to introduce a substituting technology? Do we observe incumbents hybridizing their current dominant technology with some features of a potential new technology that is announced as "coming soon"? Do we observe some incumbents actively developing the new technology?
- *A sleeping beauty about to wake up*: Do we have some burst technology introduced some years ago that could eventually lead to a pathfinder? Do we see a newly introduced technology plateauing that could resume its substitution?
- *User and customer unfulfilled or poorly fulfilled needs and matters of dissatisfaction*: To what extent are the current customers satisfied with the offerings they obtain from incumbents? Are there specific needs that are not properly fulfilled, in search of solutions that do not exist yet due to the limits of the current dominant technology?
- *Pending new regulation*: Are there regulatory threats on our current technology or candidate technologies for the future of our industry?
- *Pressures from the environment*: Is the industry under pressure to deal with specific issues (environmental preservation, carbon emission, safety [health, accidentology], waste of rare resources, etc.)?
- *New business models*: Do we see business model innovations taking place around bold ideas and new technological ways? Do we see much start-up activities? Are venture capital funds rushing into the sector?
- *Scientific breakthrough upstream*: Is the industry waiting for some upstream scientific breakthrough or new inventions to transform the status quo?

Airbus and Boeing have grown as the two dominant leaders in aeronautics. After the era of propellers (technology N) in the early days, jet engine (technology N+1) established itself in the 1950s to become the dominant design for the decades ahead. Yet, environmental concerns now put a lot of pressure on air transportation. In this context, a candidate new technology (N+2) emerged in the form of electricity-powered planes. In addition, hydrogen fuel is around the corner as well. So, we have a technology situation in aeronautics that somewhat mirrors the automotive industry, probably with ten to 20 years lag. This may still sound rather futuristic, except for the 400 start-ups that emerged worldwide around the promise of batteries in aeronautics, with heavy funding (both private and public) poured into the new ventures. Obviously, something is going on. This is a typical signal of a window of bifurcation. This does not guarantee that a paradigmatic shift is bound to happen in the next years. Yet the likelihood of a significant change around greener planes becomes quite plausible. The two main incumbents are financially powerful but too big to be agile enough to be directly active on the potential disruption. However, one can expect that they will both pay a lot of attention to new developments on that front, ready to license in successful solutions or acquire start-ups that would make a breakthrough.

In this context, a basic principle of management suggests staying alert to carefully monitor the state of the system, including checking whether there are inhouse risks of blindness: Are some of our teams or managers denying the obvious (e.g., a tendency to keep repeating "that technology will not work", "will be too expensive", "will not

Tab. 2: List of factors signaling a potential window of bifurcation ahead.

Factors signaling a potential window of bifurcation ahead
-Technology N making little or no progress (cost and/or performance)
-Pending new technologies (N+1, N+2, N+3 identified and about to be ready for launch, intense patent filing, R&D contracting and partnering)
-Potential new entrants
-Moves by incumbents (improving N, hybridizing N with N+1, developing their own N+1 or N+2, negotiating with potential new entrants)
-Existence of a sleeping beauty that looked as a burst but about to wake up as a pathfinder
-User and customer unfulfilled or poorly fulfilled needs, and matters of unsatisfaction
-Pending new regulation
-Environmental concerns
-New business models emerging
-Start-up activities
-Venture capital funds rushing into the sector
-Scientific breakthrough upstream

permit proper and efficient scale up", "will never reach the quality of offering that our technology provides", etc.)?

The key point is for managers to monitor the state of the system, looking at the conditions prevailing to detect any significant sign of instability, see Table 2. This is a matter of doing the usual homework as far as competitive intelligence and technological scouting are concerned. On top of that, if the situation can be characterized as changing and turning somewhat unstable, it is important to pre-identify what could operate as a trigger relay, in the sense of a triggering mechanism of a potential bifurcation. The challenge is to be in a position to prepare for it, watch it come ahead of the crowd and react when there is still time.

Figure 34 illustrates the concept of bifurcation windows. It plots the trajectory for the ten patterns on the same diagram, starting from a base case. Note that (a) this diagram only represents the share of N+1 over time: N and N+2 are not shown and (b) the reverting case is implicit in replacing N+2 by N.

Typical bifurcation windows are represented as rectangles on the trajectories. Note that these are shown *for the sake of illustration only*. The existence of a bifurcation somewhere does not mean that the industry crossed a window of bifurcation around that time. Similarly, bifurcation windows may have been encountered on other occasions, with no trigger of a bifurcation.

A key point is to monitor the trajectory as it unfolds to check if and when the likelihood of a bifurcation is strong. On the basis of the responses given to the set of questions above, an assessment can be made on whether the state of the system is normally stable or entered what can be considered a window of bifurcation.

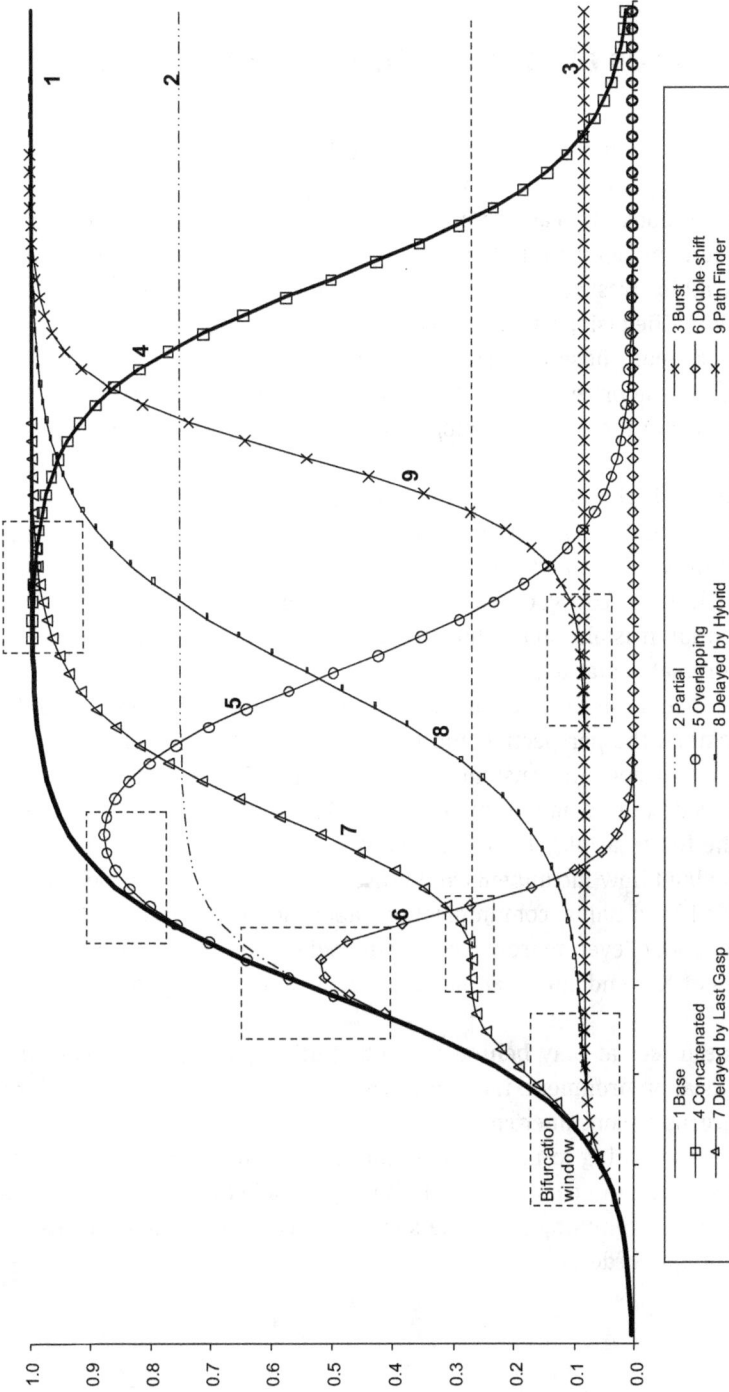

Fig. 34: Bifurcation windows along potential substitution trajectories for N+1.

Chapter 15
Underlying Forces at Work behind the Patterns

So far, I have not really discussed the underlying mechanisms that govern the emergence of the substitution patterns observed.

In as much as the book aims at helping to think about technology strategically, especially in situations of significant change, I need to dive into the forces at work behind the two variables (resistance to N+1 and timing of next disruption) and the four shape factors identified (slope, plateau, partial and downturn).

I briefly touched upon those underlying forces earlier, such as the market response over time given the price, the new functionalities offered to users, the overall perceived performance of the new technology N+1 (and then N+2, N+i) compared to N, etc.

More specifically, this chapter discusses how the N+1 vs. N substitution starts on some niche markets around early adopters. It is about the major issue of crossing the chasm and the role of word of mouth spreading via the most vocal early users in social networks while the unit cost goes down, thus permitting N+1 to address an even larger market potential. It is also about how the new functionalities fulfilled by N+1 may extend the addressable market.

In a way, I looked so far at the issue of technology dynamics from the supply side. Here, we need to extend the perspective and look at the perception of the same dynamics from the demand side – the customers and users. This is typically the perspective of marketers based in firms on the supply side, looking at their prospects for N+1.

Yet, some of the forces at play behind the substitution patterns are also on the supply side. This is about how incumbents and other players resist N+1 through a variety of levers (their brand name, communications about loopholes in the new technology, information about "even more novel" technologies coming soon, etc.). This is also how promotors of N+1 and later N+2 play their own game to compete in the strategic arena.

Yet again, some forces at play behind the substitution patterns can also stem from the socio-political environment, including regulatory, societal trends, health or environmental concerns or consumerism.

So, we have forces relating to market acceptance of the new technology on the demand side, forces relating to competition on the supply side (incumbents, new entrants) as well as forces stemming from the socio-political environment. I discuss these forces below, in that order.

https://doi.org/10.1515/9783111397979-019

Forces Relating to Market Acceptance

A first perspective on market interest for a new technology is to adopt the classical view of economics where utility and price combine to drive the decisions of buyers on the demand side. This assumes that prospective customers and users are attracted by the potential of improvements of the new technology that could bring a significant jump in performance. Yet this is classically moderated by the price to pay for that promise.

Figure 35, adapted from Brice Dattée, illustrates the potential impact of the sequence of improvement of technology N+1 vs. N, both for technological performance and utility per price over time. While it is not necessarily easy to measure utility per price in practice, it is worth discussing Fig. 35 conceptually.

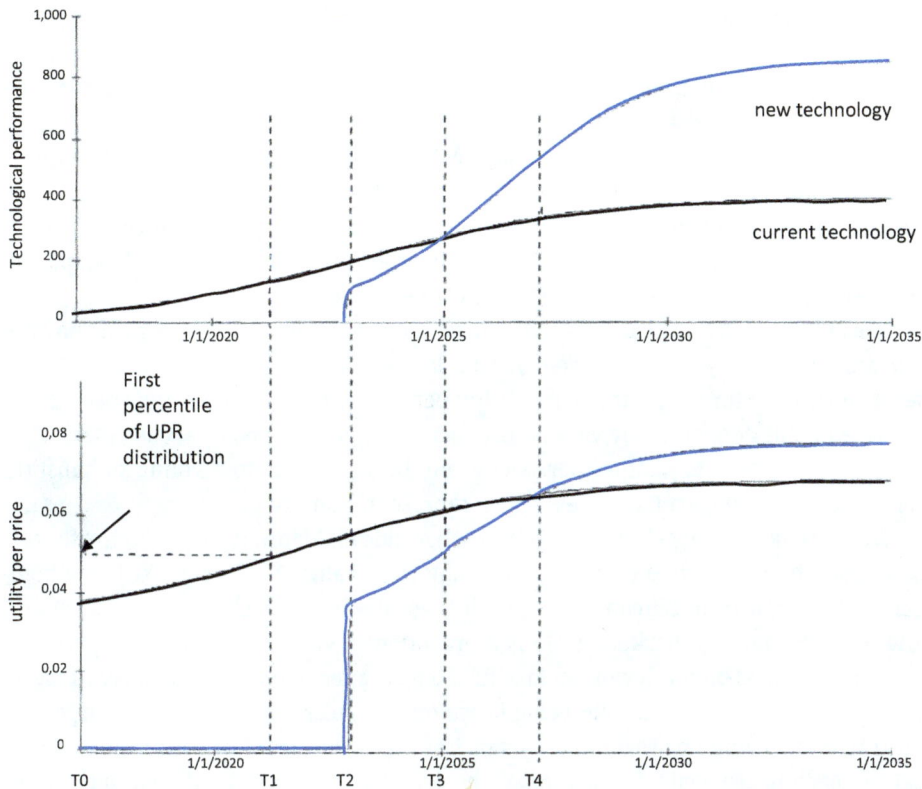

Fig. 35: Technological performance and utility per price for N+1 vs. N.
(UPR = utility/price ratio)

Before time T2 (on the x-axis), in the absence of any competing technology N+1, N is dominating and/or still penetrating the market due to its reasonable utility per price despite its soon-to-be-limited performance. Both utility per price and performance are implicitly assumed to be better than those of the previous technology N-1 (not shown on Fig. 35). When technology N+1 comes in, initially with a lower though promising technological performance compared to N and a lower though promising utility per price, N+1 can only convince the technology addicts among the potential customers. These anticipate that N+1 will significantly improve its performance and utility per price in the future. Their engagement for N+1 creates a market niche that can serve as a preliminary reference for the next groups (early adopters and then early followers), creating an installed base that helps test and improve the reliability and performance of N+1. At T3, N+1 is at par with N on technological performance. This helps N+1 capture more market segments and thus scale up, lowering costs and improving utility per price. At T4, the two utility per price curves cross, N+1 taking the lead both on intrinsic technological performance and utility per price. From there, the substitution dynamics can accelerate.

The differences in technology performance and utility per price for N+1 vs. N drive the speed of adoption of N+1 and thus the slope of the substitution (first shape factor attached to "resistance to N+1").

A similar line of thinking can apply to N+2 coming in to squeeze N+1 (with or without some remains of N in case of "partial" height). The downturn of N+1 relates to the relative advantage of N+2 vs. N+1 regarding technological performance and utility per price. In this sense, the same underlying market forces drive the fourth shape factor (downturn) as for the first shape factor (slope).

This view is fully aligned with the S-curve representation of technological substitution. This assumes a rather homogeneous market responding to the same driving forces (technological performance and some utility per price notion), even if the speed of response and thus adoption may vary according to categories of potential customers.

We need to turn to another perspective on the same issue to account for substitution patterns that depart from the S-Curve representation.

In his book *Crossing the Chasm*, a best-seller indeed, Moore typically addresses this issue from the perspective of a firm launching N+1 against N. His context is the high-tech sector, seen from Silicon Valley, with several editions including 1991, 1999 and 2014. His viewpoint is marketing. He is a practitioner who reflects on his experience. His contribution is both relevant and useful. Some academic readers are likely to regret that the book is assertive despite being based on examples which serve the purpose of illustration but cannot be regarded as empirical validation. This is a classic methodological reproach heard against practitioners' books – and legitimately so. Yet, in the present case, one should consider that such a contribution brings an interesting framework that can serve as a set of hypotheses to be tested rigorously through scientific means.

Moore calls upon Rogers' technology adoption life cycle stemming from earlier work by Bohlen and Beal. He further introduces the concept of the chasm as a wide split between the early adopters and the early majority. This was illustrated in Fig. 9, Part I, Chapter 4, also shown below as Fig. 36.

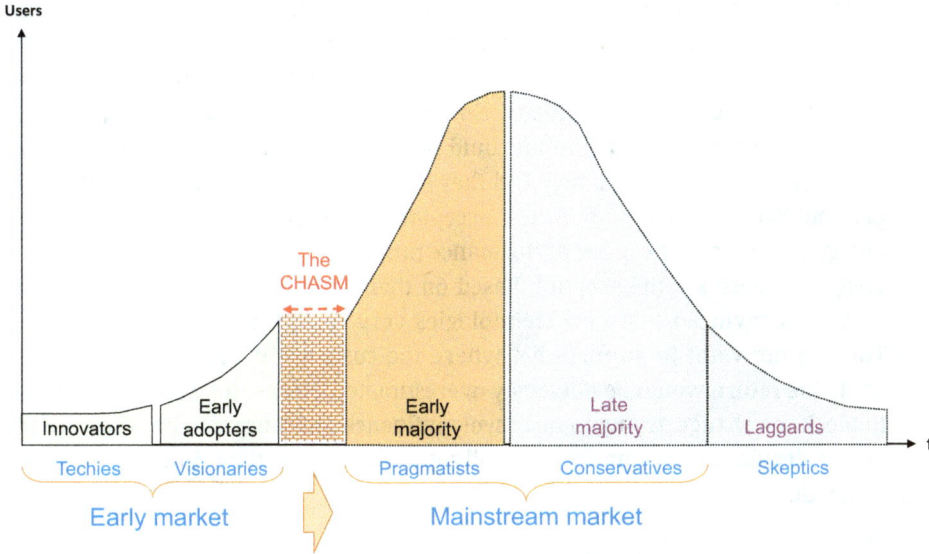

Fig. 36: The technology adoption life cycle and Moore's chasm (also Fig. 9).
adapted from Moore (1991)

Moore's key point is market heterogeneity. Moore argues that all potential customers
are not alike. He describes at length the differences among them:

– *The innovators*: they love technology per se and are interested in going for the
new technology for the sake of technology. They are the techno addicts, the
techies.
– *The early adopters*: they are the visionaries. They want to be at the forefront of
innovation. They feel that they can sense the potential of a new technology for
some new market opportunities. They are ready to debug offers that are not fully
baked because they believe that this is the price to pay for playing the game of
running at the frontier of the state of the art – and benefiting from it. In a way,
early adopters are positive to the new as much as innovators are. There is a difference though. Innovators love technology. In contrast, early adopters view technology as just a means to an end. Instead, they love dreaming up new business
ventures through innovation, matching new market opportunities with the promises of the new technology. Early adopters have (or believe they have) an intuitive
visionary sense of what to do with the new technology, in the form of something
unique that was not possible before.
– *Early majority*: these are the pragmatists. They are not looking for change or new-
ness per se, as they prefer to stay away from trouble. Typically, they are not
ready to debug the new technology; not their taste, not their job. However, they
search for a significant gain in performance in their operations at the cost of
some investment and change management. With that in mind, they may be ready

to bear some reasonable risk to benefit from the new technology, as long they can be assured that the new solutions should deliver a reliable performance.

- *Late majority*: these are the conservatives. They do not want to take any chances with unsure technological options. However, they do not want to miss the last boat on something important that could become the industry standard. If almost everybody else is on board, they feel they should join the party to stay in the competition. Yet, they would not find it acceptable if the promoters of the new technology would not deliver the performance promised.
- *Laggards*: these are the skeptics. Based on their intuition or experience or both, they are convinced that new technologies very seldom deliver their promises. They do not want to go for a bet where the costs are usually underestimated while the return would be obviously overestimated. Hence, they will do their best to block the change, trying to negatively influence other users-to-be. They are the last to decide for the change, typically grumbling that they do it against their own will.

Moore thus starts recognizing that the market is made up of heterogeneous profiles, with market segments that have very specific perceptions and expectations, especially when it comes to new technologies and change. In addition, he suggests a rough estimate of each of the market categories. About two-thirds for early majority and late majority, each one-third; about one-quarter for early adopters and laggards, each 13%; and about 5 to 6% for innovators, meaning that the bulk of the market is majority, while the sequence of entry starts first with innovators and then early adopters – a small minority indeed. Thus, the importance of reaching the two majority categories.

From there, Moore goes one step further. He argues that all groups expect previous switchers (on their left on Fig. 36) to serve as references and reassurance messengers before making the decision to switch from N to N+1. Referencing is the key mechanisms here, as word of mouth spreading from market segments to the next is the most efficient and least costly effort, saving time-consuming and expensive ad spendings. Except, and this is the core point, the psychological profile of the members of some of the groups devalue the reference given by the preceding group on their immediate left on Fig. 36. This is particularly so for the pragmatists (the early majority) who tend to distrust the visionaries of the early adopters group. Moore speaks of a catch-22 here. The pragmatists will not switch unless they see credible references and hear convincing word of mouth. Yet, they want to stay away from listening to the most sizable group who went for the new technology so far, namely the visionaries (the early adopters) whom they see as dangerous dreamers and gamblers. Thus, the chasm on Fig. 36.

This mechanism of reputational and behavioral mistrust among market segments is extremely dangerous for the wave of market cannibalization that the promoters of N+1 aim at surfing. Conversely, it operates as a "natural" defense mechanism for the incumbents entrenched on N. In other words, putting it from the perspective of the forms of patterns that we observed, a plateau or a partial height (limited extent of final market penetration by N+1) are typical consequences of the chasm, i.e., a profile misfit between market segments (pragmatists vs. visionaries). The mistrust hinders the referencing and word-of-mouth mechanisms, thus stopping subsequent major market segments to decide for the switch to N+1. In other words, the existence of a chasm in the technology adoption life cycle of Fig. 36 is a typical driver of the first variable that emerged in Chapter 13, namely resistance to N+1. The chasm was not created by the incumbents or the regulators, nor societal pressures. The chasm results from heterogeneous behaviors on the demand side of the market. Yet, it forms a sizable roadblock for the development of N+1, thus feeding the resistance to N+1 and three shape factors (plateau, partial and slope).

When a firm promoting N+1 reaches the chasm, Moore's proposition is to focus on a very limited sub-segment of the early majority category. The targeted subsegment should be small enough to be compatible with the intruder's available technical and commercial resources. Moore argues that the intruder should fight its way through in a very focused way so as to capture beyond 50% market share on that bounded subsegment. His point is that leadership on a market subsegment is the proper way to secure a base of references capable of convincing and reassuring other sub-segments. This leads to the analogy of the bowling alley: striking one pin (leadership on one market sub-segment) will get other pins down in a snowballing effect (adjacent market subsegments will follow naturally). Thus, the strategy of narrow affordable focus.

> The case of diabetes treatment discussed in Chapters 6 and 8 in Part I provides an illustration of a variant of the catch-22. When the human insulin was launched by Eli Lilly and Novo about the same time in the UK in the early 1980s, the new product (stemming from the first application of biotechnologies in the pharma industry) turned out to receive little market interest. The diabetics who had been successfully treated for years with animal insulin were doing fine. As a result, they were not too keen on taking the chance of switching to a radically new technology. Neither were their GPs. Without being aware of the concept of chasm that Moore published ten years later, marketers at both Novo and Eli Lilly chose to focus the commercial effort for human insulin on the newly diagnosed diabetics. These would not have the same doubts. They would be more open to the latest technology. Six months later, over 50% of the new diabetics were treated with human insulin, the new technology. From there, the dynamics of demography would do the growth of human insulin. This illustrates a slightly different kind of focus to cross the chasm, where word of mouth and referencing may have played a role, but not fully in Moore's sense. However, the logic of focusing on a smaller market segment to create a visible (if not sizeable at first) customer base remains.

Yet, there is more to the story. Other forces, this time on the supply side, can play a role in driving the two variables and their associated shape factors.

Forces Relating to Competitive Moves (Incumbents, New Entrants)

Incumbents have successfully promoted technology N in the past. They gained a profitable market position. They entrenched in that position through incremental improvements on cost (thus price), quality, reliability, technological performance, add-on services, etc. The incumbents are likely to see N+1 as a threat. Once they have identified the threat, they are likely to react. As discussed before, they often first tend to spend time and resources to improve technology N in an attempt to bridge the technological gap with N+1 (be the technological performance of N+1 a promise still or already a reality). We saw earlier that this is the typical driver of a last gasp. It can also explain a slowing down of the growth of N+1 (slope), a temporary halt (a plateau) or a permanent stop (burst or a partial substitution) in the growth path of N+1.

In other words, the incumbents' attempts to improve N against the irruption of N+1 contribute to the resistance to N+1, thus driving three shape factors (slope, plateau and partial). The main difference between those three shape factors is the fate of N+1. A less steep of a slope does not prevent N+1 to win in the end, unless the slope becomes flat, yielding a plateau in a last gasp where N+1 eventually resumes its growth to substitute for N (that is, N is still bound to lose). Conversely, partial height means that N succeeded in remaining in the game, as N+1 could only capture a share of the market, whatever the height reached in the end. Depending on the height, this ends up as a partial success or defeat for N or N+1.

Instead of blindly searching for improvements on N, incumbents may quickly realize that defending N as such may be a lost cause. The intermediate hybrid, a variant of the above, is when some incumbents hybridize N with some features of N+1, launching an intermediate technology which I call N+½, somehow mimicking N+1 in the hope of slowing down if not stopping the invasion by N+1. Apart from the hybridization and the timing (N+½ is developed as a counterattack, hence after N+1 entered the market, unless visionary incumbents had correctly anticipated the arrival of N+1 and acted preventively), this defense against N+1 is similar to the case of direct improvement above. It is still a defense that some incumbents organize around N, by improving N into N+½, borrowing some of the novelty and features of N+1.

In other words, this intermediate hybrid pattern, relating to a specific proactive response from some incumbents, also drives the resistance to N+1 and the three same shape factors (slope, plateau and partial) in a similar way as above.

Yet, there are other options available for incumbents (those firms entrenched on N). They can announce that some N+2 which they have been contemplating, if not developing, for some time is expected on the market. In doing so, they may scare potential innovators and early adopters away from N+1, thus reinforcing the resistance to N+1.

Once CIT-Alcatel had successfully developed TDM switches as early as 1970, through some bold (but strategically sound) leapfrogging move, they started commercializing the new technology.

Ericsson was running behind and ITT even more so. Alcatel's competitors toured their clients, the telcos around the world, with a very clear narrative that was reported to me as something like: "You know us well. We are reliable and dependable. Trust us. Alcatel went for a very risky technology. Our advice is to be careful. We too are developing the next technological generation, but in a much safer way. Wait for our next offerings. With us, no debugging will be needed. You can count on us as we count on your loyalty to your preferred supplier." This typical incumbent's speech worked as resistance to N+1.

Incumbents may also have developed another candidate for the role of N+1, i.e., the substituting technology, and decide to launch it to prevent new entrants to launch their own – or as a counterattack if new entrants already did so. Both entry deterrence and counterattack by incumbents tend to reinforce the resistance to N+1.

Alternately, incumbents may partner with one of the potential new entrants. This move gives them access to technology N+1, keeps them in the loop, limits the competition from that partner while being in a strong position to compete against the other new entrants (conversely, the alliance provides the new entrants with intimate knowledge of the industry, client intimacy, good knowledge of the distribution channels). This strategy weakens the resistance to N+1, thus affecting three shape factors (slope, plateau and partial) accordingly.

Instead, incumbents can enter an alliance (or a crash internal program) to develop N+2 as speedily as possible to squeeze N+1 between an organized defense of N and an announcement of a pending N+2, legitimizing the announcement through the credibility of the alliance (or the resources allocated to the internal technological development program). This strategic response to N+1 obviously aims at increasing the resistance to N+1, inducing doubts among the demand side about the relevance of a switch to N+1. It also affects the timing of next disruption, suggesting that N+2 could arrive before N+1 becomes dominant, thus generating an overlap, if not a double shift – a scary perspective for new entrants who plan to amortize their investments on N+1. This drives the fourth shape factor (downturn).

Other strategic moves by the competitors (and potential new entrants) in the arena include early announcements by promoters of some N+2 of the arrival of their offerings, thus contributing to the resistance to N+1 and/or the timing of next disruption squeezing N+1 into an early downturn.

The case of recorded music in France discussed in Chapter 4 and illustrated by Fig. 8 offers a paradoxical illustration of the effect of an early announcement by N+2 and a simultaneous opening of a new form of usage for N+1. Since about 1970, vinyl discs (N) were being substituted for by audiotapes (N+1). When N started its downturn in 1978, indicating that N+1 had clearly won, Japanese electronics firms opportunistically announced their CD technology (N+2) for the years to come. This announcement induced doubts on the market, leading N+1 to plateau from 1978 to 1987. Yet, when launched on the French market in 1983, the CD (N+2) plateaued as a burst until 1986 when it started a steep growth. Strangely enough, instead of declining from that point, N+1 (tapes) resumed its growth the following year. This lasted until 1990 when N+1 hit its downturn, this time fully overwhelmed by N+2. The reason for this unexpected revival of N+1 was that car manufacturers had started offering audiotape players on new cars, thus causing a paradoxical rebound of N+1 despite the expected substitution by N+2. In fact, customers on the demand side had been both expecting and postponing a switch to N+2 since the announcement of N+2 in 1978. When N+2 was launched, it did not fully convince as it required buying a CD player at the very moment when car manufacturers offered tape players as standard in new cars, considerably expanding the audiotape player base, thus creating market buoyancy for N+1 (tapes). Thus, the paradoxical rebound of N+1 around 1987, just when N+2 (the CD) was finally taking off.

Forces Stemming from the Socio-political Environment

Other forces can drive the two variables (resistance to N+1 and timing of next disruption), thus the four shape factors (slope, plateau, partial and downturn). These underlying forces behind the variables and shape factors driving the patterns can be societal trends or pressures (consumerism, environmental concerns), or concerns followed by government bodies on health, defense and security matters about sensitive technologies, materials, components or systems, with public involvement such as public procurement, regulatory bans, etc. These forces can push N out, support N+1 (or conversely N+2) thus contributing to weaken or strengthen the resistance to N+1.

> Eutelsat is a company operating satellites, especially for telecoms and TV broadcasting. They secure slots out in space from the World Radiocommunication Conference of the international telecommunication Union (ITU), the UN body awarding orbital positions. Eutelsat calls upon the services of launchers (Arianespace, SpaceX, etc.) to position satellites on geosynchronous orbits (36,000 km above the Earth). These are critical spots from which they can cover the same geographical zone on the ground 24/7. This is typically fit to conveying TV signals. Suddenly in 2015, financial market analysts realized that the younger generation is no longer ready to watch live TV, preferring instead on-demand services via the internet. In other words, the market of geosynchronous satellites for TV is likely to fall as the new generations replace the previous generations over time. The stock market reacted very negatively: Eutelsat's share value dropped by 48% during the first five months of 2016. Altogether, the share value was divided by four between April 2015 and September 2020. Eutelsat was well placed on technology N (satellites) but was challenged by a shifting demand that called for an existing technology N+1 (TV on the internet) already available and ready to capture the market. In that context, the resistance to N+1 was weak. As a result, the future of Eutelsat, stuck with technology N and the remaining declining market, became bleak.

While the above example is about a societal change weakening N and calling for N+1, the opposite situation can be encountered as well. The underlying forces listed above can push against the arrival of N+1, thus contributing to strengthen the resistance to N+1, slowing down the slope, introducing a plateau or limiting the height (the final market penetration reached is only partial) in the growth path of N+1.

If those external forces arrive late enough for N+1 to have already reached market dominance or even fully substituted for N, then N+1 may be weakened not so much in its capacity to overcome N (job already done) but in its capacity to resist the next disruption. As a result, some N+2 technology can be drawn in earlier than expected, accelerating the downturn of N+1 (a concatenation or even an overlap). Or N+1 can even be pushed out. In the absence of any N+2 available to fill the void, this leads to a reverse pattern whereby N makes a comeback to take over N+1.

In other words, external forces can both weaken or strengthen the resistance to N+1, thus driving the shape factors affecting the left part of the trajectories (Fig. 33: slope, plateau, partial). Yet those forces can have a late influence on the time path of N+1, namely if they only appear once N+1 has already succeeded in substituting for N, at least to some extent. Those forces can push N+1 out, or at least weaken its capacity to resist the next disruption. In that sense, those external forces contribute to drive the second variable, timing of next disruption, and thus the fourth shape factor (downturn).

There is still another force relevant for the analysis of the underlying mechanisms driving the patterns of technological substitution.

The promoters of N+1 (identified here to new entrants, for the sake of simplicity, although we have seen that they may not all be new entrants) are playing their own part. Typically, they decide upon the timing of entry for N+1, the resources they allocate to support the entry, the prospects they target, the way they cross the chasm, the announcements they make, the alliance they form, etc. These actions will lower the resistance to N+1 and thus will drive three shape factors accordingly (slope, plateau, partial). The promoters of N+1 may also choose to ally with future new entrants betting on N+2 as a way to secure a path into their future. This opens two strategic options for the alliance: (1) entering on both N+1 and then N+2 in sequence; or (2) leapfrogging directly to N+2. A first, entry via N+1 may be relevant to build market knowledge, client intimacy and a reference base, while sensing user needs concretely. If N+1 was to fall short of expectations, there would be a second chance to leverage the new knowledge for N+2. However, that first strategic option would mean sending to the market a signal of anticipated failure on N+1. Skipping N+1 and accelerating on N+2 may sound a risky strategy but could spare important resources and help reduce lead times, while clearly indicating that the alliance no longer believes in N+1, thus sending a strong signal to the market: wait for N+2.

In other words, N+1 allying with N+2 would internalize the possibility of running for both, thus giving a chance to N+1, while preparing for N+2, hence openly betting in advance on the downturn of N+1. Leapfrogging to N+2 without N+1 would be reinforcing the resistance to N+1 and accelerating the downturn on the right side of the N+1 time path.

The above analysis listed various forces at work behind the patterns. They relate to the two variables and four shape factors identified as drivers of the patterns (Tab. 3). This contributes to identify early signals to be followed with care (announcements, alliance formation, timing of entry, discontinued options, etc.). In turn, these can help sense when, how and to what extent the time path for N+1 could depart from the S-shaped curve. Such careful analysis can offer room for agile strategies, anticipating the timing, speed and form of ongoing or potential future substitutions.

Tab. 3: Underlying forces behind the two variables and four shape factors.

Underlying forces driving the variables and shape factors	Resistance to N+1	slope	plateau	partial height	timing of next disruption	downturn (N+1)
market acceptance and interest — technological performance & utility per price (N+1 vs N)	support to N+1	steep	always possible	always possible		
referencing, bringing reassurance	support to N+1	steep	always possible	always possible		
chasm	roadblock against N+1	flater	likely	possible		
Incumbents — Improve N	against N+1	flatish	possible	possible		
Hybridize N with N+1	against N+1	flatish	possible	possible		
call upon client loyalty	against N+1	flatish	possible	possible		
develop own version of N+1 (signal N is likely to lose)	support to N+1	moderate	doubtful	doubtful		
Partner with/ acquire promoter of N+1 (signal N is to likely to lose)	Support to N+1	moderate	doubtful	doubtful		
Strategic moves by firms in the arena or potential entrants — develop and/or pre-announce N+2	induce doubts on N+1	flatish	possible	possible	squeeze on N+1	early
partner with/ acquire promoter of N+2	induce doubts on N+1	flatish	possible	possible	squeeze on N+1	early
Promoters of N+1 — invest heavily (sales and technical customization)	Support to N+1	steep	unlikely	unlikely		
Follow Moore's techniques to cross the chasm	Support to N+1	steep	unlikely	unlikely		
partner with/ acquire incumbent (thus accessing market knowledge) — sequence: defending N then N+1	reasonably favorable to N+1	moderate	uncertain	uncertain		
going for N+1 only (trust in N+1: blindness or vision?)	a bet, favorable to N+1	possibly steep	doubtful	doubtful	possibly early	possibly early
partner with/ acquire promoter of N+2	uncertain	uncertain	uncertain	uncertain	possibly early	possibly early
Promoters of N+2 — Accelerate development of N+2	induce doubts on N+1	flatish	always possible	always possible	squeeze on N+1	early
early announcement of N+2 arrival	induce doubts on N+1	flatish	always possible	always possible	squeeze on N+1	early
partner with/ acquire incumbent (thus accessing market knowledge) — sequence defending N then N+1	reasonably favorable to N+1	moderate	uncertain	uncertain	no squeeze	early
leapfrogging to N+2	induce doubts on N+1	flatish	always possible	always possible	squeeze on N+1	in due time
partner with/ acquire promoter of N+1 — sequence: promoting N+1, then N+2	induce trust on N+1	steep	unlikely	unlikely	no squeeze	in due time
leapfrogging to N+2	induce doubts on N+1	flatish	possible	possible	squeeze on N+1	very early
External pressures against N or N+1 or N+2 — regulatory ban, consumerism, societal opposition, environmental concerns — against N	opens the floor for N+1	Steep	very unlikely	very unlikely	abort early	abort early
against N+1	roadblock against N+1	flat	just a burst	just a burst	abort early	late
against N+2	likely favorable to N+1	moderate/steep	always possible	always possible	always possible	late

Yet, even with more insight into the underlying drivers behind the time dynamics of substitution, uncertainty about future developments and market acceptance will unavoidably remain high, thus advocating for more foresight thinking rather than a forecasting stance. Periods of uncertainty call for strategy.

This calls for the systematic assessment of a variety of scenarios, enhancement of strategic and organizational flexibility and reactivity, and agility to shift to other options. This also calls for a specific look at what technological substitution disrupts, namely organizational competence. I will argue that strategizing technology and technological change can be best addressed by adopting a competence perspective. This is what Part III is about.

Summary of Key Points of Part II

(1) In the realm of technological evolution, technological substitutions are where the action is. Significant technological innovations represent business situations with plenty of room for strategy. Technological substitutions are strategic opportunities to recompose the competitive dynamics in business arenas. By technological substitution I mean radical and micro-radical innovations in the sense defined in Part I (Tab. 1-A).

(2) Part I was about representing technological innovation and its strategic consequences in a given industry. A framework was developed and presented. In this context, Part II focused on technological substitution because this book is about using technology strategically: technological substitutions are typical moments when strategy can make a difference. Part II developed an add-on framework to represent technological substitutions beyond the traditional S-curve. In that sense, Part II offers an addendum to the framework presented in Part I. Overall, this addendum provides a conceptual structure to think about radical technological substitutions strategically.

(3) Ten substitutions patterns were observed, named and described. These stem from the management academic literature and from Brice Dattée's doctoral work.
    Those ten patterns are in fact inter-related. They are variations around the base case and the concatenation that correspond to the S-curve model and a sequence of S-curves respectively.

(4) The ten patterns can be used as building blocks to recompose more complex trajectories. I further argue that many, if not most, trajectories can in fact be decomposed into these building blocks. Time will tell whether the ten patterns carry with them some form of genericity or not.

(5) Two variables (resistance to N+1 and timing of next disruption) driving four shape factors (slope, plateau, partial and downturn) account for the variety of patterns observed.
    Three of the shape factors (slope, plateau, partial) stem from the first variable, resistance to N+1, affecting the left-hand side of the N+1 time path, while the fourth factor (downturn) stems from the second variable, timing of next disruption, affecting the right-hand side of the curve.
    In short, technological substitutions can depart from the traditional S-curve representation due to the resistance to N+1 and/or the intrusion of N+2 before N+1 had time to fully win over N.
    The two variables (resistance to N+1, timing of next disruption) and the four shape factors (slope, plateau, partial, downturn) – respectively meaning: How fast? With a delay along the way? To what extent? For how long once dominance is reached? – provide descriptive analytical tools to capture the variety of time path identified in the ten patterns

https://doi.org/10.1515/9783111397979-020

(6) A mapping of the ten patterns illustrates a continuum captured by the two variables and the corresponding four shape factors. This illustrates how the patterns are variations of the base case (S-curve).

(7) At some points along the time path of a technological substitution, the dynamics may lead to sudden bifurcations in the trajectory, with shifts from one pattern to another. These are typical situations where the dynamics of change in a techno-socio-economic-political system may bifurcate. These specific situations can be viewed as bifurcation windows during which the dynamics can bifurcate into another pattern with significantly different strategic consequences. The proposition is as follows: *as the techno-socio-economic-political system in which the technological substitution takes place enters a bifurcation window, it reaches an unstable state that makes it more likely for the trajectory to suddenly respond to a trigger relay that may appear, thus shifting away from the dynamics that prevailed so far, leaving a pattern for another.* A bifurcation window can be characterized by a set of factors, as discussed in Chapter 14.

(8) There are underlying forces at work behind the patterns. These relate to:
 – market acceptance of, and interest in, the new technology (N+1),
    Technological performance and utility per price (N+1 vs. N)
    market heterogeneity that creates a chasm,
 – strategic moves by firms in the arena or potential new entrants
    Incumbents, promoters of N+1 or N+2: developing or improving technologies, entering alliances, making announcements
 – External pressures (regulatory, environmental, societal) against N, N+1 or N+2

(9) All in all, the ten patterns, the two variables and the four shape factors, the mapping of patterns, the bifurcation windows and the underlying forces (demand side, strategic moves on the supply side, external forces) provide a richer descriptive framework of technological substitutions than the traditional S-curve representation. In a way they provide a grammar for representing technological substitutions.

(10) Technological substitution disrupts organizational competence. I argue that strategizing technology and technological change can be best addressed by adopting a competence perspective. This is what Part III is about.

References for Part II and Further Reading

Abernathy, W. J., & Utterback, J. M. (1978). Patterns of industrial innovation. *Technology Review*, *80*(7), 40–47.

Anderson, P. & Tushman, M. L. (1990). Technological discontinuities and dominant design: A cyclical model of technological change. *Administrative Science Quarterly*, *35*(4), 604–633.

Blackman, A. W. (1974). Market dynamics of substitutions. *Technological Forecasting and Social Change*, Vol 6, 41–63.

Bohlen, J. M., Beal, G. M. (1957). The diffusion process. Special Report. (Agriculture Extension Service, Iowa State College) vol. 1, No. 18. : 56–77.

Burgelman, R. A., & Grove, A. S. (2007). Let chaos reign, then rein in chaos – repeatedly: Managing strategic dynamics for corporate longevity. *Strategic Management Journal*, *28*(10), 965–979.

Dattée, B. (2006) The dynamics of technological substitutions and successful innovations. University College Dublin and Ecole Centrale Paris, joint PhD thesis.

Dattée, B., & Durand, T. (2009). Patterns of technological substitutions. Working paper, S&T, Ecole Centrale Paris.

Dattée, B., & Durand, T. (2023). Technological substitutions: Emergence challenges and subsequent battles. Working paper, Cnam, Paris.

Dupuy, J.-P. (2000). Philosophical foundations of a new concept of equilibrium in the social sciences: Projected equilibrium. *Philisophical Studies*, *100*(3), 323–345.

Fisher, J. C., & Pry, R. H. (1971). A simple substitution model of technological change. *Technological Forecasting and Social Change*, *3*, 75–88.

Foucault, M. (1966). *Les mots et les choses: Une archéologie des sciences humaines*. Gallimard.

Geroski, P. A. (2000). Models of technology diffusion. *Research Policy 29*(4–5), 603–625.

Henderson, R. M. (1995). Of life cycles real and imaginary: The unexpectedly long old age of optical lithography. Research Policy, 24 (4) 631–643.

Maguire, S. (2003). The co-evolution of technology and discourse: A study of substitution processes for insecticides DDT. *Organization Studies*, *25*(1), 113–134.

Mahajan, V., & E. Muller (1996). Timing, diffusion, and substitution of successive generations of technological innovations: The IBM mainframe case. *Technological Forecasting and Social Change 51*(2), 109–132.

Moore, G. A. (2002). *Crossing the Chasm: Marketing and Selling High-Tech Products to Mainstream Customers*. New York, HarperCollins.

Norton, J. A., & Bass, F. M. (1987). A diffusion theory model of adoption and substitution for successive generations of high-technology products. *Management Science*, *33*(9), 1069–1086.

Pasquet, N. (2002). Pour une compréhension complexe des processus de bifurcation technologique: le temps-devenir : Le cas de l'énergie solaire photovoltaique. PhD thesis, Laboratoire Strategie & Technologie, Ecole Centrale Paris.

Rogers, E. M. (1983). *Diffusion of Innovations* (3rd ed.). or (2003) (5th ed.). New York, The Free Press.

Rosenberg, N. (1976). On technological expectations. *The Economic Journal*, *86*(34), 523–535.

Sainsbury David (2020) "Windows of opportunity - How Nations create wealth", Profile Books, London.

Snow, D. C. (2008). Extraordinary efficiency growth in response to new technology entry: The carburetor's "last gasp". Working Paper #1668643, Harvard Business School.

Sohn, S. Y., & Ahn, B. J. (2003). Multigeneration diffusion model for economic assessment of new technology. *Technological Forecasting and Social Change*, *70*(3), 251–264.

Suarez, F. F., Utterback, J. M., Von Gruben, P., & Kang, H. Y. (2018). The hybrid trap: Why most efforts to bridge old and new technology miss the mark. *MIT Sloan Management Review*, *59*(3), 52–57.

Sull, D. N. (1999). The dynamics of standing still: Firestone Tire & Rubber and the radial revolution. *Business History Review*, *73*(3), 430–464.

https://doi.org/10.1515/9783111397979-021

Tripsas, M. (1997). Unravelling the process of creative destruction: Complementary assets and incumbent survival in the typesetter industry. *Strategic Management Journal 18*(Summer Special Issue), 119–142.

Utterback, J. M. (1994). *Mastering the Dynamics of Innovation*. Boston, MA, Harvard Business School Press.

Further Reading

Adner, R. (2002). When are technologies disruptive? A demand-based view of the emergence of competition. *Strategic Management Journal, 23*(8), 667–688.

Adner, R., & Kapoor, R. (2010). Value creation in innovation ecosystems: How the structure of technological interdependence affects firm performance in new technology generations. *Strategic Management Journal, 31*(3), 306–333.

Adner, R., & Kapoor, R. (2016). Innovation ecosystems and the pace of substitution: Re-examining technology S-curves. *Strategic Management Journal, 37*(4), 625–648.

Adner, R., & Snow, D. (2010). Old technology responses to new technology threats: Demand heterogeneity and technology retreats. *Industrial and Corporate Change, 19*(5), 1655–1675.

Bass, F. M. (1969). A new product growth model for consumer durables. *Management Science, 15*(5) 215–227. Theory Series (January 1969).

Bhargava, S. C. (1995). A general form of the Fisher-Pry model of technology substitution. *Technology Forecasting and Social Change, 49*(1), 27–33.

Bijker, W., & Law, J. (Eds.). (1994). *Shaping Technology/Building Society: Studies in Sociotechnical Change*. Cambridge, MA, The MIT Press.

Butler, J. E. (1988). Theories of technological innovation as useful tools for corporate strategy. *Strategic Management Journal, 9*(1), 15–29.

Carnes, C. M., Hitt, M. A., Sirmon, D. G., Chirico, F., & Huh, D. W. (2022). Leveraging resources for innovation: The role of synchronization. *Journal of Product Innovation Management, 39*(2), 160–176.

Chandrasekaran, D., Tellis, G. J., & James, G. M. (2022). Leapfrogging, cannibalization, and survival during disruptive technological change: The critical role of rate of disengagement. *Journal of Marketing 86*(1), 149–166. https://doi.org/10.1177/0022242920967912

Christensen, C. M. (1992). Exploring the limits of the technology S-curve. Part I: Component technologies. *Production and Operations Management, 1*(4), 334–357.

Christensen, C. M. (1992). Exploring the limits of the technology S-curve. Part II: Architectural technologies. *Production and Operations Management, 1*(4), 358–366.

Christensen, C. M., & Rosenbloom, R. S. (1995). Explaining the attacker's advantage: Technological paradigms, organizational dynamics, and the value network. *Research Policy, 24*(2), 233–257. https://doi.org/10.1016/0048-7333(93)00764-K

Christensen, C. M. (1997). *The Innovator's Dilemma*. Harvard Business Review Press.

Christensen, C. M, Suarez, F. F., & Utterback, J. M. (1998). Strategies for survival in fast-changing industries. *Management Science, 44*(12), S207–S220.

Christensen, C. M., & Overdorf, M. (2000). Meeting the challenge of disruptive change. *Harvard Business Review*, March-April: 67–76.

Christensen, C. M. (2006). The ongoing process of building a theory of disruption. *Journal of Product Innovation Management, 23*(1), 39–55.

Cooper, A. C., & Schendel, D. (1976). Strategic responses to technological threats. *Business Horizons, 16*(1), 61–69.

Dattée, B. (2007). Appropriability, proximity, routines and innovation. Challenging the S-curve: patterns of technological substitution. DRUID Summer Conference, Copenhagen, CBS, Denmark, June 18, 2007.

Dattée, B., & Weil, H. B. (2007). Dynamics of social factors in technological substitutions. *Technological Forecasting and Social Change, 74*(5), 579–607. https://doi.org/10.1016/j.techfore.2007.03.003

Dattée, B. (2017). Convex drops in technological substitutions. *Journal of Engineering and Technology Management, 45*: 54–73. http://www.sciencedirect.com/science/article/pii/S0923474817301741

Dosi, G. (1982). Technological paradigms and technological trajectories: A suggested interpretation of the determinants and directions of technical change. *Research Policy, 11*, 147–162.

Durand, T. (1992). Dual technological trees: Assessing the intensity and strategic significance of technological change. *Research Policy, 21*, 361–380.

Finkelstein, S., & Sanford, S. (2000). Learning from corporate mistakes: The rise and fall of Iridium. *Organizational Dynamics, 29*(2), 138–148.

Foster, R. (1986). *Innovation: The Attacker's Advantage*. New York, Summit Books.

Furr, N. R., & Snow, D. C. (2015). Intergenerational hybrids: Spillbacks, spillforwards, and adapting to technology discontinuities. *Organization Science, 26*(2), 475–493.

Gort, M., & Klepper, S. (1982). Time paths in the diffusion of product innovations. *The Economic Journal* 92(367), 1 September 1982.

Greve, H. R., & Seidel, M. D. L. (2015). The thin red line between success and failure: Path dependence in the diffusion of innovative production technologies. *Strategic Management Journal, 36*(4), 475–496.

Henderson, R., & Clark, K. B. (1990). Architectural innovation: The reconfiguration of existing product technologies and the failure of established firms. *Administrative Science Quarterly, 35*(1), 9–30.

Hitt, M. A., Arregle, J. L., & Holmes, R. M. Jr. (2021). Strategic management theory in a post-pandemic and non-ergodic world. *Journal of Management Studies, 58*(1), 259–264.

Itami, H., & Numagami, T. (1992). Dynamic interaction between strategy and technology. *Strategic Management Journal, 13*(S2), 119–135.

Klepper, S. (1996). Entry, exit, growth and innovation over the product life cycle. *The American Economic Review, 86*(3), 56–583.

Klepper, S. (1997). Industry life cycle. *Industrial and Corporate Change, 6*(1), 145–181.

Kogut, B., & Ragin, C. (2006). Exploring complexity when diversity is limited: institutional complementarity in theories of rule of law and national systems revisited. *European Management Review, 3*(1), 44–59.

Linstone, H. A., & Sahal, D., (Eds.) (1976). *Technological Substitution: Forecasting Techniques and Applications*. New York, Elsevier.

Loveridge, R., & Pitt, M. (Eds.) (1990). *The Strategic Management of Technological Innovation*. New York, Wiley.

Martino, J. P. (1993). *Technological Forecasting for Decision Making* (3rd ed.). New York, McGraw-Hill.

Nightingale, P., von Tunzelmann, N., Malerba, F., & Metcalfe, S. (2008). Technological paradigms: Past, present and future. *Industrial and Corporate Change, 17*(3), 467–484.

Palacios Fenech, J., & Tellis, G. J. (2016). Dive and disruption. *Journal of Product Innovation and Management, 33*(1), 53–68.

Paladino, A. (2008). Analyzing the effects of market and resource orientations on innovative outcomes in times of turbulence. *Journal of Product Innovation Management, 25*(6), 577–592.

Panwar, S., Kapur, P. K., & Singh, O. (2019). Modeling technological substitution by incorporating dynamic adoption rate. *International Journal of Innovation and Technology Management, 16*(1). https://doi.org/10.1142/S021987701950010X

Sahal, D. (1981). *Patterns of Technological Innovation*. Reading, MA, Addison-Wesley Publishing Company.

Sood, A., & Tellis, G. J. (2005). Technological evolution and radical innovation. *Journal of Marketing, 69*(3), 152–168. https://doi.org/10.1509/jmkg.69.3.152.66361

Stoneman, P. (2001). *The Economics of Technological Diffusion*. Wiley-Blackwell.

Suarez, F. F., Grodal, S., & Gotsopoulos, A. (2015). Perfect timing? Dominant category, dominant design, and the window of opportunity for firm entry. *Strategic Management Journal, 36*(3), 437–448.

Tellis, G. J. (2006). Disruptive technology or visionary leadership? *Journal of Product Innovation and Management, 23*(1), 34–38.

Tidd, J. (2023). *Radical Innovation*. Edward Elgar.

Thomas, L. D. W., & Tee, R. (2022). Generativity: A systematic review and conceptual framework. *International Journal of Management Review, 24*(2), 255–278.

Tripsas, M. (2008). Customer preference discontinuities: A trigger for radical technological change. *Managerial and Decision Economics, 29*(2–3), 79–97.

Vīgants, E., Blumberga, A., Timma, L., Ījabs, I., & Blumberga, D. (2016). The dynamics of technological substitution: The case of eco-innovation diffusion of surface cleaning products. *Journal of Cleaner Production*, 132, 279–288. https://doi.org/10.1016/j.jclepro.2015.10.007

Zahra, S. A., & Covin, J. G. (1993). Business strategy, technology policy and firm performance. *Strategic Management Journal, 14*(6), 451–478.

Part III: **Strategizing Technological Change via the Competence Perspective**

Introduction

In Part I, I built a framework representing how technology evolves over time and its strategic consequences. In Part II, I complemented this framework with a focus on technological substitutions and patterns that depart from the S-curve. This "add-on" offers some form of a grammar of technological substitutions beyond the overemphasized, and arguably inadequate, S-curve representation.

In this context, Part III is focused on the competence perspective to think about technological change strategically. As technology forecasting is a risky exercise, I argue instead that a relevant way to think about technological change strategically is to call upon the concept of organizational competence.

By organizational competence I mean the competence of an organization. This is not just about the talents of individuals. It also includes what the teams and the overall organization are capable of doing collectively. This means that the organization is clearly more than the sum of the individuals working within. This is in line with the definition of management as leading collective organized action to achieve desirable outcome and performance.

The Competence Perspective in Strategic Management

The 1980s saw Porter's school of positioning dominate the thinking in business strategy. The key idea was that the position of your offerings against those of your competitors in terms of cost or differentiation (which, with niches, formed the generic strategies) would drive your performance. This ignored the firms' endowments in key resources and competence. Wernerfelt (soon followed by Barney and several others) argued that a firm well endowed with the required resources in a given competitive arena was likely to perform better than those poorly equipped. That made a lot of sense but was somehow ignored until Prahalad and Hamel repackaged the argument in a language fit to practitioners. In that sense, the 1980s turned out to illustrate a situation of scientific blindness where authors departing from an established paradigm (the Porterian positioning school) had a hard time to publish their alternate views.

This led to three parallel, complementary and somewhat overlapped streams, though at times dissonant. One is the resource-based view (RBV) of strategy put forward by a group of scholars who in the wake of Wernerfelt brought in their vocabulary drawn from economics. They kept the word "resources", suggesting that organizational competence was part of it. Yet, the use of the word resources conveyed the idea that these could be acquired on the market as long as you paid the price. RBV further called upon Edith Penrose, who stands today as the grandmother of this stream. Teece was probably the first author to connect the dots, pointing to this ascendency.

https://doi.org/10.1515/9783111397979-022

A second stream followed, using the wording "core competencies" adopted by Prahalad and Hamel. In a way, this suggested to rethink strategy in terms of competence rather than for strategic business units (SBUs). The firm was no longer seen as a set of SBUs but appeared as a portfolio of competence. The firm was no longer seen as primarily allocating resources among SBUs. Instead, the firm was seen as developing, maintaining and redeploying a range of competencies through a variety of learning taking place in an array of businesses.[27] This led to a massive interest in organizational learning, as learning (seen as some sort of a flux) was found easier to observe than competence (seen as some sort of a stock). While the first stream kept the flavor of economics, this second stream was closer to management with interest in built-in organizational capabilities (via learning) that would make the difference. In this stream, more qualitative pieces of competence such as organizational processes or culture are typically part of the competence base of organizations. (Obviously, unlike resources and physical assets, a culture or a process are not easily tradable on the market.) Yet, the resources and physical assets are included in this stream via the idea of coordinated deployment of assets and resources. In this sense, the coordinated deployment designates the organizational competence, while resources and assets that are tradable on markets are essentially ingredients whose endowment is not likely to be as strategic.

A third stream, after Teece et al., pointed out the importance of dynamic capabilities. Again, the vocabulary is different, but "capability" is a term that mirrors the word "competence" of the second stream. Still, the concept of dynamic capabilities adds an important point. The idea is that competence both habilitates and constrains. Organizational competence builds up over time through learning. In turn, the installed competence base operates as a filter or bias that permits some learning to take place as long as the resulting new competence is aligned with the existing base. In contrast, new learnings that depart from the existing competence base tend to be rejected. Let me recall the rail track metaphor here once again. The competence base operates as some form of railroad tracks. As long as the energy drives you in the direction of the tracks, things can roll. However, when technological change requires some significant new direction, the track operates like a constraint that prevents the organization from coping with the change. In this context, Teece argues that firms need capabilities to extricate themselves from the existing tracks. Typically, the moon turns around the Earth because the force of gravity exactly compensates for the centrifugal force stemming from it turning around the Earth. For the moon to escape from that trap, the only way would be an additional force that would pull it out. This is what dynamic capabilities capture. This point is essential in my discussion about strategizing when facing technological change. This is why Teece's contribution is so important.

---

27 Hereafter, I use "competencies" for bits (or sub-parts) of competence.

The key argument in this Part III has to do with a simple though powerful idea: what technological change affects is the organizational competence of incumbents. Hence, I argue that the strategic consequences of technological change should be looked at from the competence perspective. In what sense and to what extent will the competence base of incumbents be rendered obsolete or reinforced by the expected change? In what sense and to what extent will new entrants be well fit (at least better than incumbents) to the requirements of the new technology (N+1) about to substitute for the previously dominant technology (N)?

This will lead to assessing the gap between the firm's portfolio of competence and the portfolio of competence required by the future dominant technology. I will call it the competence gap.

This definition of the competence gap implies that it is firm-specific.

In turn, this needs to be done for the competitors and potential new entrants as well. Concretely, which competitors or new entrants may be better positioned with a portfolio of competence in better fit with the requirements of the new technology? In other words, when facing change, I suggest measuring the firm's competence gap relative to competitors'. Obviously, the competence gap depends upon how the change will shape (typically which new technology N+1 may substitute for the current technology N). Hence the competence gap varies according to both the firm's competence base before the change and the form that change may take (thus the new competence base needed).

Abernathy and Clark introduced the concept of transilience to capture a similar idea. They made up the word transilience from the combination of two words: transition and resilience. They view transilience as the capacity of an innovation to transform the competence base needed of a firm after the change (seen from both the technology, production and operations side, and the marketing and relation to the user side). To what extent will an entity be poorly (vs. well) positioned to survive the transition to the new? New entrants are likely to benefit from a significantly different portfolio of competence required by technology N+1, after the change, compared to the one prevailing for technology N – that is, before the change. This is particularly so for those new entrants that have been long preparing for the new technology. Otherwise, low or unsignificant renewal of the competence base is likely to benefit incumbents.

This leads to the idea of buying insurance (through competence) against technological uncertainty in the future.

While, as of 1980, it was difficult for Kodak to assess the form and probability of success of digital images, it would have been very relevant for that powerful multinational corporation to consider the option of recruiting a team of engineers and scientist in electronics and exploring the potential ways to build a competence base for digital photography, just in case that technology would win in the end.

Chapter 19 will be about buying insurance against the uncertainties (and indetermination, although this is in fact difficult – see the discussion of boundary objects in that chapter) around future technologies.

The Line of Reasoning

To anticipate the strategic consequences of technological change, I suggest assessing the intensity of change via the competence perspective. The more significant the change in competence needed, the higher the strategic turmoil in the competitive arena.

Technological change → Change in competence needed → Strategic consequences
("transilience")   (from "business as usual" to
                             "turmoil")

This suggests building a metric of the intensity of innovation based on the concept of competence. To do so, I suggest to analytically assess the share of the firm's competence base that is going to be disrupted (or reinforced) by the change and to what extent. This amounts to assessing the transilience, literally a firm's vulnerability (and conversely its potential of resilience) through the transition from technology N to N+1. In other words, I argue that what is needed is an assessment of the gap between the existing competence portfolio of the firm and the newly required set of competencies, given the new technology, what I call the "competence gap".

Yet, this line of reasoning raises a key question: What exactly is competence? I thus first need to clarify the concept of competence. This is what Chapters 16 to 18 of this Part III are about.

I start by discussing a variety of dimensions of competence in Chapter 16 before turning to learning, competence building and competence leveraging in Chapter 17. This will lead to presenting a referential for competence in Chapter 18. On that basis, I will discuss how to use the concept of competence to think about technology strategically in Chapter 19.

Chapter 16
Dimensions of Competence

There are many different distinctions around the concept of organizational competence.[28] Some of these relate more specifically to knowledge and know-how, others to resources or assets. I list them here as if they all were applicable to competencies in the broad, generic sense of the word. Only later will it be possible to limit and specify the concept of competence more clearly. Also note that the word "capabilities" may be used for competence as well. In this book, I tend to restrict the word "capability" to the concept of dynamic capabilities that I already discussed in the introduction of Part III under the sub-heading "The competence perspective in strategic management".

Classic Distinctions

The **tacit/articulated** distinction has been frequently recognized as important. Organizational learning or technology are known to be at least partly tacit, i.e., embedded in the routines and informal processes of the organization.

This distinction can be challenged. Knowledge (and at least part of what I call competence) can only be transmitted, recognized and thus evaluated through interaction. Thus, the cognitive limits of both the speaker and listener (the enunciation, the language, the attention paid, the message received and understood given the existing knowledge base of the listener, etc.) will inevitably lead to a distorted recognition of the knowledge. In that sense, knowledge is thus necessarily tacit, at least to a certain extent.

Similarly, the **individual/collective** duality of competence remains as one of the main epistemic challenges of management. From a collective viewpoint, the system is more than the sum of its parts. Adding the individual talents does not permit to grasp the collective competence.

Hedlund and Nonaka combined these two dimensions (tacit/explicit, individual/collective) to discuss the comparative dynamics of knowledge management in typical Japanese vs. Western firms. They identify several key processes, including articulation vs. internalization as well as appropriation vs. extension of knowledge. They suggest that a good way of protecting competence may actually be to have the individual members of an organization keep it as tacit as possible. This is indeed embeddedness (in individuals).

The **cognitive** vs. **behavioral** dimension of competence has been paid less attention, or in my opinion not as much as it should have. The field of management seems

---

28 Chapters 16 to 18 draw from Durand (1997a).

https://doi.org/10.1515/9783111397979-023

to have been more preoccupied with cognitive capabilities like knowledge, skills, patents or technologies than with individual or group behavior or the culture or identity of an organization. At times, the difference has even been ignored when the word "cognitive" happened to be used to include behavioral traits of an organization.

I argue that firms may benefit from their corporate identity acting as an engine for change while in other cases the existing culture may represent a significant inertia, hindering adaptation and creative strategic moves. This has to do with the issue of unlearning, which I discuss later, in relation to dynamic capabilities.

The **positive/negative** duality suggests that competence may be not only positive as an asset but also negative in the form of incompetence. When a firm suffers from a counterproductive capability deeply rooted in its organization, this should be regarded as incompetence. Although some argue that one should not try to qualify and evaluate competence as positive or negative, I argue for the opposite view. Assessing the value of the firm's portfolio of competence is useful. This needs to be done in context. Typically, for this book about technology strategies, one needs to look at the fit or misfit of the portfolio of competence with respect to the current dominant technology N as well as N+1 and even N+2.

More classically found is the **tangible/intangible** distinction. Indeed, in the very broad sense of the concept of competence, tangible assets such as equipment, buildings and products and intangible assets like brand names serve as ingredients to the firm's competence base, while more intangible elements such as organizational processes or culture contribute to the core of competence. In this sense, I do not view the firm as a nexus of contracts, thus supporting Teece et al. on that matter.

Sanchez, Heene and Thomas very rightly suggest adding a **coordinated deployment function** to the **assets and resources** categories. Along the same line, I argue that a football team is more than a set of skilled players, a dish is more than a set of ingredients. I call it "organizational alchemy". Management is precisely about organizing processes to make things happen, leveraging assets and resources and building new capabilities.

I thus suggest that the strategic essence of competence is to be looked for in this intangible organizational alchemy which cannot be easily imitated. Porter indeed argued that any tangible resource can be identified, described and thus imitated or acquired. The non-imitability criteria put forward by Prahalad and Hamel or Barney thus requires intangibility and difficulty to explain how it works. This is where, I suggest, we need to look for the strategic content of competence. In this book on technological change, when adopting a competence perspective, I argue that one needs to pay very special attention to this organizational alchemy.

There is another interesting debate about the nature of competence. Can a firm, performing well on some markets thanks to specific core competencies, be called competent for some other markets which it never tried to enter so far but where the same competencies could be valorized?

This actually relates to two possible distinctions: the **intended** vs. **contingent** and **demonstrated** vs. **potential** dualities.

Is it being competent to be lucky? The question is conveyed by a classic illustration. Think of a household buying a piece of land to have a house built and finding a geothermal source in the ground on that lot. Would you say that this family built a competitive advantage in energy? Obviously no, except they were lucky enough to tap a source of economic rent.

The rent may not have been created or tapped intentionally and may be purely contingent. Some argue that a competitive advantage is supposed to come from an intended, proactive strategy.

I challenge this view. I feel that the bottom line remains performance, wherever it originally came from. Luck may have played a role or not. An asset or a capability, if exploited, makes the firm more competent than those who do not hold this element of competence. If the family does not exploit the geothermal source, ignoring the asset, this means no rent. If they do, they benefit from a lucky move and indeed do better economically than their neighbors with no such cheap source of energy. In my view, contingency may thus be part of the competence game. This relates to the path dependence concept of industrial economics. History clearly matters as experience shaped up competence which was built through various learnings along the way. Luck may thus have played a significant role in the historical competence building. Technology N+1 may require competence that was built by some of the players in the field through past experience.

Along similar lines but with a slightly different perspective, one may distinguish the set of **demonstrated** capabilities from those which are **potential** or latent. Is your firm really competent if it holds core competencies which you claim could be used to develop new products/services for markets totally new to your firm? There is often more than a giant step from potentiality to reality. This point was clearly covered by Abernathy and Clark as their transilience map explicitly combines both the technology side and market linkages. Could your firm be regarded as competent as a company already fully established on these new markets with resources and capabilities already bundled into effective products and services? Arguably no.

> Electric utilities have a real potential in telecoms. Indeed, both business areas may be seen as a matter of cable connections and transmission. Yet those that did not enter the telecom market yet are likely to be less competent than existing telcos, e.g., in internet protocol, radio transmission and digital technologies, not to speak about customer intimacy regarding services and access to online contents.

All in all, these various dimensions help characterize what competence is about. From these I suggest a preliminary typology of competence, on Tab. 4.

This classification has at least one merit: it helps root a theoretical discussion into the ground of reality and thus may contribute to keep any further conceptualizing exercise from drifting too far away from managerial concerns.

Tab. 4: Candidate categories of competence.

Competence	
Stand-alone assets *Tangible and intangible*	Equipment, building, product, software, brand name, etc.
Cognitive capabilities *individual and collective,* *explicit and tacit*	Knowledge, know-how skills, technologies, patents, etc.
Organizational processes and routines	Coordinating mechanisms in the organization, combining individual actions into collective functioning
Organizational structure *May facilitate or hinder the ability of a firm* *to adapt to certain changes*	The structural design of the organization and its linkages to the environment (suppliers, clients, etc.)
Identity *May facilitate or hinder the ability of a firm* *to adapt to certain changes*	Behavioral and cultural characteristics of the firm. Shared values, beliefs, rites and taboos are constituents of identity

A key point should be stressed here: a clear distinction is made between (a) assets and resources of the firm and (b) individual and organizational capabilities, knowledge, processes, routines and culture. In other words, on one hand there are ingredients – tangible and intangible – which can be acquired and exchanged with basically no need for human resource transfers. These may be called non-social assets and resources.

On the other hand, there is what I regard as the organizational alchemy, i.e., intangible, difficult-to-buy and difficult-to-imitate capabilities. These clearly relate to the "integrated coordinated deployment of resources and assets" – meaning, in short, competence as management processes in the organization. I shall use this point as a building block of the model for competence in Chapter 18, extending this idea to include other elements as discussed below.

"Operations" should not be left apart. I suggest considering operations as management processes which indeed contribute to the overall set of processes performing the coordinated deployment of assets and capabilities.

I further argue that it should be relevant to extend this coordinated deployment function to strategy and culture as well.

Indeed, internal strategic alignment or policy deployment aims at sharing a strategic overall vision within the firm and bringing it down to clear and meaningful orientations for single components or members of the organization.

This echoes the polarization of particles in physics, e.g., photons in a laser beam.

In this sense, a strategic vision when shared throughout the layers of the firm contributes to the coordinated deployment of assets and capabilities, including the energy and commitment of the human resources. I shall come back to this in Chapter 18 when discussing will and motivation as key elements of competence.

Also note that this point may be extended even further to include the identity or the culture as a cement or a glue holding the organization together, thus as an element of the organizational alchemy of competence as I chose to call it.

Chapter 17
Learning, Competence Building and Leveraging

The strategic management literature paid much more attention to learning than to competence. I believe that this results from the difficulty to grasp knowledge and competence ("I know that I don't know; I don't know what I know" etc.) while it seems easier to study learning mechanisms.

Learning can be looked at as a flux, while competence can be looked at as a cumulated stock. (This has been much debated, and still is. JC Spender argues against this flux/stock analogy, for epistemological reasons – the nature of what we can observe and what we know about learning and competence. Although I have sympathy for the theoretical argument, I still think such a metaphor is useful when *speaking* with practitioners.)

Learning

The literature classically identifies various forms of learning.

Arrow and Atkinson and Stiglitz pointed to **learning by doing** as action empirically helps building up know-how and knowledge. In turn, Rosenberg called **learning by using** the learning process which takes place when a client uses a new product and/or service, thus building up knowledge and know-how about using it.

This idea was extended through **learning by interacting.** The user-designer interaction again helps building up capabilities and thus improvement on both the product itself and how to use it.

Many other forms of learning mechanisms may be added here. Among these, I insist on two which will prove useful in Chapter 18. First comes **learning by learning**. The process of learning helps build an ability to learn and learn again.

> Teachers indeed know that the role of education is as much in helping individuals learn how to learn than in providing them with knowledge. The content of what is learnt may not be as important as the process of helping students build a capability to learn more later on their own.

Second, I insist on the paradox of **learning by unlearning**. This is an essential point as, too often, individuals as well as organizations are stuck with routines and habits which put them in a difficult situation when change is needed. Paradoxically one may argue that the most difficult part of learning for the experienced ones is to unlearn what is now becoming obsolete and a factor of inertia. This is particularly true for the behavioral and cultural side of competence. This is typically what the dynamic capabilities stream addresses.

Another classic perspective on learning relates to the **formal** teaching and training part vs. what one may call the **companionship** approach. Typically, articulated

https://doi.org/10.1515/9783111397979-024

knowledge can be taught and learnt in the classroom. Conversely, tacit know-how, by nature, cannot be transferred formally and needs some form of "do it with me" or "observe, imitate" as mechanisms relevant for competence transfer. This in part relates to the learning by doing mentioned above.

There is an additional important aspect of learning which will be needed in the model of Chapter 18. Piaget showed that children learn not only through formal teaching but also and simultaneously through sensory information stemming from action. Children thus build knowledge and know-how at the same time. In turn this means that (a) formal teaching and (b) action are two sides of a same coin. This is also pointed by Senge. I shall extend this idea further in Chapter 18, applying it to interaction and attitudes as well.

Stages of Competence

An additional and important element of competence building needs to be brought in before our attempt to integrate these different ingredients into a model for competence. I suggest that knowledge builds up as information is integrated and assimilated into frameworks which ensure coherence and structure to the accumulated knowledge base. Yet, information is not just data. Information is data which were acknowledged, sieved, transformed and adapted to fit into the pre-existing structure of knowledge. The psychology literature suggests that individuals tend to reject data which do not fit their previous knowledge, while they overemphasize data which reinforce their existing understanding and beliefs.

One may thus consider that, at the organizational level as well, data need to be enacted before they reach the status of information which can then be integrated as an element of knowledge.

At the other end of the spectrum, expertise should be regarded as a much higher step than knowledge. Not only does expertise relate to a significantly more advanced level of competence, it also requires an integrated combination of knowledge and know-how, thus assuming a "state-of-the-art ability" to understand, explain and even act within the domain of competence. In a way expertise transcends competence, through both (a) a quantic jump in the level of competence and (b) a recombination and merger of various elements of competence (e.g., knowledge and know-how).

In other words, I suggest that there is a sequence of stages from data and information to knowledge and expertise:

$$\text{Data} \xrightarrow{\text{enact}} \text{Information} \xrightarrow{\text{assimilate}} \text{Knowledge} \xrightarrow{\text{transcend}} \text{Expertise}$$

In Chapter 18, I shall extend this to other forms of competence than just knowledge (namely for know-how and attitudes).

This is also suggested by Tab. 5 where a list of terms is presented. These were already used in Chapter 16, but I now specify in what sense they relate to competence.

Tab. 5: Degrees of competence.

Data		I have access to external pieces of information
Information		I know, I have learnt, I found out
Knowledge		I have integrated frameworks of information and I can explain them to someone else
Skill		I can do it
Know-how		I know how to do it, I can do it and I can show how to do it to someone else
Competence		I am more able than others at explaining what to do and how to do it (knowledge) but also at doing it (know-how)
Expertise		I am an expert at doing it, as well as understanding what to do and explaining how to do it and why it works

More specifically, one should note that this list tends to mix two significantly different forms of competence, namely knowledge (as information) and know-how (as skill or practical capabilities). This thus reinforces the need to differentiate among at least two scales of increasing competence. At the same time the list helps better specify different degrees of competence, e.g., data, information, knowledge, expertise. This list, once adapted, will constitute another building block of the reconstruction of Chapter 18.

A Continuum of Competence Leveraging and Building

The competence-based theory pays a lot of attention to the question of competence building and leveraging. I suggest that there is more of a continuum than an opposition between these two strands of the management of a competence portfolio. Table 6 illustrates this point.

When stretching to adapt to new market requirements or to new technologies, the firm may pivot around existing competencies, among which are core competencies, thus leveraging its existing set of distinctive capabilities and assets, in turn reinforcing them ("reinforcement"). The firm may also have to build new competencies, either from internal sources within the organization (thanks to a "synergetic fit" with other profit centers) or from the outside ("networking access") on an inter-organizational mode. "Adaptability" refers to the ability of some companies to permanently learn, un-learn and relearn again. This in turn relates to Teece's idea of "dynamic capabilities".

Along similar lines, although from a different angle, it is also possible to identify degrees in the difficulty encountered by the firm adapting its portfolio of competence when faced with change. Table 7 presents an assessment of the width of competence

Tab. 6: A continuum of competence leveraging and building.

Accessing competence

	Holding			Accessing	
	Same competence required	Competence held elsewhere		Inter-organizational competence	Learning capability
	"Reinforcement"	*"Synergetic fit"*		*"Networking access"*	*"Adaptability"*
Leveraging	++++ Full leveraging	+++ Internal leveraging		++ External leveraging	+ Leveraging the unlearning and learning capabilities
Building		and adaptation +		absorption and rebuilding ++	and competence building +++

Static access to competence   *Dynamic access to competence*

gaps by looking at the combination of the resource and asset gaps and the organizational alchemy gap. I argue that it is likely to be significantly more difficult for the firm to build new competence than to access resources and assets (because the latter can be acquired via markets).

Tab. 7: Width of competence gaps.

Assets and resources

		Held	Not held
	Held	Minor adjustment (leveraging) 1	Minor gap (rebuilding the assets base) 2
Deployment capabilities	Not held	3 Significant gap (rebuilding deployment capabilities)	4 Major gap (full rebuilding)

Coming back to the issue of imitability, assets and resources may be identified and accessed while complex human and behavioral traits of the organization may be more difficult, not only to imitate but also to manage and transform.

My key point here is that competence that is likely to turn out to be strategic as the firm struggles through a technological substitution should be looked for in the "organizational alchemy" category.

Most of the items discussed in Chapters 16 and 17 are now going to be integrated and in a way extended into a model of organizational competence (Chapter 18). In turn, this will help think about technology strategically (Chapter 19).

Chapter 18
A Model of Organizational Competence

Three Generic Forms of Competence: Knowledge, Know-how and Attitudes

Following Pestallozzi who referred to "head, hand and heart", I suggest to borrow from research on education in the three key dimensions of individual learning: knowledge, know-how and attitudes (Fig. 37). Given the specific concern of Part III, I need to specify:

- what is meant by each of these dimensions of competence;
- the dynamic accumulation of competence through learning mechanisms;
- the interactions among these three interdependent dimensions;
- how managerial levers can affect and leverage the potential of competence described by these three dimensions.

Knowledge corresponds to the structured sets of assimilated information which make it possible to understand the world, obviously with partial and somewhat contradictory interpretations. Knowledge thus encompasses the access to data, the ability to enact them into acceptable information and to integrate them into pre-existing frames which evolve along the way, or by creating new ones.

Know-how relates to the ability to act in a concrete way according to predefined objectives or processes. Know-how does not exclude knowledge. Yet, know-how does not necessitate a full understanding of why the skills and capabilities, when put to operations, actually work. Know-how thus in part relates to empiricism and tacitness.

Attitudes are too often neglected in the resource-based view as well as in the competence-based theory of the firm. This may be due to the historical lack of interest of economists in behavioral and social aspects. (This has significantly changed in recent years.) I believe that behavior, but even more so identity and will (determination), are essential parts of the capabilities of an individual or an organization in achieving anything. This is a matter of choice in defining concepts. I argue that a dedicated organization, eager to succeed, is more competent than a demoralized, passive one with exactly the same knowledge and know-how.

These three dimensions will be the generic axes of our competence referential.

As an illustration, while the profile of competence of a historian should clearly be positioned close to the knowledge axis, the engineer would be placed further down the know-how dimension, while the politician would be expected to be closer to the attitudes axis. These are obviously caricatures. Note, for example, that the engineer does not only deal with empirical know-how but also attempts to introduce as much knowledge as possible into their practice. This is exactly the difference between techniques (empirically-

https://doi.org/10.1515/9783111397979-025

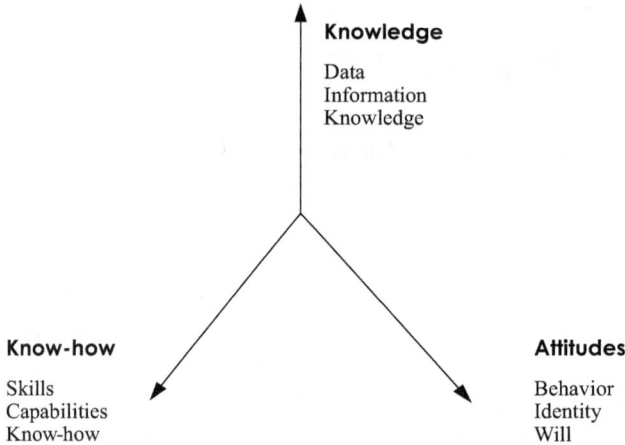

Fig. 37: Three dimensions of competence.

based with limited understanding of why it works) and technology (more science-based with solid and reliable explanations for why it works, thus making it possible to extend the technology to other applications much more easily and faster). Technical skills are difficult to extend as they are empirically built, mostly tacit, context-specific and locally embedded. Conversely, one can argue that the acceleration in technological development comes from scientific knowledge that increasingly helps technological diffusion and extension (e.g., replication of use of a technology in other contexts; combination of technologies).

Also note that the knowledge side of the competence space shown on Fig. 37 is characterized by articulated forms of competence, while the know-how/attitudes dimensions embed more tacitness.

Note also that the three dimensions of competence shown on Fig. 37 stem from individual learning. I suggest extending this referential to collective learnings as well. This is naturally a risky step which would need to be discussed at length as it requires an epistemic shift. This will not be done here.[29]

Enriching the Referential

One may then further enrich the picture by introducing some of the elements discussed in the previous chapters. See Fig. 38.

---

29 Some discussion of this matter may be found, however, in Durand, Mounoud and Ramanantsoa who advocate for interactionism and the theory of social representations, calling upon Moscovici. They see it as a way out of the internal contradiction of individual/organizational cognition, i.e., the trap of the so-called mind of an organization.

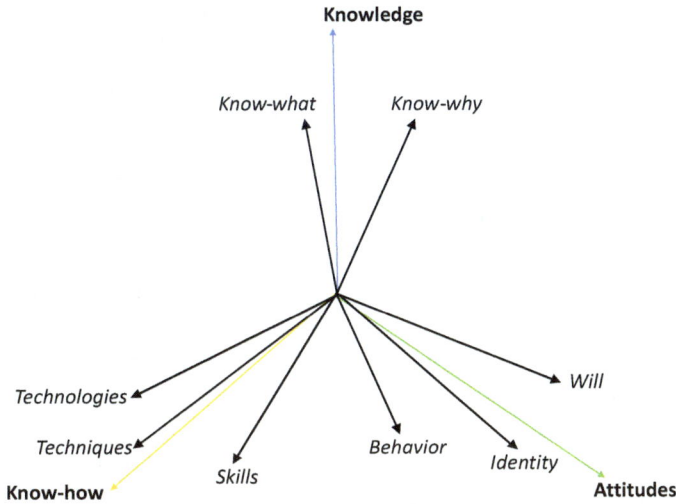

Fig. 38: Enriching the three basic categories of competence.

The "attitudes" dimension is itself composite as I suggest that it combines the behavioral dimension (know-how-to-behave), the culture or identity of the organization as well as the idea of will, i.e., determination and commitment. These are distinct items which should be recognized as such.

As an illustration of the importance of organizational behavior and its links to competence and performance, Hambrick discusses how team behavior at top management level can lead to two polar extremes: fragmentation and group think. Both situations are shown to be inefficient, thus reinforcing the idea that collective behavior may be an element of competence or, conversely, what I called incompetence.

Similarly, the "know-how" axis is also a composite dimension. It clearly relates to skills, individual and collective processual capabilities, as well as technologies. As discussed above, technologies are at least in part understood and modeled thanks to scientific knowledge. They are more than just empirical techniques. They thus lean in part towards the knowledge dimension, while techniques lean the other way.

Now turning to the "knowledge" axis, it should be noted that the "know-what/know-why/know-how" distinction put forward by Sanchez is only dealt with in part by the referential presented since only the know-how appears as one of the three generic axes. The know-what/know-why turn out to be two different variants or subcategories of knowledge. Know-what is in a sense hinting in the direction of know-how, through a flavor of intuition, without the cognitive explanation which the know-why has to offer. The know-why is actually twofold. On one hand it stands for the expertise of the knowledgeable who can explain to a skilled worker why their know-how works and how to modify and improve the corresponding skill. On the other hand, the know-why also includes a strategic understanding of why it is relevant to choose whatever strategic path that the know-what suggests. The strategic implication of this second type of know-why is far reaching.

I thus suggest that the know-why relates to strategy and strategic vision, and constitutes a very important aspect of the competence of an organization.

Managerial Levers and the Competence Base

The three basic dimensions of my referential of competence, together with the sub-dimensions which I just added, help understand key aspects of the competence base. These dimensions are descriptive, that is, they help describe what competence is about.

Yet, one should recognize that management is not necessarily capable of acting upon these dimensions.

Standard managerial levers (strategizing, organizing and motivating) are not fully aligned to the dimensions of my referential for competence:
- **Strategizing** (strategic thinking leading to a strategic vision, a strategic logic thus relating to the know-why, strategic decision making and strategy deployment). This relates to the knowledge (know-what and know-why) dimension;
- **Organizing** (the organizational structure as well as management processes). This relates more to the know-how dimension;
- **Motivating** (i.e., setting up incentives but also coaching, encouraging positive thinking and behavior, promoting dedication and will). This thus relates to the attitudes dimension.

Although these managerial levers are not aligned with the three descriptive dimensions of our model for organizational competence, it is worth discussing the interactions among the two groups (managerial levers and descriptive dimensions).

The strategic vision includes the idea of a goal set up for the whole organization and is sharable if not shared, thus leaning slightly towards the attitudes, will and commitment. This is even more so for strategic deployment, which clearly means deploying the strategic vision for the sub-parts and members of the organization.

Motivation fits in between these strategic dimensions and attitudes. Motivation combines an intent, a far-reaching goal and a positive, proactive attitude made up of will, determination and commitment. Motivation should be regarded as a key element of competence. Human resource managers are obviously well aware of this, as are line managers and sports coaches. This is indeed a key element of team building and managing. How come most of the literature on competence-based theory simply ignored this key aspect for so long? Do management researchers forget what management is all about (recruiting, convincing, embarking, generating enthusiasm, leading)? Motivation goes much beyond financial incentives.

The organization with its two basic dimensions, the organizational structure and the management processes, may be complemented by the informal organization. The organizational structure falls more on the articulated side of the referential while most of the processes are closer to the know-how axis and the informal organization is leaning towards motivation, attitudes, commitment and will.

Management processes relate to the collective capabilities of the firm, thus including the technologies. Note that processes may be regarded as twofold: on one side stand the organizational processes set up and explicitly monitored by the management; on the other, the routines which were generated historically by the organization, possibly from a distorted appropriation of some prescribed management processes, long ago forgotten. Routines in that sense may be regarded as informal processes. They thus tend to be more deeply rooted and embedded in the organization. In that sense, the routines also relate to the behavioral and cultural dimensions of attitudes, thus leaning towards this axis.

This specific positioning of the standard managerial levers (strategizing, organizing and motivating) with respect to the proposed key dimensions of competence in the model also raises the issue of the interaction between managerial tasks and competence building and leveraging. The links are not so direct. Nevertheless, they exist. Management might want to operate on the same wavelength (according to the same dimensions) as the competence base in order to better build and leverage competence.

Enlarging the Content of Coordinated Deployment

This in turn leads to the idea that the heart of the concept of competence (the organizational alchemy, as I call it), which has to do with the coordinated deployment of resources and assets, should be enlarged beyond management processes. I argue that coordinated deployment should be extended to the cultural identity, the strategic vision and even the part of the organization (formal and informal) that goes beyond the processes already covered. I argue that the identity (the shared values, rites, taboos and beliefs) operates as a cement holding the organizational pieces together at least as efficiently as any other coordinating and integrating mechanism. I further argue that a shared vision also contributes to the coordinated deployment of strategy, channeling people's energy, motivation and commitment. Finally, I suggest that the organizational structure is also a key element of the same coordinated deployment of assets and capabilities.

In other words, I suggest reviewing and enlarging the content of the coordinated deployment concept in order to encompass four elements: the management processes, the identity, the strategic vision and the structure. This is shown on Fig. 39. In so doing, I relate to Strategor's early editions and more specifically to the tetrahedron of strategic management, a representation that sadly disappeared from subsequent editions.[30]

---

30 Early editions of Strategor represented strategic management in the form of a tetrahedron made up of four faces (strategy, organization, processes, culture). Each of the four components was thus interacting with any of the other three via an edge of the tetrahedron. This extended the idea that instead of a sequence "strategy then organization to implement the strategy", the strategy/organiza-

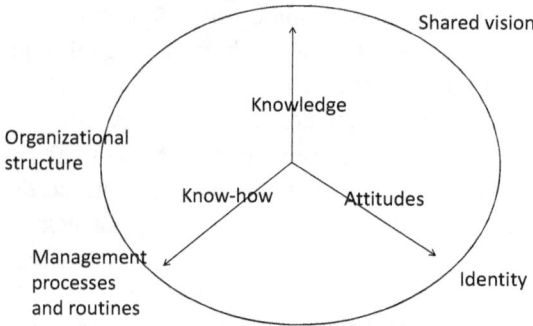

Fig. 39: Coordinated deployment (may also be called managerial orchestration).

(Note that another wording ("managerial orchestration") could be used as equivalent to "coordinated deployment".)

The Dynamics of Competence Building

This competence framework can also be enriched with the theme of competence building. As discussed earlier, competence may be seen a stock accumulated as a result of an ongoing flux of learning, reinforcing and enlarging the competence base of the organization.

The "data → information → knowledge → expertise" sequence described earlier for knowledge can now be extended and adapted to the two other axes of the referential, i.e., the two other generic forms of competence (know-how and attitudes), as shown on Tab. 8.

This illustrates the parallelism which prevails in the way learning mechanisms operate for each dimension of the referential. Knowledge is built through information, assimilation and digestion. Know-how is built through action which shapes skills and techniques. Attitudes are shaped through interaction when individuals conform to group or organizational behavior, adopt the same cultural values and share the same basic commitments.

Expertise requires one step further. As discussed, expertise needs some form of quantic jump in competence together with a merger of the three generic dimensions of competence. Figure 40 illustrates this idea graphically, detailing the learning processes at hand.

---

tion interaction is a two-way street, the pre-existing organization strongly influencing the way strategy emerges. This view of the strategy←→organization interaction can be extended to the other interactions taking place on each of the edges of the tetrahedron.

Tab. 8: Parallel learning processes and stages.

Parallel learning processes and stages		
Knowledge	**Know-how**	**Attitudes**
Data	Action	Interaction
Information	Skills and capabilities	Behavior, culture, will
Knowledge	Know-how	Attitudes
Expertise	Expertise	Expertise

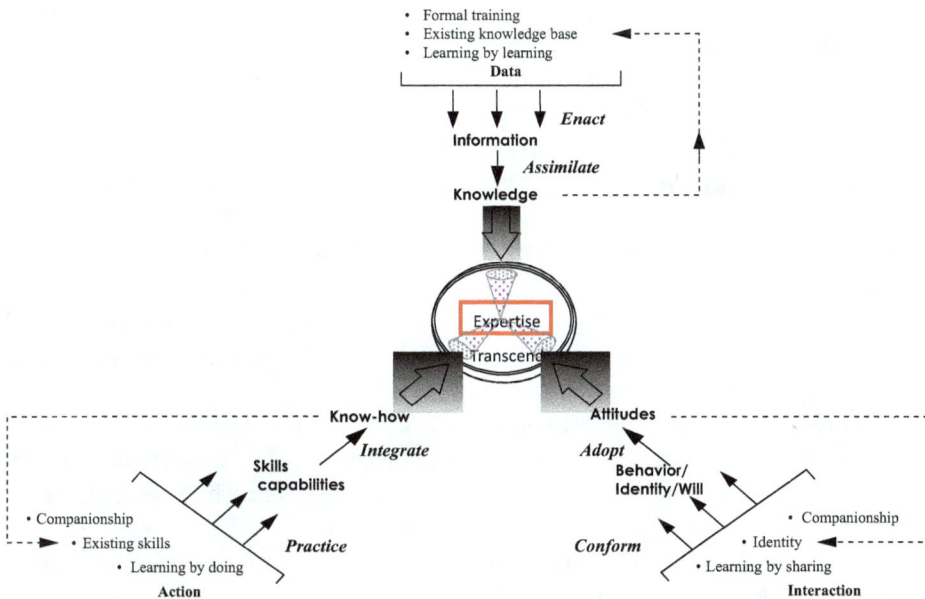

Fig. 40: The dynamics of competence building.

Four important comments may be made on this matter:

(1) The pre-existing stock of competence (the existing skills, knowledge base and identity) significantly affects the learning capabilities. It may operate as a booster to build up competence fast. It may also transform itself into a source of bias and iner-

tia, hindering any significant new learning. As discussed earlier, history matters. The "installed base" counts. This is shown graphically on Fig. 40. For each axis, the dotted arrows loop back on the pre-existing competence base which in turn influences new learnings. The result of learning is not just a function of the incoming flow of learning. It also depends upon the pre-existing base of competence.

(2) If knowledge building stems from exposure to external data enacted as information and integrated into frames, know-how is built through action and companionship while attitudes are shaped through interaction in companionship.

(3) It is action (taking place in the form of the various learning mechanisms described here) which transforms the potential competence, not yet demonstrated, into reality. Through the dynamics of competence building and learning, "what one could possibly do" becomes "what one can actually do". This relates competence learning (in the sense of competence building) to competence leveraging in a virtuous loop.

(4) Expertise combines the three generic forms of competence identified (knowledge, know-how and attitudes) into an integrated higher-level competence. Experts understand, can explain and even can do better than others, with state-of-the-art ability. Expertise is beyond assimilation and digestion. It tends to transcend competence, merging its key generic dimensions.

The Three Generic Dimensions of Competence are Interdependent

Two different aspects of interdependence may be formulated here. They are illustrated on Fig. 41.

First, building upon Piaget's work, I recognize with Senge that there is little real learning and knowledge building without action. Knowledge and know-how are in fact built simultaneously as learning needs action.

This idea can be extrapolated and extended. I argue that learning actually takes place in organizations simultaneously for the three generic dimensions of the referential. This happens, in parallel but in an interrelated mode, through exposure to external data (leading to information), action and interaction.

Secondly, I suggest looking at the case of workers highly vulnerable to technical change as they built their competence around purely empirical know-how with little or no knowledge of other technologies. When the technological process, e.g., the equipment, is changed, they lose most of their competence. Without knowledge they are not in a position to adapt to change. Know-how without knowledge can be very vulnerable.

Again, I suggest here to extend this idea to the interactions among the three generic dimensions of our referential.

What would be a collective know-how without appropriate group attitudes, i.e., without the capability to behave as a group? Similarly, attitudes without know-how may prove useless, as much as attitudes may be meaningless without knowledge and thus understanding of the stakes and challenges at hand. Pure knowledge without relevant know-how is sterile, and knowledge without attitudes may even prove counterproductive.

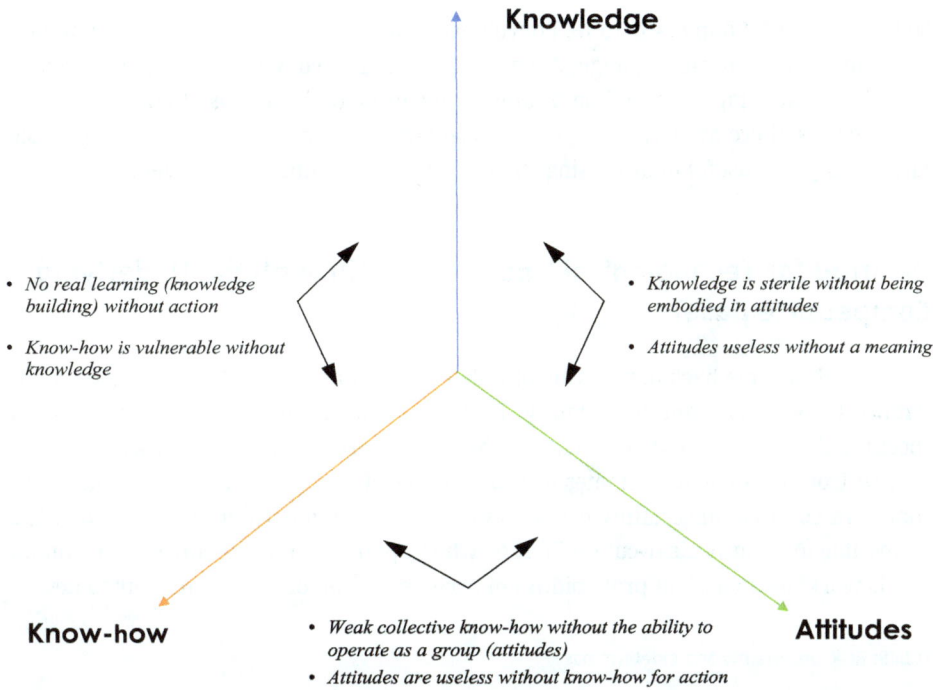

Knowledge

- *No real learning (knowledge building) without action*

- *Know-how is vulnerable without knowledge*

- *Knowledge is sterile without being embodied in attitudes*

- *Attitudes useless without a meaning*

Know-how

- *Weak collective know-how without the ability to operate as a group (attitudes)*
- *Attitudes are useless without know-how for action*

Attitudes

Fig. 41: The three dimensions of competence (knowledge, know-how and attitudes) are interdependent.

In other words, exposure to data, action and interaction are three parallel and interrelated modes of learning, building up competence simultaneously. Conversely, an unbalanced competence base, leaning more towards one of the three generic dimensions of our referential, may prove inappropriate.

In this sense, the three generic dimensions of competence in our referential are interdependent.

Chapter 19 will deal with using this model of competence to strategize technological change.

Chapter 19
Using the Concept of Competence to Think about Technological Change Strategically

So far in Part III, Chapters 16 to 18, I developed a model of competence intended to help think about technological change strategically. As the discussion hinted, the concept of organizational competence, while intuitively meaningful, is not easy to operationalize. Nevertheless, there are strong implications stemming from the concept of competence. These will prove useful in discussing change. This is what Chapter 19 covers.

Insuring for Technological Uncertainty (through the Underlying Competence Base)

I first need to come back to the issue of indeterminacy and Knight's key conceptual difference between risk and uncertainty. Table 9 combines Knight's distinction with the specific subcategory of indeterminacy within the uncertainty category. Risks can be calculated from reasonable estimates of probabilities of occurrence and valuation of outcomes. In contrast, uncertainty cannot, either because indeterminacy is such that it is impossible to identify clear-cut options, or when options can be identified, no computation is workable by lack of probabilities of occurrence and/or valuation of outcomes.

Tab. 9: Risk, uncertainty and indeterminacy.

Context	Risk	Uncertainty	
Visibility on options	Options known (as of today)	Options identified (as of today)	Indeterminacy (What are the options?)
Mode of assessment	Estimates of probabilities of occurrence and assessment of outcomes permit computations	By lack of probabilities of occurrence and value of outcomes, no computation possible	Unknown unknowns are by definition difficult to assess
Tools & heuristics	Net present value, real options	Build competence base to prepare for potential futures	
		Judgement	

On that wavelength, I argue that technology is mostly uncertain, rarely a matter of computable risks in Knight's sense. This means that apart technical experts' and business leaders' judgements, there are not many ways of strategizing technological

https://doi.org/10.1515/9783111397979-026

change. This is where I argue that thinking about technology strategically via their underlying set of competencies is an interesting way to address the matter.

How can a firm prepare for technological change? I suggest circumnavigating the trap of technological forecasting. While strategic decisions need to be made at some stage to place bets on some technologies, top management obviously lacks visibility. I suggest looking at the underlying competence base as an insurance policy for the future.

Consider a firm active on a set of business arenas, responding to a range of market needs F_i (these include the function, sub-functions and sub-sub-functions discussed in Part I, Chapter 9). For each of these sub-(sub-)functions F_i to be fulfilled on the market, the management can call upon their R&D to list the various technological options that are thinkable for the future – seen as of today. In addition, they should use the lists of all thinkable, currently available, and past technologies to draw dual technology trees (see Part II, Chapter 8) for each of these functions F_i. This leads to listing the technological options that are candidate for N_i+1, as shown on Fig. 42. Management should not necessarily resist the temptation of pointing out which in their opinion (judgement) is likely to win the race to substitute for the corresponding current dominant technology N_i and become the next dominant technology N_i+1 (or N_i+2). But they should be careful of not blinding themselves with such forecasts.

In the case of indeterminacy, it may become difficult to identify technological options because the fog is too thick. The case of quantum computing mentioned in the book's introduction is a typical illustration of this difficulty. In such a case, I argue that instead of an array of options, one can use one technological option named "quantum computing" and pursue the analysis on that basis.

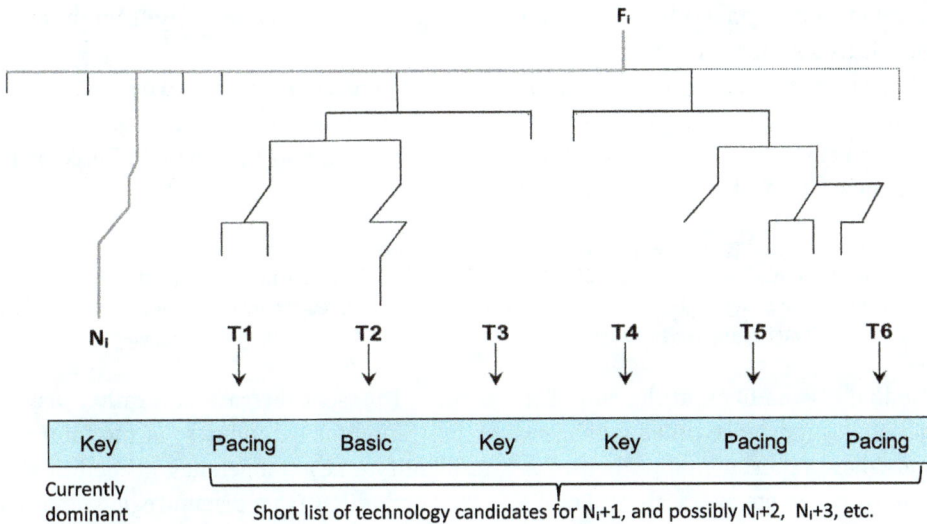

Fig. 42: Technological options for the future of a market need F_i.

In addition, those technologies preselected for a short list to substitute for N_i, thus potentially becoming N_i+1 or N_i+2 or even N_i+3, can be qualified according to usual categories such as emerging, pacing, key, basic (obviously stemming from the notion of a life cycle of technologies) or any relevant equivalent classification. ("Emerging" means very early candidate technology, not yet fully tested and validated; "pacing" means very promising new technology that has already proven useful and is currently gaining interest and momentum; "key" means strategic technology that stands as a source of a competitive advantage today; "basic" means readily available technology that can be sourced on the market with no strategic advantage attached anymore. Such categories follow some form of a technology life cycle, where pacing technologies are former emerging technologies that confirmed their potential; key are former pacing that became really strategic; basic are former technologies of any kind that are now widespread enough to be easily sourced.)

Going one step further on this analytical path, it is worth building a matrix where the technological options T1 to T6 appear in columns (Fig. 43). However, this analysis requires listing the underlying competencies that each of these technological options (in column) would need, should that option win the technological race. This may sound difficult to do, but, in practice, it is more feasible than it seems. These competencies 1 to 9 are shown as the lines on Fig. 43. The number of Xs in each cell of the matrix signals the importance of a competency for a technology. As an example, competency 4 will be essential to develop and implement technology T1, as would competency 3 for T2, or 8 for T6 or 9 for T4. However, competency 4 should not be needed for T2, T3, T4 or T5.

Building the matrix shown on Fig. 43 requires information gathering (mostly qualitative, e.g., through interviews, not only – although mostly – with scientists and development engineers, but experts in other functions as well, possibly from production, logistics, distribution, marketing, purchasing, HR, etc.).

Note that in situations of indeterminacy, it may indeed be difficult to define technological options. However, I argue that it is paradoxically easier to identify key competencies behind the few options identifiable, if any, and the foggy residual of unknown unknowns integrated into a single meta-option.

> Should top management at Kodak in the 1980s have been more open, they could have considered building a minimal competence base in digital imaging, hiring a team of engineers in electronics, digital storing, digital displays, etc. These would have monitored the dynamics of digital technologies for imaging and learnt along the way how to refine and complement the competence needed.

Along the same lines, at the end of the chapter, I present the case of a rather vague notional competence called managerial orchestration for the industry of the future. I show how experimentation helped a firm identify a key competency needed in the context of remote digital control of distributed operations from distant regional hubs.

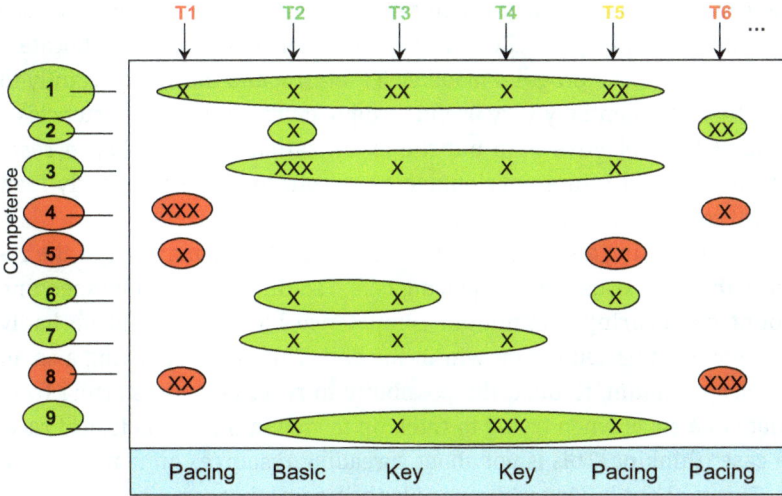

Fig. 43: Technological options and underlying competence.

Once the matrix shapes up, it becomes possible to think about technological uncertainty[31] strategically thanks to the transversal view offered by the underlying competence perspective.

Assume that the technical consensus in the organization at hand says that the future of the business will gravitate around technologies T2, T3 or T4. This is because they "appear" today as the most reasonable and viable options. This means that the internal technical consensus suggests placing bets on competencies 1, 3, 6, 7 and 9. Fair enough. Yet, there is a catch. By choosing these technologies, and thus (though indirectly) these competencies, one would simply ignore competencies 4 and 8, meaning that the organization would not prepare for technologies T1 or T6 (or T5, though to a lesser extent).

The technical consensus internally results from the researchers and technologists not believing in T1 or T6 (two pacing technologies probably seen as a bit too futuristic), while T2, T3 and T4 are obviously perceived as more convincing. In following the technical consensus, the organization would follow their view. Why not? Strategy is about resource allocation. The firm has limited resources and cannot afford to develop all technologies. So, choices have to be made. Understood.

Yet, T2 is basic, thus not very interesting as a source of strategic advantage because it can be easily sourced by any competitor, while T3 and T4 are key but possibly aging already. (Could it be that the internal consensus is rather conservative, placing bets on established technologies only?) Hence, why not follow the essence of the internal consensus with a slight addendum: not putting all of the available resources on

---

31 In the broad sense of uncertainty and indeterminacy, as shown on Tab. 9.

today's internal consensus. What about keeping a bit of slack to pay for an insurance contract against the uncertainty attached to future technologies? Why not allocate a bit of resources to monitor the progress made on T1 and T6, and more importantly to build a limited – though potentially very useful – competence base on competencies 4 and 8 just in case? The objective is to put the organization in a position to react quickly, with agility, should future developments turn out to shape differently than what the technical consensus suggests today.

This is not about keeping all options open. This is about focusing most of the resources on where the consensus suggests placing bets. Yet, this is done while spending a limited amount on securing a minimum competence base that could be badly needed should some unexpected option win in the end. This is about paying a small price, an insurance premium, to build the possibility to react fast, not starting from scratch at too late of a stage when trying to catch up to stay in the technological race. This is "just in case" thinking. This is not about spreading resources on many technological options. This is about buying insurance via the underlying competence.

One does not buy car insurance every year because the probability of an accident is high. In fact, the highest probability is no accident next year. However, should one have an accident, the coverage of the insurance will transform a bad or very bad event into something that may be a bearable adverse episode in life.

> At Kodak in the 1980s, Georges Roques chose to buy insurance for the group regarding digital imaging. Roques was the CEO at Kodak France at that time. He felt that the group was making a mistake in blindly betting on chemical imaging only, denying the future of digital images. He chose to set up a group to investigate the future of digital imaging. Just in case. He did it secretly because he knew that the headquarters of Kodak in Rochester, USA, would oppose his project. He was trying to buy insurance for the corporation. This went well, until the headquarters heard about it and ordered him to stop the venture. Roque sadly obeyed. When things eventually turned sour for Kodak in 1993, the board hired George Fisher from Motorola for a turn around. However, it was already too late. One morning, Roques, already retired, receives a call from Rochester. Fisher is calling to pay him tribute. He explains that he tried to understand what had happened to Eastman Kodak, reading the minutes of the Execom meetings before he was asked to join. He goes, "You were the only one to do the right thing. I just meant to recognize what you tried to do for the corporation."

Following the technical consensus boils down to go along the forecast resulting from the "experts". The history of technology is full of promising technologies that never made it, while on several occasions poorly regarded competing options or unexpected new technological options suddenly appearing in the landscape turned out to spread like wildfire, cannibalizing entire businesses. I argue that technological forecasting is as risky and difficult as macroeconomic forecasting. I suggest staying away from technology prophets and rely on analysis of the underlying competence. The powerful and resourceful Eastman Kodak of the 1980s was in a position to afford the building of a competence base in electronics and digital technologies. In rejecting the buying of insurance on the future of digital photography, top management's blindness destroyed the firm.

Typically for the case illustrated on Fig. 43, it is possible to pre-explore competencies 4 and 8 at minimum cost. Contracting with university labs to finance two PhD candidates, each one working in a team specialized in the specific sub-field, one on competency 4 and the other on competency 8, attending conferences and building a scientific and technological network during their doctoral work. At the outset, if the technological uncertainty remains, they can be offered a position in the organization to bring in worldwide access to up-to-date knowledge in the field, just in case that would be needed, i.e., should T1 or T6 unexpectedly turn out to take the lead.

> The whole point made above fits the issue of the fourth industrial revolution as illustrated in the introduction of this book (Chapter 1). Key technologies that are likely candidates to structure the industry of the future are identified: additive manufacturing or 3D printing; machine learning and artificial intelligence; robots and cobots; internet of things and machine to machine; predictive maintenance; big data and big analytics; digital imaging and augmented virtual reality; smart manufacturing, etc.
>
> In fact, each of these technologies is an umbrella term with very loaded content. If one starts looking below each of these umbrellas, digging into the contents, it is possible to cluster the bits and pieces into sub-technologies. Going one step further, through group discussions gathering experts for that purpose, it is possible to identify the underlying competence required. This means hard work, but the outcome may be of very high value: the sets of competence identified at the outset point to what the workforce and industrial companies as organizations need to be trained for (see Appendix).
>
> I further argue that this needs to be done not just on the technical side (scientists, engineers, technicians, operators on the job floor). It also needs to be done as well on the managerial orchestration side to manage the organizational transformations, strategize the rearrangements in the value chains, etc. (I illustrate this last point at the end of this chapter when discussing boundary objects.)

The Competence Gap

I defined the competence gap as the distance between a firm's competence base and the competence portfolio needed to survive a given change when facing the requirements of the new technology. The wider the competence gap, the more likely the firm will prefer to find new ways of leveraging its competence base, moving to new businesses. The narrower the competence gap, the more reasonable it is for the incumbents to try to bridge the competence gap by accessing whatever new competence is now needed – assuming this is feasible.

I argue that generating an estimate (even qualitative) of the competence gap is a useful lead indicator of the intensity of a forthcoming change for a firm in a business. This intensity may range from business as usual (typically the evolution from 4G to 5G to 6G in mobile telephony has a minor strategic impact as each incumbent's competence base tends to be entrenched by the change) to a major disruption (typically if one day fusion becomes dominant for electricity production).

In fact, when thinking about change strategically, competence can be seen from two complementary, though distinct, perspectives. The first perspective assumes that the competence gap is bridgeable, while the second perspective assumes it is not.

(1) Given an activity that a firm wants to stay in despite a technological substitution coming in, what is the portfolio of competence needed? How wide is the competence gap? (Typically, incumbents are likely to search for competence that would help them face the requirements of the new technology [N+1 or possibly N+2]. They logically try to bridge the competence gap, provided their initial appreciation is that it should be feasible.)

(2) Given an existing portfolio of competence that was fit to N but is likely to be rendered obsolete and useless by N+1 and/or N+2, at least to a significant extent, what can be done with the existing portfolio? How to best leverage what the organization is good at? (Typically, incumbents fully disrupted by a paradigmatic change may choose to redeploy on other businesses. Conversely, candidate new entrants in the business arena are firms that were searching for opportunities to best leverage their own portfolio of competence. In their search, these candidate new entrants may have come across the N to N+1 transition and seen it as an opportunity. They anticipate that they should be able to leverage their competence base to cover most of the requirements imposed by the change. In turn, incumbents pushed out from the business arena by the arrival of new entrants surfing N+1 may look for new businesses fit to their portfolio of competence.)

Strategies when Facing Change: Trigger or Shape, Stretch or Redeploy

The generic question of this book can be formulated as: How can a firm act when faced with technological change? Addressing this question through the competence lens will lead to four major strategic options. Note that I discuss these while remaining at a level of analysis where competence is understood at a meta-level – without going deep into fine granularity. Also note that in this section I will speak about change in a broad sense, though keeping in mind that the book is focused on technological change.

As a core point of the book, especially in this Part III, I argue that organizational competence is a central concept to think about change strategically. This led to the idea of competence gap to help evaluate how fit or unfit the firm is to the new competence requirements brought about by the change.

I need now to introduce the concept of "power to influence" (that goes beyond market power) to describe how a firm may influence the process of change. I stick here to the evolutionary perspective that I have adopted throughout the book. When faced with change, firms may contribute to generating the new trajectory, at least in part. In fact, since there are many players participating to the process of change, each contributing to shaping the future of the business, at least to some extent, most players cannot expect to control the dynamics of the industry. Influencing is already a significant strategic achievement.

So, we have two concepts to think about change strategically: on the one hand the firm's competence gap, and on the other hand the firm's power to influence.

Combining these two dimensions (competence gap and power to influence), leads to four strategies available to firms facing change (Fig. 44):

- *Trigger* the change (when the firm senses that it is well positioned to benefit from the change). This means that the competence gap is minimum while it may be more significant for most other players, including candidate new entrants. Triggering is a clear, direct way of using its power to influence;
- *Stretch* (to reach out for pieces of competence needed to bridge the competence gap as power to influence is low);
- *Redeploy* (abandoning the business arena because of not enough power to influence while there is no or little hope to bridge the competence gap);
- *Shape* (using the firm's power to influence to direct the change closer to the firm's portfolio of competence and, if possible, away from the competitors', thus reducing the competence gap for the firm while increasing it for competitors).

The resulting two-dimensional model of strategic behavior when facing change is illustrated on Fig. 44.

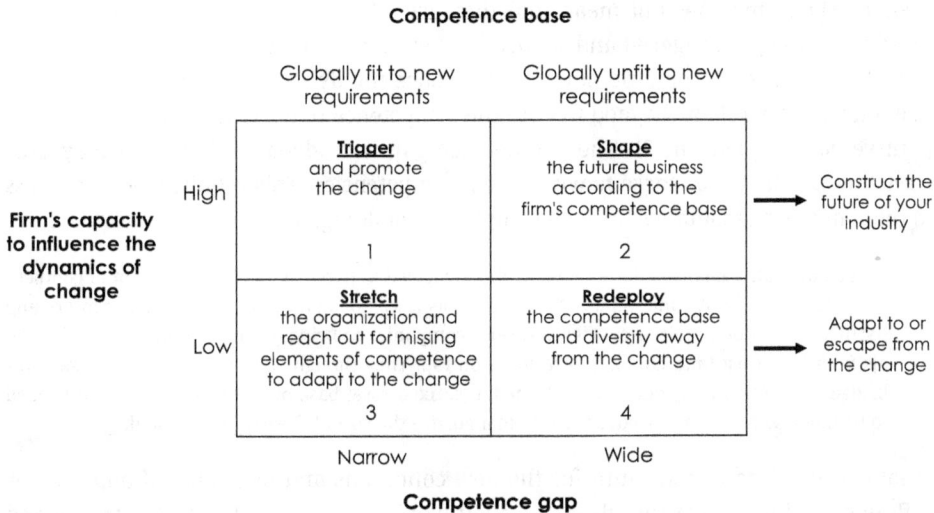

Fig. 44: Strategic options when facing change.

When the firm has both a significant influence on the dynamics of change and a good fit to the corresponding competence requirements (quadrant 1) it may advantageously promote and even trigger the change to displace competitors and build a defendable, long-lasting position. This is the typical strategy of innovators and first movers, attempting to destabilize existing market leaders.

> Salomon in outdoor sport products is a remarkable example of an innovator that chose to trigger change through innovation in the various markets which the firm entered historically (skis, roller skates, bikes, hiking shoes, golf).

When the firm has some potentially significant influence on the dynamics of change while being rather poorly fit in terms of competence base (quadrant 2), it may then try to use its power to influence. This will be done by pushing the change to require competence closer to the firm's reach, while pushing further away from competitors' capabilities. Through a proactive strategy, the firm thus tries to shape and construct the business for its own benefits.

> The bottled water leaders, Nestlé and Danone, struggled to influence the legislation in most countries to protect their mineral water brands from direct competition from local bottlers. Through active lobbying based on scientific published work and medical clinical testing which they fund, these leading players actively shaped their industry.

These two first types of situations are described at length in strategic management literature. However, not all firms can have a direct influence in reshaping their industry (and technological evolution in their industry). In fact, quite the opposite. Most of them have only a marginal effect on the future of the competitive game prevailing in their market. This does not mean that they are left with no strategic options when faced with changes triggered and shaped by their environment.

Although with no or little power to influence the dynamics of their industry, the firm may be in a relatively good fit with the competence requirements of the new competitive game (quadrant 3). The competence gap is bridgeable. The firm may thus stretch to reach out for these newly needed competencies. This requires getting access to these missing capabilities through competence building, partnerships or acquisitions.

> In the hospitality business, large hotel chains struggled to live through the new form of competition brought in by Airbnb. Some of them such as Accor bought apartments in city centers and partnered with or acquired concierge service companies to bring a combination of Airbnb rentals with breakfast (and concierge) services on top. They thought that the competence gap was bridgeable, except they were left with the large, fixed asset base of hotel rooms that still needed to be filled with a decent occupancy rate to amortize the cost of the capital invested.

Finally, if the firm is both unfit for the new conditions and incapable of opposing or influencing the change (quadrant 4), they would have a hard time to stretch and bridge the competence gap. It may thus be best to escape from the turmoil of the change, redeploying its competence base to diversify away from what used to be its business.

> TV magazines were confronted with TV menus and scanning systems announcing programs and presenting previews directly on the TV set, thus helping viewers select their programs amongst hundreds of channels. The previously very profitable TV magazines had little choice but to abandon their traditional program sections and convert into more classic magazines, typically covering TV, the media and show business. Indeed, there was little hope for them to learn the competence required to supply the TV navigation systems to select channels and programs through the remote control. The competence gap was too wide. The development of video on demand from streaming platforms reinforced this evolution.

This strategy of redeploying away, if repeated over time, may in fact lead firms to create a path for themselves by pivoting around their competence base to develop new activities.

> Zodiac was founded in 1896 as a manufacturer of airplanes and airships. After WWI, Zodiac became primarily a supplier of canvases for airships. It then moved on to manufacture soft canvas dinghies, inflatable beach buoys and garden pool covers. The company came close to bankruptcy in the early 1970s and refocused on boats. From then on, they defined their mission as providing technical flexible canvas for any form of application. They kept pivoting around their portfolio of technologies to serve a variety of sectors. In the process, they subsequently found the niche of airplane escape slides that they quickly captured as this was typically where their competence was at its best. In so doing, they re-entered the sector of aeronautics that they had left several decades earlier. As they became tier one suppliers to main airplane manufacturers, they offered to design and manufacture passenger seats, thus going beyond the technical flexible canvas. In turn, they ended up building a specialized competence in optimizing cabin space. This led them to offer services to custom design cabin space for airlines in close relation with the airplane manufacturers. They subsequently decided to sell most of their non-aeronautics activities (boats and pools) and renamed the company Zodiac Aerospace. In 2018, they were bought by Safran, the airplane engine manufacturer, historical partner of GE Aerospace. This illustrates how a company can grow by pivoting over time around technological competence and/or client intimacy. Thus, the strategic role of the competence base.

In passing, although this is not properly documented in the literature, I argue that market linkages (customer intimacy and trust) are most probably more difficult to build from scratch in the middle of a business transformation than technological competence. In rock climbing, one has four holding grips to stick to the cliff (two hands and two feet). Moving up the cliff means moving grips – but one grip at a time. In my view, when choosing which competence (which grip) to let go, I would recommend keeping a stronghold on the market/customer relation whenever possible. Although this book is about technology strategy, I argue for securing customers first.

Operationalizing Competence: Working with the Concept of Competence in Practice

So far in Chapter 19 I have used the concept of competence to suggest insuring for future technological change via the underlying competence. I also discussed the key role of the competence gap as some form of a qualitative metric of change. I then added the concept of power of influence to discuss strategies for the firm facing change (technological change in this book). This led to four strategies: trigger or stretch, shape or redeploy. The rationale is based on the competence gap combined to the power to influence.

At this stage, it is important to come back to the difficulties attached to putting to work the concept of organizational competence.

Nature of Competence: Subcategories

Chapters 16 to 18 have discussed at length categories such as tangible resources (assets, infrastructure, land, buildings, equipment, etc.). There are also less tangible resources (knowledge, technologies, know-how, blueprints, brands, reputation, client intimacy, etc.). In addition, there are human resources seen either individually (the individual talents who are mobile as they can be recruited elsewhere) or collective (this is key for the concept of organizational competence). The resources and assets do not fully fit under the word "competence" as they are tradable on the market, keeping in mind though that competence includes the coordinated deployment of resources and assets. Behind the "coordinated deployment of" (or orchestration or organizational alchemy), additional categories are to be listed here: organizational processes; organizational culture; shared sense of missions; shared objectives (and even strategy); individual and collective behaviors (both internally and connecting to the outside: clients, prospective clients, suppliers, stakeholders at large).

This enumeration does not bring anything new after Chapters 16 to 18. It does not clarify much either of how to operationalize the concept of competence. However, it confirms what I hinted before: the concept of organizational competence, although intuitively meaningful, is blurry and not easy to grasp – thus the difficulties in operationalizing the concept. Yet, the lists are useful to check which items can be identified as potential bottlenecks in adapting a competence portfolio to change.

Behavior, VRIO, Small "o" and Metabolism

In Chapter 18, I argued that the strategic heart of competence was likely to be found in the "know-how-to-behave", typically the culture or identity that operates as a cement or a glue keeping the organization together. This also includes the shared values, the motivation of the teams and individuals, the shared goals, the individual and collective behavior, etc.

Interestingly, this turns out to be the bottom line of the VRIO proposition as I see it:

The widespread VRIO proposition aims at analyzing when it is that a resource or a competence is strategic, in the sense it will make a difference vis-à-vis competitors.[32] The VRIO proposition suggests that a resource, a capability or a competence is strategic if it brings _Value_ (to the customers and the stakeholders), it is _Rare_ (thus difficult to access), difficult to _Imitate_ and if the _O_rganization can make good use of it. Barney adds that there are in fact two Os in VRIO: capital "O" relates to the usual formal description of the organization (the structure and the processes), while lowercase "o" addresses the informal organization with the organizational culture or identity, the shared value, the organizational processes as they are – not just as they were formally designed and prescribed initially. Barney insists on the key role of small "o". I could not agree more.

Using a human biology metaphor, I argue that the strategic core of organizational competence, in the sense of the capabilities to achieve things together as a firm, is to be found not in its skeleton, nor even in its anatomy, but in its metabolism.

Here is an illustration of my point. A member of the top management team of the Danone Group once described to me what he viewed as the three factors explaining why that agro-food corporation had been so successful in its M&A strategy:

> A team of business developers did the classically expected work on deals under negotiations. Yet, on top, they conducted systematic reviews of any target of potential interest for the group, just in case one day such targets could be for sale. These anticipatory reviews aimed at putting the group in a position to react extremely fast when the fruit would finally be ready to be picked.
>
> A fleet of business jets making it possible to be where needed when needed to negotiate an acquisition, come back to the headquarters to report on progress, discuss and receive instructions, go back to the negotiation front and iterate fast to close the deal before less agile competitors would wake up.
>
> A culture at the headquarters, inherited from the founder Antoine Riboud: very Latin, reactive, possibly even a bit too speedy and at times not organized enough, but extraordinarily agile. While operations were managed in very precise ways with plenty of monitoring, the upper echelon was much more flexible, capable to suddenly focus on an urgent deal that should not be missed because of lack of attention when the window of opportunity had opened. This was agility at the top.
>
> Clearly, when it came to acquisitions, leadership at Danone had fully understood the importance of speed and agility.
>
> In what sense could the three resources and competencies pointed out above as providing speed and agility to the Danone Group at that time be seen as founding a source of competitive advantage?
>
> A fleet of business jets? These are resources that can be bought on the market. One just need to pay the price. This is not what will establish a sustainable competitive advantage against major competitors. This resource is imitable because purchasable.

---

32 Note that VRIO stems from RBV, the resource-based view – thus the use of the word "resource".

A business development team? It is possible to recruit very good professionals on the market. Again, it is expensive, but quite doable. And it is then possible to ask the team to conduct the work of scanning and assessing potential targets in advance. This ingredient is also imitable.

A very special top management culture, made up of responsiveness, agility and informality? Well, this is rare, very specific, non-easily imitable, not tradable on the market, deeply embedded in the identity of the organization and cultivated, if not managed, as such. This item of competence can be seen as a source of competitive advantage – provided the other speed ingredients are there.

Any resource that is easily acquired on a market is not enough to establish a long-lasting strategic advantage. (In our focus on strategy when facing change, a competence is strategic if it is essential for the firm to bridge the competence gap.) Obviously, the price to be paid for scarce resources or rare competence runs the risk of absorbing all or most of the rent that one hopes to derive from the combination of the resources mobilized. However, paying for these resources makes it possible to conquer the coveted strategic position, or in our focus on change, to survive the change successfully.

On the other hand, a competency can contribute to making the difference, strategically, if it is difficult to imitate, collective, tacit and diluted in the history and culture of the firm. A corporate culture is not easy to find for sale in the market.

In short, look for the essence of strategic competence in the metabolism of an organization, not so much in its anatomy or skeleton.

Granularity

So far in this chapter, I have used the concept of change in a broad sense. In particular, I have not entered into the sensitive matter of competence granularity.

The discussion of future-proofing via the competence hidden behind the curtain of change, the competence gap, the four strategies when facing change (trigger or stretch, shape or redeploy): all of these did not need to clearly define the level of granularity adopted in the analysis.

The field of strategy is not always explicit regarding the wavelength of the concepts used. Typically, the concepts of competitive advantage, or value chains, or business arena, or competitors and competition, or differentiation (and many similar concepts) can be viewed both as multilevel concepts or abstract notions somehow floating somewhere in the theoretical space of strategic management studies.

This applies even more to RBV and the competence perspective. In that sense, coming on top of blurry categories as I argued, unclear granularity does help operationalize the concept of competence.

The English proverb "for want of a nail the shoe was lost" stems from an old European story in the form of a verse dating back as early as the thirteenth century, with variations in German, medieval French or English that goes as follows:

> For want of a nail the shoe was lost,
> for want of a shoe the horse was lost,
> for want of a horse the knight was lost,
> for want of a knight the battle was lost,
> for want of a battle the kingdom was lost.
> So a kingdom was lost – all for want of a nail.

The message is crystal clear: a simple nail can be strategic. The chain of causality includes various layers of resources, hinting that the issue can be looked at from those various levels of granularity.

A variation of the verse substitutes a messenger for the knight, hinting that processes (information transmission) could be strategic:

> . . . for want of a horse a rider never got through,
> for want of a rider a message never arrived,
> for want of a message an army was never sent,
> for want of an army a battle was lost, . . .

This version suggests that a simple tangible resource such as a nail can be important because it can drive or at least affect more important processes.

The bottom line of the verse would seem to suggest that any tiny resource or piece of competence, even at a very fine-grain level, should be analyzed when scanning for strategic pieces of competence. This would be in congruence with the common surprising observation that business leaders are often concerned with small details. This may indeed be the case, due to personal experience or to show how deep they can go into controlling the business system they lead. Yet, I would not go too far in that direction.

Scanning and assessing a firm's portfolio of competence or the new competence base required by an anticipated change cannot dive into that level of detail. A combination of intuition, common sense, analytical rigor and judgement is needed here. One should keep in mind that the analysis should focus on strategic elements of competence. This is not about a systematic inventory of competence.

Entry Points for Strategic Competence Identification

I suggest following a process similar to risk analysis. Natural entry points can typically be:
- *functional departments*: marketing, sales, distribution; logistics, production, purchasing; R&D, innovation; business development; finance, controlling; HR; etc.;
- *key processes*: strategy and planning; budgeting; recruiting and training; managing partnerships and M&As, post-M&A integration; innovation, project management; operations optimization, investment plans; designing and implementing transformation plans; etc.;

– *businesses*: looking at specificities per lines of business; reporting; economies of scale and economies of scope; etc.;
– *geographies*: business development internationally; reporting and control of international operations; interregional interactions;
– *culture*: identity, values, organizational behavior internally and externally, etc.

Starting at a rather meta-level of analysis, a quick first scan can help identify items of competence that could be critical. Then, investigating the chains of causality on those items can help point out critical elements of competence, whatever the granularity.

> The irruption of human insulin in the business of diabetes treatment did not affect the distribution capabilities of incumbents. R&D purchasing and manufacturing were more likely to be affected, thus suggesting digging more into these items to understand in what sense and to what extent they were to be affected. In turn, the subsequent irruption of continuous glucose monitoring (CGM) devices totally changed the manufacturing competence required. The knowledge and know-how about measuring the glucose level was held by the pharmaceutical incumbents. Yet, the digital transmission to a mobile via Bluetooth was a different story. This led most insulin suppliers to consider forming partnerships or outsourcing the supply of the device.

The exercise is a bit different when it comes to identifying the competence required by a technology (or more generally a change) that still needs to shape up concretely before it can be observed. This is the case in the situation of indeterminacy.

I first argue that a new technology, even still uncertain in its form and content, can be characterized by a set of competencies that it is likely to carry with it. In a way, I basically argue that while technology forecasting is risky (meaning it is difficult to predict which among a set of candidate technologies will win the race in the end, if any), assessing what will be the logical ingredients needed to implement a technological change is much more feasible.

In addition, the concept of boundary objects can help here.

Boundary objects

This concept stems from sociology. It designates what stakeholders in a common endeavor (say, for example, a project) produce and recognize as intermediate outputs of the project. Those boundary objects may be physical objects such as mock-ups or prototypes, documents such as maps, sketches or plans, or narratives, speeches, PowerPoint presentations, podcasts or videos, lists of potential targets, partners or supporters, or even categories or taxonomies. These boundary objects are likely to be interpreted in a variety of ways by the various stakeholders depending on which community they belong to. This flexibility in interpretation is what makes boundary objects a useful resource. Boundary objects contribute to keeping stakeholders together despite their differences when representing the project. As the project unfolds, going from one boundary object to the next, the stakeholders will adapt their own representation of the future outcome and eventually converge.

When a technology is fundamentally new, with no previous sectors of implementation, the expected new technology can keep most of its secrets, including new competence requirements. Yet, joining the discussions among experts on the matter (scientists, technologists, production engineers, marketers, HR) can help get access to boundary objects that may give indications about how the anticipated change could shape up over time. In other words, as they are produced along the way or envisioned before the trigger is pulled, boundary objects can help identify competencies that might be needed, should that technology eventually make it to dominance.

In the case of the fourth industrial revolution, it is obvious that such a context will make full use of digital technologies. As mentioned in the introduction of the book and earlier in this chapter, the industry for the future will require new competencies both technical and managerial. Technological change may strongly affect technical competence for industrial operations. Yet, there should be more to it. The managerial orchestration of the transformation expected from the new technologies may require new competencies as well, of a very different nature than for the technical, but possibly of similar extent.

In this context, one (among many) of the hopes of the industry of the future is to collect data from operating plants distributed across territories. This is planned to be done in real time, from a distant central hub, say one per region. The promise is that big analytics will help find new ways of optimizing operations, by monitoring and comparing the dynamics of similar systems on several sites. This is typically expected to support predictive maintenance.

Corp Z experimented with such arrangements in Europe, Asia and the Americas. When looking closely at this use case which can be seen as a provider of boundary objects, it appears that a key lesson of such experiments is that communication and collaboration among teams is of the essence. The data collected help the center see what local teams cannot see. Yet, the local teams see things that the center cannot see. These are complementary, as long as they communicate. Yet, several barriers are present to prevent fluid communication between the central regional hub and the local plants. Language comes first. Job-floor operators or their direct supervisors are rarely fluent in a common language, typically English at Corp Z. When something urgent pops up, life shows how difficult and misleading communication can be. Second comes culture. The local teams have been used to taking care of their own unit. A reporting system was in place for sure. Yet, they were in charge. Having Big Brother's eyes over one's shoulder is not easy and does not help pick up the phone more often than before. Third, there is a flavor of suspicion. Local teams logically fear being made redundant. In fact, Corp Z insists that this is not the purpose of the project. They speak highly of the value of the local experience of seasoned technicians who are pillars of the teams distributed over the scattered units (Corp Z operates many small units – about five to ten or so employees on each site – providing B2B service to industrial customers who need supply of various products and specific support solutions).

All in all, the Corp Z experiments conducted in three important regions of the world generated feedback (vital importance of communication) that can be seen as boundary objects around one of the many changes potentially brought about by the industry of the future when it comes to managerial orchestration.

Although the fourth industrial revolution is still fuzzy and complex, I argue that the interpretation of the boundary objects reported here illustrates how the competence framework developed in Part III can be used:

– Experiments at the frontier of industrial practice can help grasp potential future industrial transformations, both technically and managerially.
– A key element that stems from the case is that the essential competence needed to cope with the change will not so much be the technicalities of the capture,

structuring, transmission, storage and analysis of data. There might be a bit of that. Yet, a key competence needed relates to cultural change, inter-site and site-center collaboration, languages, trust, internal communication, and respect of the human professional experience and technical memory on-site compared to legitimate (possibly sometimes overplayed?) expectations from big analytics.

In addition, this example illustrates how an analysis of the competencies underlying technologies can shed light on a context of indeterminacy.[33] I indeed argue that managerial orchestration is an umbrella label used in a context of indeterminacy to designate an array of managerial ways to orchestrate the transformation of industry. In other words, as suggested earlier, the item "managerial orchestration" designates the bulky indeterminate set of aggregated sub-items not yet disentangled from one another and thus not yet identified (what forms of key competencies could be needed for managerial orchestration of the transformation attached to the fourth industrial revolution?).

In other words, as I argued earlier, in the case of indeterminacy, it may still be possible to identify potentially needed competencies while not being able to identify technological options as such.

The arrangements experimented in the case described point to the extremely strong need for enhanced collaboration, communication, cooperative behavior and trust (between the distributed plants and the regional central hubs). This is typically a non-purely technical, behavioral competence set, illustrating the importance of what I called the metabolism part of competence.

---

33 For the sake of the illustration, managerial orchestration is assimilated here to a technology in the metaphoric sense of a "managerial" technology. This is to keep the logic of the analysis. In fact, managerial orchestration is a challenge that requires organizational competencies (including behavioral competencies as we see in this example).

Summary of Key Points of Part III

(1) Competence is an interesting way to assess the ability of a firm to cope with change when technology disrupts competition in a business arena.

(2) By competence, I mean both the competence of individuals and more importantly, if not primarily, the organizational competence, meaning the collective capabilities of an organization.

(3) The key point is that what is being challenged by technological change is the competence base of the incumbents. When substituting for the soon-to-be-former dominant technology N, the future new dominant technology N+1 will require a new set of competencies. Some of the incumbents' competence may turn out to be reinforced by the change while some other parts may be rendered obsolete.

(4) The competence gap captures the distance between the portfolio of competence of a firm and the new set of competencies needed for a new technology. Hence the competence gap varies according to firms and the technologies candidate to become the next dominant technology.

(5) To clarify the concept of competence to think about technological change strategically, I put forward a model of competence.

(6) A first building block of the model stems from the key distinctions encountered describing the dimensions of competence: tacit/articulated, individual/collective, cognitive/behavioral, positive/negative, tangible/intangible, intended/contingent, demonstrated/potential, assets and resources/coordinated deployment function.

(7) A second building block of the model is a classification of competence connecting the concepts to managerial categories. Resources and assets are apart from what I call the "organizational alchemy" that both echoes and extends the classic concept of orchestration or coordinated deployment of assets and resources. The word "competence" is kept for what falls under the "organizational alchemy" category.

(8) Another building block of the model identifies different forms of learning (through information, action and interaction) as well as a sequence in competence development, also referring to the competence building/leveraging continuum. Indeed, like muscles build up through exercising, competence is being reinforced while being leveraged.

(9) Using these ingredients as building blocks, a model of competence emerges around three generic forms (knowledge, know-how and attitudes). The latter is too often neglected in the literature on competence/resource-based view. Usual managerial levers for action (strategizing, organizing, motivating) are added, showing that they do not fully align to the three generic descriptive dimensions of the competence referential. This points to an unavoidable mismatch between managerial keyboards and the competence base of the organization.

(10) Strategy and vision, as well as the organizational structure and processes, are introduced in the model. This leads to the idea of enlarging the content of the coor-

https://doi.org/10.1515/9783111397979-027

dinated deployment of assets and resources to include not only management processes but also the identity, the shared vision and the organizational structure. I argue that these are the four elements of the organizational alchemy (including coordinated deployment/orchestration) that form competence.

(11) The most strategic among the four elements is likely to be the behavioral dimension (culture or identity, shared value, individual and collective behavior, sense of a shared mission, ways to interact internally and externally, etc.). This is the most important element of the organizational alchemy in my view because of scarcity, non-imitability, non-tradability, deep embeddedness in the heart of the organization, and, I argue, because it can be a source of significant value – and a strong source of organizational inertia when it comes to change.

(12) The dynamics of competence building is added to the model, discussing the unique status of expertise and the importance of the pre-existing competence base influencing the flow of learning. (The existing competence base both habilitates and constrains.)

(13) The three generic descriptive dimensions of competence in the model are interdependent, reinforcing each other as learning takes place simultaneously in all three directions.

(14) The competence gap can be seen as some form of a qualitative metric of change.

(15) The concept of competence suggests futureproofing in the form of an insurance for the uncertainty attached to future change. The underlying competence base provides a way to do so. This means complementing the internal technical consensus via an addendum to keep some resources to pay for insurance on some specific competencies that may prove useful should the internal consensus turn out to be wrong. This is done just in case a quick refocus would be needed as the change unveils. This is about insurance to stay agile, "just in case".

(16) When facing change, one of the challenges facing the firm is the competence gap – and how to narrow it down.

There are two ways of narrowing the competence gap. One is to try to influence the change to transform the newly required set of competencies to bring it closer to the firm's competence base; the second is to try to bridge the gap by accessing the missing elements of competence.

Influence (in the sense of power to influence) is usually limited for most of the players in a competitive arena. Bridging the competence gap by stretching to reach out for missing competence is usually more of an option – unless the competence gap is too wide.

According to the capacity of the firm on either of these two levers (influencing or bridging), and depending on the width of the competence gap, the analysis leads to four strategic options: trigger, shape, stretch or redeploy.

(17) All in all, the concept of competence is difficult to operationalize because it is blurry and not easy to grasp in practice. Business intuition and managerial judgement are needed to conduct identification and analyses at relevant levels of granularity.

(18) The informal behavioral part of the "alchemy of competence" is where strategic competence is more likely to be found. This is what Barney describes as small "o". This is what I metaphorically describe as the metabolism of an organization.

(19) The list of organizational sub-parts of a firm is a sensible concrete way of scanning an organization in search of key competencies to survive a technological change: functional departments, key processes, businesses, geographies. The specific subcategory "attitudes/small 'o'" can be added to the list because of its sensitive strategic importance. Starting at a rather meta-level of analysis, a quick first scan can help identify items that could be critical. Then, investigating the chains of causality on those items can help point out critical elements, whatever the granularity.

(20) Corp Z's experimentation to feed data collected from distributed plants into central regional hubs was used to foreshadow typical new requirements of the "industry of the future" (and digitalization). The arrangements experimented in the use case point to the extremely strong need for enhanced collaboration, communication, cooperative behavior and trust (between the distributed plants and the regional central hubs). This is typically a non-purely technical, behavioral set of competencies that illustrates the importance of what I called the metabolism part of competence. A sensitive matter, indeed.

References for Part III and Further Reading

Abernathy, W. J., & Clark, K. B. (1985). Innovation: Mapping the winds of creative destruction. *Research Policy, 14*(1), 3–22.

Arrow K. J. (1962). The economic implications of learning by doing. *Review of Economic Studies,vol 29*, issue 3, 155–173.

Atkinson, A. B., & Stiglitz, J. E. (1969). A new view of technological change. *Economic Journal*, vol. 79, issue 315, 573–578.

Barney, J. B. (1986a). Strategic factor markets: Expectations, luck and business strategy. *Management Science, Vol 32*, Issue 10, 1231–1241.

Barney, J. B. (1986b). Organizational culture: Can it be a source of sustained competitive advantage? *Academy of Management Review, Vol 11, N°3, 656–665*, https://doi.org/10.5465/amr.1986.4306261

Durand, T. (1997a). The alchemy of competence. Working paper, S&T, Ecole Centrale Paris.

Hambrick, D. (1989). Guest editor's introduction: Putting top managers back into the strategy picture. *Strategic Management Journal, 10*(S1), 5–15.

Hedlund, G., & Nonaka, I. (1992). The dynamics of knowledge. In In P. Lorange, J. Roos, B. Chakravarty and A. Van de Ven (Eds), *Strategic Processes*. Blackwell Business.

Moscovici, S. (1988). Notes towards a description of social representations. *European Journal of Social Psychology, Vol 18*, Issue 3, 211–250.

Pestalozzi, J. H. (1797). *Mes recherches sur la marche de la nature dans l'évolution du genre humain*. Payet Lausanne.

Piaget, J. (1948). *La naissance de l'intelligence chez l'enfant*. Delachaux et Niestlé.

Porter, M. E. (1996). What is strategy? *Harvard Business Review, 74*(6), 61–78.

Prahalad, C. K., & Hamel, G. (1990). The core competence of the corporation. *Harvard Business Review*, May-June 1990, 79–91.

Rosenberg, N. (1972). *Technology and American Economic Growth*. New York, Harper &Row.

Sanchez, R., Heene, A., & Thomas, H. (1996). Towards the theory and practice of competence-based competition. In R. Sanchez, A. Heene and H. Thomas (Eds), *Dynamics of Competence-Based Competition*. Elsevier, London, 1–35.

Senge, P. M. (1990). *The Fifth Discipline*. New York, Doubleday.

Schneider, S. C., & Anglemar, R. (1993). Cognition in organizational analysis: Who's minding the store? *Organization Studies, 14*(3), 347–374.

Strategor. (1988, 1993). *Stratégie, Structure, Décision, Identité : Politique Générale d'Entreprises*. (Five authors: Garrette B., L Lehman-Ortega, Fredéric Leroy, P Dussauge, R Durand, B Pointeau, O Sibony), InterEditions.

Teece D. J., Pisano, G., & Shuen, A. (1997). Dynamic capabilities and strategic management. *SMJ, 18*(7), 509–533. https://doi.org/10.1002/(SICI)1097-0266(199708)18:7<509::AID-SMJ882>3.0.CO;2-Z

Teece, D. J. (2007). Explicating dynamic capabilities: The nature and microfoundations of (sustainable) enterprise performance. *Strateg. Manage. J., 28*(13), 1319–1350. https://doi.org/10.1002/smj.640

Wernerfelt, B. (1984). A resource-based view of the firm. *Strategic Management Journal, 5*, Vol. 5, No. 2, pp. 171–180.

Further Reading

Abetti, P. A., (2000). Critical success factors for radical technological innovation: A five case study. *Creativity and Innovation Management, 9*(4), 208–221. https://doi.org/10.1111/1467-8691.00194

Ansoff I. (1986). Competitive analysis on the personal computer *The Journal of Business Strategy* Volume 6 Issue 3, pp. 28–36. https://doi.org/10.1108/eb039117

https://doi.org/10.1515/9783111397979-028

Atuahene-Gima, K. (2005). Resolving the capability-rigidity paradox in new product innovation. *J. Mark.* *69*(4), 61–83. https://doi.org/10.1509/jmkg.2005.69.4.61

Barney, J. B. (1991). Firm resources and sustained competitive advantage. *Journal of Management, 17*(1), 99–120. https://doi.org/10.1177/014920639101700108

Barney, J. B. (2001). Resource-based theories of competitive advantage: A ten-year retrospective on the resource-based view. *J. Manag. 27*(6), 643–650. https://doi.org/10.1016/S0149-2063(01)00115-5

Barney, J., Wright, M., & Ketchen, D. J. (2001). The resource-based view of the firm: Ten years after 1991. *J. Manag. 27*(6), 625–641. https://doi.org/10.1177/014920630102700601

Bettis, A. R., & Prahalad, C. K. (1995). The dominant logic: Retrospective and extension. *Strategic Management Journal, Vol 16, N°1*, 5–14.

Brusoni, S., Prencipe, A., & Pavitt, K. (2001). Knowledge specialization, organizational coupling, and the boundaries of the firm: Why do firms know more than they make? *Adm. Sci. Q., 46*(4), 597–621. https://doi.org/10.2307/3094825

Christensen, J. F. (1995). Asset profiles for technological innovation. *Research Policy, 24*(5), 727–745. https://doi.org/10.1016/0048-7333(94)00794-8

Cooper, R. G., Edgett, S. J., & Kleinschmidt, E. J. (2000). New problems, new solutions: Making portfolio management more effective. *Research-Technology Management, 43*(2), 18–33.

Danneels, E. (2002). The dynamics of product innovation and firm competences. *Strateg. Manage. J., 23*(12), 1095–1121. https://doi.org/10.1002/smj.275

Danneels, E. (2008). Organizational antecedents of second-order competences. *Strateg. Manage. J., 29*(5), 519–543. https://doi.org/10.1002/smj.684

Dosi G., Teece, D., & Winter, S. (1992). Toward a theory of corporate coherence. In Dosi G., R. Gianetti and P. A. Toninelli (Eds.), *Technology and the Enterprise in a Historical Perspective*. Oxford University Press (preliminary remarks).

Durand, T. (1992). The dynamics of cognitive technological maps. In P. Lorange, J. Roos, B. Chakravarty and A. Van de Ven (Eds), *Strategic Processes*. Blackwell Business.

Durand, T. (1997b). Strategizing innovation: Competence analysis in assessing strategic change. In A. Heene and R. Sanchez (Eds), *Competence-Based Strategic Management*. John Wiley.

Durand, T. (2000) Forms of incompetence. In R., Sanchez and A., Heene (Eds), *Theory Development for Competence-Based Management*, Volume 6(A) in *Advances in Applied Business Strategy*. Greenwich, CT, JAI Press.

Durand, T., Mounoud, E., & Ramanantsoa, B. (1996). Uncovering strategic assumptions: Understanding managers' ability to build representations. *European Management Journal, 14*(4), 389–398.

Durand, T., & Guerra-Vieira, S. (1997). Competence-based strategies when facing innovation. But what is competence? In H. Thomas, D. O'Neal and R. Alvarado (Eds), *Strategic Discovery: Competing in New Arenas*. John Wiley & Sons Ltd.

Dyer, J. H., & Singh, H. (1998). The relational view: Cooperative strategy and sources of interorganizational competitive advantage. *Acad. Manage. Rev., 23*(4), 660–679. https://doi.org/10.2307/259056

Eggers, J. P., & Kaplan, S. (2009). Cognition and renewal: comparing CEO and organizational effects on incumbent adaptation to technical change. *Organization Science, 20*(2), 461–477. https://doi.org/10.1287/orsc.1080.0401

Eisenhardt, K. M., & Martin, J. A. (2000). Dynamic capabilities: What are they? *Strateg. Manage. J., 21*(10–11), 1105–1121. https://doi.org/10.1002/1097-0266(200010/11)21:10/11<1105::AID-SMJ133>3.0.CO;2-E

Ethiraj, S. K., Kale, P., Krishnan, M. S., & Singh, J. V. (2005). Where do capabilities come from and how do they matter? A study in the software services industry. *Strateg. Manage. J., 26*(1), 25–45. https://doi.org/10.1002/smj.433

Ferreira, J., Coelho, A., & Moutinho, L. (2020). Dynamic capabilities, creativity and innovation capability and their impact on competitive advantage and firm performance: The moderating role of entrepreneurial orientation. *Technovation, 92–93*, 102061. https://doi.org/10.1016/j.technovation.2018.11.004

Floyd, S. W., & Lane, P. J. (2000). Strategizing throughout the organization: Managing role conflict in strategic renewal. *Acad. Manage. Rev.*, *25*(1), 154–177. https://doi.org/10.2307/259268

Galunic, D. C., & Rodan, S. (1998). Resource recombinations in the firm: Knowledge structures and the potential for Schumpeterian innovation. *Strateg. Manage. J.*, *19*(12), 1193–1201. https://doi.org/10.1002/(SICI)1097-0266(1998120)19:12<1193::AID-SMJ5>3.0.CO;2-F

Grebel, T. (2009). Technological change: A microeconomic approach to the creation of knowledge. *Structural Change and Economic Dynamics, Vol 20, Issue* 4, 301–312. https://doi.org/10.1016/j.strueco.2009.05.003

Hanelt, A., Bohnsack, R., Marz, D., & Antunes Marante, C. (2021). A systematic review of the literature on digital transformation: Insights and implications for strategy and organizational change. *J. Manage. Stud.*, *58*(5), 1159–1197. https://doi.org/10.1111/joms.12639

Helfat, C. E., Peteraf, M. A. (2003). The dynamic resource-based view: Capability lifecycles. *Strateg. Manage. J.*, *24*(10), 997–1010. https://doi.org/10.1002/smj.332

Henderson, R., & Cockburn, I. (1994). Measuring competence? Exploring firm effects in pharmaceutical research. *Strateg. Manage. J. 15*(S1), 63–84.

Jones, G. K., Lanctot, A., & Teegen, H. J. (2001). Determinants and performance impacts of external technology acquisition. *J. Bus. Ventur. 16*(3), 255–283. https://doi.org/10.1016/S0883-9026(99)00048-8

Kaplan, S., & Mary, T. (2008). Thinking about technology: Applying a cognitive lens to technical change. *Research Policy 37*(5), 790–805.

King, A. A., & Tucci, C. L. (2002). Incumbent entry into new market niches: The role of experience and managerial choice in the creation of dynamic capabilities. *Manage. Sci.*, *48*(2), 171–186. https://doi.org/10.1287/mnsc.48.2.171.253

Kogut, B., & Kulatilaka, N. (2001). Capabilities as real options. *Organ Sci.*, *12*(6), 744–758. https://doi.org/10.1287/orsc.12.6.744.10082

Landini, F., Lee, K., & Malerba, F. (2017). A history-friendly model of the successive changes in industrial leadership and the catch-up by latecomers. *Research Policy*, *46*(2), 431–446. https://doi.org/10.1016/j.respol.2016.09.005

Laursen, K., Leone, M. I., & Torrisi, S. (2010). Technological exploration through licensing: new insights from the licensee's point of view. *Ind. Corp. Change*, *19*(3), 871–897. https://doi.org/10.1093/icc/dtq034

Lavie, D. (2006). The competitive advantage of interconnected firms: An extension of the resource-based view. *Acad. Manage. Rev.*, *31*(3), 638–658. https://doi.org/10.5465/AMR.2006.21318922

Lin, S.-H., Scott, B. A., & Matta, F. K. (2019). The dark side of transformational leader behaviors for leaders themselves: A conservation of resources perspective. *Acad. Manage. J.*, *62*(5), 1556–1582. https://doi.org/10.5465/amj.2016.1255

Lorenzoni, G., & Lipparini, A. (1999). The leveraging of interfirm relationships as a distinctive organizational capability: A longitudinal study. Strateg. Manage. J., Vol 20, Issue 4, 317–338.

Lundvall, B. A. (2016). Innovation as an interactive process: From user-producer interaction to the national system of innovation. In *The Learning Economy and the Economics of Hope* (pp. 61–84). Anthem Press.

McEvily, S. K., Eisenhardt, K. M., & Prescott, J. E. (2004). The global acquisition, leverage, and protection of technological competencies. *Strateg. Manage. J. 25*(8–9), 713–722. https://doi.org/10.1002/smj.425

McEvily, B., & Marcus, A. (2005). Embedded ties and the acquisition of competitive capabilities. *Strateg. Manage. J.*, *26*(11), 1033–1055. https://doi.org/10.1002/smj.484

Mikalef, P., Boura, M., Lekakos, G., & Krogstie, J. (2019). Big data analytics capabilities and innovation: The mediating role of dynamic capabilities and moderating effect of the environment. *Brit. J. Manage. 30*(2), 272–298. https://doi.org/10.1111/1467-8551.12343

Miozzo, M., DiVito, L., & Desyllas, P. (2016). When do acquirers invest in the R&D assets of acquired science-based firms in cross-border acquisitions? The role of technology and capabilities similarity and complementarity. *Long Range Planning*, *49*(2), 221–240. https://doi.org/10.1016/j.lrp.2015.07.002

O'Reilly, C. A., Tushman, M. L. (2011). Organizational ambidexterity in action: How managers explore and exploit. Calif. *Manage. Rev.*, *53*(4), 5–22. https://doi.org/10.1525/cmr.2011.53.4.5

Orlikowski, W. J. (2002). Knowing in practice: Enacting a collective capability in distributed organizing. *Organ Sci.*, *13*(3), 249–273. https://doi.org/10.1287/orsc.13.3.249.2776

Orlitzky, M., Schmidt, F. L., & Rynes, S. L. (2003). Corporate social and financial performance: A meta-analysis. *Organ. Stud.*, *24*(3), 403–441. https://doi.org/10.1177/0170840603024003910

Pereira, V., & Bamel, U. (2021). Extending the resource and knowledge based view: A critical analysis into its theoretical evolution and future research directions. *J. Bus. Res.*, *132*, 557–570. https://doi.org/10.1016/j.jbusres.2021.04.021

Porter, M. E. (1980). *Competitive Strategy: Techniques for Analyzing Industries and Competitors*. New York, The Free Press.

Prahalad, C. K., & Hamel, G. (1994). *Competing for the Future*. Harvard Business School Press.

Ritter, T., & Gemunden, H. G. (2004). The impact of a company's business strategy on its technological competence, network competence and innovation success. *J. Bus. Res. 57*(5), 548–556. https://doi.org/10.1016/S0148-2963(02)00320-X

Sarkar, S., Osiyevskyy, O., & Clegg, S. R. (2018). Incumbent capability enhancement in response to radical innovations. *European Management Journal*, *36*(3), 353–365. https://doi.org/10.1016/j.emj.2017.05.006

Sirmon, D. G., Hitt, M. A., & Ireland, R. D. (2007). Managing firm resources in dynamic environments to create value: Looking inside the black box. *Acad. Manage. Rev.*, *32*(1), 273–292. https://doi.org/10.5465/AMR.2007.23466005

Teece, D. J. (1996). Firm organization, industrial structure, and technological innovation. *Journal of Economic Behavior and Organization 31*(2), 193–224. https://doi.org/10.1016/S0167-2681(96)00895-5

Teece, D. J. (2010). Business models, business strategy and innovation. *Long Range Plan*, *43*(2–3), 172–194. https://doi.org/10.1016/j.lrp.2009.07.003

Teece, D. J., & Pisano, G. (1994). The dynamic capabilities of firms: An introduction. *Industrial and Corporate Change*, *3*(3), 537–556.

Tripsas, M., & Gavetti, G. (2000). Capabilities, cognition, and inertia: Evidence from digital imaging. *Strateg. Manage. J.*, *21*(10–11), 1147–1161. https://doi.org/10.1002/1097-0266(200010/11)21:10/11<1147::AID-SMJ128>3.3.CO;2-I

Troise, C., Corvello, V., Ghobadian, A., & O'Regan, N. (2022). How can SMEs successfully navigate VUCA environment: The role of agility in the digital transformation era. *Technol. Forecast. Soc. Chang. 174*, 121227. https://doi.org/10.1016/j.techfore.2021.121227

Volberda, H. W., Baden-Fuller, C., van den Bosch, F. A. J. (2001). Mastering strategic renewal: Mobilising renewal journeys in multi-unit firms. *Long Range Planning*, *34*(2), 159–178. https://doi.org/10.1016/S0024-6301(01)00032-2

Von Hippel, E. (1976). The dominant role of users in the scientific instrument innovation process. *Research Policy*, vol 5. issue 3, 212–239.

Von Krogh, G., & Roos, J. (1995). A perspective on knowledge, competence and strategy. *Personnel Review*. Vol. 24 No. 3, pp. 56–76.

Von Krogh, G., & Roos, J. (1995). Conversation management. *European Management Journal*, Vol. 13, Issue 4, 390–394.

Warner, K. S. R., & Waeger, M. (2019). Building dynamic capabilities for digital transformation: An ongoing process of strategic renewal. *Long Range Plan.*, *52*(3), 326–349. https://doi.org/10.1016/j.lrp.2018.12.001

Wernerfelt, B. (1995). The resource-based view of the firm: Ten years after. *Strategic Management Journal*, Vol. 16, No. 3, 171–174.

Winter, S. G. (2003). Understanding dynamic capabilities. *Strateg. Manage. J.*, *24*(10), 991–995. https://doi.org/10.1002/smj.318

Yang, K.-P., Chou, C., Chiu, Y.-J. (2014). How unlearning affects radical innovation: The dynamics of social capital and slack resources. *Technological Forecasting and Social Change, (87)*, 152–163. https://doi.org/10.1016/j.techfore.2013.12.014

Zahra, S. A., & George, G. (2002). Absorptive capacity: A review, reconceptualization, and extension. *Acad. Manage. Rev., Vol 27*, N°2, 185–203.

Zollo, M., & Winter, S. G. (2002). Deliberate learning and the evolution of dynamic capabilities. Organ *Sci. 13*(3), 339–351. https://doi.org/10.1287/orsc.13.3.339.2780

Part IV: **Managerial Implications – Path Creation
in Practice**

Introduction

In Part I, I built a framework representing how technology evolves over time and its strategic consequences. In Part II, I complemented this framework with a focus on technological substitutions and patterns that depart from the S-curve. In Part III, I suggested to adopt a competence perspective to think about technology strategically, clarifying the concept of competence, introducing the competence gap and calling upon competence to insure against technological uncertainty.

In Part IV, I discuss ways to operationalize the overall framework stemming from Parts I to III. More specifically, I discuss the role of a chief technology officer (CTO) in preparing top management decisions in relation to technology strategy. This obviously includes monitoring technological continuity, preparing for the future and, at times, facing upcoming technological change triggered by internal developments or coming as an external shock.

In other words, this part aims at helping practitioners make use of what I covered in the three first parts of the book.

https://doi.org/10.1515/9783111397979-029

Chapter 20
The CTO – Who is Minding the Technology Store?

Technology strategy, the topic of this book, is a task for top managers, those in charge of a business or a set of businesses.[34] Yet, the corresponding tasks may be covered or at least nurtured by an array of departments in the classic organization of a firm: research, development, or R&D; technical department, innovation (at large), strategy; legal; or at times manufacturing or production, and even IT. There are many configurations according to a firm's sector, size, age or traditions. I observe that the topics of research, science, technology, development, innovation, technical processes, methods and process designs, and innovation are too often aggregated into some strange mix that turns out to be misleading, if not counterproductive. The acronym RDTI (research-development, technology, innovation) is often used to capture the mix., I will add the technical dimension as well, thus retaining RDTIT as the umbrella name, in the sense that I will clarify below.

I argue that a chief technology officer (CTO) is the most adequate position to fulfill the role of thinking about technology strategically. More precisely, I argue that the position of a CTO is specifically designed to prepare for, and deal with, technological change, assessment of strategic options when facing change, selection and planning for future evolutions in periods of continuity.

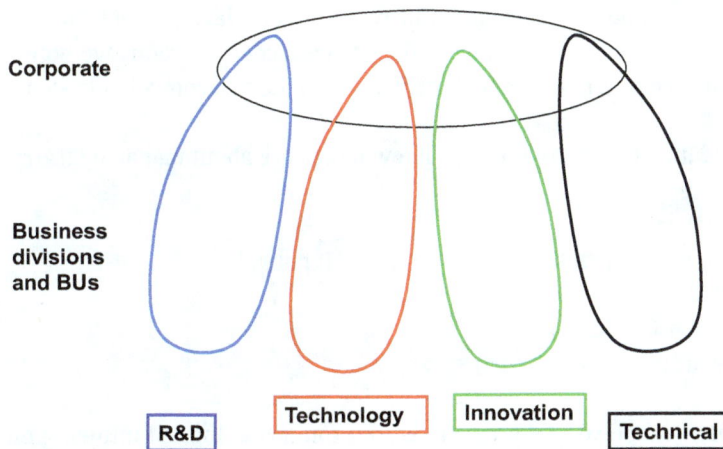

Fig. 45: The four petals of RDTIT (R&D, technology, innovation, technical).

There is a need to clarify the specific role of a CTO with respect to other players who follow technological matters in a variety of capacities in the organization.

---

34 The title of this chapter is borrowed (and adapted) from Schneider and Angelmar (1993).

https://doi.org/10.1515/9783111397979-030

In this context, I suggest that four stylized (archetypal) complementary roles (or what I will call "petals") can be identified for the management of RDTIT in the firm: these are R&D, technology, innovation and technical. See Fig. 45 showing four petals covering the corporate as well as the business divisions and the business units (BUs).

R&D

This petal is mostly found in companies dealing with technology, one way or the other. Research is seen as a necessity to investigate new topics and follow scientific progress. It is viewed as an investment to explore future technological options and prepare for the future. Note that there is no optimal way to decide an adequate amount of yearly spending on research. Most players tend to adopt a level of research expenditure around the average spending in the sector (measured as percentage of sales).

Development is a different sport. While research calls upon Doctors (PhDs) to access and build new scientific knowledge, development needs engineers to find solutions for users' needs. Development is in fact twofold. On the one hand, development searches for technological solutions to fulfill the requirements of marketing briefs. On the other hand, development is also expected to optimize, improve and rationalize existing product/service offerings and the production processes attached. In other words, development covers both design and optimization.

In this sense, the systematic juxtaposition of research and development into the widespread R&D acronym is often misleading as it conveys a counterproductive notion of two sides of the same coin, if not a single function where the two components would be merged.

The tasks covered under R&D are the most known: they are about managing R&D:
- securing R&D funding;
- programming R&D projects;
- monitoring work progress on the projects in the R&D portfolio;
- cooperating with external R&D partners;
- ensuring adequate use of R&D results;
- managing R&D staff (with HR support).

R&D has some hierarchical power, with resources, but somewhat limited influence on business decisions:
- power of running budgets and teams;
- status (and image) of a cost center;
- access to insider information/scientific knowledge;
- risk of a techno-push attitude;
- needs marketing and strategy counterparts.

R&D is typically led by a VP for R&D.

Technology

In contrast, the tasks covered under the technology petal of RDTIT are less commonly described; they are about thinking about technology strategically:
- scanning for new technologies;
- managing technology intelligence (scientific as well – with R&D);
- assessing technologies;
- building technology roadmaps;
- monitoring and maintaining the portfolio of technologies;
- monitoring and maintaining the portfolio of technological competence;
- monitoring and maintaining the technology ecosystem of the firm.

Technology has no hierarchical power but significant influence on business decisions:
- small team, small budget but significant power to influence (e.g., to impose internal standards);
- influence via legitimacy of knowledge and CEO support;
- some access to strategic issues;
- risk of a techno-push attitude;
- needs marketing and strategy counterparts.

The technology petal of RDTIT is led by a CTO.

Innovation

The tasks covered under the innovation petal of RDTIT are often misunderstood. They are about promoting innovation (in the sense of insuring that each and every part of the organization is keen to innovate). It is not about innovating and managing innovation projects from the top. It is about designing, deploying and managing innovation processes throughout the organization:
- organizing the internal innovation processes;
  - ideation
  - maturation
  - managing innovation projects
- setting up innovation teams;
- managing open innovation processes;
- running incubators;
- deploying the innovation processes in divisions and Bus;
- promoting best innovation practices;
- mutualizing ideas and innovation projects across Bus when relevant.

Innovation has no or limited hierarchical power and some indirect influence via the innovation processes carefully designed and hopefully deployed throughout the organization:
- no budget, small team, no power;
- influence via importance of innovation;
- need to convince Bus and divisions management;
- Limited access to strategic issues (essentially to select ideas and project proposals);
- Need to call upon inter-functional teams;
- Risk of failing to disseminate innovation processes in the organization due to difficulties in penetrating divisions and Bus. Instead, risk of focusing on managing a portfolio of innovation projects at corporate to demonstrate an ability to manage innovation – thus missing the objective of promoting innovation throughout the organization.

The innovation petal of RDTIT is led by an innovation process owner or chief innovation officer (CIO).

Technical

Finally, the tasks covered under the technical petal of RDTIT are often blurry, encompassing part or all of the above plus the focus that I describe below. A technical department is often found in small to medium-sized enterprises who cannot afford R&D plus a CTO plus an innovation officer.

I need here to clarify the difference between the concepts of technology and technique.

Technique corresponds to the empirical knowledge that stems from practice. The day-to-day operations generate a considerable amount of feedback on what works and what does not. Mistakes often lead to burnt fingers, meaning that practical knowledge tends to be learnt the hard way. Avoiding making the same mistakes again and again is the essence of technical knowledge. It is practical, empirically driven to a large extent, while also being nurtured by professional technical standard-setting and sharing of best practices in an industry.

In contrast, while also a technique, technology relies on mechanisms and principles that are explained by science. A technique may work without a full understanding of why and how it works. However, the reasons why a technology works are provided by scientific knowledge. This means that technology can be replicated in other contexts and other applications, with reasonable expectations that it should work. This does not necessarily apply to techniques that will need costly and timely experimentations before being extrapolated to new situations.

It can be argued that the mushrooming development of technologies in recent times had to do with the considerable recombining potential of technologies, opening new venues for innovation. In sharp contrast, techniques required lengthy and costly testing before combinations can prove feasible.

The above distinction should not lead to oppose the concepts of technology and technique. They are complementary. Despite the progress of science, there will always remain some form of empirical techniques, even in the very high-tech sectors.

It is the responsibility of the technical department to capitalize on past learning, memorize the "best ways" in operating procedures, set up and enforce internal standards.

More specifically, the tasks of the technical department are about managing and sharing technical knowledge. This is about learning the lessons learnt through operations, that is the experience stemming from past finger-burning experiences that were followed by "never again". In this sense, one of the technical department's roles is to manage the dos and don'ts learnt over the years:
- defining technical standards;
- organizing technical support to units;
- technical knowledge management;
- sharing technical expertise;
- monitoring the community of technical experts, including the community of practices (CoPs) although, in principle, these are self-organized and do not necessarily accept falling into the firm's hierarchies – something that often upsets management.

From an anthropologist's perspective, Jean Lave and her former student Etienne Wenger wrote a key book that popularized CoPs. This generated much interest among practitioners. The concept was so much used that it was distorted along the way. Lave later told me that she did not recognize her baby. From her studies of learning in context, she had conceptualized the idea of CoPs as self-generated, self-organized entities gathering individuals joining in to share their experiences and knowledge as a way to both learn even more and transmit. In firms' hierarchical structures, the CoPs were created from the bottom of the organization when isolated workers would be looking for peers to interact with. It was also for them a way to escape the weight of hierarchies imposing their rules and norms. (Interestingly enough, observations of CoPs showed that layers of status were recreated inside CoPs, thus reproducing their own internal hierarchies, apart from those prevailing in the formal firm's organization.)

The chief knowledge officer of a major German firm once told me a striking anecdote. The powerful leader of a major division in the company was facing a difficult problem. He heard about a CoP existing in the group that could bring him the competence needed to find solutions to his problem – or so he thought. He thus invited the CoP's key members to a meeting and asked them for help. To his surprise, the CoP's representatives responded bluntly: "Who are you exactly to place orders onto us? We do not belong to your division. We have no time for your request." The division head, accustomed to more respect for his position, status and level of responsibility, had expected obedience and diligence. He was shocked. That day, he learnt that CoPs may not be easily controlled. This however should not prevent the technical director of an organization from establishing good working relations with the CoPs and in a subtle and positive way monitor their activities.

Note in passing that this suggests that CoPs should be careful to enroll both technicians and technologists because merging their conversations can only add value to the firm's body of technological and technical knowledge.

With limited hierarchical power, technical directors can exert their influence given the respect for the knowledge they have accumulated over the years:

- back-office power to secure choices, especially in operations and industrialization;
- limited teams, but visible;
- influence of a service provider to units;
- no direct access to strategic issues.

The technical petal of RDTIT is led by the technical director.

These respective roles (VP of R&D, CTO, CIO, technical director) are obviously complementary, with a few overlaps where coordination is needed. When the firm's size and activities do not justify the four positions, there may be joint roles. Yet, the decomposition presented above points to the conceptual differences between the four petals of RDTIT.

In addition, the four petals are present at both the corporate level where their head sits and in the business divisions and Bus in the form of a network of correspondents deploying the role closer to the businesses across the organization. This is illustrated on Fig. 46.

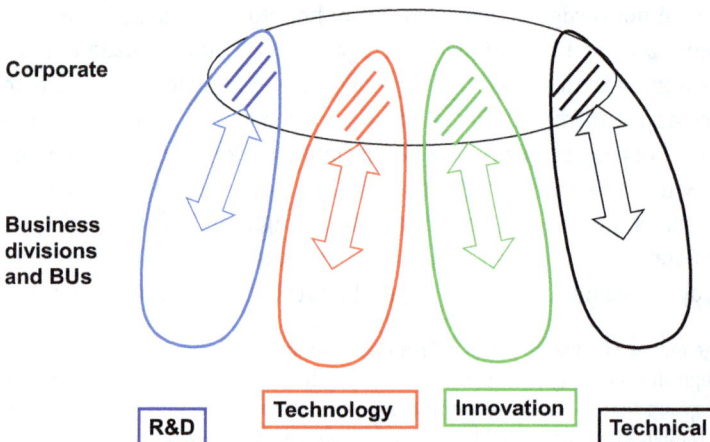

Fig. 46: The four petals of RDTIT with their corporate head and deployment in the businesses.

The role of each of the four petals of RDTIT that I have described primarily correspond to the hatched areas on Fig. 46, i.e., seen from a corporate viewpoint. Those roles are also deployed in the divisions and BUs, following similar issues at the level of the organizational units, avoiding overlaps among BUs and divisions (R&D), deciding on shared technologies for BUs and divisions (technologies), promoting best practices and mutualizing ideas and projects across BUs (innovation), or providing additional technical support, running technical days, coordinating with the purchasing department when buying new equipment (technical).

Note that the case of the technical petal may depart from this overall structure as the role of a technical director may in fact be best placed at the division level because learning the lessons of past practices is often more relevant when it takes place closer to operations.

All in all, the above discussion of the diversity of roles attached to RDTIT (research & development, technology, innovation, and technical), leads to identifying a CTO role as key for the subject of this book. Technology strategy to create a path for the firm into the future is a specific task per se, typically falling under the responsibility of top management, with the CTO running the show.

Chapter 21
Using the Overall Framework

This book is about designing and deploying strategies when facing technological change. It is about the firm creating a path for itself into the future, surfing the waves of technology. This is typically what a CTO will do to inform top management decisions on such matters. One might even say that the essence of a CTO's job is to feed top management with appropriate documented options regarding technology strategies, while making sure that the organization is competent on potentially important technologies – or prepared and agile enough to build or access competence quickly when needed.

Managing Portfolios and Preparing for Technological Change

In practice, the firm operates in a variety of businesses, taking part in a variety of added-value chains, calling upon a variety of technologies (with a variety of underlying competencies). And each of these technologies evolves at its own pace, in its own ways. As a result, the CTO needs to manage a portfolio of technologies (and a competence portfolio), each in their specific context and dynamics.

Most of the time, in the diversity of the businesses, technology will be evolving incrementally – that is in a continuous way along a trajectory to improve the dominant product design as well as the production and delivery processes. At times, however, the technology will undergo more significant changes, typically micro-radical innovations, that will require anticipation, assessment, decisions about which sub-technology to go for and transformation. And on very special occasions, a paradigmatic shift associated to a radical technological innovation might require the same "anticipation-assessment-decision-transformation" sequence, this time with much more at stake and possibly little time to respond.

This essentially reflects the representation of technological evolution discussed in Part I. Micro-radical change within the same current paradigm punctuate long periods of continuity before a major disruption brings about a new paradigm imposing new rules of the game, with a radically new technology requiring a significantly new portfolio of competence.

In short, technology strategy for path creation requires facing three types of situations: continuity, micro-radical change and paradigmatic shift.

https://doi.org/10.1515/9783111397979-031

Levers to Face Technological Change

Figure 47 presents a mapping of the levers available to management when it comes to monitoring (and preparing for) technological change (including triggering change), as well as acting to benefit from, or at least coping with, the resulting dynamics.

The columns from left to right on Fig. 47 cover the logical steps of watching out for and monitoring technological evolution (its dynamics and context), analyzing internally all the potentially weak or sensitive points to be addressed in more detail and accessing the technologies and underlying competence that could be needed further down the road. At times, this may have to be done more urgently, if "what could be coming next" was not anticipated and prepared for properly enough – transforming the CTO task in a desperate run behind technological change.

More specifically, the mapping of Fig. 47 starts (on the left-hand side) with doing the managerial homework of listening to weak signals, and for that matter strong signals as well, before anything else. Given the focus of this book, this obviously includes technology scouting as a key component of this collecting of background information. In addition, this calls upon standard business intelligence practices: market research, societal trends, environmental challenges or regulatory evolution, etc. This also includes competitive intelligence to find out what competitors are preparing, technology-wise and beyond.

In addition, beyond the above monitoring of what is happening outside the firm, there is another basic piece of homework to do: this is about conducting technology reviews on the diversity of existing businesses, as well as on candidate new businesses that top management is considering for future ventures (e.g., diversification). To start with, this means covering the value chains that the firm is taking part in. In turn, this also means systematically assessing the opportunities for one or several of three complementary challenges: improvement, regeneration and diversification. These are the three generic ways to use technology to create, consolidate, maintain and grow strategic positions in a business. More precisely, the issue is for each of the businesses to assess how important it is for the firm to develop or access specific new technologies (and their underlying competence). This is usually called technological resource development. These new technologies and pieces of competence are expected to contribute to improving or regenerating existing businesses and/or permit exploiting diversification opportunities.

The "analyze" center column on Fig. 47 shows a list of tools. I have introduced the concept of dual technology trees in Part I (Chapter 8) and the window of bifurcation (together with the concept of trigger relay) in Part II (Chapter 14). I have not yet covered an interesting tool (technology roadmapping) developed by David Probert (Farrukh et al.) and his team at the University of Cambridge. I will do it in a subsequent section below.

Once a list of technologies potentially needed for the future has been generated, the next task is to list the underlying competencies attached. Both lists (technologies

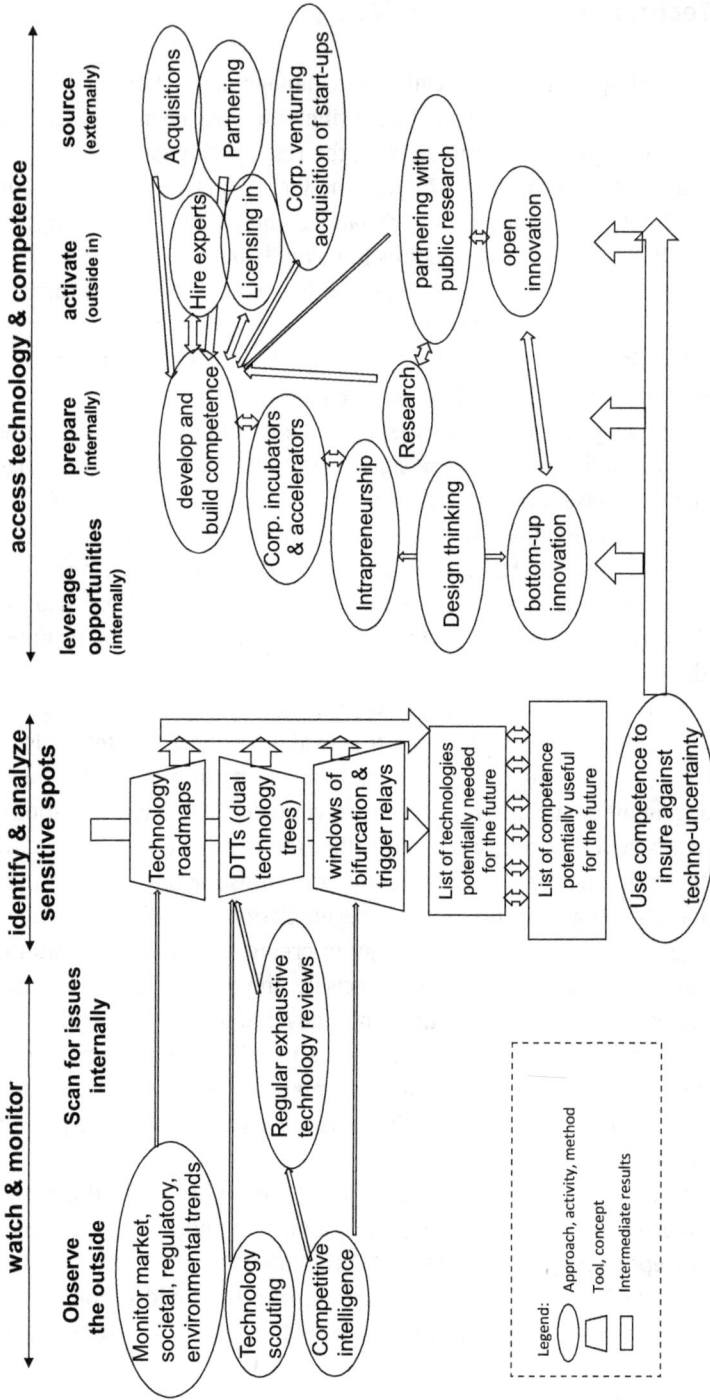

Fig. 47: Levers to face technological change.

and competence potentially needed and useful for the future of the businesses) constitute essential first-stage outcomes of the strategic thinking process regarding technology for the firm to create a path for itself into the future. The rationale discussed in
Part III, consisting of insuring against technology uncertainty via the corresponding
underlying competencies, fits right here (bottom of central column on Fig. 47).

On that basis, the right part of the mapping on Fig. 47 identifies ways to prepare
the firm for technological change by offering a series of activities or actions to access
or develop the technologies identified and/or build the missing bits and pieces of competence attached. Typically, this connects back to the usual role of research, the programming of which is logically influenced by the technological exploration conducted
on the left part of Fig. 47. (Obviously, the endogenous dynamics of scientific progress
is also to be taken into account in programming research.)

In this context, the firm can hope for serendipity, at least to some extent. Being
active on the technological front through a committed effort to search in a variety of
directions can generate new ideas and venues for business regeneration or expansion. Serendipity may offer some unexpected ways not being searched for. The key
for it is to stay alert, searching and scanning for new opportunities. Searching for
something and finding something else is the definition of serendipity. A dose of opportunism is fair play in the quest for a path into the future of the firm. Planning for
serendipity or even counting on it would be demanding too much. Yet, seeing and
seizing what serendipity brings, if and when it does, is for those prepared for it. In
the context of this book, serendipity requires the firm to be actively in search for
ways to surf the waves of technological evolution.

All in all, the key aim of the right part of Fig. 47 is to access the needed technologies or prepare for them by developing and building competence accordingly. This
can be done internally in planned ways -see the "prepare" column. On the next column just on the left (leverage), this can also be done internally by opportunistically
leveraging innovations that come from within the firm on bottom-up or intrapreneur-
ial modes and then developed through the support offered to such endogenous innovative activities by the firm's infrastructure (e.g., R&D, corporate incubators and
accelerators). This loops back to the theme of serendipity and opportunism.

When issues are pressing, when they suddenly became a matter of urgency, it
means that all the preparatory work described above failed to deliver adequate protection to the firm against exogenous technological shocks. It is too late to leverage
competence to insure against technological uncertainty. It is no longer time to plan
for medium- or longer-term solutions. In most instances, things need to be treated immediately. Given the usually long lead times of technological development (a matter
of months at best, and more often years), the only option left is to look for existing
solutions outside. See the far right "source" column on Fig. 47. This can be done
through acquisitions (fast, at least in principle, and expensive – with well-known difficulties as post acquisition reorganizations are plagued with cultural clashes, or when
the acquired company is a start-up with overcontrol and rigid processes that annihi-

late the entrepreneurial spirit that previously prevailed in the start-up). This can be done by licensing in (costly, with some loss of technological control), hiring technology talents from the outside (may take time to pay off and individual talents remain mobile, thus the issue of control remains) or by entering alliances with firms that bring in the coveted technologies (may sound less costly than acquisitions but may mean significant loss of control).

All in all, the mapping of Fig. 47 provides steps and tools to face technological evolution.

I present technology roadmaps next and then discuss the key issue of lead times when it comes to technology. On that basis, I then review the strategic options available in each of the three situations identified earlier (periods of continuity, micro-radical changes, paradigmatic shifts).

Technology Roadmaps

The technology roadmapping technique aims at articulating an anticipation of market trends and users' expectations with the technologies that are likely to be required to fulfill these evolving needs. In other words, this technique essentially contributes to connecting the marketing and technology perspectives – a classic issue indeed. In this sense, technology roadmaps help identify, visualize and plan for opportunities of modalities, that is the encounter of users' needs with technological solutions, as discussed in Part I at the end of Chapter 9.

Concretely, the analysis goes layer by layer. See Fig. 48 where the horizontal axis is time. The *roadmapping* starts with a market foresight where societal trends, future customers' needs, environmental concerns, etc. are reviewed and staggered over time, thus constituting the first layer on Fig. 48. The second layer translates expected needs into product/service offerings that should be developed, again staggered over time. Then the layer below presents the technologies that will be needed to design, produce and distribute the new offerings. Again, the sequence in time when these technologies will be necessary is shown on the roadmap. These three layers stand at the heart of a roadmap, articulating (a) market dynamics and evolution of needs with (b) the new offerings to be developed to fulfill customers' evolving expectations, plus (c) the technologies that the firm should have at hand by the time they are needed for the new offerings. The middle layer stands as the crease where market and technology give birth to new offerings (products and/or services). Note that in many cases, roadmaps are reduced to this middle layer only. When this is the case, it comes as an oversimplification, a misinterpretation of a technology roadmap that would miss the key point of connecting technology, new offerings and anticipated market needs. A roadmap is not a plan but a tentative representation of what may be expected in the years to come with a notional estimate of "possibly what, about when".

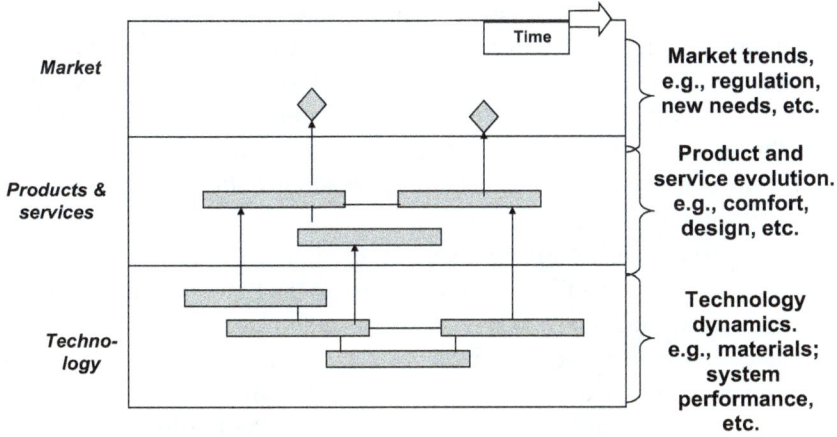

Fig. 48: Structure of a roadmap.
Source: Technology Roadmapping, Farrukh, Phaal and Probert, Ifm, University of Cambridge

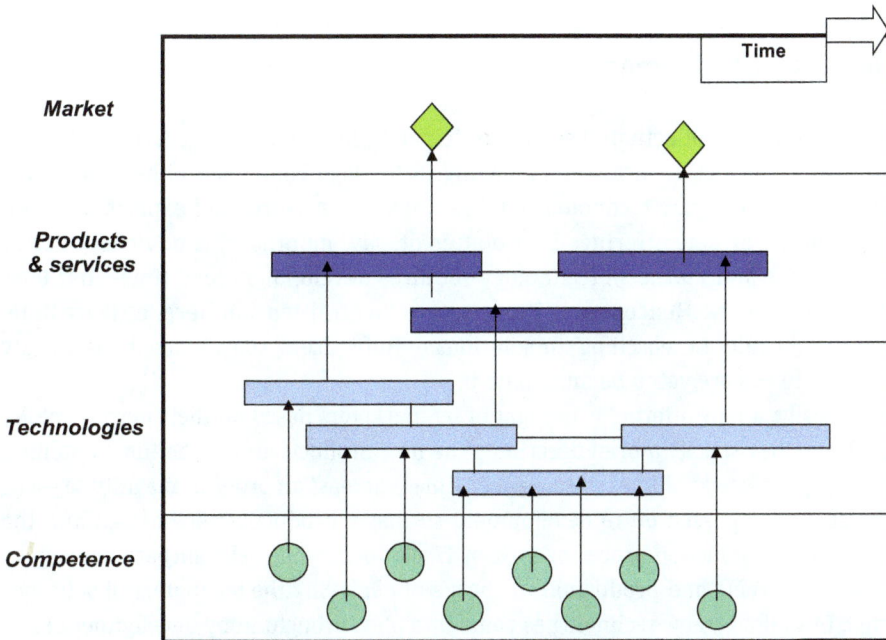

Fig. 49: A four-layer roadmap including competence.
Source: adapted from "Technology Road-mapping, IfM, University of Cambridge, 2001"

Addenda to the above three-layer roadmap can be thought of, extending the initial scheme. Typically, a fourth layer covering competence can complement the analysis. Again, the underlying competencies (those needed to master the technologies) can be staggered over time and displayed on the same representation. This yields a four-layer foresight representation (Fig. 49) that captures what can be said, as of today, about "what competence for what technology, for what new offerings, for what market needs in the years to come".

Note that one could choose to add layers on the upper part of the roadmap as well, this time by decomposing the market aggregate of the first layer into sub-layers such as customer needs, societal trends, regulatory evolution, etc.

A technology roadmap as the one shown on Fig. 49 helps visualize when competence and technology may be expected to make it possible to offer new products and services over time. This is particularly important because the lead times to develop new technology (and for that matter new technological competence) may be much longer than what the visibility on market evolution permits. This is a key point: technology requires to be prepared long before one can tell which technologies exactly will end up being needed.

Technology Lead Times

Marketing is a difficult activity because anticipating medium- or long-term evolutions of users' needs is a risky task. Yet, managing technology is not easy either. More specifically, developing new technologies takes time. When marketing expects the commercial launch of new offerings in a matter of, say, months (this obviously varies with industries and markets), technology requires development lead times that tend to measure in years. Hence, there is a major structural tension here, at least timewise, when it comes to searching for solutions to fulfill users' specific needs, especially when these needs are yet to be anticipated.

Classically, a new offering is thought of by marketers based on their market intelligence. Then, they specify a brief describing the new product/service, the functionalities, price range, expected volumes of sales over time – at least an order of magnitude – etc. The brief is then passed on to development so that a product/service design and the corresponding production processes (and/or IT platform when relevant) are developed. Then come sourcing and production in charge of deploying the technological solutions selected. In so doing, new technologies come into play, brought in by development engineers. This classic sequence means that technologies are searched for only once marketing has had a chance to foresee future needs. In practice, this is not desirable given the lead times prevailing in the realm of technology.

An Improvement of the above process came from concurrent (or parallel) engineering. Instead of viewing a new product development as a sequential pipeline process, the core idea of concurrent engineering is to start downstream phases of the development before the upstream phases are completed. This has several advantages. (1) All the functions that are expected to contribute to the development project are part of an inter-functional team that gathers all members right from the beginning. As a result, each function can start exploring the solutions that may be needed from them further down the road, thus leaving more time to prepare for it. (2) Parallelism leaves room for interaction and discussion among functions before key decisions are made (like freezing the product design). This authorizes early feedback on decisions not yet made. Typically, when choices made by upstream function are likely to lead to subsequent serious difficulties, if not impossibilities for other functions in the next steps of the project, red flags can be waved, thus avoiding long and costly iterations at a later stage. As an example, buyers may express concerns regarding the sourcing of some materials they know little or nothing about and manufacturing may argue that the product design will require asking equipment suppliers to develop specific new machines, thus generating additional costs and long lead times incompatible with the brief deadlines on commercial launch, etc. (3) The project duration can be significantly reduced thanks to avoiding useless iterations. This in turn can help cut the project costs as well.

Despite the value of parallel engineering in project management, this is not enough to prepare technology for future needs at large. I argue here that technology strategy has to prepare for future needs much more in advance. Technology roadmapping is another step in that direction, visualizing the need to anticipate technology development or sourcing well in advance of unclear needs. Yet, again, that still may not be enough.

This is where, I argue, the principle (presented in Part III, Chapter 19) of insuring against technological uncertainty by placing bets on competence to build internal agility is a way forward.

All in all, when technology is concretely needed, chances are it is already too late. This suggests preparing for the diversity of underlying competencies that could be needed. (Obviously, this is done with the knowledge available as of when the strategic thinking process regarding technology takes place.) In any case, technological resource development should be done deliberately ahead of time.

With this in mind, we can now turn to strategizing technology in each of the three main business situations previously identified: continuity, micro-radical innovation and paradigmatic shifts.

Periods of Technological Continuity

Business *doxa* seems to have taken for granted that change is all over the place, all the time. The mere theme of technological dynamics seems to convey a sense of disruption. Worrying acronyms such as VUCA (volatile, uncertain, complex, ambiguous) illustrate what seems to have become a shared belief that we are living in a world where everything changes permanently, relentlessly, at a faster pace than ever, in a reign of chaos and uncertainty.

I follow Henry Mintzberg who has consistently questioned such beliefs, asking whether prior generations were living in a motionless world (what about those who saw the early years of telephony, automotive, aeronautics, antibiotics, nuclear energy, computers, mobile phones? Our great-grandparents, grandparents or parents were not living in a world at rest, were they? Are we really the first human beings to live in a complex fast-moving world?).

More precisely, my discussion in Part I described technological evolution as long periods of continuity, at times punctuated by disruption, some of which being possibly very disruptive. Disruption is indeed part of the story and, as some would argue, where the action is as far as technology strategy is concerned. Yet, most of the life of organizations and management within organizations is under technological continuity – obviously made up of daily competition but on reasonably stable grounds. It is thus with those periods of continuity that I choose to start looking at implementing the overall framework developed in the three first parts of this book.

Technological continuity is when things evolve smoothly, through continuous improvements, *kaizen*-like. Improving costs and quality are the main drivers. There may be product adaptation and process adjustments along the way, but no significant change is taking place.

In such periods of relative technological stability, when the focus is put on optimizing costs and quality to compete, management tends to concentrate primarily on incremental progress in operations, staying away from wild ideas. Yet, in such situations a key point is to stay alert. This means a proactive search for what might come next. This leads to ongoing activities such as competitive intelligence, technological scouting, the exploration of new ways via research, corporate venturing, tapping sources of competence (partnering with public research, acquisition of start-ups), monitoring market, societal, regulatory and environmental trends.

In other words, these are periods when unclear battles to come are to be prepared for. We discussed in Part I how a period of technological continuity (a specific stage in the sense of the Abernathy-Utterback model) ends up being followed by some form of radical change at some point (Figs. 5 and 11, and Tab. 1-A). If you want peace, the well-known Roman principle recommends preparing for war (Si *vis pacem, para bellum)*. In turn, this means paying attention to the self-denial of potential future technology shifts, blindness due to attachment to the current dominant technology and overconfidence that the status quo should last long. It is also worth being careful with the opposite stance, namely nervous, fevered excitement about what may end up as false alerts.

The craze about the autonomous car is a typical example of such overplayed challenges that did not deliver yet despite large amounts of resources poured into it.

Figure 50 shows a process combining the side of users' needs (top arrow) with technology resource development (bottom arrow). This is nurtured upstream by business (including market) intelligence and technology scouting on the left part, processed through strategic thinking and planning that are then deployed and implemented through a series of programs and projects.

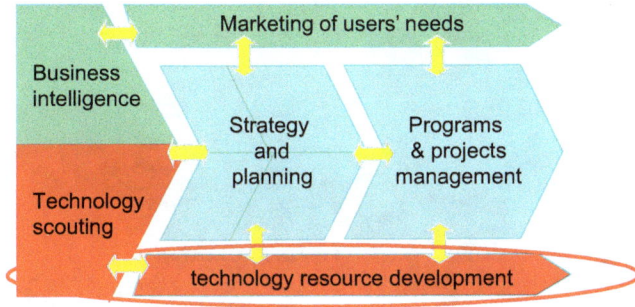

Fig. 50: Technology resource development to prepare for future business challenges.
Source: Adapted from Tetra Pak

The focus of this book deals with technology strategy. I thus focus on the bottom circled part of Fig. 50, the theme of technology resource development. The wording "technology resource" covers both technologies, in the sense of ways to offer solutions to users' needs, and technological competence, in the sense of knowledge and know-how (and know-how-to-behave, a topic discussed at length in Part III), that constitute the underlying elements to master a technology. This means building technological capabilities to prepare the firm for future challenges. This is about both constructing strategic agility fit to efficiently explore technological solutions for future users' needs as they emerge, and securing competence fit to future dominant technologies as technological evolution unfolds.

In a way, the mapping on Fig. 47, the interaction between a CCT (clarifying function F) with DTTs (Part I, Chapter 9), the technology roadmaps (covered in this chapter), and the process on Fig. 50 above all address the same issue of identifying which technologies (and competence) to prepare for. Each tool accounts for both technology evolution on the supply side and market trends on the demand side. All four aim at informing decisions (with a focus here on technology, given the theme of the book). Yet, the four tools are different and complementary.

Fig. 47: Levers to face technological change

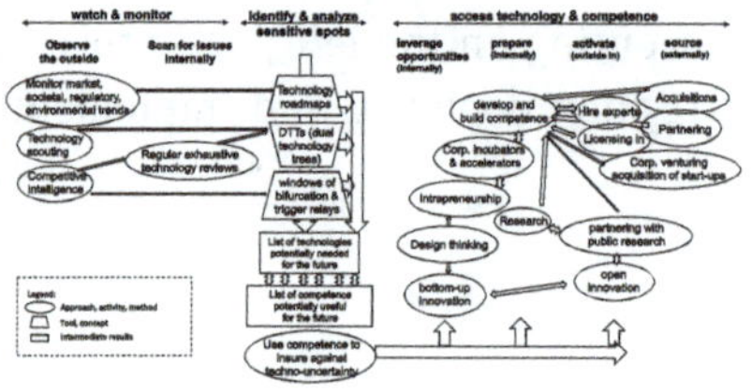

Fig. 17-B: The interaction of the (CCT) and its (DTTs)

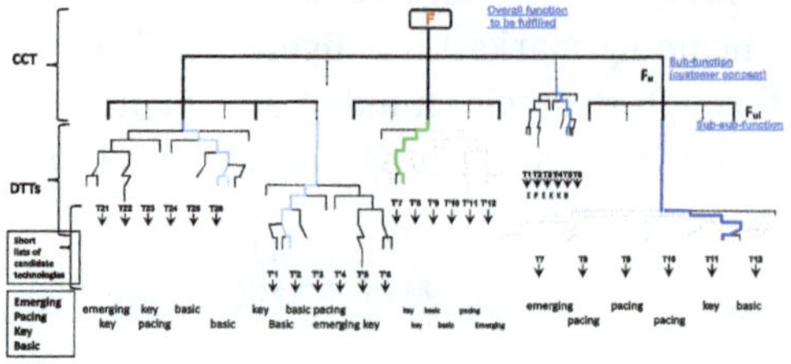

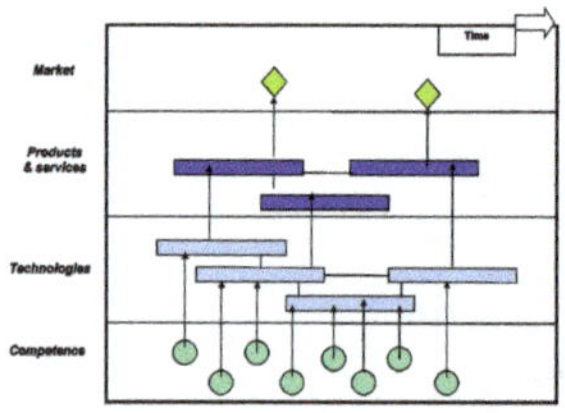

Fig. 49: A four-layer roadmap including competence

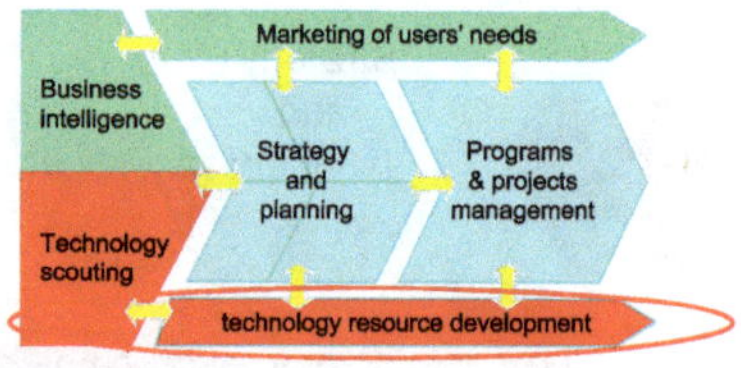

Fig. 50: Technology resource development for future business

Concretely, the above suggests the following course of action in periods of continuity:

- Accept that operations focus on incremental innovations, thus improving, adapting and optimizing as the strategic priority, as long as no major change is expected in the near future.
- In parallel, prepare for future technological battles that will eventually come to destabilize the current competitive dynamics in new ways, yet unknown, unclear, uncertain, if not indeterminate.

In periods of continuity, disruption is not expected for the next day. It is thus possible to prepare peacefully for what the future may bring.

Figure 47 offers a generic agenda for action. I discuss this in six steps.

Six Steps for a Generic Agenda for Action

Step 1: Business and Technology Intelligence – Watching the Outside and Roadmapping

Business intelligence, marketing foresight, scientific outlook and technology scouting should be conducted on an ongoing basis, as with teeth brushing for an individual. What is important is not so much the accumulation of pieces of information and data; instead, much time and care should be put into cross-checking the information and data gathered before analyses are conducted to offer both a big picture and detailed focus on matters identified as sensitive. Then it is essential that the results of all this intelligence work be circulated among those who need to see it, in a form attractive enough for them to look at it. These principles may seem simplistic. Yet, they are difficult to implement in practice for a variety of reasons, including the usual suspects: lack of time and priorities given today's operations.

This ongoing intelligence background work discussed in inter-functional groups should lead to:

- technology roadmaps, summarized in a staggered list of candidate new or renewed offerings with estimates for timing attached;
- a list of technologies to prepare for in order to launch those offerings in due time;
- and a list of the underlying competencies to grow internally or access externally to support the plan.

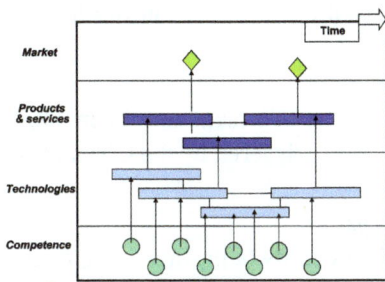

Fig. 49: A four-layer roadmap including competence. Source: adapted from "Technology Road-mapping, IfM, University of Cambridge, 2001"

Step 2: Internal Technological Reviews – Identify, List and Assess Current Technologies

In parallel, and even more importantly, the second column from the left on Fig. 47 suggests conducting technology reviews of each (significant enough) existing business. A specific business may call upon several value chains (thus the sub-sub-functions discussed in Part I, Chapter 9 around the CCT-DTT interactions). This is especially so when the offering assembles components and sub-systems, each stemming from a variety of production processes and sourcing. These reviews aim at scanning the technologies that contribute to each business at hand, checking for potential change ahead and assessing/documenting:

- the anticipated nature of the change (incremental, micro-radical innovation, paradigmatic shift);
- the level of awareness and preparation in the firm regarding the potential change;
- the list of thinkable candidate new technologies identified so far for such a change (this list should be as exhaustive as possible – obviously, as of today);
- the strategic importance of the issue;
- consider opportunities for preventive quality (see Part I, Chapter 9) if any;

- the likelihood of entering a window of bifurcation in the near future, and identification of any potential trigger relay (Chapter 14);
- what is known about new entrants and incumbents' activity on the matter;
- the opportunity for the firm to forge ahead of the flock by accelerating internal ongoing developments to trigger the change from within;
- the anticipated time horizon when the change might happen;
- the action plan already in place on the matter, the progress made in implementing the plan and the last time it was updated.

In addition, the business review can point to:
- businesses where the firm is losing competitiveness, thus possibly calling for new technologies to regain momentum;
- opportunities of diversification, thus calling as well for new technologies to seize such opportunities if relevant.

This review process is a typical joint activity between the CTO team and the management of the business units and divisions. It is likely to be triggered by the CTO and co-organized with the management of the businesses.

Four lists stem from this systematic review process:
- a list of all the technologies identified in a business entity (a business unit, a division, the firm);
- an orange list of those technologies that may be potentially challenged at a later stage, thus needing some monitoring;
- a red list of technologies directly threatened by some coming change, for which specific care and action are needed;
- a list for technologies that could help regain competitiveness on some businesses and/or diversify on promising new businesses.

From those lists, portfolios may be represented, e.g., according to strategic importance and level of internal preparation. Once done, this reviewing calls for follow-up work.

Step 3: Build or Update Plans, DTTs, Short-list Candidate Technologies for N_i+1, N_i+2, N_i+3

Based on the above, proceed as follows:
- prepare a plan or update the existing plan for each of those red technologies (appearing in the red list) and the functionalities they serve;
- prepare a plan or update the existing plan for those moving from orange to red.

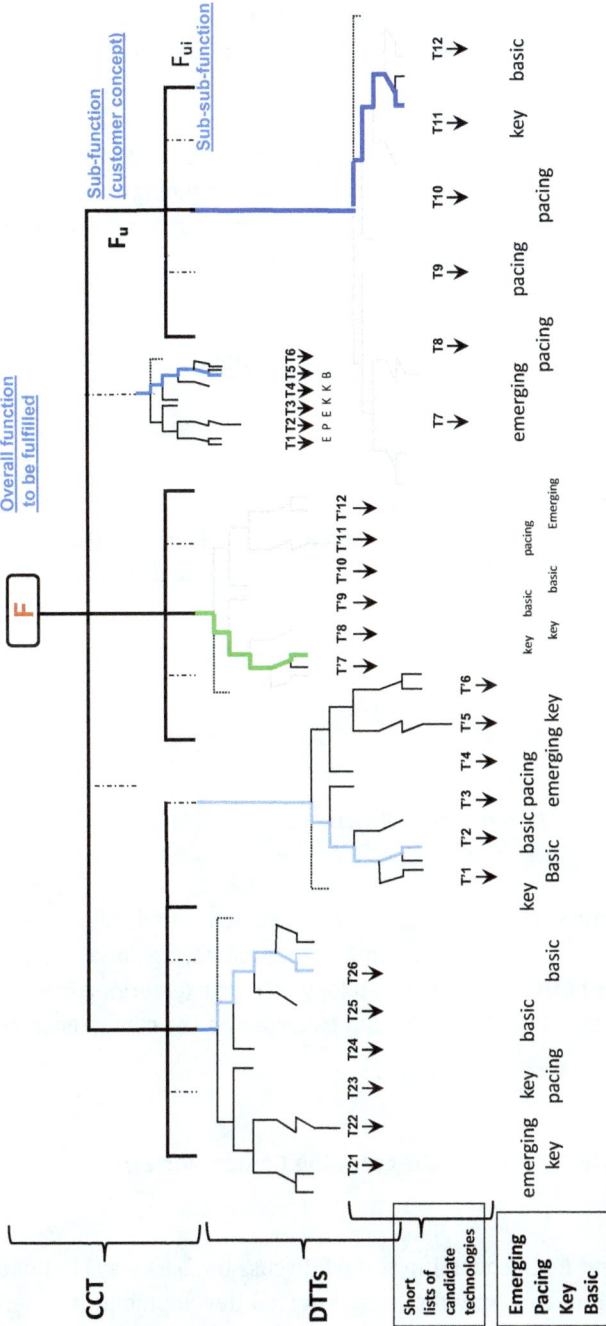

Fig. 51: CCT, DTTs and short lists of candidate technologies for N_i+1, N_i+2, N_i+3.

These plans should each include a DTT (Part I, Chapter 8). If not, build a DTT for each of the red technologies. Otherwise update the DTT. The same should be done for the most potentially sensitive technologies remaining on the orange list.

From each DTT, that is for each dominant technology where there is a substitution threat, select the most promising candidates to become N+1, N+2 or N+3 (see T1–T6 on Fig. 42, Chapter 19; also Fig. 51). Qualify the candidate technologies according to the classic categories (or anything similar), e.g., emerging, pacing, key or basic, as defined in Chapter 19 and shown on Fig. 51.

Step 4: Identify the Underlying Competencies Below the Candidate Technologies Short-listed

Then convert the candidate technologies for the red and the "sensitive" orange lists into their underlying competencies as shown on Fig. 43 (Part III, Chapter 19). From there, generate discussions with the VP R&D (or research or equivalent) to help shape the research program priorities according to the insurance principle discussed at the beginning of Chapter 19 around Fig. 43.

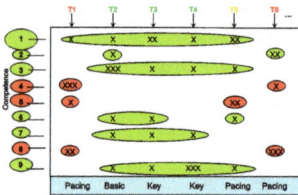

Fig. 43: Technologies candidate for F_i and underlying competencies.

Once this is done, cluster the competencies according to their relatedness. Build a portfolio of competence clusters. This portfolio can be represented, e.g., according to (1) the competence or cluster's position on the technology life cycle (emerging, pacing, key, basic) and (2) an assessment of the firm's level of expertise on the competence vs. competitions'.

Step 5: Select Best Appropriate Ways to Build/Access the Competencies/ Technologies

At that point, the CTO team and R&D leadership should discuss the best ways to build technological resources for the firm, contemplating internal development, partnerships, external sourcing or choosing to let it go (simply monitoring or abandoning). See Fig. 52. Note that from left to right, that is, from "make" to "forget" (or abandon), control of the technological resources decreases. Subcontracting can impose strict client ownership on the results while partnering (or even more so for sourcing) usually means significant loss of proprietary control.

This is where the idea of using competence as an insurance policy for technological uncertainty is most likely to be useful.

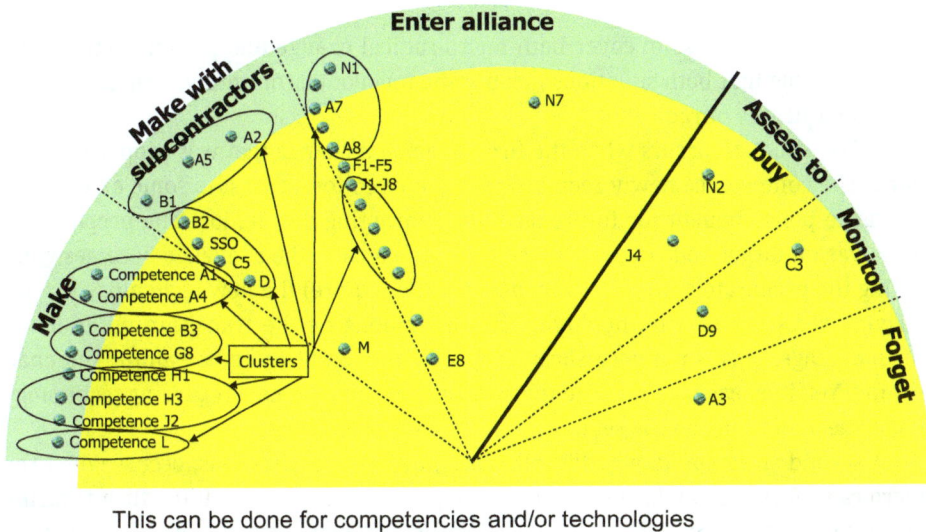

This can be done for competencies and/or technologies

Fig. 52: Building technological resources – Make, partner or buy.

Note that beyond competence, a similar representation can be drawn for technologies.

Step 6: Action Plan Stemming from Steps 1 to 5

The above five steps are likely to mean substantial work. Yet, the results should be extremely useful. Transforming the findings in an action plan is essential to transforming the business and technological intelligence and the reviews and analyses into a set of concrete actions with explicit priorities. Such an action plan should help prepare for the technological battles to come.

Again, this section deals with situations of continuity, meaning ample time to prepare for the technological future. Having done the homework is likely to help when more disruptive change will come – and it will eventually come.

Note that the activities above can put the firm in a position to trigger some of the change whenever strategically appropriate. Yet, despite all anticipation activities, it may well be that technology might bring surprises. Some N+1 technologies coming from nowhere could strike, for which the firm did not prepare well enough. This does not mean that the corresponding battles are bound to be lost. There are still strategic options left for struggling through unexpected change. This is what I discuss next.

Facing Micro-radical Change and Paradigmatic Shifts

In this section, I choose to cover both micro-radical change and paradigmatic shifts. Indeed, I argue that both situations mean some form of discontinuity, even if they differ in their degree of radicality.

A first situation occurs when the firm is facing a change that was properly anticipated. The competence newly required was prepared for, at least to some extent. The insurance policy bought for future-technology-proofing did the job. The preparatory work was on target and covered the risk. In such a case, the challenge becomes completing the preparatory work to fully develop (or acquire) the new technology (or underlying competence) and deploying it, thus managing the transition without too much damage. This is not necessarily easy. This is even likely to be painful and challenging. Yet, it is feasible thanks to the strategic thinking process regarding technology made ahead of time and the set of actions implemented.

A second situation, totally different in nature and implications, occurs when the micro-radical change and, even more so, the paradigmatic shift that the firm is facing was not properly prepared for. (In other words, this book was not read or may have been read but proved useless.) This is when the firm needs a "strategy for the unprepared".

> The history of failure in war can almost be summed up in two words: Too late.
> Too late in comprehending the deadly purpose of a potential enemy;
> Too late in realizing the mortal danger; too late in preparedness.
> Douglas MacArthur (cited by Alain Bauer (2023) "Au commencement était la guerre" Fayard)

In such situations, a set of options stems from Parts I and II:
– improve N to entrench on the current position and delay the arrival of N+1 (aiming for a "last gasp", thus buying time; see Chapter 11);
– hybridize N with N+1 into N+½ (aiming for a "hybrid intermediate" serving as cannon fodder against N+1; see Chapter 11): this is what the German car industry did to resist the assault of electric cars by developing almost carbon-free "e-fuel" to keep thermal engines beyond 2035 in Europe;
– prepare N+2 (or what may look like an N+2) and communicate about it to undermine N+1: CIT-Alcatel chose such a leapfrogging strategy in telecom switchboards in the late 1960s;
– develop N+1 internally and speedily (possibly with external support) or source N+1 technology if accessible;
– acquire one of the candidate new entrants on N+1;

- partner with a new entrant on N+1;
- exit (sell the business before its value vanishes) and redeploy on new businesses where the competence base can be leveraged.

At best, these options are second best. Yet, I suggest following Bellman's principle stemming from dynamic optimization in operations research.[35] I rephrase the principle here as *"whatever the mess you put yourself in, your best interest is to optimize from there on"*. This is what the above options are for. At the end of the day, the additional cost of the strategic option selected, plus the inevitable damage made to the business, will be the price to pay for the unpreparedness. However, if one among these options ends up saving the business, it will have fulfilled its job as a rescue squad.

The above strategic options are not mutually exclusive. On the contrary, they can be combined. Typically buying time (improving N through a last gasp or a hybrid intermediate) can be complemented by announcing some N+2 technology coming soon and preparing for it.

It should be noted here that facing micro-radical change or even a paradigmatic shift does not necessarily mean urgency. It may well be that the organization finally acknowledges the expected change before it is urgent. This changes the situation significantly as more time ends up being available to react and prepare the next step.

Typically, when incumbents in the car industry saw the combination of future bans of thermal engines (e.g., in the heart of big cities) and the aggressive entry of Tesla on the market backed by public US support, there was still time to prepare actively for the electric car. Denying the future of electric cars out of blindness is understandable for top managers who made their career on thermal engines. However, procrastinating after such clear signals is a faulty lack of strategic understanding of how the environment is changing.

Along similar lines, ignoring a disruptive new technology that suddenly breaks in but remains on a long plateau at a low level of penetration does not mean that it may not become a "path finder". It just so happens that the situation offered a second chance to prepare for it. Hence, the respite should be used to prepare for a potential path finder instead of considering the matter settled as a "burst" bound to remain marginal. The breaking-in of N+1, even if it remained so far at low level of penetration, should be treated as an eye-opener. It should urge management to look for any potential trigger relay (see Chapter 14) that could transform the burst, interpretated as non-threatening, into a potentially devastating path finder.

---

35 Bellman's principle of optimality: An optimal policy has the property that whatever the initial state and initial decision are, the remaining decisions must constitute an optimal policy with regard to the state resulting from the first decision.

More generally, even when seeing change coming around the corner, management would be wise to watch out for bifurcation windows (see Chapter 14 – the list of factors potentially signaling a bifurcation window and the discussion around Fig. 34).

Two more specific situations need to be mentioned here.

The management of a firm may feel that they have done all the needed preparatory work for a paradigmatic shift coming soon. The potentially newly required competence base has been identified. Technology N+1 has been developed and is being deployed. Everything seems to have been done right. Yet, some unanticipated N+2 suddenly comes into the picture. And, bad luck, this is not a simple "concatenation" or even just an "overlap", it is a "double shift". This N+2 strikes in the middle of the ongoing investment on N+1 (see Chapter 11, pattern 7). The line of reasoning discussed above can slide, substituting N+1 for N, N+2 for N+1 and possibly N+3 for N+2. Yet the situation is very slippery as the firm has been and is still in the process of investing in N+1, thus with limited resources left to suddenly change priorities.

The second specific situation corresponds to "reverting" (see Chapter 11, pattern 10). N+1 took over N some years ago, but N+1 ends up being forced to withdraw (due to market acceptance, environmental concerns, regulatory ban, etc.) without being pushed out by some N+2. In the absence of any N+2 candidate, N takes over again. If the firm was a previous incumbent on N, things should be manageable. If the firm came in as a new entrant surfing the wave of N+1, this is more difficult. Yet, the list of options discussed above can be revisited, substituting N+1 for N and N for N+2.

All in all, the key point has to do with time, anticipation and preparedness. The principle of insuring against technological uncertainty via the underlying competence is of the essence. This requires thinking about technology strategy when potential change is not pressing yet. Technology lead times are indeed long, requiring careful scouting and balanced resource allocation to cover for risks ahead. Technology strategy is at its best when thought of and implemented much ahead of time.

Chapter 22
A Final Word on the Nine Cases Used for Illustration

Nine cases were used as examples in the introduction of this book (three past cases, three ongoing, three cases for the future). I now return to these nine cases to point out the lessons learnt, expected or yet to be learnt, from each of the cases.

Past Cases

Insulin

Technology-wise, the history of insulin shows a dominant technology N (animal insulin) overtaken by a radically new technology N+1 (human insulin) through a paradigmatic shift (stemming from biotechnologies). One of the key incumbents, Eli Lilly, licensed-in technology N+1 from Genentech and announced the new product within five years. Novo, another incumbent, felt cornered and chose to start a technological race, choosing another path (enzymatic conversion) to develop animal insulin. So, Novo's response was to go for a "me-too product" through a different process. Surprisingly, Novo won the technological race against Eli Lilly. Yet, once offered on the market (first in the UK), the new offering sold very poorly due to market inertia, requiring a more focused entry strategy (on new diabetics). It then turned out that Eli Lilly's sales of human insulin outperformed Novo's. In fact, Novo was aware of the cost disadvantage they would be carrying when choosing their technological path (enzymatic conversion) to produce human insulin. Yet, they did it intentionally because they anticipated some N+2 technology (pro-insulin) to take over in the near future. They wanted to stay alive on the market to prepare for N+2. However, they were wrong on two counts. First, they did not see that the competencies needed for pro-insulin were likely to be linked to the competence base that Eli Lilly was developing for its human insulin. Second, the next significant innovation did not come on the product itself but on the monitoring of diabetics' glucose levels. Continuous glucose monitoring (CGM) devices made it possible to inform diabetics of the level of sugar in their blood – in real time. This made the life of diabetics much easier, allowing them to administrate insulin exactly when needed. A remarkable market success.

The insulin case provides an illustration of a partial leapfrogging strategy that was aborted (going for a second-best version of N+1 to stay alive but aiming for N+2 that never came to dominance due to a shift to CGM).

The case of insulin was used to illustrate the dual technology tree (Chapter 8).

Switchboards in the Telecoms Industry

The early years of telephony relied on operators to set up connections manually (technology N-1). Then came electromechanical switches (N), a new paradigm, followed by two additional paradigmatic shifts bringing in electronic switching, first electronic space-division (N+1), second time-division multiplexing (N+2) immediately followed by time-division digital multiplexing (N+3)

https://doi.org/10.1515/9783111397979-032

which consisted an improvement of N+2, preparing the ground for wide band time division multiplexing. The next paradigmatic shift was expected to be optical switching, but the outburst of the internet led to another shift, namely the internet protocol (N+4), which is likely to remain the dominant technology for some time as successive sub-generations follow one another on a concatenation mode. Historically, each paradigmatic shift in public switching in the telecoms industry brought newcomers to take the lead before these were displaced by the subsequent shift.

The case of telecom switchboards illustrates the concept of technological trajectories and micro-radical innovations (Chapter 8). The case shows how CIT-Alcatel, a small incumbent, went for a leapfrogging strategy, and successfully so, going from N to N+2 and even N+3 while ignoring N+1 that was supported by most competitors. A brilliant strategic move at that time.

Recorded Music

Six technologies came to dominance on the market of recorded music since the early days: the phonograph technology (cylinder then disk), vinyl (mono then stereo), audiotapes, CDs, MP3, streaming. Against conventional wisdom or beliefs, the curves of sales over time do not show an acceleration in the pace of technological change. There seems to be a significant inertia on the demand side linked to the installed base (tape players, CD players, stock of tapes and CDs) not to speak of the nostalgia market for vinyl.

The case of recorded music shows:

an interesting plateau effect (Chapter 13) for the development of the audiotape (linked to the Japanese industry's early announcement of the CD);

a difficult start to the CD market (probably announced a few years too early);

a rebound of the audiotape just when the CD was finally taking off (mostly due to the installation as standard of tape players in new cars by the automotive industry at about the same time).

In addition, the business model of the industry has co-evolved with technology. In the old days, artists would go on concert tours as a way to promote their albums (recorded music) that generated their revenues. Today with the streaming paradigm, artists earn their living through the concerts. Along the way, the ticket prices for concerts have skyrocketed. The labels live on the revenues stemming from their portfolio of rights generating income on streaming, especially on recorded music from previous decades (e.g., the Beatles are still much listened to on streaming platforms). In this context, a few leading artists decided to leave their labels, choosing to tour on their own. Some of them actually embark other artists in their autonomous venture.

The case of recorded music thus provides a concrete illustration of technological change driving a profound transformation of the business model and thus the entire music industry. Although technology drove the change, one should think of the co-evolution between technology and the business model as the concept of a physical album remains despite its loss of meaning in a streaming paradigm. This is because artists need to wave an object at the camera when promoting their latest songs on TV. Similarly, fans are interested in the materiality of an object.

Ongoing Cases

Electric Cars

After over a century of lock-in, where a technology N (thermal engines) remained dominant worldwide, a paradigmatic shift was launched towards electric batteries (technology N+1). This did not come from the industry itself, nor from clear market demands, but from public regulation decisions to ban carbon-emitting cars in cities and territories. Technology N had sub-technologies (e.g., number of pistons or cylinders [V4, V6 or V8], fuel [petrol, diesel, bioethanol]). Technology N+1 has sub-technologies as well (hybrid, rechargeable hybrid, full electric).

Interestingly enough, incumbents have long been hesitant to switch to electric cars, and to some extent still are. Some even kept arguing that diesel became the most efficient clean technology thanks to filters. Others waited for customers to get accustomed to batteries, thus preferring rechargeable and non-rechargeable hybrid sub-technology in the meantime. For switching to full electric models, the issue of autonomy was key. Tesla's aggressive and bold move for full electric forced the industry to follow suit.

A technology N+2 is still pending, namely around hydrogen (H2) and fuel cells – thus emitting water. Hydrogen is produced from the electrolysis of water, a costly process that needs electrical energy. On top, there are issues with safety as hydrogen tanks can be dangerous in situations such as fires, explosions etc.

Interestingly enough, German car manufacturers pushed their government to oppose the EU ban on thermal engines beyond 2035. Their idea was to keep thermal engines by switching to methanol. See the discussion of the green methanol case in the box below. Clearly the German automotive industry has had difficulties with the idea of abandoning the strategic advantage they built around thermal engines. Thus, their search for a solution to keep the engine sound alive for the enthusiasts. I discussed the case of intermediate hybrid (Chapter 11, pattern 9) as a way for incumbents to delay the arrival of N+1 as a defensive move to stick to their competence base around N. Let's keep in mind that N+½ (hybrid intermediate) rarely makes it to become N+1 or N+2. It essentially serves as cannon fodder to delay the arrival of N+1.

Another interesting aspect of the case of electric cars relates to the pending N+2 technology (hydrogen). Should the N+1 electric technology fully succeed in overtaking the thermal engine technology N, it means that the petroleum industry and the network of gas stations will be strongly affected. As electric recharge stations will have taken over, a new lock-in will be in place, consolidated by the installed base of electric cars. Indeed, at the same time, car owners will have invested in electric cars, thus thinking twice before switching again to yet another technology. This raises the question of the feasibility for hydrogen fuel (N+2) to displace N+1 once an electric ecosystem is fully established. This is particularly true in the automotive industry, where the weight and size of parts and sub-systems and their unit cost are key: the cost of producing hydrogen is not likely to decrease that fast, nor the weight and size of the hydrogen propelling sub-systems.

The case of electric cars provides a good example of a paradigmatic shift to N+1 while a N+2 technology (hydrogen) is still pending, with plenty of uncertainties attached. In addition, the case shows an intermediate hybrid calling upon some traits of N+2 to save N (a variant from the standard case of the intermediate hybrid [pattern 9 presented in Chapter 11] where N hybridizes N+1).

3D Printing

3D printing covers process technologies that add successive layers of matter to form a desired part or component. There are several dozens of such processes. These are developed by firms on the supply side, offering new solutions for a set of problems yet to be identified. On the demand side, companies interested by the promises of potential savings scan among those technologies to see which ones could help them for specific issues they face. In a way, 3D printing technologies are solutions in search of problems to be solved.

Most technology providers offering 3D printing solutions are usually specialized in only one or two of them. On the demand side, users are primarily industrial firms wondering how they could benefit from 3D printing. The development of 3D printing requires the encounter of problems to be solved (for firms unaware of the existence of 3D printing solutions to deal with specific problems they may have had for a long time) with solutions offered by technology providers and now rendered possible by the paradigm of additive manufacturing. Each of these awkward encounters of 3D printing solutions with a problem they might solve is a specific case of what we called a modality (see end of Chapter 9): By modality, I mean a 'nesting space', a 'window of encounter', where and when a specific business opportunity for a technology is framed and materializes as an application. This is where and when a technology and a user need meet and mate in some form of a fertilization and developmental process. In short, the development of 3D printing is a paradigmatic shift that unfolds as a low-key, noiseless ongoing process taking place at a decentralized level through some form of trial and error. This looks like seepage slowly progressing underground, through some form of capillarity.

The case of 3D printing illustrates the concept of modality that I introduced in Chapter 9 (last section of the chapter). The case also shows a paradigmatic shift that takes place slowly and noiselessly, penetrating industry step by step, through the accumulation of many specific innovations (the "modalities"), where a specific sub-technology fulfills a specific user need.

Blockchain

The blockchain is a digital technology that can transform the monitoring of sensitive documents, data or information that need to remain traceable over time. It is about creating and keeping up-to-date distributed digital registries. The technology offers a substitute to the public legal registries, the network of public notaries, the trusted third parties, medical records, archives of transactions (e.g., in banking or supply chains), diplomas and degree awarded in education, etc.

As such, the blockchain comes as a paradigmatic shift in a variety of sectors where the new solutions offered by the technology can prove useful. (This echoes the theme of modalities discussed above for 3D printing.) Some of these sectors have already started implementing the technology. Yet, the process of substitution proves to be rather slow. Snowballing in such a context does not seem to find any form of collective trigger and self-reinforcement. One could argue that several blockchain-enabled paradigmatic shifts take place in parallel, each encountering a specific chasm (in Moore's sense). Crossing the chasm in one sector does not seem to do so in other sectors of application.

Several reasons can explain this slow process. First, the players that are to be substituted for by the blockchain often have much to lose and little to gain in the change. Hence, they logically tend to resist the change. A classic issue indeed. Second, the technology (and the way it provides the service that it promises) is difficult to explain, difficult to grasp and somewhat worrying when it comes to call upon digital storing instead of certified paper documents. Third, if cryptocurrency is just one among many uses of blockchains, the extreme volatility of crypto-currency markets brings an undesirable flavor of uncertainty and risk to the blockchain world. Fourth, some of the blockchain applications (typically for cryptocurrencies) require a lot of energy, hinting that the blockchain does not fully fit in a world with a desperate need of greening the economy to save the planet. Fifth, the blockchain calls upon a community of geeks (the so-called "miners") who operate as insiders with their own jargon, rules and culture that keeps the flavor of some libertarian origins. This, combined to the difficulty to comprehend what it is all about, tends to cover the blockchain paradigm with a veil of suspicion that ends up leading to a perception of a lack of transparency from the very same people whose aim was to bring protection against the risk of opacity attached to central systems of certification and central power.

The case of the blockchain provides an additional illustration of how, when too many modalities are at stake, an otherwise powerful paradigmatic shift can be slowed down.

Future Cases

The Industry of the Future (Including the Fourth Industrial Revolution)

While still fuzzy and complex, the case of the industry of the future could be seen as already ongoing. This is partly true, at least to a certain extent – but only partly. The technologies that are going to be increasingly called upon in the industrial transformation have been around for some time. What is new is the increasing magnitude of their capacities (speed, accessibility, bandwidth, storage, computing, unit cost decrease, etc.) and thus the extent of their transformative power. One could view the anticipated change in industry not so much as a paradigmatic shift stemming from a giant leap of any single technology, but having more to do with the combined continued emergence of a cluster of technologies that bears with it a major transformation. And this transformation is not only yet to materialize, but it is in fact difficult to grasp, describe and anticipate.

The Appendix illustrates how the competence framework developed in Part III can be used in this case.

In addition, reports from experiments at the frontier of industrial practice (use cases) help grasp potential future industrial transformations, both technically and managerially.

More specifically, a key element that stems from a set of experimentations is that a key competence needed to cope with the change will not only be the technicalities of the capture, structuring, transmission, storage and analysis of data. For sure, there will be a lot of that. Yet, a key competence needed relates to cultural change, inter-site and site-center collaboration, languages, trust, internal communication, and respect of the human professional experience and technical memory on-site compared to legitimate (possibly sometimes overplayed?) expectations from big analytics.

This suggests that a major technological transformation (in fact made up of a combination of many sub-technological transformations) needs to be addressed, not only from a technological viewpoint, but with a complementary managerial orchestration perspective as well.

MSR and Fusion in the Future of Nuclear Energy (Gen IV and Fusion)

This is a very complex topic. To make a long story short, I first briefly set the stage:

The world's energy equation for the future is likely to be unbalanced, with more need than supply.

Fossil fuels are no longer an option due to carbon emissions and climate change, not to speak about resource shortages (less so for coal though, but a serious environmental nuisance altogether).

Renewable energy is obviously a must (solar, wind, geothermal, biomass, ocean – currents, waves, tides).

Renewable sources of energy (solar, wind) suffer from intermittence. They are low when demand peaks (winter, evening) and vice versa. Covering peak demand with renewables would mean oversizing the investments, increasing unit costs and spending natural resources for partly dormant infrastructure.

As long as no significant solution is available for energy storage, nuclear energy is very likely to be needed to ensure the baseline.

Nuclear energy raises three major issues: safety, waste treatment and storage, and proliferation (use of uranium enrichment technology for nuclear weapons).

The above helps understand why some governments around the globe choose to keep some level of nuclear energy despite societal concerns. Thus, the need for an outlook on future nuclear technologies.

The nuclear industry is capturing future technologies under the Gen IV family, plus a clearly longer-term option, fusion. Yet, I suggest here that the molten-salt reactor (MSR) technology may also be seen as a long-term option, possibly between Gen IV and fusion.

In a way, calling upon the labeling used in the book, one could summarize technology evolution in nuclear energy in the form of the following sequence: pressurized water reactors (PWRs) stand as technology N, fast breeder reactors (FBRs) were expected as N+1 before being abandoned, at least for the time being. The European pressurized reactor (EPR) results from continuous improvements of PWRs and can thus be seen as a sub-technology of PWRs. There could then be a technology emerging from the Gen IV family to stand as N+2. It is difficult to say which one may win, if any of them. Then, two candidates can be considered for the longer term, MSR for, say, N+3, and fusion for N+4.

There is a paradox here. Fusion is some form of a new Promethean dream of replicating on Earth the energy of the sun. One of the technologies experimented requires dealing with matter at an extremely high temperature (150 million degrees), maintained in levitation (via magnetic fields) to confine the plasma (as no available material could cope with such temperatures). This literally demands technological prowess. Yet, paradoxically, fusion is actively investigated and even experimented on in the world, e.g., at the international ITER project at CEA Cadarache in southeast France. This may sound surprising because, with many major roadblocks ahead, the technology is still futuristic, uncertain and long term. When asked to assess when they envisage that fusion could come to reality, researchers tend to say, "Well, 50 years at minimum." In plain language, this means "not in my lifetime". And I have received that same answer again and again over the last 40 years as I kept asking the same question. In other words, the time horizon for fusion keeps sliding away.

In contrast, the MSR technology, a promising option, remains significantly less explored despite a prototype operating in the 1950s in the US. MSRs are a nuclear technology in which the fuel, a molten salt, is also the coolant. Safety in MSRs is considerably increased by design as the fuel is already in the form of molten salt that, in case of emergency, can be drained out of the heart of the reactor in a containment where it solidifies, thus removing the risk of leakage into the environment. As no water cooling is involved, the risk of hydrogen generation and possibly explosion is also avoided. MSRs can be much smaller than PWRs and, in fact, rather compact. In addition, MSRs stay around atmospheric pressure, significantly simplifying their design and operation, while their temperature of about 700°Celsius permits higher efficiency in producing electricity. Regarding the issue of waste, MSRs can burn their own production of long-lived actinides extracted through chemical separation and reloaded into the fuel in a closed cycle. The need for geological containment of waste is significantly reduced to about 300 years.

However, MSRs use thorium or sodium. In a way, MSRs are sometimes seen as liquid metal coolant reactors. This means that the competence base required is no longer one attached to uranium but moves to a significantly different scientific and technological corpus of knowledge and industrial know-how. This means that incumbents active on PWRs, including EPRs, are likely to be cautious, if not strongly biased against the fully new added-value chain of thorium, from upstream sourcing to waste processing, from MSR plant design to operations.

We have here a plausible explanation of why MSRs are not being explored so much compared to fusion. I argue that this is because MSRs would require a major change in competence without the immense promises of fusion.

In any case, MSRs are not a panacea. They carry with them their own problems. Corrosion is an issue. So is the effect of radionuclides potentially conveyed through the fuel to the equipment (pipe pumps, etc.). On top, MSRs may be distorted to facilitate the production of nuclear material for weapons, thus proliferation.

The case of future nuclear energy technologies provides a good example of incumbents staying away from a technology (MSRs) that is likely to lead them to restart from scratch. The competence gap between PWRs and MSRs is very wide.

At the same time, public research from 35 countries joined forces for yet another technology (fusion) that could disrupt the industry to an even more significant extent, while carrying the uncertain promise of solving for centuries the nagging problem of energy supply for humankind on Earth.

Quantum Computing

The prospect of significantly improving computer technology (speed and volume of data processed) is a fascinating promise for the future. However, quantum computing is a typical paradigmatic shift that is yet to come and that we know too little about. At this stage, it is still too early to think of the transformation that could stem from such a shift, when and if it comes.

Note that the "if it comes" is not just a formal precaution in my writing. It is to acknowledge that future developments are uncertain and cannot be taken for granted.

The scientific principles – although intuitively difficult to grasp as quantum physics remains a surprising representation of matter – are established and proven valid. The technological ways of applying such principles are understood and being developed and tested. However, there will be many steps, and this will take time.

The expected outcome remains: more data handling, more processing capacity, faster. The computer industry has been doing it for so long that it sounds like business as usual. Yet, this time, it is about jumping into a new world where it is no longer possible to both locate particles precisely and measure their speed. As the "yes or no" leaves the floor to a greyish "in between", the bits are replaced by qubits.

A strategic question derives from the above. Will the computer industry be capable of coping with the potential coming change from within, or will the process rely upon bold start-uppers seizing the opportunity of quantum computing? The term "deep tech" was coined precisely for such cases when new technology is rooted so deep in science that technological developments may require ad hoc linkages between researchers in basic science upstream and those engineers developing the technologies. There again, it is a bit early to describe the set of competencies that those players aiming at surfing the wave of this potential paradigmatic shift will need. There is still too much indetermination. The only concrete step in that direction would be to establish close links to public research labs active in quantum physics.

All in all, this case of quantum computing provides a typical example of indetermination, where strategizing technology has to wait until the fog starts dissipating – at least in part.

Summary of Key Points of Part IV and a final word on the carbon-free methanol vs electric cars

(1) The topic of the book is about designing and deploying strategies when facing technological change. This is part of RDTIT (R&D, technology, innovation, technical). The technology petal typically captures what a CTO does to inform top management decisions on such matters. One might even say that the essence of a CTO's job is to feed top management with appropriate documented strategical options regarding technology, while making sure that the organization is competent on potentially important technologies for the future – or prepared and agile enough to build or access competence quickly when needed. This obviously includes monitoring technological matters in periods of continuity, preparing for the future and, at times, facing upcoming technological change triggered by internal developments or coming as external shocks.

(2) Using the framework developed through Parts I to III requires scouting and monitoring the outside to identify potential technological change, reviewing the technologies and competencies at work internally and developing or accessing technologies and competencies identified as potentially important for the future.

(3) To do so, concepts and tools discussed in the book can serve the purpose (dual technology trees, windows of bifurcation and trigger relays, portfolio of technologies, portfolio of competence, calling upon the underlying competencies as an insurance policy for technological uncertainty).

(4) Technology development lead times tend to be long, meaning that technology should be prepared for long before marketing can capture users' needs and write specifications in their briefs. In this context, technology roadmapping is a useful additional technique to prepare for the technologies that could be needed in the future.

(5) Part I described technological evolution as long periods of continuity, at times punctuated by disruption, some of which being possibly very disruptive. This leads to three main business situations where strategizing technology is needed: continuity, micro-radical innovation, paradigmatic shifts.

(6) Paradoxically, periods of technological continuity are the best time to think about technology strategically. These are periods when unclear battles to come are to be prepared, thoughtfully.

Six steps are suggested to implement the mapping of Fig. 47.

Step 1: Business and technology intelligence – watching the outside and roadmapping
Step 2: Internal technological reviews – identify, list and assess current technologies
Step 3: Build or update plans, DTTs, short-list candidate technologies for N_i+1, N_i+2, N_i+3
Step 4: Identify the underlying competencies below the candidate technologies short-listed
Step 5: Select best appropriate way to build/access the competencies/technologies
Step 6: Action plan stemming from Steps 1 to 5

https://doi.org/10.1515/9783111397979-033

(7) When facing micro-radical change or even paradigmatic shifts, there are still strategic options left for the unprepared:

improve N to entrench on the current position and delay the arrival of N+1 (aiming for a "last gasp", thus buying time; see Chapter 11, pattern 8);

hybridize N with N+1 into N+½ (aiming for an "hybrid intermediate" serving as cannon fodder against N+1; see Chapter 11, pattern 9);

prepare N+2 (or what may look like an N+2) and communicate about it to undermine N+1;

develop N+1 internally and speedily (possibly with external support) or source N+1 technology if accessible;

acquire one of the candidate new entrants on N+1;

partner with a new entrant on N+1;

exit (sell the business before its value vanishes) and redeploy on new businesses where the competence base can be leveraged.

(8) A final word on the nine cases listed in the introduction and developed in the subsequent parts:

Regarding the three past cases:

The case of insulin illustrates the dual technology tree (Chapters 6 and 8).

The case of telecom switchboards illustrates the concept of technological trajectories and micro-radical innovations (Chapter 5). It also displays a successful leapfrogging strategy.

The case of recorded music shows an interesting plateau effect (Chapter 13) for the development of the audiotape, a difficult start of the CD market and a rebound of the audiotape just when the CD was finally taking off. These shapes significantly depart from classic S-curves. The case also illustrates how technological evolution may bring about new business models.

Regarding the three ongoing cases:

The case of electric cars provides a good example of a paradigmatic shift to N+1 (electric cars) while a N+2 technology (hydrogen) is still pending. The case also shows an intermediate hybrid (methanol as green fuel) calling upon some traits of N+2 (not N+1) in an attempt to save N, or at least delay the fall of N.

The case of 3D printing illustrates the concept of modality (Chapter 9, last sections). The case also shows a paradigmatic shift through the slow and noiseless accumulation of many specific innovations (the modalities), where a specific sub-technology fulfills a specific user need in a specific sector.

The case of the blockchain provides an additional illustration of how, when too many modalities are at stake, a paradigmatic shift can be slow.

Regarding the three cases for the future:

The case of the industry of the future provides an example of an ongoing slow building of the combined continuous evolutionary effect of a set of digital technologies. This could result in a major transformative power, in the form of systemic change without a clear paradigmatic shift on any single new technology. In such a case, managerial orchestration of the change may be as important as preparing for the technologies.

The case of future nuclear energy technologies provides an example of a technology N+2 (MSRs) likely to lead incumbents to abandon most of their assets and competence base attached to N (PWRs and EPRs [uranium-based]) – a prospect they dislike, while an international consortium of 35 countries explore technology N+3 (fusion).

The case of quantum computing provides a typical example of a situation of indetermination, where strategizing technology has to wait until the fog starts dissipating.

A final word on the "Carbon-free methanol vs electric cars"

The introduction of this book began with the case of European car manufacturers put under pressure in the early 2020s to shift technology from thermal engines to electric batteries. I described how several leading German car makers proposed to adopt "methanol as a green fuel", and raised the question of what to think of such a strategy.

In light of the framework developed in this book, I view the innovative idea of a green fuel (methanol) as a hybridization of technology N (thermal engine) with N+2 (hydrogen), leading to some N+½ (hybrid intermediate). This is a variant of pattern 9 (intermediate hybrid) discussed in chapter 11, whereby incumbents attempt to undermine N+1 by improving N thanks to some key features potentially introduced by N+1. In the case at hand however, the idea is rather to hybridize N+2 (hydrogen), not so much N+1 (electric). The methanol strategic option could thus be labelled a hybrid intermediate N+½+1. By construction this would be part of the technology N paradigm (thermal engines), a micro-radical innovation close to N, pursuing the same envelope trajectory.

Note that under pattern 9 of Chapter 11, I also discussed the fact that a strategy of hybrid intermediate is essentially defensive. Seen through the lens of Part III, it helps incumbents stick to their competence base around technology N, i.e., their comfort zone. In addition, N+½ (hybrid intermediate) rarely makes it to N+1 or N+2. At best, a hybrid intermediate strategy delays the arrival of N+1, thus essentially serving as cannon fodder. A useful finding arises from the discussion of pattern 9 in Chapter 11: incumbents' imaginations are limitless but prove inadequate in most cases. It suggests that the "methanol as a green fuel" strategy may end up being dubious, if not a non-starter.

Yet, there may be more to it. *Indeed, the future of automotive may see another revolution as hydrogen stands as a candidate N+2 technology.* In this context, I need to stress that the "methanol as a green fuel" option requires the production of carbon-free hydrogen as a necessary step. This means that developing that specific technological path would to a large extent prepare for what may be regarded as the candidate N+2 technology for energy in automotive, namely Hydrogen.

Should N+1 (electric) win the first round against N (thermal) despite the N+½+1 attempt (methanol as a green fuel) and furthermore, should N+2 (hydrogen) contest the electric (N+1) dominance, it is likely that those who would have bet on the intermediate hybrid (methanol) option would be much more advanced for a full hydrogen option (N+2) than competitors who would not have made this choice. While the issue of carbon-free energy sourcing would therefore have been dealt with, there would remain technical and cost roadblocks that would still need to be lifted on the vehicles themselves. For cars, the *weight and size of parts and sub-systems and their related costs are key and likely to remain significant. This raises the question of whether hydrogen (N+2) can displace N+1 once an electric ecosystem is fully established, not just on the fuel front, but on the vehicle side as well.*

Should the above scenario unfold, then the "methanol as a green fuel" strategy could play a significant role in the end, benefitting its proponents and implementors.

It could transform an otherwise rather weak and defensive strategy into a winning strategy.

References for Part IV and Further Reading

Farrukh, C., Phaal, R., & Probert, D. (2003). Technology roadmapping: Linking technology resources into business planning. *Int. J. Technol. Manage.*, *26*(1), 2–19. https://doi.org/10.1504/IJTM.2003.003140

Further Reading

Afuah, A. (2000). How much do your competitors' capabilities matter in the face of technological change? *Strateg. Manage. J.*, *21(3)*, 387–404.

Ahuja, G., & Katila, R. (2001). Technological acquisitions and the innovation performance of acquiring firms: A longitudinal study. *Strateg. Manage. J.*, *22*(3), 197–220. https://doi.org/10.1002/smj.157

Albright, R. E., & Kappel, T. A. (2003). Roadmapping in the corporation. *Res.-Technol. Manage.*, *46*(2), 31–40. https://doi.org/10.1080/08956308.2003.11671552

Argote, L., & Ingram, P. (2000). Knowledge transfer: A basis for competitive advantage in firms. Organ. *Behav. Hum. Decis. Process.*, *82*(1), 150–169. https://doi.org/10.1006/obhd.2000.2893

Argyres, N. S., & Silverman, B. S. (2004). R&D, organization structure, and the development of corporate technological knowledge. *Strateg. Manage. J.*, *25*(8–9), 929–958. https://doi.org/10.1002/smj.387

Bergek, A., Berggren, C., Magnusson, T., & Hobday, M. (2013). Technological discontinuities and the challenge for incumbent firms: Destruction, disruption or creative accumulation? *Res. Policy*, *42*(6–7), 1210–1224. https://doi.org/10.1016/j.respol.2013.02.009

Buhalis, D., Harwood, T., Bogicevic, V., Viglia, G., Beldona, S., & Hofacker, C. (2019). Technological disruptions in services: lessons from tourism and hospitality. *J. Serv. Manage.*, *30*(4), 484–506. https://doi.org/10.1108/JOSM-12-2018-0398

Carvalho, M. M., Fleury, A., & Lopes, A. P. (2013). An overview of the literature on technology roadmapping (TRM): Contributions and trends. *Technol. Forecast. Soc. Chang.*, *80*(7), 1418–1437. https://doi.org/10.1016/j.techfore.2012.11.008

Cassiman, B., & Veugelers, R. (2006). In search of complementarity in innovation strategy: Internal R&D and external knowledge acquisition. *Manage. Sci.*, *52*(1), 68–82. https://doi.org/10.1287/mnsc.1050.0470

Cetindamar, D., & Pala, O. (2011). Chief technology officer roles and performance. *Technol. Anal. Strateg. Manage.*, *23*(10), 1031–1046. https://doi.org/10.1080/09537325.2011.621297

Cetindamar, D., Phaal, R., & Probert, D. R. (2016). Technology management as a profession and the challenges ahead. *J. Eng. Technol. Manage. 41*, 1–13. https://doi.org/10.1016/j.jengtecman.2016.05.001

Cooper, R. G., Edgett, S. J., & Kleinschmidt, E. J. (2000). New problems, new solutions: Making portfolio management more effective. *Research-Technology Management*, *43*(2), 18–33.

de Alcantara, D. P., & Martens, M. L. (2019). Technology Roadmapping (TRM): a systematic review of the literature focusing on models. *Technol. Forecast. Soc. Chang.*, *138*, 127–138. https://doi.org/10.1016/j.techfore.2018.08.014

Durand, T. (1992). The dynamics of cognitive technological maps. In P. Lorange, J. Roos, B. Chakravarty and A. Van de Ven (Eds), *Implementing Strategic Processes*. Blackwell Business. 165–189.

Durand, T. (1996). National management of technology and innovation: Integrating the firm's perspective into government policies. In H. Thomas and D. O'Neal (Eds), *Strategic Integration*. John Wiley & Sons Ltd.

Durand, T., Farhi, F., & Brabant, C. (1997). Organising for competitive intelligence: The technology and manufacturing perspective. In W. Bradford Ashton and Richard A. Klavans (Eds.), *Keeping Abreast of Science and Technology – Technical Intelligence for Business*. Colombus, Battelle Press.

https://doi.org/10.1515/9783111397979-034

Durand, T., & Dubreuil, M. (2001). Humanizing the future: Science and soft technologies. *Journal of Future Studies, Strategic Thinking and Policies, 3*(4), 285–295.

Durand, T. (2003). Twelve lessons from 'Key Technologies 2005': The French technology foresight exercise. *Journal of Forecasting, 22*(2–3), 161–177. https://doi.org/10.1002/for.856

Durand, T. (2004). The strategic management of technology and innovation. In *Bringing Technology and Innovation into the Boardroom: Strategy, Innovation and Competences for Business Value* (pp. 47–75). EITIM, Palgrave Macmillan.

Eggers, J. P., & Kaplan, S. (2009). Cognition and renewal: comparing CEO and organizational effects on incumbent adaptation to technical change. *Organization Science, 20*(2), 461–477. https://doi.org/10.1287/orsc.1080.0401

Gambardella, A., & McGahan, A. M. (2010). Business-model innovation: General purpose technologies and their implications for industry structure. *Long Range Plan. 43*(2–3), 262–271. https://doi.org/10.1016/j.lrp.2009.07.009

Garms, F. P., & Engelen, A. (2019). Innovation and R&D in the upper echelons: The association between the CTO's power depth and breadth and the TMT's commitment to innovation. *J. Prod. Innov. Manage., 36*(1), 87–106. https://doi.org/10.1111/jpim.12441

Gerdsri, N., Assakul, P., & Vatananan, R. S. (2010). An activity guideline for technology roadmapping implementation. *Technol. Anal. Strateg. Manage., 22*(2), 229–242. https://doi.org/10.1080/09537320903498553

Gold, A. H., Malhotra, A., & Segars, A. H. (2001). Knowledge management: An organizational capabilities perspective. *J. Manage. Inform. Syst., 18*(1), 185–214. https://doi.org/10.1080/07421222.2001.11045669

Groenveld, P. (1997). Roadmapping integrates business and technology. *Res.-Technol. Manage., 40*(5), 48–55. https://doi.org/10.1080/08956308.1997.11671157

Hagedoorn, J., & Duysters, G. (2002). External sources of innovative capabilities: The preference for strategic alliances or mergers and acquisitions. *J. Manage. Stud., 39*(2), 167–188. https://doi.org/10.1111/1467-6486.00287

Jones, G. K., Lanctot, A., & Teegen, H. J. (2001). Determinants and performance impacts of external technology acquisition. *J. Bus. Ventur. 16*(3), 255–283. https://doi.org/10.1016/S0883-9026(99)00048-8

King, A. A., & Tucci, C. L. (2002). Incumbent entry into new market niches: The role of experience and managerial choice in the creation of dynamic capabilities. *Manage. Sci., 48*(2), 171–186. https://doi.org/10.1287/mnsc.48.2.171.253

Kogut, B., & Zander, U. (1996). What firms do? Coordination, identity, and learning. *Organ Sci., 7*(5), 502–518. https://doi.org/10.1287/orsc.7.5.502

Laursen, K., Leone, M. I., & Torrisi, S. (2010). Technological exploration through licensing: new insights from the licensee's point of view. *Ind. Corp. Change, 19*(3), 871–897. https://doi.org/10.1093/icc/dtq034

Lee, C., Lee, K., & Pennings, J. M. (2001). Internal capabilities, external networks, and performance: A study on technology-based ventures. *Strateg. Manage. J., 22*(6–7), 615–640. https://doi.org/10.1002/smj.181

Leten, B., Belderbos, R., & Van Looy, B. (2007). Technological diversification, coherence, and performance of firms. *J. Prod. Innov. Manage., 24*(6), 567–579. https://doi.org/10.1111/j.1540-5885.2007.00272.x

Lichtenthaler, U. (2008). Open innovation in practice: An analysis of strategic approaches to technology transactions. *IEEE Trans. Eng. Manage., 55*(1), 148–157. https://doi.org/10.1109/TEM.2007.912932

Lichtenthaler, U., & Ernst, H. (2009). Opening up the innovation process: The role of technology aggressiveness. *R D Manage. 39*(1), 38–54. https://doi.org/10.1111/j.1467-9310.2008.00522.x

McEvily, S. K., Eisenhardt, K. M., & Prescott, J. E. (2004). The global acquisition, leverage, and protection of technological competencies. *Strateg. Manage. J. 25*(8–9), 713–722. https://doi.org/10.1002/smj.425

Medcof, J. W. (2008). The organizational influence of the chief technology officer. *R D Manage., 38*(4), 406–420. https://doi.org/10.1111/j.1467-9310.2008.00526.x

O'Reilly, C. A., Tushman, M. L. (2011). Organizational ambidexterity in action: How managers explore and exploit. Calif. *Manage. Rev., 53*(4), 5–22. https://doi.org/10.1525/cmr.2011.53.4.5

Patel, P., & Pavitt, K. (1997). The technological competencies of the world's largest firms: complex and path-dependent, but not much variety. *Res. Policy*, *26*(2), 141–156. https://doi.org/10.1016/S0048-7333 (97)00005-X

Petrick, I. J., & Echols, A. E. (2004). Technology roadmapping in review: A tool for making sustainable new product development decisions. *Technological Forecasting and Social Change*, *71*(1–2), 81–100. https://doi.org/10.1016/S0040-1625(03)00064-7

Phaal, R., Farrukh, C. J. P., & Probert, D. R. (2004a). A framework for supporting the management of technological knowledge. *Int. J. Technol. Manage.*, *27*(1), 1–15. https://doi.org/10.1504/IJTM.2004. 003878

Phaal, R., Farrukh, C., and Probert, D. (2004b). Technology roadmapping—A planning framework for evolution and revolution. *Technological Forecasting and Social Change*, *71*(1–2), 5–26. https://doi.org/10. 1016/S0040-1625(03)00072-6

Phaal, R., & Muller, G. (2009). An architectural framework for roadmapping: Towards visual strategy. *Technol. Forecast. Soc. Chang.*, *76*(1), 39–49. https://doi.org/10.1016/j.techfore.2008.03.018

Ranft, A. L., & Lord, M. D. (2002). Acquiring new technologies and capabilities: A grounded model of acquisition implementation. *Organ Sci.*, *13*(4), 420–441. https://doi.org/10.1287/orsc.13.4.420.2952

Ritter, T., & Gemunden, H. G. (2003). Network competence: Its impact on innovation success and its antecedents. *J. Bus. Res.*, *56*(9), 745–755. https://doi.org/10.1016/S0148-2963(01)00259-4

Rothaermel, F. T., & Boeker, W. (2008). Old technology meets new technology: Complementarities, similarities, and alliance formation. *Strateg. Manage., J. 29*(1), 47–77. https://doi.org/10.1002/smj.634

Rothaermel, F. T., & Hill, C. W. L. (2005). Technological discontinuities and complementary assets: A longitudinal study of industry and firm performance. *Organ Sci.*, *16*(1), 52–70. https://doi.org/10.1287/ orsc.1040.0100

Schneider, S. C., & Anglemar, R. (1993). Cognition in organizational analysis: Who's minding the store? *Organization Studies*, *14(3)*, 347–374.

Srinivasan, R., Lilien, G. L., & Rangaswamy, A. (2002). Technological opportunism and radical technology adoption: An application to e-business. *J. Mark.*, *66*(3), 47–60. https://doi.org/10.1509/jmkg.66.3.47. 18508

Tippins, M. J., & Sohi, R. S. (2003). IT competency and firm performance: Is organizational learning a missing link? *Strateg. Manage. J.*, *24*(8), 745–761. https://doi.org/10.1002/smj.337

Vojak, B. A., & Chambers, F. A. (2004). Roadmapping disruptive technical threats and opportunities in complex, technology-based subsystems: The SAILS methodology. *Technol. Forecast. Soc. Chang.*, *71*(1–2), 121–139. https://doi.org/10.1016/S0040-1625(03)00047-7

Walsh, S. T. (2004). Roadmapping a disruptive technology: A case study: The emerging microsystems and top-down nanosystems industry. *Technol. Forecast. Soc. Chang.*, *71*(1–2), 161–185. https://doi.org/10. 1016/j.techfore.2003.10.003

Warner, K. S. R., & Waeger, M. (2019). Building dynamic capabilities for digital transformation: An ongoing process of strategic renewal. *Long Range Plan.*, *52*(3), 326–349. https://doi.org/10.1016/j.lrp.2018. 12.001

Yoon, J., & Kim, K. (2012). Detecting signals of new technological opportunities using semantic patent analysis and outlier detection. *Scientometrics*, *90*, 445–461. https://doi.org/10.1007/s11192-011-0543-2

Zhang, Y., Robinson, D. K. R., Porter, A. L., Zhu, D., Zhang, G., & Lu, J. (2016). Technology roadmapping for competitive technical intelligence. *Technol. Forecast. Soc. Chang.*, *110*, 175–186. https://doi.org/10.1016/ j.techfore.2015.11.029

Zhen, T., Xuan, Y., & Jing, Z. (2012). Trusting relationships of CTO-CEO and CTO's participation in technology strategy based on empirical study of Chinese high-tech firms. *Chin. Manag. Stud.*, *6*(1) 137–159. https://doi.org/10.1108/17506141211213889

Appendix: Competencies Underlying Key Technologies for the Fourth Industrial Revolution

This appendix aims at providing a concrete example of the analysis of the competence base required for a new technology (or a set of new technologies). The example draws from the case of the industry of the future seen from the perspective of the fourth industrial revolution.[36]

Industry in several Western countries has been hurt over the last decades by two parallel dynamics. First, the structure of their economy has evolved with increasing employment in the service sectors while industry was following a similar downward path as agriculture with a time lag of about a century or so. See Fig. 53 for employment by sector in the US.

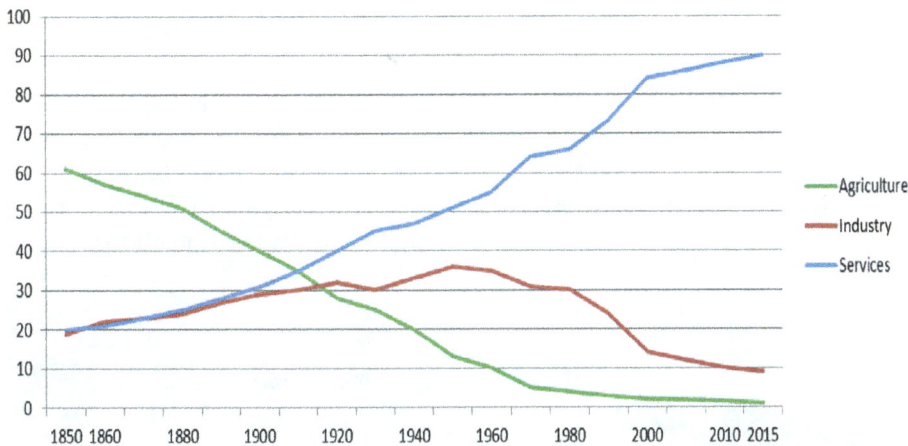

Fig. 53: Dynamic of employment in the US economy by sectors (1850–2015).

Second, several Western countries have seen their industry hollowed out through offshoring. As a result, the UK, the US and France have seen the share of industry in GDP fall from some 20% to 25% in the 1970s to around 10% in the 2020s (Italy and even Germany also saw a decrease but not to the same extent). See Tab. 10.

As far as offshoring is concerned, it is likely to be irreversible as reshoring would be difficult and most probably unsuccessful. (In most cases the gap in labor cost that led to offshoring is still in place.) Thus, the issue is about reindustrializing, not reshor-

---

36 The content of this appendix awes to Jean-Pierre Chevalier, Brice Dattée, Audrey Perrocheau, Alexis Pokrovsky, Majda Seghir and Benoit Tezenas du Montcel. They contributed through a working group that I gathered at Cnam around the theme of Competence for the *"Industry of the future"* (2022–2023).

https://doi.org/10.1515/9783111397979-035

Tab. 10: Share of manufacturing (% GDP) over time (1970–2015).

	1970	2010	2015
France	19.7%	10.1%	10.0%
Germany	31.4%	20.0%	20.5%
Italy	23.8%	14.2%	14.2%
United Kingdom	24.7%	9.0%	8.7%
USA	23.3.%	12.2%	12.0%

Source: Fabrique de l'industrie from United Nations

ing. It is conceivable to reindustrialize to keep (or recreate and keep) a layer of industrial activity similar to the layer of agriculture remaining in these countries. Reindustrializing is thinkable by surfing the coming waves of technological change – much in line with the topic of this book.

In fact, there are several viewpoints or strands possible to envision the future of manufacturing and more generally industrial activities. Figure 54 shows the perspective of stakeholders: business leaders, the workforce, academia, society at large (non-profit organizations, fab labs, communities of practice). Figure 54 does not show the demand side explicitly as B2B is covered by "businesses", while consumers (B2C) fall under "users". Figure 54 also shows the perspective of both technological change (technology) and managerial orchestration. These last two items are the two viewpoints that I adopt hereafter.

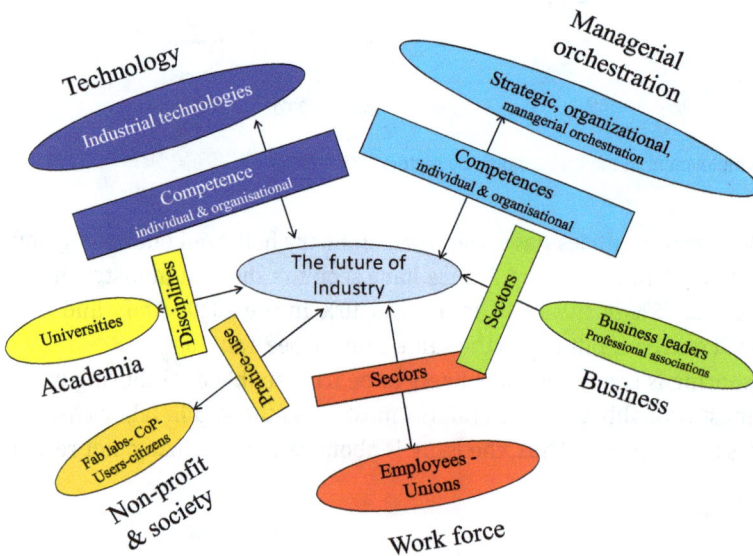

Fig. 54: Strands to think about the fourth industrial revolution.

The fourth industrial revolution, including what is sometimes called Industry 4.0, can be seen as a paradigmatic shift, a wave of technological change (or a set of waves) to surf, staying away from head-on competition with low labor-cost countries. The backbone of the major industrial transformation yet to come is expected to be made of a set of candidate technologies that are already identified (as of today):

– 3D printing
– artificial intelligence/machine learning
– internet of things
– robots/cobots
– big data/big analytics
– predictive maintenance
– drones
– digital imaging/augmented virtual reality
– digital twins
– network infrastructures/IT
– smart manufacturing

More may appear along the way, but the above technologies are very likely to play a role, one way or the other, in the transformation to come.

Conceptually, I follow Brice Dattée in viewing technology as a transformation process that starts with an input (material, energy and/or information) to generate an output (a part, component, hardware/software and/or refined information, a model or decision), see Fig. 55. This applies to the topic of this appendix, namely industrial activities.

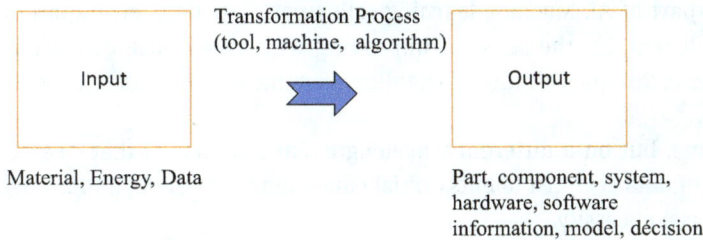

Fig. 55: Technology as a transformation process.
Source: Brice Dattée (private communication)

Note in passing that beyond the list of key technologies that are candidates to structure the industry of the future, managerial orchestration of the change should be added, meaning strategizing rearrangements in the value chains, managing the organizational transformations attached, etc.

The technologies likely to structure the industry of the future offer an opportunity to regain part of the industrial ground lost over the last decades by advanced economies. This requires preparation, including thinking about technology strategically.

Several available descriptions of the disciplines, roles and competencies behind candidate technologies for the industry of the future can be found, stemming from academia or practice.

A typical academic perspective would identify scientific and engineering disciplines behind the technologies. For example:

- 3D Printing: materials, energy, mechanics, chemistry, digital 3D
- artificial intelligence/machine learning: applied math, algorithmics, computer science, coding
- internet of things: electronics, networks, waves, computer science (hardware/software), digital platforms, sensors, processors, actuators, local hub boxes, networks, IS, cloud
- robots/cobots: mechanics, electronics, optics, computer science (IS/programming)
- predictive maintenance: statistics, TQM, computer-aided maintenance.

Beyond the above academic (scientific and engineering) perspective, there are many similar attempts made in the professional grey literature offering decompositions of some of the loaded terms, such as "data science" into: data visualization; pattern recognition; statistical analysis; probability models; computer modeling; machine learning; artificial intelligence (AI).

Or the "skills needed for data science": mathematics and statistics sharing an overlap of machine learning with computer science and IT, sharing an overlap of software development (for applications) with business knowledge and know-how.

Or "deep learning" (enabling computation in neural networks) as a subset of machine learning (with supervised, semi-supervised, unsupervised and reinforcement learning), itself a sub-part of AI. Machine learning calls upon statistical techniques to enable computers to learn – in the sense of improving with experience over time, while AI covers all the techniques aiming at enabling machines/computers to process information and data.

On the same theme, but on a different wavelength, Saporta argues that, "Faced with a large shortage of data scientist talents, initial education is not enough to fill the gap: lifelong learning is a necessity."[37]

Going one step further, there are also lists of roles or positions related to data science in organizations, e.g., for automotive (Fig. 56). As an illustration, the French society of automotive engineers issued such a description of roles: data project manager; data architect; data steward; data engineer; data analyst; statistician; data and IA scientists; business owner.

37 Saporta, G. (2018). Training data scientists: A few challenges. *International Journal of Data Science and Analytics*. Vol 6 – 201–204. https://doi.org/10.1007/s41060-018-0114-1

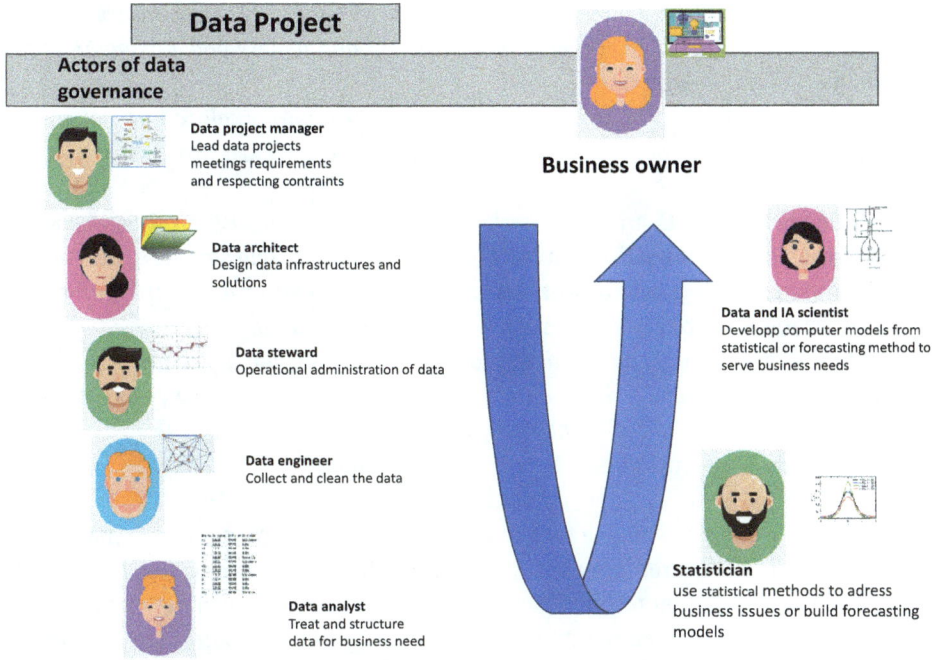

Fig. 56: Data-linked roles in automotive industry.
Source: Sia (French Society of automotive Engineers – SIA)

Along the same lines, a taxonomy of such roles (with short descriptions of the content attached) is adapted from Syntec Numérique and Kantar:

– **Chief data officer (CDO):** *create an environment providing easy and quick access to data. They shape the platforms, systems, software and ecosystems so that everyone can perform analyses independently. Accountable for the quality of the data content.*
– **Chief analytics officer:** *use statistical tools and methods to organize, exploit and synthesize data efficiently. They identify the most important and relevant data to be extracted for optimal decision making. They also manage the implementation of the data treatment process.*
– **Data protection officer:** *in charge of information, advice and control of data governance (particularly individual data). As an example, they ensure compliance with the European data protection regulation (GDPR).*
– **Data architect:** *intervene upstream of data processing to organize the collecting and cleaning of raw data. Define and optimize the infrastructure for collection, storage and handling.*
– **Data engineer:** *develop the infrastructures defined by the data architect and build robust and reliable technical solutions. They carry out the integration of the supervised data and check their quality. Ensure data integrity via the follow-up of data flows, especially at interfaces.*

- **Data steward:** *quality manager; senior role with authority. They ensure that the data is relevant, available, compliant, consistent and understood. Custodian of the knowledge about data.*
- **Data scientist:** *process, analyze and add value to data. Explore new sources of data. Competent in building and coding methods and algorithms to sort out and analyze data.*
- **Data consultant/data analyst:** *translator between data and business. They define key performance indicators. Use data tools to explore, organize and structure raw data.*
- **Data vizualisation consultant:** *exploit data in context; propose straightforward visualizations to convey key messages drawn from the data.*
- **Dataops engineer:** *Lead the data machinery; they organize the process of data analysis, develop new functionalities and automate quality. They ensure that the production systems are efficient, with readily available outputs.*
(Source: adapted from Syntec Numérique and Kantar)

Should nothing else be available for my intended analysis here, namely preparing for the industry of the future, these lists of scientific disciplines, sub-technologies, skills and roles linked to digital technologies for industry would be much better than nothing. Yet, I suggest digging more into it to serve my purpose of thinking about technologies for the future of industry strategically.

As discussed in Chapter 19 (around Fig. 43), technology forecasting is a risky exercise. We cannot be certain of which technologies will play a significant role in the future of industry. However, we can buy insurance policies against technological uncertainty by identifying and preparing for the underlying set of competencies that may play a role, one way or the other, in the change to come.

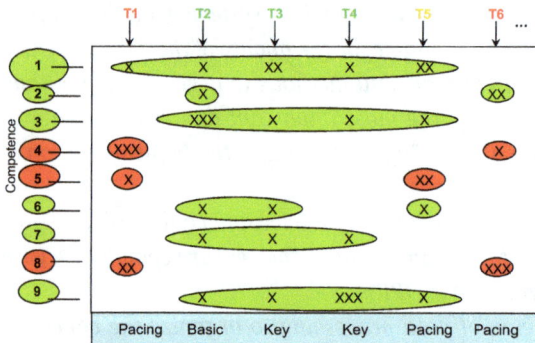

Fig. 43: Technological options and underlying competence (from Chapter 19).

Typically, digging into 3D printing for the sake of illustration, we need to segment what stands behind the loaded terms "3D printing" and "additive manufacturing". Depending on the granularity, we find seven sub-technologies, or even 37 or more. Remaining at the first level of seven sub-technologies for this illustration, we get: extruding materials, photopolymerization, melting-sintering on a power bed, matter spraying, glue spray, depositing matter with energy addition, merging layers.

Table 11 shows the first six sub-technologies in columns and the underlying competencies identified in line.

Note that several labelings of the lines in fact correspond to elementary "tasks" behind which specific technical competencies are attached. I shall come back to this after two other illustrations with machine learning and then internet of things (IoT).

The case of machine learning differs from the above in the sense that sub-technologies are replaced by various types of learning in columns, as shown on Tab. 12. Another example comes from the IoT, where this time the columns do not show sub-technologies or types of learning, but sectors of application (Tab. 13). In addition, the boxes in the matrix assess the criticality of a line for the column (sector).

Note that Tab. 13 is primarily for the sake of illustration, with only the column for aeronautics filled out (as well as the line for real-time requirements).

As pointed out earlier in commenting on Tab. 11 regarding 3D printing, several labelings of the lines in the matrix in fact correspond to elementary tasks. Yet, specific technical competencies (technical know-how and scientific knowledge, as well as more general knowledge) can be readily identified behind these tasks.

Note that the terms that appear in the tables are those used by experts who were interviewed on each of the three cases.

More specifically, some of the items (lines on Tabs. 11 and 12) include verbs such as: design, model, trace, adjust, select, set up, finish; design and create (an object or a system), take into account (think of), remove (material leftover), check (functionalities), etc.

Verbs are also used in the gerundive form as: selecting, dealing with, operating, monitoring, conducting, building, hosting, benchmarking.

Other wordings use substantive forms: acquisition-visualization, optimization, preparation, selection, collection, analysis, validation, problem definition, explanation, dissemination, documentation, compliance, evaluation, predictions.

All these terms relate to action through the specification of a task.

Going one step further, Tab. 13 uses yet another set of labels having to do with objects: components, middleware, software, systems, networks. I will call these "artifacts" that are needed to be designed and built (or sourced and understood) to be put to use efficiently in shifting to a new technology – such as IoT in this instance.

All in all, this suggests that, in the search for underlying competencies below the candidate new technologies, the building of matrices such as those shown on Tabs. 11 to 13 leads to competencies, tasks or even artifacts.

Tab. 11: 3D printing: Competencies by Sub-technologies.

Competency	Extruding materials	Photopolymerization	Melting-sintering on a power bed	matter spraying	glue spraying	deposition of matter with energy addition
•Knowledge and selection of materials	x	x	x	x	x	x
•Design and Modeling						
•Model development taking needs and constraints into account	x	x	x	x	x	x
•Familiarity with CAO softwares and files formats and tracing of files (digital integrity)	x	x	x	x	x	x
•Acquisition–visualization (e.g. use of 3D scanners, stereography, multispectral video cameras,...)	x	x	x	x	x	x
•Modeling multi-material printing	x	x	x	x	x	x
•Topological optimisation/generative design	x	x	x	x	x	x
•Lean material consumption	x					
•Selecting shapes and rate of material filling	x	x	x	x	x	x
Selecting internal structure	x	x	x	x	x	x
Model preparation for printing: selecting the supporting base material	x	x	x	x	x	x
Model preparation for printing: slicing the file in layers	x	x	x	x	x	x
Piling up and optimizing several parts on the same base			x	x		
•Model Preparation for printing: positioning/orientating the part (anisotropy/isotropy)	x	x	x	x	x	x
Chasing with distortion, anomalies, and printing defaults which cooling anomalies for materials and performing test printings	x	x	x	x	x	x
Adjust layer thickness (printing duration and surface condition)	x	x	x		x	x
•selection of granularity and surface conditions (to yield a smooth and homogeneous surface)				x		
Select colors (for color printing)						
•Production						
Machine set-up (work station, base level, adjustment of printing head)	x	x	x	x	x	x
Powder conditioning, ventilation, cooling	x	x	x	x	x	
•Operating the machine	x	x	x	x	x	x
•Knowledge and know-how: extrusion process and melting of plastics	x	x				
Monitoring the resin tank		x				
Knowledge and know-how: laser- material interactions (sintering and melting)			x			x
Knowledge and know-how: material behavior		x		x	x	
Knowledge and know-how: interactions glue-material					x	
Knowledge and know-how: interactions ultraviolet laser – photosensitive material		x				
•Chemical processes of polymerization		x				
•Conducting and monitoring the printing process	x	x	x	x	x	x
•Monitoring the cooling phase to limit retraction	x				x	x
•Post-processing :	x	x		x	x	x
removing the setting (base, stand, accessories and material)	x					
removing the base and cleaning the parts, post-polymerization, finish (polishing)		x				
remove the part and the leftover of powder from the powder tank			x			
disposing of leftovers (using mechanical tools or chemical solvents)						
finish - surface post-processing	x	x	x	x	x	x
•First level maintenance	x				x	x
Sintering to solidify the part – post-printing	x	x	x	x	x	x

Tab. 12: Machine learning, tasks and underlying competencies.

		Supervised Learning	Unsupervised learning	Semi-supervised learning	Reinforcement learning
Developers of software and tools					
	Heuristics/Algorithmics				
	Scientific computing				
user: data collection and processing					
	Data collection				
Preparation	Data analysis				
	Data validation				
	Problem definition				
	Feature Engineering				
	Model Building				
Modeling	Evaluation and Benchmarking				
	Model/prediction explanations				
	Information dissemination				
	Documentation and compliance				
	Ethics by design, GDPR, etc.				
Model deployment hosting					
Post-Deployment	Monitoring and management				
	Effecting model predictions				

Tab. 13: Internet of things (IoT): Matrix for sectors by tasks – underlying competencies.

Technological chain to identify the underlying competencies	Main domains of use (each with specific challenges/needs/specific requirements)								
	Automotive	Aeronautics	Space	Medicine	Building	Manufacturing	Energy	Telecoms	Consumer electronics
Electronics									
Design and making of chips, components and cards		X							
Microprocessors, SoC, sensors, actuators		X							
Local hubs: intermediary integration systems		X							
Edge computing /fog computing		X							
Software/systems for IoT - (object linked and local integration)									
Operating systems and control sensors/actuators		X							
Middleware		X							
networks and protocols		X							
Safety/Security		XXX							
Apps (Machine Learning, computer aided decisions, ...)		X							
Software-Cloud-IoT (upward flow)									
Protocols and networks		X							
Middelware and integration systems		X							
Data collection		X							
Data analysis		X							
Thinking about the piece and the whole simultaneously		X							
(Designing the object while viewing the whole system, and vice versa)									
Properties (non fonctionnal)									
Criticities Safety		X							
Security		X							
Data security		X							
Real-time requirements	XXX	XXX	XXX launchers	XX	vary with apps	vary with process	XXX	vary with apps	
Managing breakdowns with severe consequences		XXX							
Development process norms		XXX							
Certification requirements		XXX							
Main functionalities									
Measurement and communication		X							
man-machine interface		X							
Comfort Optimisation		X							
Process Optimisation		X							
Energy Optimisation		X							
Quality of service		X							
Cost		X							

It is quite logical that the decomposition of a technology in the columns on Tabs. 12 and 13 or sub-technologies on Tab. 11 lead to a set of tasks, or even artifacts, that stand as the expected outcome of a task.

Creating an artefact that is needed to proceed with the deployment of a new technology, or an action to be performed, when spelt out, can be presented as a task. And a task calls for knowledge and know-how. Knowledge of: the context, the overall process, the expected outcome, the interdependencies with other tasks, the key performance indicators (KPIs), etc.; Know-how of: the concrete form of action, the roles played by colleagues, the proper timing in a sequential process, the dos and don'ts, etc.

In other words, each of the three types of item that appear on the lines of the matrix (artifacts, tasks, competencies) relate to competence.

Calling upon the framework for competence developed in Part III suggests that knowledge and know-how, together with attitudes (know-how-to-behave), combine to form competence (both individual and organizational).

In this sense, the lines of Tabs. 11 to 13 provide an insight into the competencies required by the technology (and sub-technologies when appropriate) at hand. The competencies identified through the decomposition process may thus be labeled according to an artifact, a task or a piece of knowledge or know-how.

However, two important issues appear at this stage.

First, granularity is a concern. How far down should one go in decomposing the technology and sub-technologies into elementary artifacts, tasks or competencies? This is an important practical issue. A reasonable level of granularity should be aimed for between two extremes. On the one hand, going too deep into finer grains would run the risk of being overwhelming, up to the point of getting drowned into too many sub-sub-items, losing sight of the overall objective of the analysis. On the other hand, remaining at a meta-level (very coarse granularity) would lead to running the risk of missing the target of identifying underlying competencies below the surface (technology). As often, an in-between solution is likely to be the most reasonable option. To do so, an iterative search process is a fair way to go: decomposing the sub-technologies more than really needed, realizing that it is just getting too messy because of too fine a granularity, going back a level up and checking that things are then both workable and relevant.

A typical reality check on this matter is to ask engineering professors specialized on the specific topic whether they see what course(s) they could design to educate students for the "artifacts / tasks / competence" and thus prepare them for the sub-technologies and technologies at hand. Should their answer be positive, the analysis is on target. If not, it would mean that another iteration may be needed, probably going down the granularity scale.

Secondly, the main focus apparently put on individual competence as a result of the analysis, with little attention paid to organizational competence, is the other concern. The exercise summarized in Tabs. 10 to 12 for the sake of illustration seem to essentially point to individual competence. This obviously stems from the way the corresponding matrices are built, decomposing technology into sub-parts, including tasks and artifacts calling upon elementary pieces of competence that are seemingly attached to individuals.

This, however, would be a wrong reading of the analysis. The decomposition into artifacts, tasks and then pieces of competence does not imply that the corresponding competence is to be borne by individuals only. The collective dimension remains an important part of what an organization needs to be capable of doing when leveraging new technologies. The illustration at the end of Chapter 19 (Part III) about the use case of Corp Z made the point. The experimentation conducted at Corp Z was about monitoring units distributed over territories from a central digital hub. A key outcome of the experimentation was that in such new settings, much more than before, communication and collaboration among teams is of the essence. Thus, the importance of the managerial orchestration.

This means that the "reality check" (as suggested three paragraphs above) should not be limited to course contents offered to individuals. The design of a program to educate the workforce of an organization, including the management line, should not only address the technicalities of the candidate new technologies. It should also include the collective capacity to handle the new technologies, including the managerial orchestration of the new normal, yet to come, as well as the organizational transformation to go from current operations to the future steady state.

In short, the line of reasoning stemming from the three illustrations of Tabs. 11–13 can be summarized as a flow in the competence by technology matrix (Fig. 57).

Technologies ⮕ sub-technologies ⮕ ⮕ technological chain ⮕ artifact tasks/competence ⮕ ⮕ Accessing

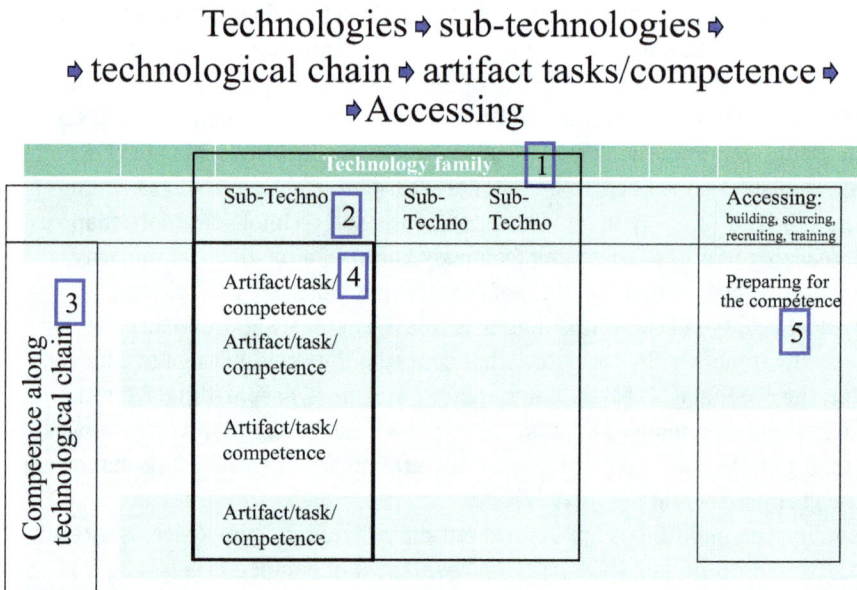

Fig. 57: From technology to competence (and vice versa).

The sequence starts with the technology family (1), often a loaded term which may have to be decomposed into sub-technologies or sectors of application or type of learning or equivalent (2) in columns. The sequence proceeds to the technological chain (3): the chain of steps called upon to apply the technology in context is itself decomposed into artifacts, tasks or competencies (4), that are translated into competencies, thus permitting to prepare a future portfolio of competence fit to the requirements of the new technology. This is where the buying an insurance policy against technological uncertainty can prove useful. In other words, step 5 on Fig. 57 is where strategic thinking can take place as discussed below.

Indeed, taking a step back and looking at the illustration stemming from the above analyses of 3D printing, machine learning, and IoT, the exercise should proceed in a similar way with the other candidate technologies for the future of industry. Then, the resulting matrices "competence by technology" should be merged into one large matrix. The various technologies are in columns and the competencies are in lines. At that stage, redundancies (typically identical line headings) can be merged into one single line: this corresponds to competencies that are transversal to several technologies (columns). This is when a specific piece of competence can be of interest for more than one technology.

From there, strategic thinking can take place using the idea of buying an insurance policy against technological uncertainty. Typically for a competence item that does not seem likely (as of today) to be essential, it may be acceptable to do nothing special about it or to build a minimum knowledge and know-how base to permit agility and further quick build-up if need be – should the technologies calling upon that competence take the lead. In contrast, should that piece of competence seem to be essential, it may be appropriate to develop the competence aggressively (or sourcing it) especially if it could be needed for several technological options that are assessed as potentially important for the future (seen as of today).

Yet, given the competencies listed on Tabs. 10 to 12, I need to stress here that there are not so many transverse competencies appearing under the three meta-technologies addressed (3D printing, machine learning and IoT). There are a few exceptions though, e.g., applied math, algorithmics, model development, coding.

This opens the door to an interesting discussion about the role of digital technologies in the industry of the future. Some quotes from interviews that I conducted with CTOs bring some insight into the matter:

"Engineers of tomorrow will have to think their task through the lens of heuristics and algorithms. The knowledge and know-how base will have to be seen holistically as one of a system engineer looking at the process and technologies in their totality, with all interdependencies attached. Thinking by disciplines will be much less relevant."

"Preparing technologists for digital technologies in industrial activities cannot be done cheaply, on the side. It cannot be an add-on either. It will require a basic layer to form a solid platform on which the rest of the training will grow."

"In industrial firms, the power is likely to go to those who think business, not to IS, data analysts or digital geeks."

Should this point of view turn out to be sound, then education in technology, engineering and the management of industrial operations will need a serious rethinking.

"Human-machine interface will have to be revisited as 'computer-aided decision making' does not mean 'decision made by the machine'.

Thus, the need to build data visualization tools to help decision making (this relates to the issue of fit between cognitive maps).

And the need to improve the tools and the ability to read, understand and benefit from computer-aided representations of data and information to better inform the decision-making process."

"Digital tools are increasingly capable of addressing more than one added-value step: typically, digital design tools are also offering to manage the production process, inventories, assets, shipments or invoices. Roles and positions are blurring. As a result, organizations can lose their way.

What used to be a tool for a specific task is becoming a platform that covers everything from design to operations, to after sales services, including all the data attached."

The above analytical exercise of this appendix triggers some strategic thinking.

Let me illustrates some of the issues that the appendix brings about.

The above analyses of the competence needed for the industry of the future raise the question whether the industry of the future will go through a paradigmatic shift or, the technologies already being in place, whether this future of industry will essentially be business as usual (more of the same) with ongoing evolution more than radical transformation. There should be more digital in most industrial activities for sure, but will it be a game changer? The jury is still out. Yet, it seems, seen as of today, that it is not so much a totally new set of technologies that may trigger a paradigmatic shift, but the extent to which existing technologies (they have been around for years already) will expand their capacity of data treatment and accessibility through speed and bandwidth. The computing power, speed and accessibility are likely to keep growing exponentially, thus most probably leading to a paradigmatic shift.

Surfing the wave of such a change will not be easy for many countries and firms that attracted industrial activities primarily by offering lower labor costs. In addition, opportunities for new added-value services will open for those capable of surfing the wave of the industry of the future. They will have the possibility of exploiting the data gathered through operations, thus potentially triggering virtuous circles of business success. This should benefit most to those starting early in the new game, especially those capable of making use of the data for business purposes, typically offering new services to clients and users.

On top, this change will take place in a context where decarbonation will be a major challenge as well, adding both constraints and additional opportunities to forge ahead in a technology-based competition.

Yet, there is more to it.

As already discussed, beyond the technology side of the expected paradigmatic shift likely to affect industrial activities in the future, there is also a "softer" side that I suggest to call the managerial orchestration of the transformation. See Fig. 54.

Radical technological change is not just a matter of technology selection, development and deployment. It is also a challenge for management to build new strategies, reallocate resources and trigger and conduct organizational change.

The paradigmatic technological shift will not take place without the technologies. It will not unfold without the managerial orchestration either. In other words, radical technological change requires both technological and managerial competence. This means that specific managerial competencies are very likely to be needed to weather and conduct the transition.

While one of the key arguments of the book was built around the "competence by technology matrices" (see Chapter 19 and the previous discussion in this appendix), it is not obvious to adapt the framework to analyze managerial orchestration.

I will now discuss managerial and soft competence. There is however no obvious list of candidate columns in what would be the equivalent of Fig. 57. Nevertheless, I suggest looking at use cases, identifying the list of tasks and competencies that are called for such cases. I thus suggest using use cases in a column of a "competence by use case" matrix.

In turn, this raises another difficult question: Which use cases are available to anticipate what forms of change may need to be managed?

There are existing practices that can be seen as use cases. There are also ongoing experimentations that can offer emergent use cases, such as online monitoring of remote industrial sites, as already discussed at the end of Chapter 19. There are conceivable use cases, anticipated but not yet fully experimented. For example, the idea of a flow of communication between cars on the same road to inform drivers about hazards to be encountered along the way: when a car just skidded on a patch of ice, a warning is immediately shared with neighboring vehicles. All these are either observable or at least realistic enough to be considered as such. There are also visionary use cases, significantly more futuristic, such as the idea of an instant PDCA (plan-do-check-act) loop in industrial processes. Digital technologies compress temporal sequences and could offer real-time treatment of the data of the whole PDCA loop at once or in a matter of seconds, thus making it possible to increase the capacity and speed of process improvement. See Fig. 58.

Observable or quasi-observable use cases appear on the left part of Fig. 58, while indeterminate use cases appear on the right. While the "indeterminate" futuristic use cases are difficult to analyze as of today, the "observable" categories are more reachable, even the anticipated ones. In this context, the illustration below will cover two emergent use cases: online monitoring of distributed sites and monitoring of a fleet of aircraft turbines.

I have already mentioned the online monitoring of distributed industrial sites over a territory from a central hub (end of Chapter 19). Let me dig a bit more into it.

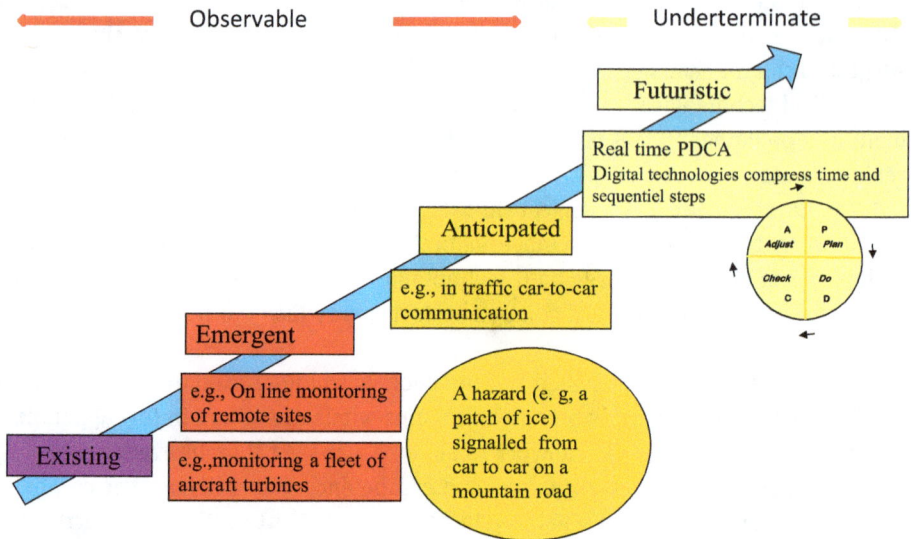

Fig. 58: Finding outward-looking use cases.

This use case (at Corp Z) can be divided into three main stages: design the change; conduct the transformation; monitor the distributed sites online.

Each stage can be subdivided into managerial tasks that call for specific competencies.

(1) *Design the change*:
  - (a) identify and list key processes, tasks and existing and planned role allocation;
  - (b) select technical options;
  - (c) architecture and design the data management system and decision tools;
    - data cleaning and curation;
    - data analyses to feed experts and decision-making processes;
  - (d) think of cybersecurity right from the beginning;
  - (e) prepare a staggered deployment plan;
  - (f) specify protocols for crisis management;
  - (g) risk analysis of the whole change project.

(2) *Conduct the transformation*:
  - (a) adopt project management mode;
  - (b) use methods and tools for managing change;
  - (c) allocate key tasks and processes between center and sites;
  - (d) test crisis management protocols;
  - (e) train, train, train – shared language, multicultural and collaborative stance.

(3) *Monitor the distributed sites online*:
- (a) develop a very intense sense of collaboration – collaborate, collaborate, collaborate;
- (b) manage portfolio of assets and their renewal over the long term – machines, IT, OT (in the sense of "operational technologies" that, in short, cover industrial IS) ;
- (c) manage talents (HR pool);
  - avoid risk of jeopardizing local human capital – technical expertise and leadership;
  - protect, maintain and support technicians' competence;
  - grow HR talents on digital and IT;
  - train to understand and use outputs stemming from data tools;
- (d) manage meetings where staff from center and sites interact and socialize;
  - train for efficient work between local and central teams;
- (e) monitor risks;
  - cybersecurity – control and integrity of data, digital thread;
  - dependence to tools, service providers, intermediaries.

The tasks listed (and the underlying managerial competencies) are mostly classic, e.g., process and task allocation (1a, 2c). However, some of these items deserve particular care in this context, typically collaboration and culture of sharing (3a, 2e, 3d) support key expertise – technical staff (3c), crisis management (1f, 2d), cybersecurity (1d, 3e).

In other words, the managerial orchestration of this type of industrial transformation is not likely to focus primarily on digital technologies (although their implication will have to be taken care of). Instead, the focus will be on softer issues of culture, communication, language, crisis management and HR support.

The second illustration of the theme of managerial orchestration is a use case stemming from aeronautics. A company, T, producing aircraft engines (turbines) develops new added-value services by managing the fleet of their turbines that are installed on planes. They keep track of the state of each turbine individually, tracing the flights, mileage, flight times, type of freight (including load), kerosene consumption, climate conditions, vibrations, temperature profile during flight, number of landings, special events that may have occurred, repair and maintenance, etc.

In order to understand how T operates the management of "their" turbine fleet and the additional service provided, the structure of the sector needs to be briefly introduced. Firm T sells turbines to aircraft manufacturers who sell the planes to either airlines or cargo companies, or aircraft rental companies owning a fleet of planes that are then rented to airlines and cargo operators, or for private or chartered use. Thus, T follows the turbines beyond the aircraft manufacturer to the owner of the planes and the operating companies (airlines or cargo). Through the usual maintenance services of the turbines, T has access to and manages detailed data about each turbine of their portfolio (fleet). This is confidential information that is shared with the planes' owners. This makes it possible to custom design (and optimize) the management of the turbine life cycle (planning and nature of maintenance, nature of repair when needed, decommissioning) as well as setting technical parameters according to next flight plans (distance, load, climate conditions).

Analyzing the types of tasks and competencies needed for this use case is illustrated below:

Business Objective: Offer New Added-Value Services on Optimized Management of Assets (Turbines)

– Build a systematic database of the running conditions of operations of the turbine (at present time and historically, since the first flight)
– Capture an exhaustive array of data to create models (digital twin)
– Allow Predictive maintenance
– Improve cost of ownership

Manage the Digital Chain (Data Capture, Curation and Analysis; Augmented Decision)

– Beyond control command – data capture plans, data curation and decision models
– Manage interactions between digital twin and technical specialties (fluidics, thermodynamics, mechanics, materials (including alloys), etc.)
– Revisit the technical department structure to set up a role for data management
– Revisit the communities of practice and knowledge management accordingly
– Manage the HR and organizational implications

Manage the Inter-organizational Setting in the Value Chain

– share the gains derived from better asset management and cost of ownership
– deal with the issue of data ownership – the data belong to the client.
  – Legal perspective or business model viewpoint (value extraction from data – with or without intermediaries)?
– If business model viewpoint with intermediaries: expect the latter to speak the language of the digital community, not that of the business

Learn How to Use the Output Stemming from Decision Tools

- Use tools to simplify life for the technicians (their assigned tasks and their overall job)
- Make sure that seasoned technicians accept it when tools identify things that they missed out (while technicians can sense things that tools may not catch).
- Understand heuristics and algorithms to avoid black box effect.
- Awareness of tools' limitations

Security Protection

- Risk of dependence to tools and providers
- Cybersecurity

In a way similar to the discussion around Fig. 57 above, it is possible to follow the sequence that goes from a use case to the managerial orchestration competence that stands behind it (Fig. 59).

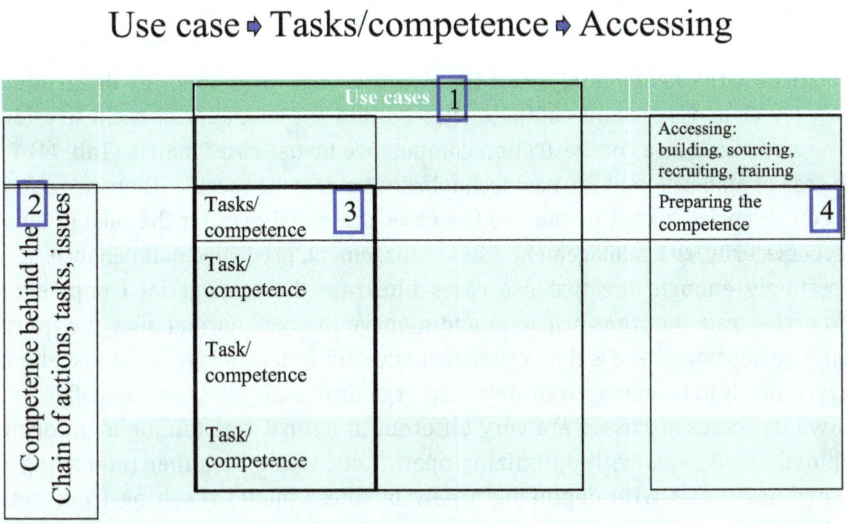

Use case ➔ Tasks/competence ➔ Accessing

		Use cases 1			Accessing: building, sourcing, recruiting, training
2 Competence behind the Chain of actions, tasks, issues	Tasks/ competence 3				Preparing the competence 4
	Task/ competence				
	Task/ competence				
	Task/ competence				

Fig. 59: From use cases to competence for managerial orchestration.

The sequence starts with the use case (1), seen as a chain (2) of tasks and/or competencies (3) called upon to orchestrate the application described in the use case. In turn, this permits to prepare (4) for the corresponding competencies and thus build a future portfolio of competence fit to the requirements of the managerial orchestration of the application at hand.

Interestingly enough, the competencies that emerge in both illustrations above (online monitoring of distributed industrial sites; managing a fleet of turbines to provide added-value services) are labeled around verbs and substantives that can be grouped in three categories:

- **management**: list and allocate roles, design protocols for crisis management, organize cybersecurity, train (collaboration, multicultural, team communication), manage HR talents, manage socialization in between teams, organize predictive maintenance, revisit technical department structure, revisit community of practice and knowledge management, reorganize project management;
- **strategic management**: select technical options, plan, analyze and monitor risks, manage asset portfolio, decrease cost of ownership, share the gains, address issue of proprietary data in inter-organization business models, protect and secure against risks (cybersecurity, dependence to tools and providers);
- **managing the technical**: architecture and design data management system, build data base, capture data and build models, manage interactions between digital and technical specialties, prepare technical staff to being challenged by tools (and vice versa), train for heuristics and algorithms, raise awareness of tools' limitations.

More specifically, the above analysis of the two use cases presented for illustration points to very clear issues and competencies behind the managerial orchestration that can be structured as a "orchestration competence by use case" matrix (Tab. 14).

Each case of application of the new technologies tends to be specific. There are a few common competencies shared by the two use cases presented here for the sake of illustration: cybersecurity, risk management, asset management, predictive maintenance.

Interestingly enough, the two use cases illustrate the managerial competence needed to orchestrate the transformation and manage the new normal after the transformation. The key point here is that a paradigmatic shift in technology is not just about technology, it needs to be managed strategically, organizationally and operationally.

The two use cases discussed are very different in nature. One (online monitoring of distributed sites) deals with optimizing operations, while the other (managing a fleet of turbines) deals with deploying a new business model resulting from new value-added services to clients.

I stress below some typical examples of competencies clearly emerging as a need from at least one of the use cases.

Strategic competence is needed to:

- design new business models leveraging the data made available;
- design partnerships (here in value chains) accordingly;
- protect and secure the business and the system put in place;
- manage risks and crises.

Tab. 14: The "orchestration competence by use case" matrix for the two illustrative use cases.

	Online monitoring of distributed sites	managing a fleet of Turbines
Strategic management		
Design strategy		New business model – added-value services; strategizing and managing partnerships; data ownership; sharing gains
Competence to search for new business models		calling upon illustration from use cases to stimulate collaborators and teams; foster interactions between marketing - technologists - strategists
Protect and secure	cybersecurity; Risk management; crisis management	cybersecurity; limit depedence to tools and providers; risk management
Organize and manage		
Manage complex organizational settings	multicultural; Center-site and inter-site languages; Collaborate, collaborate, collaborate; Strike balance between autonomy and collaboration; Call upon remote expertise	interorganizational worldwide operations along the value chain
Use Data to optimize operations	inter-site benchmarking; Process optimization; Asset management; predictive maintenance	Asset management; predictive maintenance

In this context, new added-value services offered to clients may require vision, creativity and iterations through trial and error to converge towards offerings that best fit clients' needs. This echoes the competence expected from high-tech start-ups searching for problems to be solved by the new solutions stemming from new technologies. In this sense, studying use cases, including from other sectors of application, can help envision what may be done of new technologies.

- Weathering the change and managing the transformation calls for both strategic thinking of technology and change management. The first item is my topic in this book. The second is a classic managerial competence – classic does not mean easy, by the way.

- Managing the new normal after the change is yet another challenge. The issue of collaboration was identified in the use case on the online monitoring of distributed sites. It is a typical example of another classic issue that may become critical. Management can act in advance to prepare the teams for it and will have to constantly act to promote smooth collaborative behaviors in the new setting.

- In both use cases discussed, strategizing and optimizing, respectively, are made possible by the data capture and modeling provided by the digital technologies. This means that the corresponding competencies attached to managerial orchestration need the technological substrate in the first place.

In turn, this leads to augmented decision making as decision makers learn how to use the outputs of the models, another new competence required by the new setting. This again stems from technology in the first place.

I can extend the implication of the above observations in the form of an obvious but important proposition: there is a need to develop competence to manage the technical-managerial complementarity.

Typically, curating and analyzing data, including tracing the integrity of data and the treatment operated on raw data, may be seen as a technical task. However, using the outputs of the models fed by the data to permit augmented decision-making falls on the managerial side.

Another illustration is provided by ergonomists having a foot on both sides (technical and managerial) when thinking about human-machine interfaces for a job – thus combining a technical and a human/HR viewpoint. Similarly, designers (and for that matter ergonomists as well) need to combine a technical and a marketing viewpoint when thinking up new offerings for users.

All in all, technology and management are intricately intertwined when facing a technological paradigmatic change. Hence, in such contexts, competencies to work at the technical-managerial interface are more than ever likely to be needed.

My observations of a variety of companies over the last four decades led me to a possibly simplistic but strong hypothesis: a line of divide between the world of technologies and the realm of management still exists in many organizations. Among other things discussed in this book, I suggest that this matter be dealt with when facing potential significant technological disruptions.

Index

https://doi.org/10.1515/9783111397979-036

www.ingramcontent.com/pod-product-compliance
Lightning Source LLC
Chambersburg PA
CBHW061804210326
41599CB00034B/6871